# Lebanon

# LEBANON

## The Challenge of Independence

EYAL ZISSER

I.B.Tauris *Publishers*
LONDON · NEW YORK

Published in 2000 by I.B.Tauris & Co Ltd
Victoria House, Bloomsbury Square, London WC1B 4DZ
175 Fifth Avenue, New York NY 10010
website: http://www.ibtauris.com

In the United States of America and in Canada distributed by
St Martin's Press, 175 Fifth Avenue, New York NY 10010

ISBN 1 86064 537 2

A full CIP record for this book is available from the British Library
A full CIP record for this book is available from the Library of Congress

Library of Congress catalog card: available

Set in Monotype Garamond by Ewan Smith, London
Printed and bound in Great Britain by WBC Ltd, Bridgend

# Contents

# Acknowledgements

This study could not have been completed without the help and support of many people throughout its various stages. I am grateful to the staff of the archives of the French Ministry for Foreign Affairs in Paris and Nantes, the archives of the French Army in Vincennes, and the archives of the Public Record Office in London, of the Centre for Middle East Studies of St Antony's College, Oxford, and of the Israel State Archives. Some of the best scholars of Lebanese and Syrian history have been kind enough to lend an attentive ear to my project and to offer wise advice. I owe many thanks to them all, and primarily to the late Albert Hourani and Elie Kedourie. I also wish to thank my colleagues at the Dayan Center for Middle Eastern and African Studies and the Department for Middle Eastern and African History at Tel Aviv University and in the Department of Near Eastern Studies at Cornell University, where this project was completed, for assistance and encouragement. Special thanks are due to Mr Nadim Shehadi, Director of the Centre for Lebanese Studies in Oxford, who kindly shared with me his rich knowledge and deep understanding of Lebanon's history, and opened the Centre's archives for me. Personal thanks are due to the Colton family, who not only generously granted me a fellowship that made it possible to devote my time to research, but also kept abreast of my project and encouraged me during the ordeal of writing, and to my wife Shirley and my children Liron, Lilach and Toam, who patiently stood by me throughout this long ordeal. I extend special thanks to Professor Itamar Rabinovich who supervised the doctoral dissertation on which this book is partially based. Without his encouragement and support, this study would not have been completed.

# Preface

The subject of this study is the political history of Lebanon in the years 1943 to 1952, that is, in the first decade of independence. These years coincided with the presidency of Bishara al-Khuri, the country's first president, elected in September 1943 and forced out of office in September 1952. His role as one of the founding fathers of modern Lebanon and his personal part in forming the distinctive character of the Lebanese polity were not just a chapter in his own biography; they made his incumbency an epoch in the history of his country.

How to write a history of modern Lebanon has long been a matter of controversy, regardless of whether western or Lebanese researchers were engaged in doing so. Given the heterogeneity of Lebanese society, this was perhaps inevitable. Each segment of that society clung to its individual identity and developed its own particular historical memory. From the beginning of independence, these memories formed part of the arsenal each side drew upon when struggling over the character of the state and, in particular, over who should hold a position of hegemony in it.[1] The controversy was further fed by varying (not to say conflicting) ways of explaining the unique course of modern Lebanese history, a history rich in success and prosperity, but also beset by strife and dissension. The crises culminated in the civil war that lasted from 1975 until 1989 and all but precipitated the country's total ruin.

Since 1975, the controversy has centred round two points: first, the question whether the course of modern Lebanese history is all of one piece, with a thread of continuity holding its various episodes together; or whether it is a series of disparate events marked off by complete breaks, either between the distinct periods dividing the era of statehood, or between them as a whole and the country's pre-state past.[2] Second comes the issue (frequent in any historical discussion) of determinism versus contingency.

Both questions lead back to the basic issue of Lebanese history (as well as Lebanese politics): was the framework established first by the French (in 1920) and later (in 1943) by the Lebanese themselves, a genuine, legitimate, viable entity, or was it rather an artificial conglomerate unlikely to survive? Would its political, social and economic elements eventually congeal or were they destined to fall apart?[3]

Indeed, studies of Lebanese history, particularly those written after the

start of the civil war, fall into two broad categories. Works such as Elie
Kedourie's and Meir Zamir's take the deterministic point of view.[4] They hold
that the establishment of the Lebanon devised by the French had sealed the
country's fate. After all, its boundaries did not change with the advent of
independence in 1943; even more importantly, the composition of the population stayed the same. Together they formed the background of the 1943
National Pact which – for better or for worse, but more often for worse –
laid down the lines of the country's political development for the following
few decades. The outbreak of civil war, thirty-two years later, was no more
than the inescapable consequence of the pact's implementation.

These historians view Lebanese history in the twentieth century as a long
series of upheavals and crises. Severe as these were, they could not change
the country's history radically – its course was, after all, predetermined – but
they accelerated its rhythm. The establishment in 1920 of 'le Grand Liban'
by the French, these authors felt, was a complete break with the Ottoman
past. Similarly, the National Pact was another radical break, this time with
the French mandatory regime which, for all intents and purposes, had been
a period of Maronite hegemony exercised under French tutelage. By necessity,
this approach led to the conclusion that the Lebanese state (both that of
1920 and that of 1943) was an artificial creation lacking legitimacy and,
having regard to its basic character and essence, incapable of survival in the
longer term. A second school of thought, represented by scholars such as
Kamal Salibi, Albert Hourani, Nadim Shehadi and Ghassan Salama, refuse to
regard Lebanese history as having been decreed by fate.[5] They interpret it in
terms of continuity and coherence, consider the Lebanese state as legitimate
and viable, and point to the many years of prosperity as evidence corroborating their view.

One cannot help feeling that the work of many of the researchers dealing
with the subject, and in particular those analysing Lebanese politics, were
influenced by the 'spirit of the times', that is by the specific circumstances
of Lebanon at the time of their writing. Scholars writing before or during
the 1960s (such as Leonard Binder, John Entelis, Iliya Harik, Elie Salem,
David and Audrey Smock, and to a large extent Michael Hudson as well)
tend to describe the Lebanese state as viable and are inclined to think of
earlier stages of Lebanese history as leading naturally to the prosperous
entity they knew in their day.[6] Others were more sceptical even then but, not
being witness to the destructive experience of the civil war, refrained from
peremptory judgement.[7] By contrast, authors writing in the mid-1970s or
later took a much more gloomy view of Lebanese legitimacy and survival.
This led them to a deterministic mode of thinking which made it seem that
Lebanon had been poised on the road to self-destruction ever since 1920.[8]

The voluminous struggle over the valid interpretation of Lebanese history
failed to elicit much interest in the events of 1943–52. Researchers inclining
to a deterministic view thought of that decade as marginal and as devoid of

influence on what was in any case destined to follow. For them, an understanding of Lebanon had to be anchored in an analysis of the emergence of
Greater Lebanon, of the National Pact, of the 1958 crisis and, most of all,
of the civil war. But their counterparts, too, did not find much to attract
them to this particular period, at least not beyond the initial struggle for
independence and the formulation of the National Pact. Most scholarly
histories of either school therefore devote no more than a few lines to the
entire decade.

The point of departure of the present study is, by contrast, that the first
ten years of Lebanese independence are of major importance for the understanding of the country's subsequent history; it was then that the state's
character was fixed and its future path marked out.

It is true – and indeed most scholars make that point – that the roots of
modern Lebanon reach down into the earlier circumstances of Mt Lebanon
and the adjacent areas such as they had been shaped over several centuries;
yet the Lebanese state of 1920 and that of 1943 marked new departures and
ushered in a 'new order' there. This new order reflected, and sometimes led
to, processes of modernization which transformed Lebanese politics, its
society and its economy. The transition from Ottoman rule to the French
mandate and from the mandate to independence, and its repercussions in
Lebanon itself and in its immediate environment, posed the most serious
challenges the new-born state as well as its leaders had to contend with. It
compelled the Lebanese elite, particularly the Maronite and the Sunni notables,
to combine elements of the old order with the new; or, to be more precise,
to try and preserve as much as they could of the old principles while giving
them modern trappings. These notables felt strongly that only by doing so
could they guarantee the new state's existence and ensure its political, social
and economic stability, thus preserving their own status as elite. These views
became the underlying principles of the Lebanese state and its political system
for a long time to come and still inform the thinking of Lebanese leaders
today. Hence the close link between the formative period of Lebanese
independence – the decade here reviewed – and the course of subsequent
Lebanese history.

At the centre of the events of 1943–52 stands the figure of Lebanon's first
president, Bishara al-Khuri. His personality and his policies are a reflection
of the most salient characteristic of the first years of independence: the need
to blend the old with the new, with all the dilemmas and tensions this implies.
It was this attempt which made Khuri a controversial figure. Some saw him
as a brilliant politician capable of finding the middle ground between the old
order and the new and thus able to lay the foundations of Lebanese independence and to ensure political stability. By doing so, they would add, he made
it possible for Lebanon to hang together until this day. In a preface to Khuri's
memoirs, published in 1960, Emile Khuri wrote: 'Khuri put into place the
foundations of the Lebanese state where no conception of statehood had

[previously] existed and endeavored to create a sense of homeland where the term "homeland" had not been known at all.'[9] – Other observers regarded him as the man who had mistakenly perpetuated the traditional Lebanese methods, carrying over into the era of independence all the faults and defects of the former system. He had acted, so they felt, from an erroneous belief that this would guarantee the country's existence in the future, as well as ensure his own position of power. These observers have tended to describe Khuri's tenure as a period of corruption and inefficiency which thereby set the low standards of public service which remained characteristic of Lebanon ever since.[10] This would lead them to the conclusion that Khuri's errors of omission and commission not only brought about his own downfall in the short term, but also, in the long term, launched Lebanon on the series of crises which culminated in the civil war.

This, then, is the background against which the present study has been undertaken: a wish to re-examine and reassess the relevance of these years, as well as of the role of Khuri and his government, in the course of modern Lebanese history.

The book is divided into four parts preceded by an introduction. The latter briefly traces the history of Lebanon from 1920 until the early 1940s, depicting the antecedents of independence. Part One deals with the struggle for independence and Khuri's personal contest for the presidency. It touches on the Franco-British rivalry in the Levant – this being the background against which events in Lebanon were acted out; describes the 1943 parliamentary and presidential elections; deals with the National Pact, formulated by Khuri and Riyad al-Sulh, then Khuri's closest political associate; and gives an account of the crisis of November 1943, the first serious challenge the newly independent state had to face.

The next part gives an account of the first years of independence when the French and British presence in the country was still casting shadows on the scene. It describes the final removal of Lebanon from the French sphere of influence and the emergence of an indigenous Lebanese foreign policy in both the global and the Arab arena.

The subject of the third part – the years 1947–50 – could well be called the Khuri administration's 'mid-life crisis'. True, it was then that Khuri reached the peak of his power, but it was also the time when his administration lost a great deal of momentum and suffered a number of crises which threatened its stability. The parliamentary elections of 1947 were indeed a victory for Khuri and led to his re-election as president, but they were followed by the upheaval of the 1948 Arab–Israel war and by the 1949 crisis in the country's relations with Syria. Particular attention will be paid to the confrontation in 1949 between Khuri and the Syrian National Party (PPS, Parti Populaire Syrien) under the leadership of Antun Sa'ada.

Part Four carries the story forward to the years 1951–52 and thus to Khuri's fall from power. It gives an account of the growth of domestic opposition and the break with Sulh, as well as of the crisis in Lebanon's relations with the western powers. It ends with Khuri being forced to relinquish the presidency.

The study draws on a large variety of primary and secondary sources. It brings together relevant archival material from official records and private collections in Britain, France, the United States and Israel. Some of the documents used have only become available during the last decade. In Britain, Foreign Office, War Office documents, all kept at the PRO, have been used. So have papers from the private collection of Major-General Sir Edward Spears, kept at the Middle East Centre, St Antony's College, Oxford. In France, use has been made of the Service Historique de L'Armée de Terre, of the papers of the Beirut High Commission now in Nantes, of the Quai d'Orsay, and of General Georges Catroux, now at the French National Archives. In Israel, Foreign Ministry documents now at the State Archives or the Central Zionist Archives have been consulted. Another source has been US State Department material available in photocopies at the Centre for Lebanese Studies, Oxford. Together, these documents reflect events in Lebanon as seen and interpreted by western, Arab and Israeli diplomats, other officials or military men. Wherever relevant, personal memoirs of British, French, Israeli, Syrian and, of course, Lebanese public figures, diplomats and army officers have been used as well. Much weight has also been given to published collections of official papers, as well as to items from the Middle Eastern press and regional broadcasts, first and foremost to those of Lebanese origin. These were made available to me at the French Bibilothèque Nationale, the British Library and the newspaper collections of the Hebrew University of Jerusalem and of Tel-Aviv University. Such items, particularly those from Lebanon, give us valuable clues to the way current developments were seen by those close to the event both geographically and chronologically. It is my conviction that a careful cross-reading of the sources of such various character, together with a study of research work done over the last decades, makes it possible to arrive at a balanced judgement of the events of 1943–52 and hence of their proper place in the story of Lebanon.

# Introduction: The Birth of the Lebanese State

On 1 September 1920, General Henri Gouraud, the French high commissioner of the Levant, proclaimed the establishment of the state of Great Lebanon, from Nahr al-Kabir in the north to Ra's al-Naqura in the south, from the Mediterranean in the west to the Anti-Lebanon in the east. It encompassed what had been the Ottoman administrative district (*Sanjaq*) of Mt Lebanon (the '*Mutasarrifiyya*', in Ottoman parlance), but was considerably larger, for the French added areas not formerly part of the '*Mutasarrifiyya*': the town of Beirut; the coastal strip south of it, including Tyre and Sidon; the town of Tripoli and the adjacent area of Jabal 'Akkar in the north; the Biqa' (the rift valley lying between Mt Lebanon and the Anti-Lebanon); and Jabal 'Amil (the southernmost region of Lebanon).[1]

This decision by the French was not as illogical or as devoid of historical good sense as has often been claimed since it was anchored, at least in part, in a centuries-old past which had given Mt Lebanon (the core area of the new state) a unique historical, political, social and economic character. This provided both a factual base and a conceptual justification for building a state around it.

Its mountainous and virtually inaccessible nature had long made Mt Lebanon a haven for persecuted minorities, for Maronites, Druse and, along the southern slopes, even for Shi'is. In the mountains, the Maronites were clearly in the majority. Unlike the other Christian communities, such as the Greek Orthodox or the Greek Catholic, they had originally been an Arab tribal group which had made their new religion into a bonding agent for their members. Over time, it acquired a communal identity and, in the nineteenth century, a national one as well. It ended up demanding self-determination and ultimately a state of its own.[2]

The link the Maronites established with Roman Catholic Europe, in particular with the Vatican and with France, added to the unique features of the mountain region and eventually became an important component in the consolidation of the Lebanese entity. The link with France went back to the time of the Crusades, growing in intensity as French interests in the Levant amplified. Beginning in the nineteenth century, this led to stronger cultural and economic and eventually political French involvement in Mt Lebanon. This policy peaked with the French military intervention in the Maronite–Druse civil war of 1860 and the political involvement the following year in establishing an autonomous region in Mt Lebanon (the above-mentioned *Mutasarrifiyya*) and in its subsequent administration, until the outbreak of the First World War.[3]

It was not France, however, which gave Mt Lebanon its special status. Politically speaking, it had a semi-autonomous standing within the Ottoman empire for centuries before. The so-called 'Emirate of Mt Lebanon' (*Imara*) had been formed in the late sixteenth century and lasted until the middle of the nineteenth. From 1591 until 1697 it was headed by a Druse dynasty, the Ma'anids. Their most famous member was the Amir Fakhr al-Din whom many considered as the real founder of the emirate and hence, in a sense, of the future state of Lebanon.[4] When the last of the Ma'anids died in 1697 without leaving an heir, the emirate passed to the house of Shihab, kinsmen of the Ma'anids but Sunni Muslims. In 1758, two Shihab emirs became Christians of the Maronite persuasion and other members of the family followed suit. The Shihabs went on to rule over Mt Lebanon until 1842. Most prominent among them was Emir Bashir II (1788–1840).[5]

The salient aspect of the emirate (some elements of which actually go back to the Mamluk period) was its special political, social and economic regime which in many ways prefigured the Lebanese system of today. It has become customary to liken it to medieval European feudalism. Real power in the mountain region was in the hands of families of notables, both Maronites and Druse, who collected the taxes there, each in its particular district. Each such local tax region was called *muqata'a* and the tax farmer was called *muqata'ji*. Their grip on power over their *muqata'a* and its inhabitants was well-nigh absolute.[6]

The emirate survived for such a long time because it provided a framework accommodating both the dominant local power-holders and the outside forces. The Ottomans regarded it as an instrument for guaranteeing quiet and stability in the mountain region and ensuring the regular collection of taxes there. The Druse notables for their part thought of it as an instrument for ensuring the status quo and thus perpetuating the feudal order of things and all the social, economic and political benefits they derived from it. The Maronites, finally, viewed it as the vehicle for their community's prosperity and, during the reign of Bashir II, came to think of it as the kernel of a separate political entity. At the same time, each of the three groups had, of course, its own ideas of what the future of Mt Lebanon should be and its own aspirations and ambitions. The Ottomans intended to reassert their full authority and to make Mt Lebanon part of one of the adjacent provinces. The Druse thought in terms of fuller autonomy which would set them free from direct Ottoman control. The Maronites (once the emirs had converted to their faith), wanted the emirate to develop into a purely Maronite institution.[7] But then the existence of the emirate was predicated on the recognition by all that none was strong enough to realize its ambition; hence only compromise would enable them to live together and to preserve the peace.

This recognition reflected a basic fact of life in the mountain area, both under the Ottomans and in the Lebanese state, namely that the essentially heterogeneous nature of the area required a strictly controlled formula for the coexistence of its component parts and for the division of power and of resources among them. The exact nature of the compromise formula was prescribed by the relative strength of the mountain communities in each given period. Their proportionate strength was the function of several variables: the relative demographic weight of each in the total population; its political and social consolidation; its economic vigour; its military strength, often enough tested in actual combat; and finally the backing and support from the outside which each was able to enlist.

The history of Mt Lebanon and that of the later Lebanese state therefore represent a continuum of various laboriously constructed formulas for coexistence which, taken together, lasted for a long period of time. But underlying their effectiveness was a given balance of local power to which they gave formal expression; when that balance changed, they collapsed. Perhaps what defeated them was the inability of the communities to set up institutions capable of examining them anew at each turn, and of revising the formulas in conformity with the changes as they were occurring. In the absence of such an apparatus, the transition from one formula to the next proved so complex and difficult that often enough the sides attempted to resolve it by the use of force. But such a period of bloodshed was eventually followed by a new accommodation. The new formula, it usually turned out, was rather similar to the preceding one and very different from what the contenders had aspired to when they challenged the old one.

To illustrate: the emirate came to an end when local and regional circumstances were altered by the onset of modernization as well as by increasing Ottoman, Egyptian and western intervention. This was particularly true of the reign of Bashir II. Lebanese society had begun to change; the various Christian communities proved more susceptible to the impact of modernization and to outside influences than did the Druse. The Christians therefore became the principal economic and political beneficiaries of the new situation.[8] It was at this time that the Maronites, under the leadership of their church (which had by then turned itself into the community's most powerful agency), began to develop a national identity and to demand to turn Mt Lebanon into a Maronite political entity. Conscious of the local and regional changes, a segment of the Maronite community started challenging the status quo. In part, their challenge was directed against the status quo within the community itself. The peasant revolt against the feudal lords (1858–61) weakened the great Maronite families and accelerated the rise of the church to a prominent position of power at the expense of the notables. But most of all, the Maronite community challenged the position of the Druse; more precisely, the standing of the Druse feudal lords dominating the southern slopes of Mt Lebanon. Their status had already been weakened by political and social changes under Bashir II: the rapid growth of the Maronite population; the settlement of many Maronites in the south, until eventually they formed the majority there; and the overall weakening of the economic position of the feudal lords, both Maronite and Druse, through the development of alternative hubs of economic activity emerging in the Christian urban centres. To all these, we must add the impact of intrusions from the outside: Ottoman, Egyptian and, especially, French and British. French involvement in particular led some of the Maronites to feel that they were growing strong enough to change things in Mt Lebanon unilaterally for their benefit. The growing tension between them and the Druse erupted first in 1840 in a long and bloody struggle over domination in the mountain area, challenging the old idea of coexistence there. Political strife soon acquired communal and religious overtones. Fighting went on until 1860 and ended, as so many other armed clashes had before, without a clear-cut decision in favour of one side or the other.[9]

The establishment in May 1861 of the Mt Lebanon autonomous district, the *Mutasarrifiyya*, became a milestone on the road to the future Lebanese political entity. Resulting from an agreement between the Ottoman empire and the western powers, it marked the end of the old order and laid down a new formula which shaped communal relations in Mt Lebanon until 1914. Autonomy towards the central government in Istanbul was successfully maintained. It was a time of quiet coexistence, even of cooperation between Maronites and Druse, both of whom had learned the lesson of the wars and had come to understand that neither was strong enough to impose its will on the other. True, the Maronites constituted 58 per cent of the mountain population and the Christian communities as a whole some 80 per cent, but they had failed to defeat the Druse. The latter, though only 11 per cent of the mountain population, had been able to secure victory in combat because of their communal cohesion and the warlike qualities for which they had always been known. But they knew that they could not overcome the Maronites because of the latter's foreign, mainly French, support. Each side had thus come to acknowledge its limits, and therefore preferred coexistence in the *Mutasarrifiyya*, for all its drawbacks, to continued strife – at least until the next opportunity arose to come out against the status quo in Mt Lebanon. That opportunity occurred in 1920.[10]

The outbreak of the First World War led to the abolition of the *Mutasarrifiyya*. The Ottomans proclaimed martial law in Mt Lebanon in October 1914 and upon the resignation of Ohannes Pasha, the governor of the *Mutasarrifiya*, in June 1915, they abrogated the protocols and the imperial decrees that governed the privilege status of Mt Lebanon. Neither of these steps, however, weakened the Maronite sense of identity. When the war was over, the leaders of the Maronite church began a campaign for the establishment of an independent Maronite state under French protection. This was to be a continuation of the previous autonomous area, but within rather wider borders and with the Maronites enjoying absolute hegemony.

The account so far would make it appear that the French decision to set up a Lebanese state had at least as much logic and was as justified as the creation of the other new Middle Eastern states established by France or Britain (Syria, Transjordan, Iraq). The new state was built around Mt Lebanon as its acknowledged core area, a core which had distinct historical roots of its own and had been internationally recognized at least since 1861. Moreover, the French decision was supported by an important local community, the Maronites; indeed, it came in response to their demands.[11]

But then the Greater Lebanon of 1920 was not confined to Mt Lebanon. It included further areas which in the past had only slight links with the mountain region. Instead, both in their historical development and their present economic and social conditions they had much stronger bonds with Damascus and the interior of Syria and with northern Palestine. Moreover, their population differed greatly from the mountain people. The Biqa' and parts of southern Lebanon, for instance, had in the past been part of the province (*vilayet*) of Damascus and the majority of the inhabitants there were Shi'is. Tripoli and its environs had long formed a separate Ottoman *vilayet*. Its principal economic links were with the interior of Syria, in particular with the towns of Homs and Hama whose exit to the sea was through the port of Tripoli. Most of the inhabitants were Sunnis. Beirut for its part did indeed have close economic ties with Mt Lebanon, but had in the past been an independent *sanjaq* of its own. At least half of the people of Beirut were Sunnis. Finally, the coastal strip south of Beirut had for most of its history been a *vilayet* of its own, with either Sidon or Acre as the seat of the local Vali; Sunnis and Shi'is together formed the majority of the population there.[12]

The establishment of Greater Lebanon thus caused a major change in the numerical proportions of the Lebanese population. According to the 1932 census, the share of the Christian communities taken together fell from 80 per cent to 54 per cent. That of the Maronites alone – the 'hard core' of the new entity – was reduced from 58 per cent to 29 per cent. As against the Christians, the Muslims (Sunnis and Shi'is together) now accounted for 48 per cent. Though slightly outnumbered by the Shi'is, the Sunnis, with 22 per cent, took the lead, both politically and economically speaking. Most were opposed to the very idea of establishing a Lebanese state and con-sistently demanded that all, or most, Lebanese territory should be made part of the Syrian state. Account must also be taken of the fact that the rate of natural increase was higher among Muslims than among Christians; moreover, there were more Christians than Muslims among the emigrants who, since the middle of the nineteenth century, left Lebanon for abroad in growing numbers.[13] Both factors aggravated the danger which such demographic imbalance would present for the future of the country.

The figures in Table 1.1 raise the question why the French chose to set up a state with such a configuration. At first glance, the French decision seems no more than the logical conclusion of French Levant policy such as it had evolved in the preceding seventy years or so, a policy supported, and in some measure even propelled forward, by certain political and economic pressure groups in France. It aimed at French hegemony in the Levant as well as at the establishment of a permanent French presence there strong enough to guarantee it. Several factors combined to sustain it: the belief in France's mission as the defender and protector of the Christians in the Levant; the desire to strengthen its grip on North Africa by creating a second French stronghold further east; the expectation of economic gain; and finally a desire to gain some territorial recompense for the great sacrifices France had made in the First World War.[14]

To underpin this policy by setting up a greater Lebanese state which the Maronites would run virtually on their own therefore seemed an appropriate response to this combination of motives. It appeared all the more logical in the light of the Muslim population's resolute opposition to any kind of French presence. It suited the overall principle of *divide et impera* which shaped the pattern of French regional policy; France split the area of geographical, or 'natural', Syria into four more states: Aleppo, Damascus, the 'Alawi state in northwestern Syria, and the Jabal al-Duruz (the Druse Mountain) in the south. Furthermore, two autonomous regions were set up: the Jazira and Alexandretta.[15]

It turned out, however, that a great many French people were opposed to the creation of Greater Lebanon or soon came to regret its establishment. They began to grasp the disastrous consequences likely to follow from its demographic composition as well as the damage it was bound to inflict on France's future relations with the Arab nationalist movement then gathering momentum. Among the erstwhile supporters and subsequent opponents was Robert de Caix, General Gouraud's secretary. At first he had thought of Greater Lebanon as a useful prop to strengthen the French position in the Levant. But after a short stay in the region he changed his mind radically and spoke out in warning. 'We know of no reason to annex Tripoli to Lebanon,' he wrote in July 1920. 'It is a Sunni Muslim center, rather fanatic, and not wishing at all to be incorporated in a country with a Christian majority.' Speaking of the choice of Beirut as the seat of Lebanon's government, he wrote that it was 'most questionable whether such a large city ... which will no doubt contain half the Lebanese population in a few years, is the most desirable capital for the Mountain, whose character might be greatly altered by the move'.[16]

Such views became quite common in France. Already in 1919, French Prime Minister Georges Clemenceau had tried to come to an agreement with Faysal who, with British encouragement, was soon to be proclaimed king of Syria in Damascus. Under the compromise proposal, France would dissociate

TABLE 1.1 Composition of the population in the autonomous region of Mt Lebanon and in Greater Lebanon.

| Community | Mutasarrifiyya (1911) | (%) | Greater Lebanon (census of 1932) | (%) |
|---|---|---|---|---|
| Maronites | 242,308 | 58.3 | 227,800 | 29.0 |
| Greek Catholic | 31,936 | 7.7 | 46,709 | 5.9 |
| Greek Orthodox | 52,356 | 12.6 | 77,312 | 9.8 |
| Other Christian Communities | 3,026 | 0.8 | 45,125 | 5.7 |
| All Christians | 329,626 | 79.4 | 396,946 | 50.4 |
| Sunnis | 14,529 | 3.5 | 177,100 | 22.5 |
| Shi'is | 23,413 | 5.6 | 155,035 | 19.8 |
| Druse | 47,290 | 11.4 | 53,334 | 6.8 |
| All Muslims | 85,232 | 20.5 | 385,489 | 49.1 |
| Jews | 86 | — | 3,518 | 0.5 |
| Total | 414,944 | 100 | 785,933 | 100 |

*Note*: Inclusion of the Druse among the Muslims follows the practice of the original statistics.
*Sources*: Akarli, *The Long Peace*, p. 107; Zamir, *The Foundation of Modern Lebanon*, p. 98.

itself from the demand of the Maronites for a Christian Lebanese state and would agree for Mt Lebanon to be incorporated in the Kingdom of Syria. In exchange for being acknowledged as the representative of the Arab national movement, Faysal would recognize the special status of France in the Levant. For a variety of reasons, the proposal was not acted upon.[17] French hesitations led the Maronite patriarch, Elias Hawayik, to launch a public relations campaign in French government quarters and among the public at large with a view to keeping French policy in line with his community's demands. As M. Zamir has shown, the campaign contributed greatly to France's eventual decision to set up the kind of Lebanon the Maronites wanted and to make it almost exclusively dependent on France.[18]

It was in this way that the Maronites were able to impose on the other communities a form of coexistence such as they had long aspired to in the area of Mt Lebanon, but which was now to be applied within the wider borders of the Lebanese state-to-be. Their *diktat* was naturally opposed by large sectors of the population, most of all by the many Sunnis who had now adopted an Arab identity cast in the mould of the Arab nationalist movement. They felt that the new state was being forced upon them against their will and that, moreover, it totally contradicted the basic tenets and aspirations of Arab unity. It was the point that a large part of the population of the future Lebanese state negated its very existence which, even more than merely the precarious demographic imbalance, led historians to criticize the French decision as historically unjustified and politically unsound. Here, in their view, lay the roots of Lebanon's future vicissitudes and, ultimately, of the 1975 civil war.[19]

But then for a long time, at least until the end of the 1960s, the new Lebanon proved impressively viable; its constituent communities not only coexisted but cooperated successfully, and reached a remarkable level of prosperity. The country's success was due to the ability of the two major communities – the Maronites and the Sunnis – to arrive at a new formula for coexistence, this time a mutually agreed one. This formula, gradually worked out in the 1930s and 1940s, revised the Maronite–French *diktat* of September 1920 and was based on mutual consideration and an intelligent assessment of demographic realities and the demographic balance of power. On the part of the Maronites, it reflected a growing recognition that it was beyond their power to preserve for long a Greater Lebanon under their own outright hegemony and under French protection. On the part of the Sunnis, the new formula was an acknowledgement that a separate Lebanon had become an established fact which their community was not strong enough to undo. Both trends eventually found their ultimate expression in the National Pact of 1943.

The new formula made it possible for all the communities (or, perhaps more precisely, for their elites) to work out new and agreed patterns of public life. It drew its inspiration from old patterns which had existed in and around Lebanon during the centuries of Ottoman rule, and thus gave the new state a stronger bond with the past of the area over which it extended. It provided a foundation of constancy which made it possible to move from the Ottoman order to a modern polity with comparative smoothness and ease: first to the French mandate; next, and more effectively, to independent statehood. It provided historical continuity and hence political, social and economic stability and, in the final analysis, allowed the Lebanese elites to maintain their positions of prominence.

Acceptance by the elites – most importantly, by the Maronite and Sunni ones – of the new Lebanese political framework as well as of the elements of the old order preserved within it, seemed to follow unavoidably from the unique character of the country's society. The mosaic pieced together in 1920 left them no other option. This singularity of the Lebanese social and political system requires some elaboration.

Historical research usually analyses the history of Lebanon (and, before it, of Mt Lebanon) in terms of Christian–Muslim or overall inter-communal tension and strife. But that means focusing on a single aspect and disregarding other facets. The first point to be made is that the Christians and the Muslims of Greater Lebanon were never politically and socially cohesive units.[20] The Maronites – the largest single Christian group – formed approximately 60 per cent of the Christian population (see Table 1.1). The other Christian communities were less than enthusiastic when it came to following the Maronite lead and to sharing Maronite concepts of the future of Lebanon. Salient in this respect was the Greek Orthodox community, the second largest Christian group. Unlike the Maronites, the large majority of whom lived in Mt Lebanon, the Greek Orthodox had co-religionists spread out over the entire Middle East. Again unlike the Maronites, the Orthodox never developed a feeling of national identity. Beginning in the middle of the nineteenth century, with the onset of modernization and in the wake of the *Tanzimat* (the Ottoman reforms) which granted formal civil equality to the local Christians, they started to seek a common denominator to link them with the neighbouring Muslim population. Alternatively, they probed for a new framework of inter-communal coexistence which would enable them to make the best of the new political and economic opportunities now open to them. Eventually, the emerging Arab nationalism provided the sought-for common denominator and became the identity badge of most of the Orthodox.[21] Another model suggesting itself was Syrian, rather than Arab, nationalism. It was adumbrated around the middle of the nineteenth century in the attitudes and teachings of the scholar Butrus al-Bustani (himself, incidentally, of Maronite origin). Bustani's writing was, however, an expression of local patriotism rather than of nationalist sentiment. Indeed, Syrian identity, limited as it may have been, enveloped Bustani in the more compassing mantle of Arab and Ottoman identity. The most prominent spokesman of this school was Antun Sa'ada, a Greek Orthodox who, in the early 1930s, founded the Syrian National Party (the PPS) and led it until his execution in 1949.[22] One way or another, Greek Orthodox loyalty to the idea of a Maronite Christian national home in Lebanon had been dubious from the start and was to remain so.[23]

The Muslim camp, too, was not characterized by cohesion or unity of ranks. The Sunnis (the second largest group in the population) had their strongest political, social and economic ties with the Syrian interior. Since the end of the First World War (and in some cases even earlier) they had become Arab nationalists. This, as we have seen, led them to demand the inclusion of all or part of Lebanon in Syria.

The Shi'is had little in common with them. They were predominantly rural people, and were considered the most backward sector of the population. Most lived in villages in the Biqa' valley and the south (Jabal 'Amil). They followed local feudal leaders who had a strong grip on the villagers. Most of them had no wish to see Sunnis resume domination over their areas. The French had to do no more than recognize them as a separate religious community in order to gain the support of most of them for the kind of Lebanon France envisaged.[24]

The Druse for their part went on pursuing their age-old ambition of securing an autonomous status for their areas (the southern part of Mt Lebanon) and to be left free to run their daily lives in their own manner.

The establishment of Greater Lebanon disadvantaged them: in Mt Lebanon, they had been the second largest component; in Greater Lebanon, they became a small community (a mere 7 per cent of the total). Yet the majority of the Druse leaders soon made their peace with the new realities, perhaps from a recognition that a union with Syria would place them in an even worse condition.[25]

The bipolar Christian–Muslim pattern is thus not sufficient to understand the Lebanese system nor does it enable us to account fully for the history of modern Lebanon (and perhaps not for that of Mt Lebanon either). Only in rare cases did any of the communities close ranks effectively in pursuit of a single common aim. On most issues, each community was, to a greater or lesser extent, divided against itself. A conspicuous example of this trend is the split within the Maronite community during the civil war years of 1975–89. A substantial part of the community supported the Jumayyils, but other segments were followers of the Faranjiyyas and the Eddes, and resolutely opposed the Jumayyils. In other words, loyalty to family was, and often enough still is, capable of overriding communal loyalty. Most certainly during the period reviewed in this study, many Lebanese acted first of all in the name, and for the sake, of the family to which they belonged as kinsmen or whose clients they were.[26] It must be recalled that the roots of the political, social and economic system of the Lebanese state reached back to the old patterns of Mt Lebanon where the local authority of families of notables (Druse or Maronite) over their particular area and its inhabitants was virtually absolute. A similar situation existed in the Shi'i area. True, social and economic development during the nineteenth century, and in particular the establishment of the *Mutasarrifiyya*, had eroded the standing of the notables; the establishment of Greater Lebanon, furthermore, had given greater weight to the coastal cities (most of all to Beirut) at the expense of the mountain region. This in turn had strengthened the Beirut economic elite in comparison with the rural notables of the feudal type.[27] Yet during the first half of the twentieth century, the majority of Druse and Shi'i rural areas, and many of the Maronite ones, continued to be under the domination of families traditionally regarded as the local notables, and in particular those called *za'im* ('leader'). The use of this term – originally brought in from Egypt – and the role of the men so called became the most characteristic element of the Lebanese system which gave such predominance to Shi'i, Druse and (to some extent) Maronite semi-feudal lords, as well as to Sunni political 'bosses' in the major cities.[28] Similarly, among the Sunnis of the coastal cities the Ottoman system under which urban notables (*a'yan*) held sway had been largely preserved. Here, too, the processes of modernization had lessened, but not abolished, their authority.

As we have seen, communal identity and some sort or other of communal coexistence lay at the basis of the Lebanese system; more than that – of Lebanon's very existence. This naturally implied that resources and positions of power should be shared out proportionally among the communities, in accordance with whatever accepted formula for coexistence was being applied at any given moment. But our account has also shown that the recipients of benefits were not so much the members of the communities but rather their acknowledged representatives, i.e. the notables. In other words: to enjoy benefits or to advance to positions of influence or power in the Lebanese polity as a whole, a family had first to achieve prominence within its own community. This usually meant that they had to struggle hard against others contending for the same prizes. (We find a similar situation among Sunnis elsewhere in the Ottoman empire – a useful reminder of how firmly the practices of Lebanese statehood were anchored in the overall patterns of the Ottoman era.)

From time to time, families of notables formed alliances meant to protect, or to promote, the fortunes of their affiliates in the struggle for positions in the wider Lebanese framework. Such alliances, most of them short-lived, were often concluded in order to fight off a challenge on the part of some other community who pressed for a revision of the coexistence formula of the moment. In other cases, alliances were made in order to enable the confederates themselves to try and change the formulas in favour of their community – which meant, in actual fact, in their own personal or familial favour.

Among the most conspicuous encounters of this kind was the prolonged struggle between the Junbalats and the Arsalans in the Druse community, the origins of which dated back to the period of the emirate. Among the Shi'is, the As'ads, Zayns, Khalils and 'Usayrans competed for the hegemony in Jabal 'Amil; in the Biqa', the Hamadas and Haydars were the principal rivals. In the Sunni community of Beirut, the chief families of notables – the Sulhs, Yafis and Salams – were the leading competitors; among the Sunnis of Tripoli, the Karamis, Muqaddams and Jisrs led the struggle. An example from among the Maronites was the political contest between the Khuris and the Eddes from the 1920s until the 1940s, and between the Faranjiyyas, Jumayyils, Chamouns (Sham'uns) and Eddes from then on and until the early 1980s. There were also instances of fierce competition within a single family, between brothers, uncles or other kinsmen, for first place in the family and for control of the family's wealth. In the period here reviewed, Riyad al-Sulh and his cousin and brother-in-law, Sami al-Sulh, provided a salient example for this kind of contest. So did Rashid Karami and his cousin Mustafa, both of whom wanted to step into the shoes of Rashid's father, 'Abd al-Hamid Karami, after the latter's death. The tension between Bishara al-Khuri and his brother Salim was of a similar nature.

To begin with, then, Lebanon had no room for ideologically-oriented parties. When they did appear, beginning in the 1930s, they were often enough 'front' organizations for certain notables who expected to maintain their strength with the help of a party organization. In other cases, parties were launched by lesser-known notables as a vehicle for their rise to prominence within their community. Such men preferred the guise of a party for their personal endeavours in order to exploit the growing political awareness of ordinary Lebanese. This could, of course, be done only by acting in conformity with the new rules of political conduct. The party called Phalanges Libanaises (al-Kata'ib), set up by Pierre al-Jumayyil in 1936, was intended to appeal principally to middle-class, urban Maronites, but served most of all as a springboard for propelling the Jumayyils into a position of power in their community. Another party, the National Call (al-Nida' al-Qawmi), which appealed mainly to lower-class Sunnis in Beirut and Sidon, was a political tool in the hands of the Sulhs.[29]

These practices explain why no community was able to rally behind a single leader or a single family. The resulting delicate balance of interests underpinned the Lebanese political system and gave it durability. Since no community was quite cohesive, none was able to enter the fight with its full potential force. Similarly, the splits within the broader camps – the Muslims and the Christians – neutralized some of their latent power and thus mitigated tensions to some extent. Interference from the outside sometimes upset the balance, at other times it reinforced it by giving added weight to certain communities or to the weaker families within them. Overall, the balance of power, benefits and interests rendered the notables more pragmatic, led them to display greater openness, made them more amenable to compromise, and obliged them to cooperate with each other. It helped to ensure the pluralist character of the society and the state, and allowed the elites to turn away from infighting to some extent and devote some energy to coping with the country's basic problems and the issues of modernization which threatened its stability.[30]

Having described the characteristics of the Lebanese system and dwelt on its ability to survive and even prosper for a number of years, it is time to return to the country's history from the establishment of Greater Lebanon onwards and to examine how far it was moulded by the factors we have listed.

Despite the circumstances in which it was set up – a Maronite *diktat* enforced by French bayonets – the French mandatory period was a vital conduit leading to Lebanese independence. It was under the mandate that the idea of a Greater Lebanon turned into an established fact. For one thing, the question marks which had, during most of the 1920s, hovered over the delineation of the country's boundaries were gradually removed. The borders had been challenged both by some factions prominent in the Sunni community and by Syrian nationalists. But the French, too, were originally hesitant and considered a possible revision with a view to excluding from Lebanon some chiefly Sunni areas, for instance the town of Tripoli and the adjacent Jabal 'Akkar. Paradoxically, the eventual French, Syrian and Lebanese Sunni recognition of the original borders led (as we shall see below) to the emergence of a Maronite faction which now opposed them. For another, it was under the mandate that Lebanon's state institutions and administrative apparatus were set up and that the country was given a constitution. Thirdly, it was in this period that public attitudes, especially on the part of the Sunnis, changed towards acceptance of the state in its present configuration. Already back in the mid-1920s, this led to the greater integration of Muslim notables – again, particularly of Sunni Muslim notables – into the fabric of Lebanese politics and into the country's administration. More than that: in the 1930s we can discern the beginnings of that Maronite–Sunni understanding which was to make Lebanese independence possible.

In November 1925, Henri de Jouvenel became high commissioner. He is credited with having contributed greatly to the consolidation of the Lebanese state, chiefly because of the constitution that was proclaimed during his tenure of office. The constitution was neither imposed by the French according to their own ideas nor did it express the traditional Maronite concept of what a Lebanese state should be. Rather, a variety of notables, including Sunni leaders, were able to make their input before the draft was finalized. Among them were Charles Dabbas, a Greek Orthodox, and Michel Chiha, a Roman Catholic. Their part in the work of constitution-drafting provided the first glimpse of a change in the Maronite as well as in the overall Christian view regarding the nature of the Lebanese state. It pointed to a transition from Maronite and Christian hegemony to the concept of a 'state for all the communities', or more precisely: a state for notables from all communities. The constitution was in many ways a return to the *Mutasarrifiyya*-type of politics or, more broadly speaking, to Ottoman political patterns. This is evident from the application of communal affiliation as the fundamental political principle. With only a few amendments, the mandatory constitution later became the constitution of independent Lebanon. As such, it still stands at the centre of the present Lebanese political system.[31] In its original form, it was ratified in May 1926 by the Lebanese Council of Representatives and gave a further impetus to the emergence of elected institutions. A Chamber of Deputies was formed the same month; so was a Senate but, unlike the chamber, it existed only for a year. Dabbas was elected president; a cabinet was formed and Auguste Adib Pasha, a Maronite, was appointed prime minister.

Once these political arrangements were in place, they in turn further accelerated the gradual change in the political concepts of both Maronites and Sunnis. The Sunnis who, as we have seen, had at first negated the very existence of the state, began to accept it as an accomplished fact. But their acceptance was conditional on two points which formed a 'red line' they were not prepared to cross: first, that a fair share of the appointments and benefits in the gift of the state should go to them ('fair' meaning 'in proportion to their numerical strength in the population as a whole'); and secondly, that the Arab character of the country should not be in dispute (and, concomitantly, that Lebanon's links with the West should not go beyond what was acceptable for an Arab country). The Sunni elite of Beirut formed the vanguard of these new trends. They, as well as some other Sunni notables, had begun to understand that only through acceptance and integration could their community promote its political standing and economic prosperity. None of them wanted the Sunni community to play second fiddle to the Syrian leadership, as would necessarily happen if Sunni areas were added to a greater Syria. Another consideration was that Sunnis were engaged in joint economic ventures with Christian business partners.

Yet these attitudes had not quite become common ground for the Sunni community as a whole. Many still clung to the old ideas. A series of conferences called 'the Conferences of the Coast' were held in 1926, 1928, 1933 and 1936 to provide a forum for airing their views. During the 1930s, the prominent figure in their camp was 'Abd al-Hamid Karami from Tripoli. His attitudes were shaped both by pan-Arab and by Muslim religious sentiment. (He had himself been the Sunni mufti of Lebanon for a while, until the French dismissed him.) Tripoli's political and economic competition with Beirut and its close commercial links with the Syrian interior (which we have mentioned earlier) played their part in reinforcing such sentiments. But Karami's attitudes also had a great deal to do with power struggles within the Sunni community, most of all in his home town. There, he was in competition with the Muqaddams and the Jisrs as well as with the family of Ahdab. Already back in the 1920s, the latter had come round to an acceptance in principle of the Lebanese state, found their place in the establishment and had thus gained a round over their competitors.[32] Muhammad al-Ahdab had been consulted at the time the constitution was being drafted. Other participants from Tripoli were Muhammad al-Jisr (then deputy speaker of the Senate) and Khayr al-Din al-Ahdab. Also making their way into the establishment during this period were 'Abdallah al-Yafi from Beirut and Khalid Shihab from South Lebanon. Each became prime minister during the 1930s.

Other members of the Sunni elite, however, sought to bolster their standing in the community by continuing to negate the Lebanese state or at least opposing Sunni integration in it. Apart from the above-mentioned 'Abd al-Hamid Karami, this line was taken by Salim 'Ali Salam. But it soon turned out that their approach flew in the face of realities. It eroded rather than reinforced their standing and enabled their rivals to overtake them – both politically and economically. By the mid-1930s, therefore, when the younger generation of the Sunni elite were making their way to the top, its members opted for a more sophisticated approach: accepting realities and seeking integration, but struggling to make the state's nature more to their liking and fighting for their full share of the spoils. They expected this combined option to further their cause among the ranks of the broader Sunni public. The Sunni population at large had, on the one hand, become more committed to Arab nationalism but, on the other hand, wished to attain an improvement in the fortunes of their community. In retrospect, it is possible to say that this approach also served the younger leaders' interests in their contacts with members of the Maronite elite. The latter came to regard them as more authentic representatives of the Sunni community and thus as more valid interlocutors in any discussion of the country's future.

Riyad al-Sulh's life story, with its mid-career turn from rejection of, to integration in the state, seemed to trace and to symbolize the history of his community.[33] He was born in 1894 in Sidon to a wealthy, well-established family of urban Sunni notables, some of whose descendants would later become prominent leaders of the community. Riyad was educated at Christian schools: the Lazarist (high) School of Aintoura, run by Jesuits, and the Faculty of French Law at St Joseph University in Beirut. Among his fellow-students were future leaders of the Maronite community: at Aintoura, he studied together with Bishara al-Khuri (with whom he would later share power) and at the university he formed a lasting friendship with Emile Edde. He later continued his law studies at the university of Istanbul.

Prompted by his father Rida' and following the direction taken by many of his own generation, Riyad joined the ranks of the Arab nationalist movement. During the Turkish oppression of the nationalists at the outbreak of the First World War, he and his father were sentenced to exile in Anatolia. After the collapse of the Ottoman empire, both joined Faysal in his short-lived kingdom of Syria (which included Lebanon). Rida' became Faysal's minister of the interior and Riyad was appointed civil governor of Sidon.

When the French took over the Syrian–Lebanese coast in 1919, Riyad al-Sulh's pan-Arab record, his antagonism towards France and his opposition to the establishment of Greater Lebanon made him *persona non grata* with the French authorities. In August 1920, he was sentenced to death (commuted to imprisonment) *in absentia* on a charge of his anti-French activity. The sentence was later commuted to exile abroad. He went to Egypt and later moved to Geneva where he was active on behalf of the Syrian–Palestinian Congress. In 1924, he was allowed back into Lebanon but, after taking part in the Syrian revolt of 1925, he was exiled once more. It was only in 1929 that he was permitted to return, after his old friend Emile Edde, now the country's prime minister, had pleaded with the French on his behalf. So had Kisrawan al-Khazin, a close associate of Edde's and a friend of Riyad's father.

In 1932, Riyad married Fa'iza, niece of Sa'adallah al-Jabiri of the Jabiri family of notables from Aleppo and one of the leaders of the National Bloc in Syria, later to become his country's prime minister. Sulh's close ties with the Syrian national leadership led, in 1936, to an invitation to join the Syrian delegation going to Paris to negotiate a treaty with France. Under the treaty, Syria was to become independent, but would still have treaty obligations towards France in defence and other matters. The treaty contained a clause under which Syria recognized Lebanon unequivocally as a separate state.

Though never ratified because of French reservations, the signing of the treaty became the backdrop to a change in attitudes towards the Lebanese state on the part of a number of Lebanese Sunni leaders. Riyad al-Sulh was one of them. True, Syria's recognition of Lebanon had been a inescapable part of its quest for independence, but Lebanese Sunnis interpreted it as an abandonment by Damascus of its commitment to the incorporation of Lebanon (as a whole or in part) into Syria.[34]

Riyad's change of heart had, however, begun earlier than that. Already in 1934 he was reported to have told the French High Commissioner Henri de Martel that he was 'in favor of keeping Tripoli within Greater Lebanon'. Earlier still, in 1928, he had reportedly said: 'I prefer to be in a hut in an independent Lebanon rather than live in a colonized Arab empire.'[35] More than that: since the beginning of the 1930s, he had tried to get himself elected to the Chamber of Deputies and thus to gain entry into the Lebanese political establishment. The French, however, frustrated his attempts. Yet by 1937, when there were proposals to appoint a Sunni prime minister, Sulh's name was mentioned as a possible candidate. Eventually, to Sulh's disappointment, President Edde preferred to nominate Khayr al-Din Ahdab. Edde felt that if a man as charismatic and as dynamic as Sulh were to head the cabinet, the president's authority would begin to be eroded. But Sulh did not despair. He considered it imperative that he himself should take part in, and in fact lead, the process of integrating Sunnis into the political system, provided this was done under conditions acceptable to the community. To underpin his personal claim to a leading role, he entered into a dialogue with most of the leading figures of the Maronite community: Edde, Khuri, Phalanges leader Pierre al-Jumayyil, and even the Maronite patriarch, Antun 'Arida. His purpose in these contacts was to seek a Maronite–Sunni understanding on the future of Lebanon – and, in no lesser degree, to fortify his personal claim to lead his community.[36]

Among other Sunni notables who acted in a similar fashion and, for all we know, from similar motives, were two cousins of Riyad, the brothers Kazim and Taqi al-Din al-Sulh. The two, particularly Kazim, provided the ideological framework for Riyad's political moves. Both declared themselves committed to the pan-Arab world-view which had become dominant among Arab nationalists in Lebanon, having by then replaced the earlier commitment to union with Syria (or 'Syrian unity', as they would have called it). It was Kazim al-Sulh who, from the early 1930s onwards, argued that recognition of the Lebanese state and integration into its political system did not contradict a commitment to pan-Arabism. In the prevailing circumstances, he claimed, only an independent Lebanon free from French domination and maintaining its Arab character would be able to participate, together with other independent Arab states, in the quest for the hoped-for comprehensive Arab union.[37]

Meanwhile, a similar transition became apparent among Maronites. The post-demographic realities and their political implications, as well as the prevarications of French policy during the 1930s (cf. below), convinced many Maronites that exclusive reliance on France could no longer guarantee the continued existence of Lebanon as a state. Hence, the concept of Greater Lebanon as a Christian state under Maronite hegemony was no longer viable. It was the Maronite church (originally the protagonist of the old concept) which now contributed significantly to the emergence of the new attitudes. Since the 1930s, a rift, both personal and political, had become apparent between the highest church functionaries and the French mandatory authorities. It involved the archbishop of Beirut, Ignace Mubarak, and most particularly the patriarch, 'Arida (who had assumed the patriarchate only in 1932). These and other church dignitaries did not hesitate to speak out for Lebanese independence and began cooperating more closely with the Syrian national movement and therefore also with the latter's allies, the Lebanese Sunnis.[38]

At this time, two blocs were being formed, one around the former Maronite attitudes, the other representing the new ideas: the National Bloc (al-Kutla al-Wataniyya) led by Edde, and the Constitutional Bloc (al-Kutla al-Dusturiyya) headed by Khuri. Edde and his followers clung to the old vision of Lebanon being a national home for the Maronites, but recognized that this could not be created within the boundaries of Greater Lebanon. He and his associates therefore now advocated reducing Lebanon to what it had been, that is the mountain area ('Little Lebanon'). The areas in which the Muslims were in the majority, they affirmed, should no longer form part of the Lebanese state.[39]

Khuri's bloc, by contrast, favoured the continued existence of Greater Lebanon in the 1920 borders. To ensure its survival, Khuri and his political allies were prepared to give up the vision of a Maronite national home and accept the notion of a Lebanese state for all communities. It would be founded on Christian–Muslim cooperation and would form part of the Arab world surrounding it. Quite a number of leading figures from Christian communities other than the Maronites joined the bloc, among them, for instance, Dabbas and Chiha. The bloc represented some elements in the Christian economic elite of Beirut whose standing had consistently been enhanced since the 1920s. Its advance had come about at the expense of quarters formerly more powerful in the various Christian communities, most particularly at the expense of the Maronite church. From obvious political and economic motives, they preferred a polity within the boundaries of Greater Lebanon and sought a dialogue with the Muslims.

Needless to say, the emergence of the two blocs also owed a great deal to the two leaders' deep-seated personal rivalry for first place in their community. For some twenty years, beginning in the 1920s, their mutual antagonism had set the agenda of Lebanese, or at least of Maronite, politics. Their respective views of Lebanon and of the nature of its links with France were shaped against the background of their contest. Later on, in 1949, a US

Legation report put it like this: 'The biography of Bishara al-Khuri is the story of the growth of Lebanon from its days under the Ottoman Empire, through the French mandate to its present status as an independent republic.' Indeed, his career and the emergence of his political concepts largely correspond to the stages by which his country achieved independence.[40]

Bishara al-Khuri was born in August 1890 in Ba'abda near Beirut, but his family came from Rashmaya in the Jurd region of Mt Lebanon. The local population there was composed of both Maronites and Druse. The Khuris were not among the leading Maronite families, but had a record of public service in the administration of Mt Lebanon. Bishara's grandfather was a judge in the Druse district (*Qa'imaqamiyya*), his father a secretary in the administration of the *Mutasarrifiyya*.[41] Khuri wrote in his memoirs: 'Bayt al-Din [the Maronite centre of Mt Lebanon] and Ba'abda and their town quarters were the first neighborhoods to meet my eyes and capture my heart with their covert threads, whose strength exceeds that of the ropes holding a boat at anchor.'[42]

Khuri received his secondary education at the hands of the Jesuit teachers of the Lazarist school of Aintoura. There, he was able to perfect his knowledge of literary Arabic. The richness of his idiom in Arabic – of which he made ample use during his political career as well as in his memoirs – contrasted markedly with Edde's express and life-long preference for French. From 1909 to 1912, Khuri studied law in France. On his return to Lebanon, he joined Edde's law office. Simultaneously, he began to be politically active, joining an association called Lebanese Beirut (Bayrut al-Lubnaniyya) which propagated expanding Lebanon beyond the limits of Mt Lebanon and making it the Maronite national home. The association had close ties with the French consul in Beirut, Georges Picot, and this fact forced Khuri to leave Beirut for Egypt as soon as the First World War broke out. There, he continued to be active in the same cause. After the end of the war, he returned to Lebanon and soon obtained a position in the French administration. In 1921, he was appointed secretary-general of the Lebanese government; later, the French made him a senator. Later still, he was minister of the interior in the government of Auguste Adib Pasha, and eventually held the premiership three times: from May 1927 till January 1928; from January to August 1928; and from May till October 1929.

As might be expected, Khuri's memoirs do not clearly expound his views of the establishment of Greater Lebanon by the French as a Maronite homeland under French protection. A clearer, though less flattering, view may be obtained from French and British as well as from US archives. A 1932 report by the US consulate-general, for instance, describes Khuri as 'pro-French'.[43] This is borne out by his political activity before the First World War and in Egypt during the war, as well as by his joining the Progress Party (Hizb al-Taraqqi) which sought the formation of Greater Lebanon. His cooperation with the French mandatory authorities has been noted above.[44]

Khuri's close cooperation with the French stemmed not only from his support for the French presence in Lebanon but also from the fact that he did not, during those years, possess a power base of his own in the Maronite community. It was only some time later that he acquired such a base by allying himself with a number of personalities from among the Christian economic elite of Beirut. These men put financial means at his disposal and some of them became his ideological mentors. One of them was Dabbas who, during his presidency, had laboured to have Khuri appointed to the cabinet. He did so partly because of his political rivalry with Edde. Dabbas regarded Khuri as a useful political counterweight to him. Another of Khuri's supporters was his brother-in-law Henri Far'un. (In 1943 Far'un was to play a major part in Khuri's election to the presidency.) Even more important in this context was the role of Chiha, another Roman Catholic, a banker whose sister was married to Khuri. All three were part of the growing economic elite of Beirut who shared, as is shown in Farid el-Khazen's *The Communal Pact of National Identities* as well as in Carolyn Gates's *The Merchant Republic of Lebanon*, common economic and political interests and thus also a common view regarding the future of Lebanon.[45]

It is important to stress Khuri's ties with Chiha; both Khuri and Sulh were soon to become the principal advocates of a Sunni–Maronite *rapprochement*, but both acted on the basis of ideological foundations laid by others. As we have seen earlier, the ideological founding fathers of this school of thought among the Sunnis had been Kazim and Taqi al-Din al-Sulh; on the Christian side, its protagonist was Chiha. Already, in the 1920s, he had turned against the idea of a Maronite national home and had begun to speak out for a Lebanon of all the communities. Only such a pluralist approach, he asserted, could make the country a crossroads of Arab, western and Mediterranean politics, cultures and life styles. Only thus could stability be achieved and the future standing of the economic elite be ensured. Chiha's thinking derived from a view of Lebanon as a 'merchant republic' drawing its inspiration from the period of the Phoenicians. He regarded the latter as the soil in which modern Lebanon had its real roots.[46]

During the 1930s, Khuri gradually dissociated himself from the mandatory authorities. He did so under the influence of Chiha's political doctrine, but also because links with the French were no longer helpful to his political career. Indeed, they had become an obstacle on his way to the top in his community and eventually, as president, in the Lebanese state as a whole. He ran for president twice (in 1932 and in 1936) and failed on each occasion because, so he claimed, the French had frustrated his efforts.[47] Both times, his chief rival had been Edde. In 1932, Edde, feeling that Khuri's chances were better than his own, endeavoured to have the elections cancelled. He persuaded the Sunni politician Muhammad al-Jisr (see above) to run for president, arguing that the Muslims now formed the majority in the Lebanese population and the presidency should therefore go to one of their representatives. Jisr demanded that a census be taken. When this was done (in 1932 – the last time ever that a census was held in Lebanon), it turned out that the Christian communities, taken together, had maintained their majority. The French high commissioner, Henri Ponsot, none the less decided to cancel the presidential elections, as Edde had proposed. He suspended the constitution, dissolved the Chamber of Deputies (whose task was to elect the president) and prolonged Dabbas's tenure as president for another three years.[48]

These measures dealt a serious blow to Khuri's political ambitions. His prospects of winning the presidency had, at least in his own judgement, been better than anyone else's. In response to Ponsot's steps, he and his political allies now launched a campaign for the reinstatement of the constitution – a campaign which, in the last analysis, was part of Khuri's race for the presidency. To conduct it all the better, he established, in 1934, the Constitutional Bloc of which he made himself the leader.

In 1936, Khuri again tried for the presidency, but failed once more. Elections were indeed held this time, because (as a prelude to the opening of negotiations on a Lebanese–French treaty) the French had made the constitution operative again. But when the elections took place in the parliament, Edde won by a vote of thirteen against twelve. French pressures had something to do with the result, but it was also evident that Khuri lacked the required measure of support among the Lebanese notables on whose votes he depended.[49]

The treaty was signed in November 1936; France recognized Lebanon as a sovereign and independent state and, in return, Lebanon granted France special political, economic and military privileges. But it never came into force since the French parliament postponed its ratification over and over again. Nevertheless, following its signing, elections to the Chamber of Deputies were held in Lebanon and President Edde formed a new cabinet. To head it, he appointed a Sunni Muslim, Khayr al-Din al-Ahdab. Later, he replaced him by 'Abdallah al-Yafi and later still by Khalid Shihab (two more Sunnis). By making these appointments, Edde acknowledged the emergence of new realities. They attested to his desire to maintain his position not solely by relying on France; he now wished to reinforce it by rallying part of the Sunni leadership to his side. From the point of view of his personal career, this acknowledgement may have come too late, but it still ushered in a new epoch in Lebanese politics.[50]

The 1930s were thus a time of personal disappointment for Khuri. Again and again, he found himself relegated to a marginal role by his main rival, Edde, and by the French (who always had the last word). His conclusion seems to have been that – with the French against him and with Edde having the edge over him within the Maronite community – he would have to build up his power position by recourse to alternative sources of support. He did so by drawing on Chiha's doctrine as well as by falling back on his personal background in the politics of Mt Lebanon. The latter prescribed cooperation with the Muslim community, or, more precisely, with the Sunni elite. Such cooperation would lay the foundations of an independent Lebanon belonging to all its communities and forming part of the Arab world around. Once this was achieved, Muslim support, as well as the absence of French intervention, would allow him to reach the highest position in the Maronite community and would thus bring his personal career to its peak.

The course of Lebanese history during the French mandate period, as well as the careers of Khuri and Sulh, show that during these years the country made great strides towards the goal of securing its survival and of achieving independence. Institutions of government were put into place and the concept of Sunni–Maronite cooperation took shape. The two communities developed similar ideas about the country's basic character and the course it should take in the future. Both trends brought independence closer and made it more viable.

The constitution was suspended again when the Second World War broke out. The Lebanese political system went into a coma, with only a flicker of the old hopes being kept alive. The defeat of France the following year deflected attention from the domestic scene to the momentous events unfolding elsewhere and thus deepened the sense of local stagnation. Only in June–July 1941 when Free French and British forces occupied the country did a new start look possible. New options seemed to open up, but in many ways the country simply resumed its march along a road already paved in the 1930s: the road towards an independent Lebanon of all the communities. That road would also take both Khuri and Sulh to the summit of power they had so long striven to attain.

# PART ONE

# The Struggle for Independence

# First Steps Along a New Road

The French–Lebanese treaty negotiated in 1936 had been expected to open the way for Lebanon's independence, but the failure of the French to ratify it turned the clock back. The real breakthrough on the road to independence occurred only in the summer of 1941 with the entry of British and Free French forces into Syria and Lebanon. At the same time, this was a breakthrough for those Lebanese leaders whose vision was an independent Greater Lebanon in the 1920 borders, though no longer under the hegemony of a single community but belonging to them all. Regardless of the views they had held in the past, Khuri and Sulh had become the most prominent representatives of this school of thought among the Maronites and the Sunnis, respectively. Their earlier careers have been reviewed above. Now, they were set for the final lap in their race for power.

Despite the radical change in the country's basic circumstances brought about by the events of 1941, it was several more years, not until December 1946, before full independence was achieved. These years have been described in a wealth of memoirs by high-ranking British and French officers and officials as well as by Lebanese leaders active at the time.[1] Also, over the last decade, archives have released records dealing with the period and a great deal of documentary evidence has become accessible, particularly in Britain and France. This has encouraged research and a considerable number of historical studies have been published, dealing with the Anglo-French struggle in the Levant during the Second World War and with events in Lebanon at the time.[2] These studies as well as the memoirs of western actors on the Lebanese scene tend to stress the influence of the great powers and to regard it as the key to an understanding of Lebanese affairs. In their view, the role of the Lebanese themselves in their struggle for independence was mainly a function of the great-power dispute. In contrast, the memoirs of the Lebanese actors on the scene incline (quite naturally) to dismiss western, especially British, exertions and instead to bestow rather heroic dimensions on the efforts of the Lebanese; they even speak of the battle for independence as a broad national effort. The truth, as so often, lies somewhere in the middle. There can be no doubt that local groups and their leaders, most particularly those sectors of the Maronite and the Sunni elite which we have singled out above, had an important role in pressing forward towards independence. They acted, after all, in keeping with, and in continuation of ambitions which had motivated them since the 1930s. They had taken part in working out the ideological foundations which were now to govern independent Lebanon. Their principal leaders, Khuri and Sulh, had thus seized that jumping-off ground which would give them the edge in the power struggle within their communities. Neither can there be any doubt that the western powers, and most of all the Franco-British rivalry in the Levant, served as a powerful accelerator of the process. Without them, it would not have materialized at that early stage.

Operation Exporter, as the allied advance against the strongholds of the Vichy regime in the Levant was called, began on 8 June 1941 and lasted about one month. On 14 July 1941, an armistice was signed at Acre, bringing to an end the rule of Vichy over the French mandatory areas of the Levant. Almost immediately, the new situation triggered a sharp and bitter dispute between the Free French and the British. Formally speaking, the region was placed under total Free French control, but the French were not allowed to be the sole masters there. British forces remained in Syria and Lebanon and it was their presence which made it possible for the followers of de Gaulle to exercise their functions.

The French were in no hurry to acknowledge the new realities. The way they saw it, the clock had merely been turned back to what it had been on the eve of the fall of France in May 1940. In their own view, the Free French were the successor government of the Third Republic. There was, therefore, no room to make any changes in the standing of France in the Levant, certainly not before the end of the war and the restoration of France to its former strength and position.

Under pressure from the British, the Free French high commissioner, General Georges Catroux, issued a statement proclaiming France's commitment to the independence of the states in the region. On 26 September 1941, he reaffirmed this commitment in a second declaration of 'independence'.[3] But it turned out that the French had their own ideas about what precisely independence was to mean. Back in May 1941, de Gaulle had already said: 'Our position in Syria will be as follows: We will proclaim independence. But we will not declare the mandate purely and simply abolished ... We will only say that we are coming in order to put an end to the mandatory regime and to conclude a treaty guaranteeing independence and sovereignty.'[4]

Accordingly, in his letter of appointment to Catroux, naming him high commissioner and commander-in-chief of the French forces in the Levant, de Gaulle instructed him to allow representative parliaments to be elected in Syria and Lebanon. These in turn were to be allowed to form local governments. But Catroux was then to open negotiations on treaties of friendship with these governments, treaties which would form the basis of France's future relations with Lebanon and Syria.[5]

The British for their part thought along totally different lines. Being altogether immersed in the war effort, Britain's first priority in the Middle East was quiet and stability. This, it was felt in London, was best achieved by a policy of appeasement, gratifying as far as was feasible the aspirations of the Arab nationalist movement. This had already been evident in Palestine in 1939 when the White Book was published restricting Jewish immigration and limiting land sales by Arabs to Jews. In the Levant, this policy implied promoting Syrian and Lebanese claims to independence. At the same time, however, the British recognized the need for proper, even friendly, relations with the Free French. This in turn implied acknowledging France's standing in the Levant. Good relations with the Free French were required for the successful pursuit of the war in Europe. Furthermore, caution in the Levant was advisable because any change there was bound to have reverberations for Britain's standing in Egypt, Iraq and Transjordan.

It seems likely that many Britons did not sense the contradiction inherent in such attitudes. After all Britain, too, had proclaimed Egypt and Iraq independent states back in the 1920s and 1930s and had yet managed to maintain its standing and preserve its influence in both Cairo and Baghdad. What Britain was now demanding of France did not, therefore, appear to London to be an untenable or unreasonable request nor was it meant, in British eyes, to dislodge the French from the region. On the contrary, some British politicians and officials believed that in following the British line, France might well be able to do two things: to contribute to Britain's immediate interest of fortifying the war effort, as well as to maintain its own position in the Levant. This was the view Churchill put forward in an address to the House of Commons on 9 September 1941:

> We have no ambitions in Syria. We do not seek to replace or supplant France, or substitute British for French interests in any part of Syria ... However, I must make it quite clear that our policy, to which our Free French Allies have subscribed, is that Syria shall be handed back to the Syrians, who will assume at the earliest possible moment their independent sovereign rights. We do not propose that this process of creating an independent Syrian Government ... shall wait until the end of the war. We contemplate constantly increasing the Syrian share in the administration. There is no question of France maintaining the same position which she exercised in Syria before the war ... There must be no question, even in war-time, of a mere substitution of Free French interests for Vichy French interests ... I was asked a question about our relations with Iraq. They are special; our relations with Egypt are special, and, in the same way, I conceive that France will have special arrangements with Syria. The independence of Syria is a prime feature in our policy.[6]

Aware of the dispute bound to emerge once the allies had entered the Levant states, de Gaulle and Oliver Lyttelton, Britain's minister of state in the Middle East, met in July 1941 and arrived at an agreement on future Franco-British relations there. Its terms were laid down in an exchange of letters between the two. Britain recognized French rule in Syria and Lebanon, but insisted that responsibility for law and order should rest with the British forces on the spot. However, British military moves in the Levant would be subject to French confirmation. The British assured de Gaulle that they had no other aim in the region than to work for victory in the war. The French for their part affirmed their commitment to Syrian and Lebanese independence.[7]

The first difficulties arose as soon as it became apparent that the British were interpreting the clause giving them responsibility for law and order in the broadest and most comprehensive manner possible. They subsumed under it virtually all aspects of life in the Levant: social and economic affairs, local politics, and more. In the British view, events in all these spheres were liable to have repercussions on law and order. The de Gaulle–Lyttelton letters were thus unable to forestall the sharp and bitter conflict over actual control in Syria and Lebanon that now ensued.

It would appear, however, that the dispute had its roots not so much in differences of approach between British and French policy-makers – though these differences would certainly have made some friction inevitable – but mainly sprang from the conflicting ways in which instructions from the centre were interpreted and executed by the men on the spot. The British and French officers and administrators stationed in the Levant and charged with implementing the policies laid down in London and Algiers (later in Paris) soon ended up pursuing policies of their own, and these contrasted sharply with the official intent of their governments.

On the French side, this process is easy to trace. De Gaulle and Catroux differed mainly on tactics; as far as the ultimate strategic aim was concerned, viz. the maintenance of the French position in the Levant, they were altogether in agreement. At the tactical level, de Gaulle was more keenly aware than Catroux of the constraints placed on Free French policy by the struggle against Vichy and the need to rally opinion in the Vichy-controlled part of France and in the French empire to his side. De Gaulle, still under the impact of how the British had treated him after the collapse of France, was in an anti-British mood and considered it a personal obligation to make every effort to secure France's holdings in the Levant. Catroux for his part was not constrained by such political considerations. Moreover, he had a great deal of experience in dealing with Muslim populations, having served in French North Africa and having been stationed in the Levant once before, in the early 1920s. His attitudes towards the Arab nationalist movement as a whole, and towards its followers in the Levant in particular, was thus more flexible than de Gaulle's. He was more easily prepared to recognize the new realities created by the allied occupation of Syria and Lebanon.[8] But the ultimate executants of French policy were those officials on the high commissioner's staff who were actually in the field in places all over the Levant. Many of them had long held administrative posts in the region. Most remained captives of the outlook of the past: of the charms (in their eyes) of the traditional French colonial notions which regarded Lebanon, and perhaps Syria as well, as an integral part of the overall French polity. Accordingly, control over them must not be abandoned, certainly not in favour of local nationalists. Such men, they felt, were no more than creatures of Britain, forced on the country by British efforts.[9]

On the British side, things were more complex. At one end of the scale was the Foreign Office which felt committed to the support of the Free French and to the British government's promise not to harm France's position in the Levant. At the other end were military men and the civil administrators, particularly those on the spot in the Middle East, who envisaged an entirely different kind of future for the region. They tended to see the current situation as the direct continuation of the rivalry between Britain and France that had existed during, and immediately after, the First World War. To their minds, the French presence in the Levant was a threat to British interests. In keeping with that view, they held that Britain must seek to eliminate French influence in the Levant states. Glubb Pasha (Sir John Glubb), then commander of the Arab Legion in Transjordan, warned:

> The possible hostility of independent Egypt, Iraq or Syria is, in a serious crisis, of altogether minor importance as long as no foreign power has a foot in these countries. It is at least possible, if not probable that France will be resentful and hostile to Britain after this war. An elementary knowledge of human nature is enough to convince us that, if we freely restore her independence and her empire to France, she will loathe us for it. In view of this fact, it is surely tempting fate to allow her to maintain herself in Syria, or even the Lebanon, in a splendid strategic position to cut our life line to the East by invasion of Palestine, by submarine activities in the Mediterranean from Beirut or by air activity all over the Middle East.[10]

Many high-ranking British officials thought likewise. The sense of a meeting of the Middle East War Council (MEWC) of May 1943, for instance, was summed up in the following words:

> The continued presence of France in the Levant is incompatible with our political and military interests in the Middle East as well as with the peaceful development and well being of the Arab countries ... From the long-term strategic angle the presence of an unco-operative and unreliable foreign power in the Levant States represents a permanent danger ... Any form of closer political association between the Arab States or even the States of 'Greater Syria' ... a development to which His Majesty's Government have declared themselves sympathetic, is hardly possible as long as the French maintain any direct influence, political or military, in Syria and Lebanon.[11]

The real challenge to the line taken by the Foreign Office came from the activities, even the mere presence in the Levant, of the British minister to Syria and Lebanon, Major-General Edward Louis Spears. A politician and a senior officer, Spears was a close associate of Churchill's who had sent him out as soon as the allies had moved into Syria and Lebanon, to act as liaison officer between British and French headquarters there. A few months later, in February 1943, he was appointed British minister in the Levant.[12] But the actual tasks of Spears and his staff went far beyond that of liaison or diplomatic representation. Spears became a second high commissioner along-side his French counterpart, but with more force behind him and with a greater capability to make his influence felt.[13]

Before assuming his mission in the Levant, Spears had been a Francophile and a personal friend of de Gaulle whom he had personally flown out from Bordeaux and taken to London when France collapsed in 1940. Once in the East, however, he turned into a rival of de Gaulle and an enemy of France. He began advocating the relegation of France from the Levant and the inclusion of Syria and Lebanon in the British sphere of influence. An official of the Eastern Department of the Foreign Office, W. E. Beckett, noted regretfully in a minute written in June 1942: 'General Spears is inspired by an extreme disgust of the Free French ... and we are in the position where our Minister in the Levant, who should be a useful intermediary to smooth things over between our military authorities and the local powers ... is far more extreme against the French than are the military authorities.'[14]

As Beckett's phrasing shows, Spears had managed to make enemies both of the French and of senior Foreign Office officials. The Foreign Office staff had disliked his appointment from the start, regarding him as an outsider or as a political appointee forced upon them by Churchill. They soon came to perceive him as an obstacle to the conduct of British diplomacy, to the consolidation of an appropriate policy towards France and the evolution of a desirable Middle East policy. But Spears had, and continued to have, Churchill's backing and the latter, on the strength of his long acquaintance with him, gave him a free hand.[15] He tolerated no criticism of Spears, since, as Harold Macmillan (the minister of state in Algiers) noted in his diary: 'Spears is an old friend, and Winston is very loyal (too loyal, sometimes) to old friends.'[16]

But the conflicting attitudes of the British actors, whether in London or on the scene, cannot hide the fact that the British dispute with France stemmed from fundamental differences in the two powers' view of the future of the Levant: France was resolved to maintain its imperial standing; Britain wanted Syria and Lebanon to move forward towards independence (and to closer relations with Britain). Personal inclinations apart, these differences were reflected in the relations between Spears and Catroux (and later between him and Catroux's successor, Jean Helleu). To the local population, matters looked a great deal more simple. They, and most of all the Sunni elites of Syrian and Lebanese notables, found nothing to interest them in the differences between Spears and the Foreign Office or between him and Churchill, or in the distinctions between the approaches between de Gaulle and Catroux or the latter and Helleu. They may not even have understood them very well. They were convinced that all France wanted was to perpetuate its rule, while the British wanted to throw the French out and to replace them as the dominant power in the Levant. Britain was likely to apply indirect rule, through the medium of Arab nationalist quarters in Syria and Lebanon which it supported. It might even, some Lebanese feared, set up a unified Arab state. The latter would be ruled by the Hashemites, either from Transjordan or from Iraq, and would include Lebanon. As clients of the British, the Hashemites would ensure British supremacy there.

All this would not, in itself, have sufficed to overturn the old system of loyalties of the Lebanese elites. The hard core of the Maronite community continued to exist. It rallied round Edde who continued to look to France for support, because only France had the ability and the political will to sustain the Maronites in their ideology and their political aspirations; to maintain Lebanon as a state under Maronite hegemony, and to perpetuate his and his fellow-notables' dominant position in it. On the other hand, the elite groups (some Maronites, but mainly Sunnis) who had turned against France in the 1930s, now started pinning their hopes on Britain. Britain, they expected, would help them in realizing their own political ambitions: an independent Lebanon which they themselves would run. Yet their rallying to the British side, for all the enthusiastic rhetoric of their declarations of support, particularly on the part of Khuri, was not a matter of real conviction. Their aim was not so much to support London as to promote their own political interests in Lebanon. Some of those who now cheered Britain (mainly the Sunnis among them) had, after all, earlier turned expectantly to the German representatives who came to Beirut after the fall of France in 1940.[17] According to French reports, Riyad and Sami al-Sulh as well as 'Abd al-Hamid Karami had made such contacts. The British mostly dismissed such French accusations against Sunni notables now considered to be in the pro-British camp. A British report of July 1942 said of Riyad al-Sulh that he was now convinced the allies would win the war and was prepared to cooperate with them.[18] A biographical note written a few years later stated: 'He has always been anti-French and, between 1938 and 1940, flirted with the Germans. Of late he has shown more understanding for British interests and has made a number of attempts to promote Anglo-Arab understanding.'[19]

As was usual with them, the majority of the Lebanese elites remained on the sidelines – at least initially. This applied to all communities. Among others, it was true of the Sunnis Sami al-Sulh and 'Abdallah al-Yafi; of the Shi'is Ahmad al-As'ad and Sabri Hamada, and of the Druse Nazira Junbalat. These men were ready to go on cooperating with the French, but also to establish ties with the British representatives. The latter for their part classed them as 'pro-French', either on the strength of their past record or because of their present conduct, and treated them with reserve. But as the new balance of power between the French and the British became clearer to them, and especially when the idea of Lebanese independence acquired firmer outlines, they gradually revised their attitudes. This process found expression in British reports. A member of Spears's staff, Geoffrey Furlonge, for instance, wrote in mid-1944, after a meeting with 'Abdallah al-Yafi, that the latter was 'formerly considered a tool of the French and Emile Edde, [but] has undoubtedly improved considerably within the last year. He still lacks personality and force of character, but his views are lucid and he is obviously anxious to play a useful part.'[20] Yafi had of course never been a French 'tool', nor did he later become a supporter of the British. He was not as ambitious as Khuri, Edde, Sulh, Karami or others and was content to play a waiting game so as to maintain whatever measure of influence he possessed, whether the ultimate overlordship in Lebanon should remain with the French or pass on to the British, as well as in case Lebanon became independent.

Since the beginning of 1942, the focus of the dispute between Britain and France had been the issue of whether or not to revive the Syrian and Lebanese constitutions and to enable parliamentary elections to take place. Without elections, progress towards independence would not be possible. Oddly enough, the matter had been placed on the agenda by the formation, on the part of the Wafd party, of a new government in Egypt. This had come about in the wake of the incident of 4 February 1942 when British tanks had surrounded the Egyptian king's palace and had forced the choice of a Wafd prime minister upon him against his wishes. The British, wishing to strengthen the new government and erode the position of King Faruq, encouraged the Wafd to hold new elections, regardless of wartime conditions. When they decided to do so, the Syrian National Bloc launched a campaign for holding elections in Syria, too. Spears soon took up their cause, believing that elections would strengthen Britain's hand and therefore weaken the position of France. Consequently, the French – taking the same view – expressed their reserva-tions.[21] Rather than blaming the Syrian nationalists, they accused Britain of initiating the move. As Catroux put it: 'With a unanimity which would be surprising if one did not suspect it of being concerted, Spears, Nahhas Pasha and Nuri Pasha Said [respectively, the Egyptian and the Iraqi prime ministers] declare that Lebanon and Syria cannot be considered legitimately independent until they enjoy a democratic, parliamentary regime.'[22]

But unlike the conjectures of the French (and, for that matter, unlike the conclusions of several historians of the period), the restoration of con-stitutional life and the subsequent elections in Syria and Lebanon were not solely inspired by Britain's, or rather Spears's, interest in mobilizing their local allies. Both measures benefited the whole gamut of political trends in the Levant, including allies of the French, such as Edde and his followers in Lebanon. As we shall see, all political groupings were demanding elections, regardless of their attitude towards Britain.

The Sunni elite favoured elections in the belief that they would bring independence from France closer. More down-to-earth, they also expected they would allow them to recoup their losses, after they had forfeited a great deal of their influence through the suspension of the constitution, the dissolution of the Chamber of Deputies and the transfer of all authority to the French high commissioner and his men. Some of them, such as Riyad al-Sulh, expected elections to provide them with an important springboard in their struggle to reach the top position within their community.

Similar considerations were entertained by the leaders of the Maronite community, Khuri and Edde. Their views on the future of the Lebanese state and its future relations with France did indeed differ fundamentally, but both were agreed that only the reinstatement of the constitution and the holding of elections could open the road for them in their race for supremacy within their community, and hence in the state of Lebanon. Both had high expectations from the French; Edde in particular had expected them to hand power to him on a silver platter by making him president. He had, after all, been elected president in 1936, but had been dismissed in 1941 by the Vichy high commissioner, General Henri Dentz. The Free French, he probably thought, now owed it to him to reinstate him in his former position. In actual fact, however, the British and Free French takeover had left both Khuri and Edde equally far from the presidency which they had both sought so fervently for two decades. In his memoirs, Khuri did not hide his ambition. After describing the beginnings of the rivalry between France and Britain and the conflicting aims pursued by the French and British representatives, he went on to say: 'As for ourselves, our demands have remained what they were: the restoration of constitutional life and the holding of free parliamentary elections, and eventually the election of a President of the Republic by parliament, in accordance with the constitution.'[23]

Even the Maronite church came to support elections and joined the ranks of those demanding full independence. On 25 December 1941, the patriarch 'Arida convened a meeting at his seat in Bkirke under the slogan: 'There is no independence without reinstating the constitution.'[24] Khuri attended the meeting – an indication of how close he was to 'Arida at the time. In his address, he reiterated his demand for independence and for free elections (which he expected to result in his assuming the presidency).[25] At its conclusion, the meeting adopted a series of resolutions, among them a call for full independence, self-determination through free elections, the right for Lebanon to sign treaties and establish ties with foreign nations, as well as for individual liberties and the separation of executive and legislative powers, to be achieved by 'a freely elected parliament in which the Lebanese communities and regions are fairly represented'.[26]

These attitudes on the part of the Maronite church are noteworthy, because the church had originally been in the vanguard of those calling for a Greater Lebanon. But then, 'Arida had a prolonged personal quarrel with the French

authorities which had begun back in the 1930s and the French had tried hard
to prevent his election to the patriarchate (as did Khuri, who supported his
cousin 'Abdallah al-Khuri's candidacy).[27] It was this quarrel which had, in large
measure, shaped the attitudes of 'Arida (who was known throughout Lebanon
as an irate and impulsive man). But he had other considerations as well. He
also expected the overturn of the status quo to bolster his personal position.
He had come to realize that, somewhat paradoxically, the establishment of
Greater Lebanon which the church had done so much to promote had ended
up eroding its influence among Maronites and in the new state as a whole.
In its place, new centres of power had come into existence, precisely because
there now was a Greater Lebanon. Most salient in this particular context was
the rise of the Christian business elite of Beirut. Khuri had quickly understood
the significance of this shift; 'Arida followed suit. He had come to realize that
he could only restore the leading role of the church within the community
by adopting a new approach towards the Lebanese state.[28]

After the British and the Free French had moved in, 'Arida drew closer
to Khuri and began cooperating with him in the political arena, especially in
the struggle for the reinstatement of the constitution. This had been the
background to the above meeting. Khuri repaid the patriarch by publicly
acknowledging the leadership and the authority (at least, the moral authority)
of 'Arida.[29] However, these idyllic conditions proved short-lived. Once Khuri
had become president, 'Arida soon realized that the former was unwilling to
make him a partner in the decision-making process. New frictions emerged.
What is more, in 1941 'Arida had contacted British representatives, had
suggested the establishment of closer ties with them and had proposed that
Britain replace France as the protecting power in Lebanon. The British had
turned down his overtures, not wishing to provoke the French at that
particular juncture. They also took a negative view of 'Arida's character and
doubted his motives and the seriousness of his proposals.[30]

The 1941 church convention thus marked a certain turning point: it
expressed the reservations on the part of many Lebanese or even Maronite
circles towards the French mandate which were becoming prevalent at that
time. It was felt that France, in its present weakness, was no longer a
significant factor in shaping Lebanon's destiny; more than that: France had
become an obstacle on the road to independence. The roots of such sentiments go back to the 1930s, but the circumstances of the early 1940s revived
them and gave them a great deal of added impetus.

An important stage in this development was reached in June 1942, when
Khuri and Jamil al-Mardam, a prominent leader of the Syrian National Bloc,
came to Cairo to meet with Egyptian prime minister Nahhas Pasha. The
meeting had been called at the instance of Nahhas who was then eager to
bolster his domestic position by assuming an active role in the promotion of
pan-Arabism. The three participants agreed that Egypt and Syria should
become joint guarantors of Lebanese independence, while Lebanon would

undertake to affirm, and maintain, its Arab character and disengage itself from overly close ties with France. In his memoirs, Khuri recalls telling his two interlocutors that 'Lebanon wishes for full independence in its present boundaries and for the maximum feasible cooperation with the Arab states'. He went on to say: 'part of the Christian public do not share this approach of ours and affirm a totally opposite view, the main principle of which is the need for protection by a foreign [i.e. non-Middle-Eastern] power, but I myself and my associates cling to our own approach and are ready to defend and to implement it'.[31]

These last words explain the political benefit Khuri expected to derive from his trip to Cairo. His meeting there and the understandings arrived at formed a new and incisive phase in Khuri's struggle for the presidency. It illuminated like a spotlight the political gamble he was taking by staking his all on inter-Arab backing and on the expectation that this in turn would gain him the support of the Sunni notables at home. The backing of the latter would then give Khuri the edge in his own community. He would emerge as the only Maronite leader with a new vision and the capability to set the Lebanese state on a new path. Indeed, it had been Khuri's record of contacts with the Syrian nationalists which had prompted Mardam to recommend to Nahhas to summon Khuri to the Cairo meeting. A less publicized aspect of the understanding reached there apparently touched on promises by the Egyptian and Syrian leadership to support Khuri in his election campaign.[32]

These electoral promises marked the beginning of inter-Arab involvement in Lebanese domestic affairs. Egypt's intervention on the side of Khuri caused the Iraqi chargé d'affaires in Beirut, Tahsin Qadri, to suggest that his government should back Khuri's rival, Edde.[33] But the Iraqi prime minister, Nuri Sa'id, who met with both Edde and Khuri in Lebanon in July 1943, came to the conclusion that he, too, preferred Khuri as a partner. (Nuri, it must be recalled, was then working on Fertile Crescent union schemes embracing Iraq, Syria, Jordan and Lebanon, whether by merger or federation.) Following his meeting with Khuri, Nuri told Spears that when he broached the subject of a broad Arab federation, he 'had of course found Bishara [Khuri] much more nearly in conformity with his own views on Arab Federation and even apparently quite willing to consider the possibility of an independent Christian Lebanon reduced in size as an alternative to a far-reaching federation between the present Lebanon and her neighbors'.[34] Khuri's hints to Nuri were undoubtedly mere lip-service, intended to please his Iraqi guest. But they none the less attest to Khuri's desire for a dialogue, and for cooperation, with the Arab nationalist leadership outside Lebanon.

The impression Nuri came away with after meeting Edde was very different. According to Spears: 'Here Nuri Pasha, as was to be expected, found the going more difficult. Emil Edde had been much less easy to convince of the possibility of any close federation between the Lebanon and Syria.'[35] Yet Edde had said something more which seemed surprising, at least to Spears:

He [Edde] had, on the other hand … talked in rather violent terms of the dislike of the Lebanese for the idea of continued French domination, and had urged on Nuri the desirability of the Lebanon's concluding treaties (sic) with Iraq with a view to restricting French powers of interference. To this Nuri had replied in effect 'Not so fast!' Did Edde mean that in the proposed treaties the Iraqi Government were somehow to record their insistence on the French giving the Lebanese Government a freer hand? If so, this was altogether too much to expect. Apparently Edde did not further develop his views on the subject; and I was left with the impression that his motive had been simply to impress Nuri with the fact that he was as patriotic as the rest, and no French stooge.[36]

Spears's words attested to his own attitude towards Edde, but did not necessarily conform with reality. It would appear that Edde – much like Khuri and from similar motives, but belatedly and more hesitantly – was seeking for ways to reach an understanding with neighbouring Arab leaders. And doing so implied a similar approach to the local Sunni leadership. In other words, Edde too was now beginning to acknowledge the changes that had occurred on the regional as well as on the domestic scene and had started coming to terms with them. His timing had much to do with the approach of the election which, he hoped, would win him the presidency.

Despite the broad consensus, within Lebanon and in the Arab states, on the need to restore the constitution, the French remained adamant. The British were, at that particular time, reluctant to bring pressure to bear on the French on this issue. Their minds were on the exigencies of the war, their attention riveted on the current battles at El-Alamein (not so far away, after all, from Lebanon) and at Stalingrad. The upshot was that the political situation the allies had encountered in 1941 when they moved in remained unchanged until 1943.

At the time of the occupation of Lebanon, the presidency was held by Alfred Naqqash. A Maronite from Beirut, he had been appointed president on 8 April 1941 by the Vichy high commissioner, General Dentz. When Catroux became high commissioner on behalf of de Gaulle, he confirmed Naqqash in his position and in November 1941 prolonged his incumbency, finding him pliable, ready to cooperate and well aware of being altogether dependent on the French. Moreover, Catroux did not wish to involve himself in the competition between Khuri and Edde, realizing that this would eventually force him to take sides. He therefore preferred to leave things as they were. But his decision to prolong Naqqash's tenure led both Khuri and Edde to turn against him; each had expected to be called upon to replace Naqqash and had hoped thereby to gain an advance round for their coming struggle. Khuri, as we have seen, was led to adopt rather more radical attitudes, dissociating himself from France and seeking alternative bases of support among Arab nationalists at home and abroad. True, the British had also been reserved about the extension of Naqqash's tenure (they thought of him as a tool in the hands of the French),[37] but it was not their attitude which

motivated Khuri and Edde in opposing Catroux. Nor was it the influence of
the Maronite patriarch – a determined adversary of Naqqash. One of the
reasons for 'Arida's attitude was that he had not been consulted over the
extension of Naqqash's incumbency; another was that he resented Naqqash's
close ties with the Jesuits. He considered that order as an enemy of, even a
threat to, the standing of the Maronite church, or at least to his own personal
standing.[38]

During his tenure, Naqqash appointed Sunnis to the premiership. In doing
so he wished to uphold the model of Maronite president and Sunni prime
minister (first applied in the late 1930s; see above), as well as to consolidate
his own position by being seen to conform with it. His first appointee was
Ahmad Da'uq who was prime minister from December 1941 till July 1942;
the second was Sami al-Sulh (July 1942 to March 1943). Both belonged to
the same group within the Sunni elite: those who had been prepared to
become part of the Lebanese state establishment back in the mid-1920s.
They had not been required to pay a heavy price to gain entry into it. The
British, it is true, considered them pro-French but, as we have seen, these
cut-and-dried definitions were now losing their significance; all these men
were trying to do was to reinforce, or at least to maintain, their personal
standing.

Both Da'uq's and Sulh's cabinets had to contend with a long series of
difficulties and encountered considerable opposition, particularly because of
economic dislocations caused by the war. Furthermore, their rivals, as well as
many others who had not been coopted into the government, entertained
the hope that bringing down the prime ministers through public protest
would also cause the downfall of Naqqash. This was even more marked in
the case of Sulh's government than in that of Da'uq. Sulh had expected to
form a coalition in which a broad spectrum of Lebanese political quarters
would be represented. But the coalition talks broke down over the division
of government portfolios and the attempt was abandoned.[39] Among Sulh's
adversaries were Khuri's Constitutional Bloc, Edde's National Bloc, and Sami
al-Sulh's rivals from within the Sunni community. The opposition also included
the Phalanges and the Najada (the latter having been formed in 1937 as a
Sunni para-military organization working to secure Lebanon's independence
from France and to establish the country's Arab character). The two cooperated in organizing protest demonstrations to denounce the government's
inaction in the face of the current economic crisis.[40]

The fall of Sami al-Sulh's short-lived cabinet coincided with the end of
the stagnation on the domestic scene of Lebanon. After El-Alamein and
Stalingrad, the British felt sufficiently reassured to revert to the plan of
holding elections in the Levant. This time, surprisingly, the French did not
put up any serious resistance. On 29 January 1943, the Free French Committee
of National Liberation in Algiers agreed to reinstate the constitution.
Apparently Catroux – who was on the point of joining the highest echelons

of the Free French authorities then being constituted in Algiers – wanted to wind up affairs in the Near East as quickly as possible. He may have hoped that after showing flexibility over the issues of the constitution and the elections, the French would be able to claim greater British support for France's demands. The French aim was to conclude treaties with the newly-elected governments which would ensure France's future standing in the Levant.[41] Yet a long stretch of the road leading to new elections was still to be travelled. Naqqash resented not having been consulted on the matter beforehand and refused to issue a presidential decree for new elections. He was also playing for time in an endeavour to strengthen his own position in the Maronite community before the balloting took place.[42]

Naqqash's tactics caused Catroux's patience to snap. On 18 March, he dismissed Naqqash and appointed Ayub Thabit, a Protestant notable from Beirut, in his stead. Khalid Shihab, a Sunni, and Jawad Boulus, a Maronite, were appointed ministers.[43] But it soon became apparent that Naqqash's removal had not resolved the matter. Thabit did indeed agree to new elections, but two decrees he issued on 17 June concerning their modalities and their date caused a political uproar. They had been drafted by Thabit alone and were approved by the French only after the event. The public felt that their purpose was to prepare the ground for Thabit's own re-election by bolstering his position in the Christian camp. Khuri, however, took a different view: in his memoirs, he attributed Thabit's step to his lack of political experience as well as to his ambitious, egocentric and easily irritated character rather than viewing them as a piece of political scheming.[44]

Thabit's decrees stipulated that the Chamber should be made up of thirty-two Christian and twenty-two Muslim deputies, and that Lebanese residing abroad should be entitled to the vote. According to various estimates, the latter numbered some 159,000, most of them Christians.[45] A government statement published on 28 June set the balloting date for 26 and 27 September 1943. To justify the delay, it was pointed out that the summer months were the principal tourist season and thus unsuitable for an election campaign.[46]

Thabit's decrees infuriated the Muslim sector of the population, most particularly the Sunni elite who felt that they had conceded a great deal simply by agreeing to take part in Lebanese political life. They were altogether unwilling to consent to a division of parliamentary seats which disadvantaged them so significantly. On 21 June, therefore (only a few days after Thabit's decrees were issued), an all-Muslim committee was formed with the participation of all prominent Sunni leaders as well as with Shi'i and Druse representatives. The mufti of Lebanon was placed at its head. The committee resolved to demand the revocation of the decrees and insisted on taking a census. Kurds and bedouin living in Lebanon were to be counted, but Lebanese nationals abroad (predominantly Christians, as we have noted) were to be excluded from the census. If these demands were not met, the Muslims would boycott the elections.[47] However, the wording of the committee's resolutions was low-key and businesslike and betrayed a readiness to reach an eventual compromise. Only 'Abd al-Hamid Karami came out with a strong statement to the effect that he would not allow anyone to force him to support the continued existence of the present Lebanese state unless it was Arab in character and cooperated with the other Arab states. But he remained in a minority of one.[48]

The Muslims were not alone in opposing the decrees. The Constitutional Bloc, too, interpreted them as directed against itself and launched a campaign against them. On 30 June 1943, Khuri addressed a sharp protest to Catroux, accusing Thabit of cooperating with Edde with a view to furthering the latter's prospects in the forthcoming elections. He went on to warn Catroux that the resentment caused by the decrees in so many sectors of the population was bound to elicit anti-French sentiments.[49] Khuri seems to have thought of the decrees as a delaying tactic, while his own vital interest lay in holding the elections promptly. Furthermore, as described above, Khuri had based his own approach to the elections on his cooperation with the Muslim camp, especially the Sunni elite. To ensure their continued support, he did not hesitate to enter a confrontation with those in his own community who supported his rival Edde. It was not in his interests to lend support to the hard-core elements in the Maronite community whose backing Thabit had wished to enlist by his decrees.

The compromise proposal that pointed to a way out of the crisis came (not by coincidence) from Egyptian prime minister Nahhas Pasha. For reasons we have already referred to, the holding of elections in Lebanon and Syria was a matter of self-interest to him. He proposed to allot twenty-nine seats to the Christians and twenty-five to the Muslims. This came close to reflecting their shares in the population (53.7 per cent and 48.3 per cent, respectively).[50] The Sunni leaders accepted Nahhas's proposal, but the Maronite patriarch turned it down. He described the Muslim opposition against Thabit's decrees as a deliberate Muslim attack against the country's Christian majority as well as its territorial integrity.[51] While ready in principle to cooperate with the Sunni leadership, he was not willing to do so at the price of abandoning Maronite supremacy. Further mediation was therefore required to settle the crisis. The French prevailed upon Spears to step in. On 30 June, he met with both the patriarch and the mufti. A compromise was finally agreed to by all. The Chamber would number fifty-five deputies: thirty Christians and twenty-five Muslims (one more seat for the Christians than Nahhas had proposed).[52]

A few weeks later, on 21 July, Thabit was forced to resign and the French appointed Petro Trad, a Greek Orthodox, to the presidency. Once all controversial points had been settled, High Commissioner Helleu issued an order, dated 31 July 1943, fixing the size of the Chamber and the division of seats as shown above. A decree issued by Trad named 28 August as balloting day.

Where a run-off election was required, it was to take place on 5 September. The Chamber would then elect a new president on 21 September.[53] An important phase in Lebanon's struggle for independence had come to a close. The elections would now decide who would run the affairs of the state and determine its future course.

## CHAPTER 2

# The 1943 Elections

The elections, ending with Khuri's assumption of the presidency and Riyad al-Sulh's appointment as prime minister, were a clear victory for those striving for independence from France and seeking a 'Lebanon of all the communities' to form part of the Arab world. The results consolidated Christian–Muslim understandings on the future of the country, soon to be laid down in their final form in the 'National Pact'. It was the pact which made independence possible and ensured the state's existence for many years to come.

True, the elections were held in the shadow of the rivalry between France and Britain over control of the Levant and have therefore often been considered no more than a phase in that dispute. Its results have been described as decisive for the outcome of the larger struggle and as a turning point in the process of eliminating French influence from the region. Indeed, a US intelligence report, written about half a year before the elections, stated:

> Information from Baalbek (Ba'lbak) and Zahle tends to show that the forth-coming elections will be anything but free and democratic. It seems evident that the situation is actually one of political struggle between Anglophiles and Francophiles, and that both Britain and France are taking active parts. It is a matter of common knowledge that both are canvassing the regions in attempts to find the most powerful candidates definitely favorable to their designs.[1]

Once the results were known, Philippe Filliol, deputy Free French repres-entative in Cairo, acknowledged in a conversation with Lord Casey, the British minister of state in the Middle East, 'that the results of the election had been a severe blow to the French position in Lebanon ... so severe that they had to make up their minds whether to sit down under it (which would mean, he stated, elimination of French influence from the Levant) or else to react violently'.[2]

In actual fact, however, the elections were first and foremost another stage in the long struggle of Lebanese domestic quarters over who was to rule the country and what its future character should be. Viewed that way, the results were no major departure from past patterns. The elites of notables from all communities maintained their strength by adapting to the new rules of the political game dictated by the changing regional and international circumstances. The modifications that did occur happened within the communal elites, particularly in the Maronite community, where power struggles now took the shape of ideological argument. Victory went to those among the Maronite notables who interpreted the signs of change correctly and were quick to adapt to it. Khuri's camp carried the day for doing so best. In the other communities, the changes were on a minor scale. Sulh did indeed gather enough support to gain the premiership, but this did not signify any weakening of other Sunni leaders, not even those who, in the past, had been ready to cooperate with the French mandatory authorities. They now demonstrated their agility in coming to terms with the new realities. Much the same can be said of the Shi'i and Druse notables. Their communities were much less influenced by the Franco-British dispute than were the Sunnis and the Maronites. Neither did the domestic confrontation over the future of the state have the same impact on them. They therefore found it easier to act according to old personal loyalties and to vote for their traditional leaders.[3] It would be correct to say that the principal loyalty of the Lebanese notables remained exactly as before; it was devoted to their personal interests. This, they felt, would now be better served by joining those who preferred independence over French domination.

The elections were held under the same system that had been applied earlier under the French mandate. Lebanon was divided into five electoral districts or constituencies, with the number of deputies to be elected in each varying in accordance with the size of the population of the district. The seats to be filled in each constituency were divided along communal lines, intended to conform to the estimated relative strength of each community in the district. Nevertheless, each deputy was elected by all the voters in the district, regardless of their communal affiliation. Most candidates did not run on a personal ticket but rather as part of a list presenting candidates according to the communal key. The voter need not, however, accept a list *in toto*; he was free to cast his ballot on the basis of his personal preference or to vote for candidates from different lists. The average Lebanese voted on the strength of personal or family loyalty, picking a name that suited him, and was then likely to cast his ballot for the rest of that list, regardless of community. This was particularly true of the rural areas in the Biqa' and the south. There, the appearance of a local feudal chief on any particular list usually sufficed to get the voters to vote for the rest of the names he had chosen to include in it. In these areas, Shi'i votes could thus decide the fate of candidates from any of the Christian communities or even of Sunnis, providing these had associated themselves with a particular local chief and been placed on his list by him. Such candidates could win a seat even if most members of their own community preferred someone else. Inclusion in the list of a locally powerful man was thus a cherished prize. Deals for their composition were negotiated in prolonged talks and often decided by money changing hands or by other benefits being offered.[4]

In the 1920s and the 1930s, such lists had been drawn up in consultation with the local French representative who acted on instructions received from Beirut or even Paris. They would usually prefer to have a single list presented in each district and would work to have potential 'trouble-makers' – the common terms for nationalists opposed to French rule – excluded from it. But during the run-up to the 1943 elections, the French were in a weaker position, while British influence had increased. This brought Franco-British relations – tense since 1941 – close to breaking-point. Initially, at the time of his appointment, Spears had warned British officials not to let themselves become pawns in the hands of local politicians in their struggles against the French and against each other.[5] Subsequently, however, he began intervening in local politics himself.

The French none the less tried to draw up lists of local candidates identified with their cause, and to steer them towards electoral victory. Spears for his part sought to frustrate the French efforts and to encourage candidates he considered anti-French (and hence pro-British). French complaints against Spears increased in frequency.[6] In July 1943, the Foreign Office found it advisable to instruct its representatives in Beirut that, whatever their suspicions regarding the elections, they must not allow them to turn into a Franco-British contest.[7] However, it seems that Spears largely ignored the note.[8]

Yet the dispute was no more than the backdrop to the local struggles. In the last analysis, these were decided on the spot in the electoral districts. British and French pressures were indeed brought to bear during the parliamentary election campaign as well as during the run-up to the presidential elections, but to a large extent they seem to have cancelled each other out. This was borne out for instance in Mt Lebanon, and to some extent in Beirut as well, where – despite substantial British efforts – the results favoured the French. For all intents and purposes, the real struggle was between the isolationist sector of the Christian camp who wanted French overlordship to continue because they believed that France would guarantee their domestic predominance, and their opponents, both Christians and Muslims. The latter, by contrast, sought independence because they had convinced themselves that only in an independent Lebanon would they be able to make their way to the top. Both Spears and Helleu came to realize that their classification of candidates as pro-British or pro-French had become irrelevant, certainly in the longer term. Lebanese politicians did not have the interests of one or the other great power at heart; what motivated them was self-interest. This may have been particularly true of the Shi'i and Druse notables, but it undoubtedly applied to others as well. What they wanted was their share of the spoils. To illustrate: the Druse Kamal Junbalat from the Shuf mountains appeared in Edde's list for Mt Lebanon and some Beiruti Sunnis such as Yafi and Sami al-Sulh ran in lists considered pro-French. In neither case did this signify anything much about the line they were going to take once they were elected. To sum up: election results depended principally, if not exclusively, on the play of local interests and the balance of power on the spot. To regard them merely as a plebiscite on affiliation with either Britain or France is to misjudge their real significance.

## The Results of the Election

SOUTHERN LEBANON   This district had ten representatives in the Chamber. The local holders of power were a number of Shi'i families, most prominently the As'ads, headed by Ahmad al-As'ad, and their rivals, the 'Usayrans, under 'Adil 'Usayran. Two other important families were the Zuwayns and the Khalils. Ostensibly, the contest between As'ad and 'Usayran was political in character, the first being identified with the French on the strength of his record of cooperation with the mandatory authorities, the latter being regarded as pro-British and as sympathetic to the cause of Arab nationalism.[9] For this reason, the British had vetoed As'ad's appointment as a minister in Sami al-Sulh's government in July 1942 and had tried to put an end to his political career by accusing him of drug smuggling. But (unlike Rashid Muqaddam; see below) As'ad was never caught in a criminal act. When eventually a small quantity of hashish was found in his car, the blame was put on his driver.[10]

This being the local situation, the French urged As'ad to put together a list and to present it as an alternative to 'Usayran's. They even agreed for As'ad to include their arch-rival Riyad al-Sulh in it. (Sulh was running in the same district.)[11] But they did not succeed. For political reasons (and perhaps also, as the French claimed, because of British pressures), As'ad preferred to ally himself with 'Usayran and with Kazim al-Khalil, the current head of the Khalil family, and to form a single list together with them. He did eventually include Riyad al-Sulh in the list,[12] despite a considerable degree of personal tension between them. The main reason was that Edde had interceded with him on Sulh's behalf.[13] Edde may have done so simply on the strength of his long friendship with Sulh, but he may also have had his eyes on the presidential elections due to be held in the wake of the ballot for the Chamber, and may have thought it worthwhile to 'invest' in figures likely to be useful to him then. One way or another, his helping Sulh attested once again to his increasing understanding of how much the scene had changed in Lebanon and proved that he did not want to be outflanked by Khuri in chasing for the support of Sunni notables. Opposite the As'ad–'Usayran list, Yusuf Zuwayn formed a list of his own. But the latter and his allies were unable to stand up to weight of the combined As'ad–'Usayran list; they were defeated and none of them was elected.[14]

On the face of it, the victory of the combined list, which included figures like 'Adil 'Usayran and Riyad al-Sulh who were known for their opposition to the French, could have counted as a defeat for France and an achievement for Britain. The British did indeed take that view.[15] Seen in a more detached light, however, it was a victory for the established Shi'i elite of the south. Two leading families, often enough at daggers drawn in the past, had joined to maintain their positions of power under the new conditions, had decided to leave their differences to be settled at some future date, and had carried the day. But for Ahmad al-As'ad – who had earlier cooperated with the mandatory rulers – to join anti-French figures like Riyad al-Sulh and 'Usayran signalled that men like him were now ready to dissociate themselves from France and cast in their lot with the nationalist camp, both Christian and Muslim, who clamoured for independence.

THE BIQA' This district sent seven members to the Chamber. A joint list, headed by Sabri Hamada, the local Shi'i feudal leader, was drawn up. Though related to the As'ads through the marriage of his daughter, he was a political rival of Ahmad al-As'ad. His competitor for power among the local Shi'is, Ibrahim Haydar, was prevailed upon to join Hamada's list. Henri Far'un, a wealthy Greek Catholic banker from Beirut and a close associate of Khuri's, also appeared on it.[16] He had to pay Hamada some 70,000 Lebanese lira for the privilege.[17] But then he had money to spare; his major political investment was made with a view to supporting Khuri's list in Mt Lebanon. Some observers claimed that further financial contributions later enabled Khuri to gain the presidency.[18]

Hamada, Haydar and Far'un were opposed by a list headed by another Hamada, Fadlallah. Its most conspicuous member was the Maronite Musa Nammur who had been minister of the interior in Sami al-Sulh's last government. The French tried to prevail upon Sabri Hamada to include Namur in his own list, but had not been able to convince him. They now supported Fadlallah Hamada's and Namur's list which was joined by the Shi'i competitors of Sabri Hamada. But the latter was much too powerful for them on the local scene and, despite Far'un's funding, none of its members was elected.[19] The British were quick to register the outcome as a French defeat and referred to the winning list as 'Far'un's men' (even though he was a subsidiary figure in it).[20] Being close to Khuri, they identified him with the pro-British camp. But in reality, just like in the south, the motive behind the winning list was that the local Shi'i leaders preferred to join forces in order to maintain their predominant position.

BEIRUT In Beirut, which sent nine deputies to the Chamber, two lists were competing. One was headed by Sami al-Sulh (the British called it 'French inspired') and included Christian leaders like Thabit and Naqqash. The opposing list was headed by Sulh's Sunni competitors: Yafi, Sa'ib Salam and Muhi al-Din al-Nasuli. It included Habib Abu Shahla, a Greek Orthodox who was an ally of Edde's.[21] The lists point to the fact that in Beirut, no more than anywhere else, the struggle between France and Britain did not determine the delineation of the competing camps. Both lists numbered candidates known as pro-French or as past collaborators with the mandatory authorities. The real significance of the way the lines were drawn was that they reflected the contest between the city's Sunni leaders. Christian candidates joined one or the other according to their personal calculations.

Both lists had considerable success. Their prominent figures – the Sunnis Sulh, Yafi and Salam, and the Christians Thabit and Abu Shahla – were all elected, relegating candidates of the second rank from the race. The French viewed the outcome as a success for themselves. They expected to find common ground with the new deputies, some of whom had, after all, cooperated with them in the past. The British were quick to concede defeat.[22] But here, too, the Franco-British yardstick must not be too narrowly applied. The broader significance lay once again in the ability of the elite – in this case, the Sunnis – to maintain their strength and position. Whatever their former links with the French, the successful candidates soon found their way into Lebanon's nationalist camp.

In the remaining two districts – North Lebanon and Mt Lebanon – the elections came closer to being an expression of Anglo-French rivalry. In both places, the two sides intervened vigorously; yet the underlying thrust of the local balance of power did not fail to assert itself in some measure.

NORTH LEBANON North Lebanon was allotted twelve seats in the Chamber. Its geographical centre was the town of Tripoli where a bitter contest between the Karami and the Muqaddam families had been in progress for many years. The former was headed by 'Abd al-Hamid Karami, known for his Arab nationalist inclinations; the latter by Rashid Muqaddam, who was regarded as pro-French. The two families were in a state of blood feud because, in 1935, 'Abd al-Hamid Karami had killed a member of the rival family, 'Abd al-Majid Muqaddam. Karami was indicted and tried; but his plea of having acted in self-defence was accepted and he was acquitted. His attorney, interestingly enough, was Bishara al-Khuri.[23]

French endeavours focused on an attempt to bring together a pro-French list under Rashid Muqaddam, but the British were able to foil their efforts by exposing Muqaddam's involvement in smuggling drugs to Egypt. He had bribed a number of British officers to carry drugs there in British army vehicles.[24] On 21 April 1943, the British therefore arrested him, together with some other members of his family. They handed them over to the French authorities, demanding that they be put on trial and that Muqaddam's candidacy for the forthcoming elections be cancelled. The French failed to comply, merely placing Muqaddam under house arrest, but leaving him free to conduct his election campaign from there. The French justified their procedure by pointing out that most Lebanese notables, including religious functionaries, were involved in the drug trade; strong action against Muqaddam would make it imperative to deal similarly with most members of the elite. They also threatened that, should the British continue to take action against Muqaddam, they for their part would arrest Camille Chamoun, one of Britain's most prominent supporters.[25]

After prolonged discussions, the French and British authorities in the Levant reached a compromise. But when the compromise proposal reached Prime Minister Churchill's desk, he turned it down (acting largely under the influence of Spears who was then in London). The British thus reverted to their original attitude and, with Churchill's personal weight now behind their demands, the French had no choice but to give in.[26] Muqaddam had to withdraw his candidacy; for the time being, he remained under house arrest, but immediately after the elections he was handed over to the British who exiled him to Cyprus. For reasons of ill health he was soon allowed back to Tripoli where he remained under house arrest until his death on 1 March 1944. In short, the British had succeeded in eliminating from the race a man who was thought of as France's main prop in the northern part of Lebanon. Muqaddam, furious at having been abandoned (as he saw it) by the French, refused to have any part in the election run-up, and continued to claim that he was being persecuted because of his opinions.[27]

Ostensibly, then, this was a transparent example of forceful and effective British interference in favour of Muqaddam's competitor, Karami. But we have to remember that all this took place in Tripoli, a town for long the main stronghold of Sunni factions holding militant Arab nationalist and anti-French views and strong opinions even on the issue of the very desirability of a Lebanese state. Indeed, it was Farid el-Khazen who wrote: 'Tripoli was by far the most "Arab", "Syrian" or "Muslim" city in Greater Lebanon ... Politically, religiously, and economically Tripoli was perhaps the Sunni city most truly "amputated" from its Arab and Muslim hinterland.'[28]

It is therefore hard to believe that, even if Muqaddam had run, the outcome would have been substantially different. The special character of Tripoli is only one reason for thinking so. For even if Muqaddam had been elected, we must still assume that, like so many other Sunnis, he would soon have found his way into the Lebanese nationalist camp, just as Sami al-Sulh and Yafi had done before him.

Once Muqaddam's candidacy had been ruled out, the way was open for the formation of a nationalist, even anti-French list, under 'Abd al-Hamid Karami. He was joined by a number of supporters from among Tripoli's Sunni community, notably Sa'di al-Manala, as well as by Sunnis from other areas of northern Lebanon. Prominent among the latter were Muhammad al-'Abud and Sulayman al-'Ali. Most local Maronite leaders joined it as well; their group was headed by Hamid Faranjiyya, Yusuf Istafan and Wahib Ja'ja. Obviously, only their common interest in the election outcome had brought the various components together. Earlier, relations between Karami, 'Abud and 'Ali had been tense, not to say hostile. So were Faranjiyyah's relations with his Maronite colleagues on the list. The two topmost candidates, Karami and Faranjiyya, were suspicious of, even antagonistic towards, each other, despite their ostensible common stance of being pro-British and anti-French. What had brought them together was the need to join ranks for the protection of their position as notables in a period of transition that was threatening it. By the time of the next elections, in 1947, the constellation had already changed.

The French at first tried to draw Karami over to their side, but had no real chance. Then, after some efforts, they put together a list of candidates willing to run against Karami and Faranjiyya. A closer look reveals that the figures on it were not so much concerned with giving support to France as with giving vent to their personal rivalries with men on the first list. It contained names from the Muqaddam and Jisr families; among the Maronite components figured 'Awad (then government secretary and a close associate of the patriarch 'Arida) as well as Nadra 'Isa al-Khuri, affiliated with Bishara al-Khuri's family.[29] Such a list could not prosper in the shadow of Karami and Faranjiyya, and indeed the latter gained all the seats of North Lebanon.

MT LEBANON   It was here that the most significant election campaign was fought out. Not only was this the district sending the highest number of deputies to the Chamber (seventeen); it was also the district where the majority of the country's Maronites resided, forming the hard core of their community. It was here that the fight between the two camps within the Maronite population would be decided, not just for Mt Lebanon but for all of Lebanon. Khuri's Constitutional Bloc, advocating independence and the country's integration into the Arab world, and enjoying the support of Britain, was ranged against Edde's National Bloc, advocating the maintenance of the status quo and supported by the French. The elections here, despite their local framework, were in reality of the utmost importance for the future of Lebanon as a whole.[30] (This can be argued even though, alongside the two large blocs, a third list, under Fu'ad 'Amun, was running; none of its members gained a seat.)

During the campaign, copious use was made of charges of corruption, and allegations of French and British interference were bandied about.[31] When the ballot was taken, it turned out that Edde's list had obtained eleven seats and Khuri's six. Both Edde and Khuri failed to win their own seats in the first round, and run-off elections were required; in these, they both won their seats with Edde getting 22,587 and Khuri 22,287 votes.[32] From among the prominent Maronites, only Chamoun (running on Khuri's list) succeeded the first time round – an indication of his broad popularity in Mt Lebanon.

The outcome would indicate that Edde and his ideology had a decisive advantage over his rival where the hard core of the Maronite community was concerned, and perhaps with regard to the community as a whole. But some reservations should be noted.

First, here as elsewhere in the country, elections were governed by personal and familial considerations. It would be wrong to assume that the results attested to a preference for one particular ideology or set of attitudes rather than another. This was borne out by the fact that Druse votes contributed considerably to Edde's success. Kamal Junbalat figured on Edde's list and his and his family's supporters thus voted for it. But their votes went to Edde in recognition of the latter's close association with the Junbalats, rather than because of his ideology and his vision of the country's future course. Another sign that caution is indicated was Chamoun's achievement in garnering more votes for himself than were given to either Edde or Khuri. As we have seen above, Chamoun was identified as anti-French and as a confirmed friend of the British. Moreover, both Edde and Khuri had candidates from the same families running on their lists. While Kamal Junbalat ran on Edde's list, 'Izzat Junbalat appeared on Khuri's. The Maronite Khazins were represented on Khuri's list by Farid, on Edde's by Farid's cousin Kisrawan.[33]

Second, Mt Lebanon was indeed the traditional heartland of Lebanon, and of the Maronites in particular, but since the establishment of Greater Lebanon it had gradually ceded first place to Beirut. The capital's economic elite – Christian as well as Muslim – had now become the decisive factor in moulding the country's future. Whatever place we accord to the residual importance of Mt Lebanon, the focus of power and influence had long since moved to Beirut.

Third, even if we accept the claim that Khuri failed to rally the majority of the Maronite community to his side, we must still remember that he did not need such a majority. It was precisely because he judged his own community to be split somewhere along the middle that, as we have seen above, he sought the support of outside quarters: Sunni notables, some Arab leaders abroad and, of course, the British. The latter were to have the final say soon afterwards in the presidential elections, not so much by assisting Khuri but by acting against Edde. In the event, Khuri's weakness within his own community may have turned out to his advantage. Precisely because he was not fettered by a large Maronite following clamouring for a special status, he was able to show the flexibility necessary to form connection with Muslim leaders. These contacts were to lay the ground for the 'National Pact' and thus for modern Lebanon.

For all that, Edde's undisputable victory in Mt Lebanon gave the election, at least initially, a certain coloration which influenced the British and French men on the spot, as well as some Arab politicians in neighbouring countries. Even though the overall results showed a clear advantage for the Lebanese nationalist camp to which Khuri belonged, Edde's local victory first seemed the more significant event.

Spears himself, assessing the prospects of the presidential elections now to follow, observed that even though Khuri had a majority in the Chamber, he had suffered a considerable loss of prestige because of the outcome in Mt Lebanon and clearly did not enjoy broad overall popularity with the public at large.[34] Furlonge, too, remarked on Khuri's having 'lost prestige through [his] poor showing' locally and was 'unlikely to succeed unless Emile Edde is eliminated. It is said that the Bekaa (Biqa') deputies, under Henri Pharaon's (Far'un) influence, would vote solid for him and that most (though not all) of the North Lebanon deputies would do the same; he can also count on some support in Beirut. The South Lebanon deputies have ... so far refused to commit themselves.' Riyad al-Sulh, Furlonge added, was presently favouring Edde 'for personal reasons' but would 'swing over' to Khuri if he felt Edde was about to lose, 'since he is ambitious to become Prime Minister'. As for Edde, Furlonge pointed to a legal obstacle to his candidacy: the constitution stipulated that a minimum period of six years must pass before an incumbent could become president again. Only four had elapsed since Edde's dismissal in 1939, but his supporters argued that, since the constitution had also been suspended at the time, it no longer governed the present elections. Furlonge went on to say that if Edde was 'allowed to stand he has the best chance of anyone ... in view of his well-known adroitness in securing deputies' votes by promises of future preferment for them or their relatives'.[35]

## The Presidential Elections

Apart from Khuri and Edde, there were additional presidential hopefuls: Chamoun, Hamid Faranjiyya, Thabit, Trad and Naqqash all presented themselves to the Chamber as candidates.[36] But Khuri and Edde were generally considered the front-runners; after all, the Lebanese political scene had been dominated for some twenty years by their personal struggle for the presidency.

Khuri had more to contend with than his poor showing in the elections. First of all, Edde was a powerful rival; he had French backing and the support of numerous Lebanese notables. Many were men who had worked with him in the 1930s, such as Yafi and Sami al-Sulh, or who had been close to him, such as Riyad al-Sulh. Moreover, once Edde realized that his own prospects were decreasing, he did his all to spoil Khuri's chances, just as he had done back in 1932. Second, Khuri soon faced difficulties in enlisting the necessary number of votes for himself. Despite his anti-French record and his reputation for being a serious interlocutor when it came to a dialogue with the Sunnis (a reputation he had done so much to foster), he found he could not take the Sunni votes for granted. Sunni support was conditional on promises for a share of the spoils in a future independent Lebanon. Some Sunni notables had personal reservations about Khuri; as we have seen, this was even true of Riyad al-Sulh.[37] Perhaps Sulh was influenced by his old friendship with Edde; more likely, his reservations sprang from a desire to raise the price of his support for Khuri and make himself the first prime minister of independent Lebanon.

Third, the French exerted their influence against Khuri as someone who had worked against the mandate, had befriended the British in 1941, and, worst of all, had drawn close to the pan-Arabists. Finally, it turned out that, despite impressions to the contrary, the British were not enthusiastic about Khuri's presidency either. Spears had scant regard for Khuri's character and, as shall be seen presently, worked behind the scenes to promote Chamoun's prospects. Chamoun was, after all, Britain's principal protégé in Lebanon. Writing to Casey, the British minister of state in the Middle East, after Khuri had been elected, Spears noted:

> I did not have much faith at first in Edde's opponent, Beshara el-Khouri (Bishara al-khuri). He seemed to me to be very much a politician of the old school, out for his own hand, whose only claim to our interest was that he opposed everything Edde did on personal grounds. I began to realise, however, as the fight went on that Beshara was much more of a man than his opponent and the hardness of the struggle and the disgusting way the French treated him began to develop some sort of political principle in him, but his chief interest to us resides in the fact that he includes in his group some really good men. It was without enthusiasm that I began to give him some support, of the discreetest kind of course, more for the sake of his followers than for himself.[38]

In conducting his fight, Khuri demonstrated the qualities that made him modern Lebanon's most talented politician. He understood the Lebanese political system, right down into its innermost recesses, better than anyone else did, and surpassed all others in his powers of political manoeuvre. Soon enough he lined up a majority of the country's political figures in his support and eventually gained the acceptance (however reluctantly granted) of both Britain and France. He knew how to turn inter-Arab differences to his own advantage and to derive the greatest possible benefits from the rivalry between Britain and France. Playing on the latter he weakened Edde's status in spite of French support for him, and relegated Chamoun to the sidelines despite Spear's initial backing.

The overall results of the parliamentary elections had given a clear majority in the chamber to those deputies who wanted to end the political status quo created by the French in the 1920s, or at least recognized that change was inescapable and that they must place themselves alongside the forces of the future. For all that, many were still in doubt what shape the future would, or should, take. Did it lie with pan-Arabism? Or with Britain? Or perhaps still with the French from whom Lebanon could demand, and obtain, its full independence? But even the doubters knew that change there must be. That gave Khuri his advantage over Edde: the latter seemed to personify resistance to change while for many years Khuri had made himself the symbol of innovation. He had succeeded in appearing best suited to lead a 'Lebanon of all the communities', yet keep central government authority feeble enough for the notables to maintain their position. While Edde was described as charismatic, strong and likely to arouse the antagonism of other notables, Khuri was seen as a weaker, colourless character, hence better suited to be the leader of the sort of state the notables wanted.[39] The same consideration also worked in favour of Khuri as compared with Chamoun.

One by one, then, Khuri was able to overcome the obstacles that had at first barred his way to the presidency. First, he managed to neutralize Edde's influence. Despite French backing and despite the support of some Sunni notables, most prominent among them Riyad al-Sulh, many deputies regarded Edde as an obstacle to the emergence of a new Lebanon. Among Edde's opponents were the twelve deputies from North Lebanon (led by Karami and Faranjiyya) and the seven from the Biqa' whom Far'un steered away from Edde and closer to Khuri. They were joined by the six deputies from Mt Lebanon who belonged to the Constitutional Bloc, and by a number of members from the south and from Beirut.[40] All these were, moreover, encouraged by the unequivocal British opposition to Edde's becoming president. This went as far as hints on the part of British representatives that London would not acknowledge the legality of Edde's election. Immediately after the voting in the Chamber, Spears wrote to Casey:

> Edde ... is not only a consummate scoundrel who has been exposed in the past in the press and was in fact forced to resign, but he was the most complete French stooge. Not only would it have been a great disadvantage to have a man of this kind as President with infinitely wider powers than anyone we have had to deal with so far, but he would have played the game of the French by disputing with the Syrians ... We should have had as many headaches as it would have suited the French to create for us.[41]

The British conducted a methodical campaign to delegitimize Edde and to deter deputies from backing him. The legal objections mentioned above were worked out for them by Khuri; the counter-arguments were formulated by the legal adviser to the French high commissioner.[42] The British also trotted out old accusations made against Edde by the Constitutional Bloc in the past, such as a charge going back to 1941 that Edde had been involved in the cultivation of hashish and in the drug trade; or that he had illegally gained control of certain tracts of land in the Biqa'. Spears claimed that documentary evidence corroborating the charges was in existence, assuming Edde's men had not succeeded in laying their hands on it and destroying it.[43] Spears also tried to enlist the French high commissioner, Jean Helleu, with whom he was at that time on reasonably good terms, against Edde's candidacy. In a meeting with him on 17 September – that is, just a few days before the balloting – Spears showed Helleu an article published in *Le Jour* (the organ of Khuri's bloc) in 1934 which 'gave an account of disgraceful intervention by Edde in the course of justice to influence a judge to give a verdict in his favor'. The judge had written to the press about it and Spears gave Helleu copies of the relevant newspaper passages.[44]

Furlonge reported that he had 'told several enquirers' that Edde's election would be illegal and 'that we might have to refuse to recognize it. They ...

all maintained that only a public pronouncement on these lines would have any effect.' This should 'preferably' come from the French high commissioner whose declaration to this effect 'would be much welcomed as settling a point of major controversy'.[45]

When Edde began to feel that his prospects were being whittled away, he redirected his energies to the task of preventing Khuri's election and securing that of another politician whose incumbency would be more convenient than that of his old rival. As in 1932, he considered encouraging a Muslim notable to run for the presidency and contemplated the candidacy of Sami al-Sulh.[46] But (more dangerously to Khuri) he also tested the possibility of promoting Chamoun's case; this would serve two aims: to foil Khuri's efforts and to revenge himself on the French who had not backed him as he felt they should have done.[47]

Chamoun's candidacy endangered Khuri's mainly because the former was closer to the British than he could hope to be. Astonishingly enough, the French — not at all eager to see Khuri succeed — found themselves on the same side as Spears. Spears, still believing that Edde had a chance, was out to thwart him at all costs, but neither was he keen to see Khuri win. He also felt that a continued contest between the two could imperil the country's stability or at least delay the advent of independence. And independence was not only in Britain's interest, as he saw it, but was first and foremost a personal commitment on his part. Most importantly, Spears probably felt that by letting Edde and Khuri keep each other in check, he could advance the cause of Chamoun. In a letter to Casey, worded to obscure his own active intervention, Spears said: 'There was a general feeling half way through the negotiations that it would be desirable to have a neutral candidate if by this means the two old rivals ... could be eliminated.'[48] The man Spears wanted to be the 'neutral candidate' was, of course, Chamoun. Spears reported as follows on a meeting with Helleu on 18 September: 'he asked me whether I agreed that it would be a good idea for both Beshara el Khoury (Bishara al-Khuri) and Edde to withdraw. I told him I thought it would be a very good thing.' When Helleu broached the question of 'alternative candidates', Spears went on: 'I refused to be drawn, saying that this was a matter for the Lebanese to decide themselves.'[49]

Spears had already met Edde, on 14 September, and had suggested to him that he should withdraw. Edde replied that he would do so only in favour of one of four other leaders: Chamoun, Istafan, Hamid Faranjiyya, or Amin al-As'ad (but not in favour of Khuri).[50] Now, after his conversation with Helleu, Spears summoned Khuri and told him that Edde was prepared to withdraw, provided Khuri did likewise. In his memoirs, Khuri enlarged on the pressure tactics Spears used against him; they included telling Khuri that, according to the information Spears possessed, Khuri would find it difficult to obtain a majority for himself.[51] As we shall see presently, Khuri indeed declared himself ready to withdraw, but only in favour of Chamoun.[52] Spears seems to have believed that now, with both Edde and Khuri out of the running, the French would swallow the bitter pill and approve of Chamoun's candidacy. In a subsequent summing-up of the chain of events, he recalled Edde's naming the four alternative candidates he would yield to, adding: 'He included ... Beshara's (Bishara) lieutenant Camille Shamoun (Chamoun), who is very much liked and respected.' He then gave an account of his above conversation with Helleu on a 'third candidate' and the latter's suggestion for Spears to 'influence Beshara in this sense', adding: 'It was evident that his faith in Edde's chances had begun to weaken.' Spears then went on:

> I was greatly encouraged by this demarche and saw a great opportunity. I sent for Beshara and following my constant tactics of always insisting that we were taking no direct part in the matter and were only giving advice upon request, I got him with great difficulty to consent to stand down himself but he would only do so in favour of one man, Shamoun. Now I knew that Shamoun was anathema to the French but kept this to myself, merely urging Beshara to come to an understanding directly with Edde on the subject.[53]

Looked at against the background of these moves, Khuri's readiness to stand down seems odd, all the more so as his personal relations with Chamoun were unfriendly, their joint activities in the Constitutional Bloc notwithstanding. According to Khuri's memoirs, Chamoun had 'deserted' from his camp during his 1936 presidential contest with Edde and had thereby decided the outcome in favour of Edde.[54] The following year, Chamoun was delegated by the Constitutional Bloc to serve as a minister in the coalition government then being formed. But when a coalition crisis caused the bloc ministers to resign, Chamoun refused to go along with them and remained in the cabinet.[55] It would appear therefore that, in offering to withdraw, Khuri took a calculated risk, staking his prospects on the expectation that the French would never agree to Chamoun's candidacy. They did, after all, consider him as their 'principal enemy in Lebanon and as the agent of the British there'.[56]

Khuri's calculations did indeed prove correct. The French were quick to veto Chamoun's candidacy. In a report to his superiors in Algiers, Helleu wrote:

> I cannot for a moment consider agreeing to the highest post in the state being occupied by M. Camille Chamoun who, for the last six years, has been one of the most active agents of British Secret Service and who is openly hostile toward us. His accession to power would mean a total defeat, not only for the prestige of France but also for the effective maintenance of our position in the Levant.[57]

More than that: under French pressure Edde went back on his declared readiness to stand down in favour of Chamoun. This removed the ground from under Spears's plan to get the French to accept Chamoun's candidacy as an accomplished fact agreed to by both Edde and Khuri. In the light of the complications thus engendered, the French made up their minds to pin their hopes on Khuri as the lesser evil – certainly if compared with Chamoun. Similar reasoning led Spears to similar conclusions, especially as he was still wary of the possibility of Edde's success. He reported on the French change of heart in a somewhat mocking vein: '[The] French however were still so nervous that Edde might not be successful and Shamoun (Chamoun) might slip in that, reversing their policy completely, they threw their whole weight in favour of … Khuri. As … Khuri had now become the French candidate as well as representing moderate nationalist elements in the country I gladly agreed to give him what support was in my power.'[58]

We must acknowledge that, in the last analysis, both Spears and Helleu were manipulated into supporting Khuri, their initial reluctance notwithstanding. As we have seen, Spears had originally preferred Chamoun. Summing up the course of events immediately after the election, Spears wrote to Casey that, eventually, 'The French had no choice … but to support Beshara, which … from our point of view was by far the lesser of two evils and may turn out quite well.' Chamoun's election, he went on, 'would have shaken' the French, undoubtedly producing 'a major row'; the French would have done everything they could to make his tenure 'impossible'. Spears concluded that 'it was really not desirable to introduce such an element of strife'. Chamoun had done his part 'by causing the French to abandon Edde' and Spears had asked him to stand down 'on patriotic grounds'. This 'he willingly agreed to do, being a decent chap … '[59]

Chamoun's disappointment was undoubtedly the reason for his subsequent vigorous opposition activity against Khuri and his administration. (In his memoirs, Khuri derisively called Chamoun 'president for a single night'.)[60] Edde for his part did not conceal his grudge against the French for 'betraying' him. In Spears's words, after trying to split Khuri's bloc by offering to support Chamoun, Edde 'entered into direct conflict with the French. He went to see Helleu and threatened not only violent parliamentary opposition but also hinted darkly at disturbances in the mountains.' Helleu hurried to see Spears who assured him that 'if anybody in this country broke the peace or carried out a campaign likely to lead to a breach of peace, we would give the French complete support in suppressing him. Greatly reassured Helleu went off to perfect his arrangements to hamstring Edde.'[61]

The description, so far, of how Khuri became president is bound to leave the impression that his choice was first and foremost the result of Anglo-French consultations and the resulting understandings. This was indeed the charge later levelled against him by rivals such as Chamoun and Kamal Junbalat; in their struggle against him towards the end of his tenure, a decade afterwards, they alleged that he had come to power through a series of tactical moves led by Spears.[62] Documentary evidence from British and French archives, when it was eventually released, pointed the same way. But the foreign archives do not, in this particular case, provide the full picture.

True, the French, and even more so the British, had played their part in Khuri's election; more to the point, had they wished so, each alone or both together could have prevented it. But then Khuri's emergence as the leader of the pro-independence Constitutional Bloc and his dissociation from the French connection had started back in the 1930s, much against the wishes of the French and a long time before the British appeared on the scene. More than that: if Khuri was eventually able to rally a great majority in the Chamber, including many Sunnis, to his side, this was in response to his attitudes and proposed policies. The Sunni leader 'Abd al-Hamid Karami, for instance, had joined Khuri right from the start (unlike Riyad al-Sulh, who came round only late in the day). Overall, Sunni support in the Chamber was at least as decisive for Khuri's eventual success as was great-power backing.

Furthermore, beginning in the 1930s but especially in the early 1940s, Khuri took a calculated risk by linking his political future to the good-will of Arab nationalist leaders abroad (in Syria and Egypt). This, too, proved advantageous to his cause. Nahhas Pasha, for one, became committed to Khuri's election. He supported Khuri financially during his campaign in Mt Lebanon (see above) and later instructed the Egyptian consul in Beirut, Ahmad Ramzi, to help Khuri by influencing Muslim opinion in his favour.[63] Likewise, the Syrian National Bloc came to his aid. When Khuri ran into difficulties, its leaders, Quwatli and Mardam, instructed Lutfi al-Haffar and 'Afif al-Sulh to take a Syrian delegation to Beirut and persuade Sunni notables there to support Khuri's candidacy. A subsequent account stated that it was this delegation which influenced Riyad al-Sulh to make up his mind and back Khuri after all.[64] It was indeed the attitude of the Sunni deputies which put a stop to Edde's candidacy and left the stage clear for Khuri. From that point onwards, he no longer encountered any significant opposition.

The way was now open for Khuri to approach the Sunni notables, led by Riyad al-Sulh, on the issue of the division of the spoils and of the modalities of power-sharing between the communities; most importantly of all, between the Maronites and the Sunnis. On 19 September 1943, Sulh and Khuri met at 'Aley and from their discussions that day there emerged what was to become known as the 'National Pact' – the genuine, solid cornerstone of the state structure of independent Lebanon.

The following day, a majority of the deputies met in order to give official, written form to their proposal to elect Khuri as president. Karami was asked to draw up the document nominating him, and Riyad al-Sulh was the first to sign it. A day later, the Chamber convened. Forty-four members voted for Khuri, three abstained. Eight deputies, most of them followers of Edde, stayed away from the session.[65] Immediately after the vote had been taken, Khuri asked Sulh to form, and head, independent Lebanon's first cabinet. An important phase in the struggle for independence had come to a close; a long stretch of the road still needed to be covered.

CHAPTER 3

# The National Pact

Maronite–Sunni agreements on the future character and basic policies of Lebanon, on sharing power and the positions of power, and on dividing the resources of the state lay at the core of the newly independent state. We have already pointed to the first indications of an impending accommodation in the 1930s and have described how it gathered momentum in the early 1940s. It was given its final, detailed shape by Khuri and Sulh at their meeting on 19 September 1943.[1] Their agreement, the so-called National Pact, was never laid down in writing, but was considered none the less binding. What now remained to be done was to implement it.

The pact gave independent Lebanon a new conceptual foundation, different from that which had underlain the idea of 'Greater Lebanon'. Instead of a country under the hegemony of the Maronites, there arose a 'Lebanon of all the communities'. This proved acceptable to most sectors of the complex Lebanese social fabric. Moreover, the new concept had its roots in the past – a fact that added to its legitimacy in the eyes of the Lebanese. On the practical level, the pact laid down the rules which were to govern the game of politics in the country. Indeed, it gave Lebanon political stability and ensured the functioning of its political and administrative system for many years to come.

The way the Lebanese regarded the National Pact was well brought out in an editorial in the Beirut daily *Al-Hayat* of 31 August 1949 which read in part:

Tomorrow ... is 'Independence Day'. On that day, in 1920, General Gouraud issued a degree concerning the establishment of a Lebanese state in borders laid down by the mandatory authorities ... Gouraud added ... four districts as well as Beirut to Mt. Lebanon, but he did not create a Lebanese people ... This was how things remained until the era of independence began and until the compromise of 1943 was reached to the satisfaction of both sides ... In this way, the sons of the country succeeded in doing by their own exertions what the foreigner had not succeeded in imposing upon them.[2]

The view that the National Pact was the centrepiece of Lebanon's ability to function, at least during the first two decades of independence, is widely shared by researchers of the period. But its success is accounted for in contrasting ways. Some stress its innovative nature and claim that the pact was able to become the cornerstone of the state structure precisely because it marked a departure from the past. Kamal Yusuf al-Hajj, for instance, wrote: 'The National Pact consolidated, even created from nothing, a Lebanese nationality … by defining its modus operandi.'[3] Others, by contrast, detect the secret of its success in its conservative character, viz. its ability to preserve the status quo and maintain the communal balance. Making the latter point, Itamar Rabinovich notes: 'The Lebanese polity was not based on the presumed existence of a Lebanese nation but on a confederation of proto national communities, each of which claimed the ultimate allegiance of its members. This [was] a unique political system which acknowledged the primacy of its constituent religious communities and vested them with political power.'[4]

It would appear that something was to be said for either notion. The eminence of the pact lay precisely in its sophisticated combination of innovative and old elements for bridging the communal gaps. It combined political traditions which had prevailed in Mt Lebanon and, more generally speaking, in the Ottoman empire as a whole (and which, to some extent, had been preserved in 'Greater Lebanon') with characteristics of the modern, independent state – first and foremost the parliamentary system. An elected parliament had been in existence since the late 1920s and had become central to the polity in 1943, albeit operating according to a uniquely Lebanese system. The National Pact provided the Lebanese with a common framework of authority (as al-Hajj wrote) but also preserved the division between the communities (as Rabinovich asserted). In Albert Hourani's words:

> The 'National Pact' expressed the difference as well as the unity of the sects. All might speak of a Lebanese nation, and of equality among the sects, but they meant different things. For some, Lebanon was still essentially a Maronite national home, for others a Christian refuge, a secular state based an a scarcely existing national unity, or perhaps a temporary expedient until a broad, secular Arab state should be ready to absorb it. [Behind different national movements and parties … ] there lay different religious loyalties, still the fundamental reality in Lebanese society.[5]

The National Pact was built around two basic principles:

1. The allocation of positions of power and influence between the various communities in proportion to their percentage strength in the population according to the 1932 census. Accordingly, the presidency was to be reserved for a Maronite, the premiership for a Sunni and the office of speaker of the Chamber for a Shi'i.[6] In the Chamber the ratio of Christians and Muslims was to be set at six Christians to five Muslims. Other positions of influence in government and in the administration were to be shared according to the

same communal key. For example: the minister of defence was usually a Druse while the army's chief-of-staff was always a Maronite. The five provincial governors were from the main five sects (one Maronite, one Sunni, one Shi'i, one Greek Orthodox and one Druze or Greek Catholic).

2. Lebanon was to be a country 'with an Arab face' (*Wajh 'Arabi*), but not an Arab state. It was to be part of the Arab world and would, as such, seek to cooperate with the Arab states, but would maintain its sovereignty, its independence, its unique character (in other words: it would not join any of the Arab unity schemes then being adumbrated in the Arab world). It would retain its traditional links with the West, but not permit itself to be used as a bridgehead for the renewed penetration of the West into the Middle East.[7]

These principles were set forth in public for the first time in an address to the Chamber, on 8 October 1943, by Riyad al-Sulh when he presented his government, the first cabinet of independent Lebanon.[8] But while dwelling on the principles and their underlying ideology, Sulh preferred to skip over the practical details of the division of the spoils. Khuri, too, took a similar line in his memoirs where he described the pact as 'an agreement between the two elements of which the Lebanese homeland is made up, for the fusion of their aspirations in one single principle: complete Lebanese independence without recourse to protection by the west and without joining a union or confederation with the east'.[9]

Most Lebanese leaders were to do likewise for a long time to come. A salient example is provided by the acceptance speech, on 23 September 1958, of Fu'ad Shihab after his election as president. One passage read:

> I swear to honor the Lebanese constitution and I promise, and ask you to promise, faithfully to maintain our unwritten constitution, the National Pact, which has made it possible for us to believe in Lebanon, and has in fact made us believe in it – the dear, independent, sovereign and free fatherland; the fatherland which faithfully and devotedly, and to its own benefit, cooperates with its Arab sister states while maintaining ties with the entire world, based on friendship and mutual respect.[10]

In Shihab's interpretation of the National Pact, Lebanon formed part and parcel of the Arab world surrounding it and was committed to give priority to its links with it, though it would maintain its independence and sovereignty and preserve its freedom of action. Ostensibly, this would appear to go beyond Khuri's concept which could be summed up briefly in the phrase: 'Neither East nor West.' But the actual policies of both, such as they were shaped under the constraints of their time, point to an underlying identity of views. Both regarded the pact as obliging them to pursue a pan-Arab policy, though a restrained and cautious one. If Khuri (unlike Shihab) refrained from saying so, the reason was that he did not want to give the Maronite community cause to fear overly close links with the Arab countries. Another reason probably was that on this particular point his ideas went beyond those of some of his close associates, such as Michel Chiha and the latter's political allies who, as we have seen, regarded Lebanon as a meeting place of East and West rather than an integral part of the East.[11]

Ever since 1943, the nature and significance of the pact have become the subject of a prolonged scholarly controversy. In the words of el-Khazen:

> [S]tudies of the Pact have attempted to advance a particular reading of that unwritten 'document'. Interpretations ... varied with the ebb and flow of Lebanese politics. Deplored in times of crisis and praised in times of stability and prosperity, the National Pact reflected sectarian differences in post-1943 Lebanon. For some [it] came to symbolize national integration and confessional unity, for others it came to embody a 'philosophy' of confessional coexistence, still for others it was a 'capitalist confessional' deal aimed at promoting the interests of some segments of Lebanese society at the expense of others.[12]

Indeed, the pact can be considered from various angles: as a political accommodation, as a social and economic charter, or as a personal deal between Khuri and Sulh; in the final analysis, these viewpoints will mesh.[13]

Looking at its political significance, we can consider it as an agreement between the two principal power elements of the country: the Maronites and the Sunnis. It put an end – at least partially and temporarily – to the ideological controversy between them about the nature of the state, and about the practical issue of how they could coexist and even cooperate through allotting positions of power according to an agreed key. To reach this accommodation, the Maronites waived their claim to hegemony and gave up their close links with the West, especially with France. In practical terms, this signified renouncing French guarantees for the existence of the Lebanese state and accepting the necessity for Lebanon's integration into the Arab world. The Sunnis for their part gave up the idea of dismantling Lebanon through its total or partial inclusion in Syria and acknowledged the predominant status of the Maronites. Under this aspect, the pact appears as a novel formulation of the modalities of communal coexistence. As such it was meant to replace the old one jointly imposed by the French and the Maronites at the time of the establishment of Greater Lebanon. This had, in turn, replaced earlier modes applied under other regimes. As we have seen, no unilateral arrangement had lasted for long, let alone resolved the issue.

Both points apply to the 1920 French–Maronite formula. Important segments of the Maronite communities had understood its limitations already in the 1920s and 1930s. Moreover, they had grasped the significance of the regional changes of the 1940s: the eclipse of France, the rise of British influence in the Levant, the emergence of an inter-Arab political system, the establishment of an independent Syria. Their reading of the new political map had led them to see the need for placing Lebanon on new and sounder foundations. All the while, a similar trend had gradually emerged among the

Sunnis. They moved towards an acceptance of Lebanon as it was, and of the predominant, but not exclusive, power positions of the Maronites which their demographic weight, their history and their links with the West had given them. They may also have understood that any attempt to circumscribe the status of the Maronites too narrowly might drive them back into the arms of the French. Both leading communities thus learned to take a more sober look at themselves and at Lebanon as a whole. That look, in turn, engendered the National Pact.

Considered from the social and economic point of view, the pact was an agreement between the Christian economic elite and the elite of Sunni urban notables, particularly those of Beirut, meant to consolidate and preserve their social and economic positions and their saliency and predominance in economic and political affairs. For similar reasons, the elites of notables from other communities joined in, even though they were aware that they would do no better than play second fiddle.

The founding of Greater Lebanon had furthered the emergence of these elites. In particular, it had accelerated the process – first noticeable in the nineteenth century – of the development of a class of Christian businessmen and bankers in Beirut. Some were Maronites, but its most salient members were Greek or Roman Catholics and some Greek Orthodox. Their rise came at the expense of feudal families of landowners, many of them Maronites, but some also Shi'i and Druse. It was the business community which was to set the tone in Lebanon during the years here reviewed. The Sunni urban notables were the natural allies of the Christian traders and bankers; their common interests brought them together and facilitated agreement.

The Christian economic elite, just like other sectors of notables, had, right from the time of the establishment of Greater Lebanon, faced the challenge of how to maintain its role and influence under the new domestic and regional circumstances. In this respect, the pact continued the development first marked by the constitution of 1926. As we have seen, notables from the elites here described had a hand in drafting its provisions. Both the 1926 constitution and the Pact were based on the idea that the preservation of their standing made it necessary for Lebanon to become an independent state as well as a 'state of all communities' – or, more precisely, a state of the notables from all the communities. This in turn meant incorporating some elements of the previous order in Mt Lebanon and in the Ottoman empire as a whole into the new structures. The principle of communalism was, in itself, the most striking such residue from the past. So were a degree of political pluralism and the absence of a strong central government. But for all their conservative character, the new patterns also marked a shift: greater influence than previously would henceforth accrue to those sectors among the notables who had conceived, initiated and executed the transition to the new structure – that is, the Christian Beiruti economic elite and its Sunni partners.

Against this background, the principle embodied in the pact of integration into, or at least cooperation with, the Arab world acquired added significance. Alongside its political benefits it was also to serve Lebanese economic interests. It was meant to keep open Lebanon's access to the developing Arab markets; an access seen more and more as a precondition for Lebanon's prosperity, hence of the prosperity of its elites. In this context, ideology and practical interest were no more than two sides of the same coin. In both respects, the pact was a step in the readjustment to changed circumstances.

Finally, there was the element of a personal accommodation between the pact's two authors and their hope of deriving prompt political benefits from it. For Khuri, the immediate gain was the support of the Muslims, especially the Sunnis, in the Chamber for his election as president; Sulh became prime minister, largely in recognition of his contribution to devising the pact. His appointment made him the recognized leader of his community and enabled him to outface his erstwhile rivals.

This aspect later led observers to think of it as a cynical deal devised by two experienced politicians out for what they could get. Those who took this line thought of them as placing personal interest above principle and even above the true cause of their respective communities. In this version, Khuri renounced the old Maronite link with France and released Paris from its long-standing obligation of protecting the Christians of Lebanon and hence the Lebanese state. Sulh for his part was accused of having forsaken his commitment to the cause of Arab union (or at least to union with Syria) and of thus having abandoned the Muslims to the mercies of a Christian (or, more narrowly, a Maronite) overlordship, even though a rather mitigated one if compared with the period of French mandatory rule.

Such is Elie Kedourie's argument against Khuri in an article entitled 'Lebanon: The Perils of Independence', in which he stated:

> The National Pact thus meant that the Maronites were to give up French protection, indeed to make common cause with the Sunnis against the French, in return for their acceptance of Greater Lebanon. Present security was to be bartered against future performance. But covenants without the sword are words ... This radical departure in Maronite policies, so fraught with dangers and so heavy with future disasters, was undoubtedly effected under British influence, which was then predominant. We do not know whether those Maronite leaders who set their community on this perilous path weighed the risks of their adventure, or whether in their eagerness for power they persuaded themselves that General Spears ( ... who egged them on) ... would forever watch over their welfare.[14]

A comparable charge, similar in nature but in the reverse direction, was made by Khalid al-'Azm, one of the prominent leaders of Syria during the first decades of its independence. In his memoirs, he accused Sulh of having frustrated any remaining chance of a union between Syria and Lebanon. In return, he went on, the Maronites had supported him in his bid for a leadership role in Lebanon. 'Azm conceded that Sulh may not have been strong enough actually to bring about a union with Syria, but he could have brought the two states closer. Yet, had he done so, he would not have been promised the premiership.[15]

There is no denying that Kedourie's above criticism contained more than a grain of truth: Lebanon did indeed waive its special links with France, and with the West as a whole. But, as the contents of the National Pact made clear, Khuri and his associates acted from the conviction that under the changing circumstances of the region, reliance on the West was no longer the only means to guarantee Lebanon's independence. A new equilibrium, grounded in the convergence of all political elements in the country as well as of inter-Arab influences, needed to be found. This must also include a new balance *vis-à-vis* the western powers, reflecting their standing such as it now was. Acting on this conviction not only gave Khuri personal power for a full decade, but also ensured the independent existence of the Lebanese state for a period much longer than that. With regard to Lebanon's foreign policy, the pact was not a new departure, as Kedourie asserted, but rather a return to earlier concepts, though they had now been adapted to the realities of the 1940s.

For all that, the pact also had its demerits. These were later to contribute to the various severe crises in the functioning of the Lebanese political system and eventually added their share to the outbreak of the civil war. These defects have been dealt with at length in studies on modern Lebanon or monographs on the pact. We shall therefore take up only those negative elements whose effects were already felt during the period of Khuri's presidency.

Three negative aspects of the pact can be singled out:

1. A system built on a precise communal balance and an exact equilibrium between the families of notables, and calculated to a nicety to prevent any single power group from becoming stronger than any of the others wished it to be – a system like this was bound to produce immobility, if not paralysis. True, the balance went back in large measure to the 1926 constitution, but it was its reaffirmation by the authors of the pact which made it the mainstay of independent Lebanon. It resulted in determining the communal affiliation of the president and the prime minister, and the communal composition of the Chamber and had delineated their respective powers. It thus created a fabric of relations rendering decision-making exceedingly difficult and making the running of the country cumbersome at the best of times and often rendered it well-nigh impossible. In doing so, it imperilled the political system as a whole.

The 1926 constitution had ostensibly given the president very broad powers. He appointed and dismissed the cabinet as well as civil servants and was empowered to issue presidential decrees. The parliament exercised no more than a loose kind of control over the president's activities.[16] Under the mandatory regime, however, the French high commissioner had powers overriding those of the president. Often enough, the incumbent was a French puppet, with no backing from the notables and without any genuine popular support. But with the high commissioner gone, the president seemed to have come into his own, particularly versus the prime minister, the rest of the cabinet, and the Chamber.

However, inasmuch as the pact was, among other things, a personal deal between Khuri and Sulh, we must assume that Sulh had agreed to leave the multitude of formal powers in the hands of the president. He probably did so on the assumption, which proved correct, that the formal division of authority between the Maronite president and the Sunni prime minister did not tell the whole story. The weight of their actual power would make itself felt regardless of what the constitution prescribed.

Sulh relied on his own firm position with the Sunni public to give him greater authority than was formally granted him – just as he expected Khuri's weaker standing within the Maronite community to detract from his formal powers. It is worth noting that a certain weakness within their own community was characteristic of several of the presidencies following Khuri's. Their standing was affected by the continued activities of their Maronite rivals who continued contesting the president's position even after he was elected. Often enough, their conduct towards him during the six years of his incumbency was guided by a desire to occupy the best possible starting position for the next presidential race. Another source of weakness lay in the political and ideological differences which split the community. In order to win a presidential race, Maronite candidates had to adopt a conciliatory policy calculated to gain them support among Muslim deputies. Furthermore, they usually needed the good-will of other Arab countries, first and foremost that of Syria. This in itself rendered them unpopular among some sectors of their own community.

In agreeing to leave the constitutional provisions as they were, Sulh may also have hoped to benefit from the comparative advantage he held in terms of personal character: Khuri was often described as a weak and colourless personality, while Sulh was regarded as charismatic and vigorous. A British intelligence report of 1944, for instance, had this to say about them: 'There is the general realization that the Christian President is a much weaker man than the Moslem Prime Minister.' Had he possessed Edde's 'strength and determination', he might have been able to 'dominate his exuberant Prime Minister. As it is, the influence of the President is mainly a negative one, and even then not always effective.'[17]

A balance of power and interests was indeed achieved by the pact, but it was of a kind liable to render both the president and the prime minister incapable of action. Things were made worse by the fact that the pact did not address itself to only the two men who held the top positions in 1943, but was meant as a long-term settlement. As soon as the president's formal powers were no longer balanced by the personality of a strong premier (as was to happen during the last years of Khuri's incumbency), the president became too powerful. This eroded the authority of the cabinet; yet it was this body the president had to rely on as his executive, as his partner in policy-making and as his instrument for carrying out directives. True, a weak cabinet was likely to serve the president's personal interests, and often enough he acted with the express intention of rendering the prime minister's and the cabinet's position as feeble as possible. And yet an overly weak cabinet only expedited a president's eventual failure. In any event, undermining the cabinet aroused antagonism elsewhere in the political system (not necessarily within the Maronite community alone) and prompted those who saw their positions threatened to come out against the president. In such a situation, the delicate balance achieved by the pact was liable to be impaired; a period of instability was then bound to ensue.

In the situation just described, the prime minister found himself constantly between the hammer and the anvil, that is to say, between the hammer of the president – who had appointed him and could dismiss him with equal ease – and the anvil of his rivals within the Sunni community. The latter were waiting for him to come to grief, expecting to replace him as soon as he did. They bided their time, aware that while the constitution set the president's term at six years, it did not stipulate any fixed period of tenure for the premiership. The prime minister could thus be replaced at any moment. More than that: unlike the president he was dependent on the Chamber which had to confirm his assumption of office by a vote of confidence and could terminate it by a vote of no-confidence.

The Chamber was nominally autonomous and sovereign. Though both the president and the prime minister were able to influence deputies, there were always others who were independent of the central government. The deputies from the Biqa' and from southern Lebanon, for instance, owed their seats (and hence their loyalty) to local leaders who had made them deputies by placing them on their lists.

The president, then, had the advantage of his formal authority as the senior figure in the hierarchy; but often enough the prime minister was able to neutralize him. Similarly, both were often neutralized by competitors in their own communities, or else by deputies who represented particular sectors from among the notables. As a group, the notables were quick to defend their standing against any possible encroachment by the central authorities. This 'sanctified' balance which the pact had laid down thus contained a built-in capacity for one component to neutralize, or even paralyse, the others. Inevitably, there were therefore periods when the effects of the balance seriously impaired the functioning of the government. But when, on the other hand, the balance was disturbed, instability resulted; in 1952, this became serious enough to cause the downfall of the president.

2. The consecration, so to speak, of the communal principle preserved a tradition of pluralism and openness and even possessed certain elements of democracy, but it produced a weak state structure. The live elements of the Lebanese system were not the governing bodies of the state but the communities and within them the holders of communal power, semi-independent and self-willed as they were. This not only prevented the development of strong central authorities but also militated against the emergence of a sense of identification with, and loyalty towards, the state. For both reasons, Lebanon always found it difficult to respond to, let alone counter, challenges whether from within or from outside.

The defects of communalism were rendered worse by the absence of any former traditions of statehood and public service which could have imbued office-holders with a sense of responsibility towards Lebanon and its citizens as a whole. The only existing tradition was of communal, regional and familial loyalty. It was this tradition which determined the choice of appointees to positions of influence as well as the allocation of public resources, and it was this tradition which guided the officials, once they had gained their appointments, in the exercise of their functions. They were not committed to the state but to their community or their family; beyond that, the more responsibly minded among them also felt committed to the principle of communalism as such and to the maintenance of the communal balance. A system of this kind was bound to make it difficult to work out overall state policies concerned with the welfare, in the broadest sense, of citizens regardless of community.

Finally, the communal principle was harmful because, despite all efforts, it was incapable of being applied fully and fairly. In 1944, Furlonge noted:

> In the last few years this vaguely expressed principle has been allowed to develop into a tradition that every community must be represented in proportion to its numbers in every type of public function; for example ... the five provincial al-Mohafezes [governors] must be chosen one each from the five principal communities (Maronite, Sunni, Shia, Greek Orthodox, Greek Catholic). In the lower grades of the administration the tradition has, however, been less rigidly applied, partly because some communities, notably the Shias, were too backward to produce their fair proportion of eligible officials, partly because of past French favouritism of the Christians. An analysis I made in 1942 suggested that the Maronites held far too many functions, the Sunnis and Greek Catholic a roughly fair proportion, the Shias and Greek Orthodox less than their due.[18]

3. The most important drawback of the pact, much like of previous formulas for coexistence, was the lack of a method to adjust it to changing circumstances. The basic fact of the pact was that it reflected the balance of power and the proportional numerical strength of the communities as of 1943. These were bound to change: British and French influence would not remain what it was; the demographic balance could not remain static. The

fact that no provisions had been made for the pact to accommodate such changes turned it into a time-bomb. Its eventual explosion was certain; if anything remained in doubt it was only the precise moment when it would do so.

Both partners to the pact, however, preferred to ignore this aspect. True, the Sunnis did not altogether conceal their view that the pact in its present form was a temporary solution. Sulh stated that he had agreed to the presidency being held by a Maronite so that their community would feel reassured in an independent Lebanon and would not feel constrained to isolate themselves from the Arab world[19] – a hint that this might not be necessary in the long run. But there is no record of Sunni reflections on how the changes in the pact could be brought about, once they had become necessary. The Maronites for their part were content to regard the pact as a final settlement of the issue of communal relations and thought of the prerogatives it granted them as a permanent achievement.

Yet, taking an overall view and considering the alternatives, the conclusion ought to be that the pact was the lesser evil. Perhaps one might even go a step further and say that, at that particular moment, there were no feasible alternatives. That was the view expressed by Furlonge in 1944, when he wrote:

> Riyad es-Sulh has several times declared to us his intention of preparing a motion for the abolition of confessionalism before the Chamber meets in October [1944]. The President and all other members of the government seem, however, equally convinced that this reform, however desirable, would lead to an outburst ... which it would be beyond their power to master and which would only result in their own disappearance and in French intervention ... The Ministers may be right; they know their own weakness as well as we do, and are in a better position than we to judge how far the matter would convulse the country ... even the many enlightened Lebanese who admit the deleterious effects of the present system on the administration do not consider its abolition practical politics.[20]

Indeed, in 1943 both Khuri and Sulh were concerned with much more pressing and immediate problems than devising far-reaching reforms which would radically remake the political system according to which Lebanon, and before it Mt Lebanon, had been governed for so long. As early as November 1943, only some two months after they had agreed on the pact, they were required to deal with the first severe challenge to Lebanon's young independence: the crisis of the Lebanese constitution.

## CHAPTER 4

# The November 1943 Crisis

The November 1943 crisis of the Lebanese constitution marked an important stage in Lebanon's struggle for independence. Like the events recounted so far it, too, evolved in the shadow of the rivalry between Britain and France. Indeed, it was triggered by the French at a moment when they felt that their influence in Lebanon was threatened; and it was ended by the British in a manner which greatly diminished French prestige in the region. Yet it was also a significant event in terms of Lebanese domestic developments. It was the first time the Lebanese government, so recently formed, had to face a challenge and the first time that the validity of the National Pact, only just agreed upon, was put to the test. Albert Hourani regarded it as the peak of the Lebanese struggle and wrote of it: 'The events of 1943–1946 were child's play compared to the struggles through which other nations have won their independence, but they left behind them a fragile sense of unity and triumph, from which the independent Lebanon and its government could derive something of the revolutionary legitimacy which is the basis of modern nation-states.'[1]

Two points are worth emphasizing: first, it was the Lebanese government which was the leading factor in the crisis and which by its initiative obtained the amendment of the constitution, deleting all references to the French mandate from it. And it was the Lebanese government that profited most from the resolution of the crisis. Secondly, the failure of the French to turn the clock back was not caused by British intervention but first and foremost by the inability of the French to muster support among the Lebanese; not even their traditional allies backed them now. The refusal of the Lebanese public, and in particular of the notables, to go along with the French attested to a broad consensus regarding independence and was clear proof of the acceptance and validity of the principles underlying the National Pact. It was not for nothing that 22 November, the day the crisis came to a close, was later declared Independence Day. It may have been somewhat presumptuous on the part of the Lebanese leaders to relate to the crisis as the watershed in their country's struggle and to cast their own roles in it in a mould of heroic resistance; but there is no denying that this was Lebanon's first marked success as an independent state and Khuri's and Sulh's first major personal achievement.

When the crisis broke out, Lebanon – its nominal independence notwithstanding – was still effectively under the thumb of the French. The mandatory power continued to be the source of legal and executive authority, still remained in control of the country's economic resources (termed the 'common interests'), and even retained the ultimate supervision of the armed forces, the police and the internal security service. All along, ever since the Free French had moved into Lebanon in 1941, their policy had borne witness to the aim of preserving France's imperial status in the Levant. When the Free French realized that it was no longer in their power to prevent Lebanon (and Syria) from becoming independent, it became their aim to make independence contingent on the signing of treaties which would allow them to retain their influence under a different guise.

On 12 October 1943, Khuri and Sulh had met with French High Commissioner Helleu and had enquired what powers France was ready to give up in order to facilitate the emergence of an independent Lebanon. More than anything else, the two were interested in the transfer to the Lebanese government of control over the 'common interests'. These included the ports, airports, broadcasting stations, government buildings, and economic authorities like the Lebanese–Syrian customs union and the Lebanese–Syrian Bank. Helleu replied that there could be no waiver of authority until the formal end of the mandate. The original League of Nations mandate had imposed upon France an obligation towards the peoples of the Levant as well as towards the international community. This commitment, he went on, could not be revoked by the Free French Committee of National Liberation, nor could it be annulled by Syria or Lebanon. The regional states would therefore have to wait until the League of Nations could be convened again or until another body had replaced it, and was able to consider their demand for the revocation of the mandate. Helleu hinted, however, that practical matters affecting the present political conditions could be considered before the formal annulment of the mandate, provided Lebanon and Syria were prepared to sign special treaties, similar to the Anglo-Egyptian treaty or to the Franco-Lebanese treaty of 1936. These were to ensure that France's standing in the Levant would be maintained. Khuri and Sulh rejected the offer most emphatically, going to the length of proclaiming that they would rather cut off their right hands than sign such treaties.[2] Helleu reiterated this proposal at a further meeting with Khuri on 23 October and Khuri rejected it once again, justifying his refusal by reference to the legally ill-defined status of the Free French Committee in Algiers.[3]

The Lebanese leaders were aware that, at least for the time being and on this particular point, their interests coincided with Syria's. Simultaneously with the above talks, they were therefore at pains to set up a common front with Damascus. A joint approach was formulated during a series of meetings between Lebanese and Syrian leaders; at its centre was the demand for full independence and the rejection of French demands for special treaties. Both declared that their countries had never recognized the French mandate; rather, it had been imposed upon them against their will. The Free French Committee in Algiers was not, in their view, the recognized legal successor to the French government. They also recalled that Catroux had promised them prompt independence without making it conditional on their assuming treaty obligations towards France. Also, quite apart from these arguments, they demanded the prompt transfer of the 'common interests' to their own governments in order to give substance, however partial, to their newly acquired sovereignty.[4]

In the face of this negative attitude on the part of the French, the Lebanese leaders concluded quite realistically that any attempt to turn to them on the matter of the country's final status was bound to end in deadlock. They decided to take a series of immediate and unilateral measures, mostly of a symbolic kind, meant to demonstrate the independent status of their country. To cite an example: Sulh instructed government offices to conduct all internal correspondence in Lebanon's official language (Arabic) only, rather than in French as had been the custom hitherto. This was intended to negate the influence of the French advisers posted to the various ministries.[5] But the core issue was the revision of the 1926 constitution and its adaptation to the current circumstances. This meant annulling clauses such as the one declaring the French mandatory authority to be the sole source of authority in Lebanon. Sulh spoke of changes which would make the constitution 'fully suited to the epoch of independence, for it to become the source of authority for the Lebanese people and its rightful representatives – a source capable of serving as the foundation for running their affairs in the future'.[6]

The French were quick to register their opposition to such intentions, regarding them as a precedent likely to encourage the states of the region to take unilateral steps and thus detract from France's standing. The Free French Committee in Algiers therefore sent an official message to the Lebanese government, dated 5 November 1943 (and rendered here in the telegraphic style of the original): 'National Committee has examined question whether Lebanese Constitution could be modified in a valid manner by unilateral action on part of Lebanese Government and Parliament.' Since international obligations entered into by France could not be modified without its consent,

> Committee has reached conclusion that French authorities could not recognize validity of a revision carried out without such consent. Committee has felt bound to make known its decision forthwith. It wishes at the same time to emphasize that this decision is merely application of a general rule of law ... Committee do not doubt therefore that Lebanese nation will recognize justification for this declaration and will understand that in practice it does not run counter to determination of France to accord Lebanon complete independence by means of negotiations conducted between two parties in that spirit of loyal

and friendly collaboration which must ... inspire special [in French: 'particuliers'] relations uniting Lebanon and France.[7]

Khuri and Sulh reacted furiously. Khuri later noted in his memoirs that he felt all the more bitter about the note since the French had leaked its contents to the local press before it was delivered to him.[8] But it is more likely that he and Sulh were glad to exploit it to advance a political move on which they had decided earlier. The very day the message was received, they convened a cabinet meeting which resolved to bring forward the date of the next session of the newly elected Chamber so that it could take up the constitutional issue immediately.[9] Khuri rejected an appeal transmitted by a messenger from Helleu (then in Algiers) to delay the opening of the Chamber session until he, Helleu, was back in Beirut.[10]

The Chamber convened on 8 November 1943 to discuss a government proposal for amending the constitution. The French, assisted by Edde, tried to persuade a number of deputies to stay away from the session and thus to cause it to be delayed for lack of a legal quorum.[11] When they failed, Edde and his supporters proposed to wait until Helleu's return, or to refer the matter to a parliamentary committee for detailed study. They failed again. The Chamber adopted the government proposal by forty-eight votes, with seven abstentions and no votes against. Even Edde and his associates preferred to abstain or else to absent themselves. The amendments included the erasing of any reference to the French mandate in the constitution, as well as the abolition of articles which established the French mandate as the source of political power and jurisdiction in Lebanon. They entered into force the same day, as soon as President Khuri had added his signature to the Chamber's resolution.[12]

Khuri's and Sulh's resolve to push the changes through and their impatient insistence on completing the matter as quickly as possible, seem amazing. They contrast sharply with the caution and patience, not to say hesitancy, both had been wont to display (Khuri perhaps even more than Sulh) over a period of so many years. It is also remarkable that it was Lebanon rather than Syria which took the lead in the joint campaign against France, with Khuri and Sulh leaving the Syrian leadership far in behind.

One possible explanation is that the two acted from inexperience and a lack of political maturity and simply failed to consider fully what their actions were bound to entail. Sulh in particular may have been driven by an exaggerated feeling of self-confidence, resulting from his and Khuri's success in reaching the positions they had aspired to for so long. We can find such a note in the words of Sulh at a press conference he gave on 27 September. Among other things, he said: 'A gleam of patriotism is already appearing on the horizon.' He told the journalists that their pens were 'needed to nourish and sustain the national awakening ... in this country ... It is only my conviction that the national aspirations can now be realized which has caused me to accept office.' Defeatism, he went on, had 'attacked' many Lebanese during the past years of confusion. 'I therefore ask you to encourage this national awakening ... to feed the fire of patriotism in lukewarm hearts ... and to [help] throw off the heavy burden which a long tradition has unfortunately bequeathed to us. We are at the dawn of a new struggle for independence.'[13]

We can discern a similar theme in Sulh's words to the British oriental secretary, Captain 'Arab, at a meeting on 29 October: 'I ... devoted my blood to independence when [still] under age, and my blood was nearly shed' – a reference to his having been condemned to death by the Turks during the First World War. 'I am not only a politician, I am a fighter. I am going to execute my programme.' The people, he added, were supporting him 'enthusiastically'. 'I am proud to say that I have lighted in Lebanese hearts the light of independence ... I am proud of having gathered Christians and Moslems around the banner of independence.' He concluded by asking the British 'not to lose faith in me'.[14]

The French, of course, claimed that the issue of the constitutional amendments had been pressed upon the government by the British; Sulh was a British agent who would not make a move without consulting London, while Khuri was no more than a spineless opportunist unable to stand up to any pressure.[15] But a scrutiny of the British archives does not yield any evidence whatsoever for a British initiative, or even a personal effort by Spears, to press for the amendment of the constitution. In fact, it might well be argued that the revision of the constitution ran counter to London's overall interests in the Middle East where it might set an undesirable precedent in places such as Egypt or Iraq. But attention should be paid to Roshwald's observations. He wrote:

> Whether or not Spears had explicitly urged the Lebanese to abolish the mandate unilaterally seems almost inconsequential. From the telegrams he sent to London during October 1943, it is clear that he saw himself as the champion of Lebanese nationalism and took delight in watching the rapid erosion of French power. It was Spears who had created the atmosphere in which the Lebanese government dared to throw the gauntlet down before the French, knowing that if it were taken up, their duel would be fought for them by the British minister. It is certainly difficult to imagine that, during wartime and with their country under British occupation, al-Khuri and al-Sulh would have proceeded as they did, had Spears warned them not to.[16]

On balance, the French charges against Khuri personally should be taken more seriously than those against the British. There is some substance in the allegation that Khuri and the Lebanese government were not acting according to a preconceived plan but were swept along by events. Khuri himself conceded in a conversation with French officials that he proposed the constitutional amendments while under pressure from the Chamber. Most deputies, he explained, were anti-French and because of its weakness the government had to conform to their wishes. Indeed, in a meeting with the French on 23 October 1943, Khuri warned that the government could not range itself against the wave of nationalism then sweeping the country.[17] On 18 November (while under arrest), he told Catroux that he had found himself in an intolerable situation facing both the Chamber and the cabinet and had no choice but to follow their lead.[18]

Khuri's remarks need, of course, to be taken with a pinch of salt; they were after all made at a moment when (being under detention) he was trying to get back in the good graces of the French. They underline Khuri's inclination to hold the cabinet in general, and Sulh in particular, responsible for the course of events. We shall note this tendency again at other critical junctures, for instance over the execution of PPS leader Antun Sa'ada in 1949. Taken as a whole they throw light on Khuri's personal weakness opposite Sulh (a configuration already referred to in Chapter 3). We find further evidence for it, as well as for the differences between Sulh's and Khuri's approaches, in Sulh's conversation with the British representative of 29 October, part of which has already been quoted above. The British report noted that Sulh seemed to have 'matters well in hand' and said he would not 'let himself be influenced by a possible "go-slow" policy on the part of ... President [Khuri]'.[19]

Evidence from official documents is corroborated by Salma Mardam who had access to the private papers of her father, the Syrian leader Jamil Mardam, who, at the time of the events here described, was his country's foreign minister. Salma Mardam wrote:

> The Syrian government made it clear to the Lebanese government at their first meeting in early October [1943] that in dealing with the French on political matters, prudent diplomacy had to be exercised in order to avoid a head-on clash. The Syrians were also anxious to avert British interference in their relations with France and were apprehensive lest Spears's machinations succeeded in Lebanon. But the Lebanese government did not have in Lebanon the same homogeneous support as the Syrian government commanded in Syria, and was therefore less able to use the same degree of discretion in its negotiations with the French; any sign of secretiveness on the part of the Nationalists in Lebanon risked raising suspicions in their supporters' minds.[20]

This evidence, too, needs to be considered with caution: in part at least it is an attempt to explain or justify Syria's inaction during the crisis in Lebanon. Yet it does help us to understand how the Lebanese decision to bring the issue of relations with France to a head took shape. Both Khuri in his observations and the evidence from the French and British archives refer to the political pressures which were being brought to bear on Sulh to push through the constitutional amendments. These increasing pressures, stemming from the relentless struggle between Sulh and his rivals for the leadership of the Sunni community, had become all the sharper once Sulh had reached the premiership.

In this respect, the events of October and November 1943 set a precedent for the future: Sunni leaders would adopt increasingly radical and militant attitudes as a means of advancing their fortunes in the permanent power struggle within their own community, or else against rivals from other confessional groups (especially from among the Maronites). This much was true of all Sunni leaders, but the prime minister faced a double dilemma: on the one hand, he needed to keep his options open opposite the president who was his superior – at least according to the clauses of the constitution. In order to assert his position in the face of the formally broader authority of the president, he needed at times to support a radical course, at least in his rhetoric, so as to maintain the whip hand over the president. On the other hand, he needed to give himself enough leeway in confronting rival Sunni leaders who would champion extreme (often even more extreme) measures as a means to offset the advantage the prime minister had over them by being the incumbent. Over time, this outbidding game became necessary for every politician trying to move ahead in the Sunni community. The Sunni public had acquired a much enhanced national awareness and at the same time had increasingly set itself free, socially and economically, from the traditional rule of its notables. By the early 1970s, most Sunni leaders had become captives of their community's public opinion and, rather than lead, let their supposed followers drag or push them this way or that.

Taken together, the factors listed above may account for the way the constitutional issue turned into a fully-fledged crisis. The French reaction came as soon as Helleu was back in Beirut. At dawn on 11 November 1943, French soldiers raided the residences of senior government figures and arrested them. Among the detainees were Khuri, Sulh, Interior Minister Chamoun, Foreign Minister Salim Taqla, and Minister of Supplies 'Adil 'Usayran. 'Abd al-Hamid Karami, though not in the government, was also arrested. The following day, Pierre al-Jumayyil, head of the Phalanges, was detained as well. At 8 a.m. on 11 November, Beirut radio broadcast a speech by Helleu in which he announced the suspension of the constitution, the annulment of the constitutional amendments, the dismissal of the president and the cabinet, and the dissolution of the Chamber. A separate broadcast announced Edde's appointment as president.[21]

Spears had already had some warning the day before when rumours of impending drastic steps by the French began circulating in Beirut. More specifically, one of the ministers informed him that the French were on the point of dismissing the government and of dissolving parliament. Later that day, Spears met Helleu at a dinner and asked him whether there was any truth in the rumours. Helleu denied them emphatically and promised solemnly that the French would not use violence against the Lebanese government.[22] When Spears learned the truth early the following morning (from Khuri's son who had escaped during the French raid on his family's home), he hurried to inform Casey as well General Holmes, commander-in-chief of British forces in the Levant, demanding the immediate proclamation of martial law throughout Lebanon. The British, he urged, should take full control of the country and thus guarantee calm and stability. But Casey and Holmes turned him down. Casey later noted in his diary that he had opposed Spears's proposals for fear that they would result in British forces having to fire on French soldiers, and also because he saw no point in entering a confrontation with Helleu who was no more than an emissary from the Free French Committee in Algiers.[23] Holmes was rather more blunt; he later told the US consul in Beirut, George Wadsworth: 'Let us be frank about this. The man most responsible for jeopardizing our common war effort in this theater of operations is Spears. He can't see it in his overriding belief that the French must be ousted to support that effort.'[24]

It did not need British intervention for the French to understand that their latest move was a gamble that had not paid off. They had acted on the assumption that a majority of the Christians would back Helleu and would recognize Edde as the embodiment of their basic aspirations and therefore rally round him. Moreover, the French expected most of the traditional elite of notables, including some from among the Sunni elite, to stand by them. After all, many Sunni notables had cooperated with the French mandatory authorities in the past and might do so again. Some Sunni leaders did indeed act precisely as the French expected them to. Sami al-Sulh, for instance, quickly contacted Helleu to find out whether there was room for him in the new government the French were now trying to form under Edde. Under pressure from Sunni colleagues, however, Sami al-Sulh soon went back on his offer.[25] In his memoirs, he does not deny having been in touch with the French during the crisis, but claims that it was Helleu who turned to him, asking him to help in bringing the country back to tranquillity. When he declined, so Sami al-Sulh tells us, Helleu threatened to have him arrested, too. In his version, the premiership was only offered to him – by Catroux, rather than Helleu – at a later stage (for Catroux's role in the crisis, see below). He refused again, asserting that he was committed to the position of the other Sunni leaders who were demanding full independence and insisted on the release of the Lebanese detainees.[26] Sami al-Sulh's public image is captured in the following remark found in 'Adil Arsalan's memoirs: 'Nobody was so adroit in transferring his loyalty as he was.' Arsalan recalled that Sulh had been prominent among the supporters of the Axis powers; when the British and the Free French moved in, he went on, 'we said that this was sure to mean the end of the poor man, but there he was, to everybody's surprise, and [in 1942] he was even appointed prime minister'.[27]

The basic French assumption that Christian support would promptly be forthcoming turned out to be over-optimistic and unrealistic. Thus, until the very eve of the crisis, French intelligence and administrative reports spoke of continued broad support for France, especially among Maronites, and of reservations towards the line taken by Khuri and Riyad al-Sulh. Even at the peak of the crisis, on 20 November, Helleu reported to René Massigli, who was in charge of foreign affairs for the French Committee of National Liberation (FCNL): 'There is complete quiet throughout Lebanon.'[28] At about the same time, a local French report from Tripoli stated that 'nobody' there supported Khuri, Sulh or 'Abd al-Hamid Karami; rather, the prevalent view, even among politicians, was to regard the crisis merely as an Anglo-French contest not really affecting the Lebanese.[29]

Rather than let themselves be won over, however, the notables regarded the French steps as an anachronistic attempt to turn the clock back. The measures aroused not only the opposition of the notables but also that of the public at large. British attitudes, and Spears's in particular, did play a part in fostering that opposition. Many took their cue from Spears in persuading themselves that concessions by France were merely a matter of time and that ultimately the French would have no choice but to hand power back to the elected Lebanese government. Without waiting for instructions from London, or even in contravention of instructions already received, Spears set to work to bring together a united Lebanese front opposing the French steps.[30] But the anti-French attitude of the Lebanese elite had as much to do with their own convictions about the desirability of independence and the application of the National Pact as with Spears's tireless efforts. We have described how their concept of the Lebanese state evolved over the past decade or two; now they saw the French measures as totally opposed to their own vital interests.

Opposition to the French spread quickly. Despite the popularity Edde had hitherto enjoyed in the Maronite community, significant sectors in it, including the Phalanges and, more importantly, the Maronite church, now declined to back him. Helleu made a point of going to Bkirke to call on the Maronite patriarch 'Arida at his seat, but was given a hostile reception and had to listen to critical remarks by the patriarch.[31] The Maronite archbishop of Beirut, Ignace Mubarak, was a great deal more outspoken, declaring that the Lebanese would never agree to be governed by a team of 'thieves and bandits' who were collaborating with foreigners in order to destroy Lebanon and everything Lebanese.[32] Mubarak also teamed up with the Sunni mufti of Lebanon, Muhammad Tawfiq Khalid; together they signed a petition appealing to Spears to intervene in the course of events.[33]

Furthermore, the great majority of the Druse and Shi'i leaders came out against the French. The most prominent figures to give vent to their opposition were Sabri Hamada, the speaker of the Chamber, and Majid Arsalan, the Druse minister of defence. They and many of their colleagues had found their place in the new establishment of independent Lebanon and had burnt their bridges as far as the French were concerned. Among the Sunni notables, finally, no single figure of note was prepared to cooperate with the

French – and even less so with Edde. But without some Sunni support, Edde's government would not be able to function. The vigorous Sunni pressures which compelled Sami al-Sulh to go back on his original offer to the French, attested to the community's present mood.

Within days a general strike was proclaimed throughout Lebanon. There were demonstrations, mostly in the Sunni quarters of the large towns, leaving behind eighteen dead and sixty-six wounded in clashes with French forces. The students of the American University in Beirut were conspicuous among the organizers of demonstrations there; so were the students of the schools of the Muslim Charitable Society (al-Maqasid al-Khayriyya). Most Lebanese newspapers were closed by the French; only a few pro-French papers were allowed to appear. In response, an underground newspaper started coming out in Beirut. It did not identify itself and instead printed two question marks at its masthead. It was therefore generally known as '*Alamat al-Istifham* (The Question Mark).[34]

The Chamber managed to convene once more, on 11 November, with Speaker Hamada in the chair. Only a sprinkling of its members were able to make their way to the building. It declared the French steps invalid and passed a motion giving Lebanon a new flag which has remained in use since then. (The old flag had been the French tricolour, with a cedar placed over it. The matter of the flag had been on the agenda for a long time, but the government had not previously allowed it to be taken up.) While the Chamber was in session, its building was surrounded by French troops; the deputies hastily wound up the session and escaped as best they could.[35] The following day, thirty-four deputies met at the home of Sa'ib Salam in Beirut and decided to reject the French measures and not to cooperate in any way whatsoever with Edde.[36] Two ministers, Habib Abu Shahla (hitherto known as being close to Edde) and Majid Arsalan, fled to the small town of Bashamun east of Beirut and proclaimed themselves a provisional government acting, so they asserted, as the only legal government of Lebanon. This body, which became known as 'the revolutionary government' (*Wizarat al-Thawra*) or 'the Bashamun government',[37] quickly issued a series of decrees and regulations, beginning by forbidding Edde's government to draw any money and ending with a ban on the use of postage stamps with Edde's likeness on them.[38] A French detachment dispatched to Bashamun during the night of 15–16 November to arrest the two ministers encountered a force of armed volunteers at 'Aynab (near Bashamun) and withdrew. Soon enough, the Lebanese depicted the encounter as a heroic and victorious battle and it quickly became an element in the evolving myth of the Lebanese independence struggle.[39] In actual fact, Catroux, who had arrived in Beirut that day and had decided to try and cool tempers, called off the entire operation.[40]

Especially noteworthy in a scrutiny of the various reactions to the crisis was the joint response by the Phalanges and the Najada. Cooperating closely, they arranged for a series of joint protest actions such as distributing leaflets and organizing demonstrations. The French responded by arresting Phalanges leader Pierre al-Jumayyil and his assistant, Elias Rababi.[41] Both groups had started working together a year earlier when they jointly opposed the government of Sami al-Sulh. Their members were mostly middle-class, non-elite people, and their joint action proved that Maronite–Sunni cooperation was no longer a matter for the elites alone.[42] Jumayyil later admitted that he had regretted the way the 1943 crisis had evolved, but had felt compelled to oppose the French for fear of losing ground to other leaders in the Maronite community.[43] There may have been a measure of exaggeration in contemporary western diplomatic descriptions (especially in those by Spears) of the weight of Lebanese resistance, and a similar tendency is displayed in later studies; but the truth remains that the majority of notables rejected the French measures and refused to cooperate with France and that the line they took had a great deal of broad public backing.

Sharp anti-French reactions were also noticeable in the Arab world, where the inter-Arab political system was then in the early stage of its formation. Egypt, Saudi Arabia, Iraq and others registered their protests. Iraqi Prime Minister Nuri al-Sa'id even proposed joint Arab military intervention in Lebanon.[44] When the Iraqi chargé d'affaires in Beirut, Tahsin Qadri, delivered his country's protest to Helleu, the latter (to go by his own report to Algiers) told him that France had dealt with Khuri and Sulh exactly as Britain had earlier dealt with Rashid 'Ali al-Kaylani in Baghdad.[45] Yet all the while Arab leaders were aware that there were certain limits which they could not overstep without eliciting highly emotional public reactions in their own countries that would be difficult to contain. This was particularly true of Egyptian Prime Minister Nahhas who censured the French but at the same time called on Egyptians not to let their reactions turn violent.[46] The British, too, felt that a wave of anti-French feeling might well back-fire against themselves in Iraq and perhaps in Egypt as well. They hurried to restrain Nuri al-Sa'id from making militant declarations and – much to Spears's displeasure – toned down the anti-French note in British broadcasts from London and from within the region.[47]

Syria, despite its geographical proximity and its pretensions to being the standard-bearer of the anti-French struggle, did not rise to the challenge. Not only did it fail to follow in Lebanon's footsteps, not amending its own constitution until two months later, but its overall reactions also remained quite muted. As we have seen, Syrian leaders had tried to deflect the Lebanese leaders from their course at the very last moment.[48] When their attempts failed, the main thrust of their policy was to prevent the fire from spreading to Syria. As Salma Mardam put it: 'The Syrian government was aware of the urgency of taking measures to prevent public disorder in Syria and any physical attack on the French. It feared that if the situation got out of control, British military intervention might ensue, an eventuality it was determined to avoid.' She added that Mardam Bey had been indirectly warned by Daniel Lascelles of Spears's mission, who had spoken to him of the possibility of British army intervention in Lebanon in case of disturbances there.[49]

A strike was proclaimed in Damascus, but was only partially observed. A few demonstrations took place. On 15 November, the Syrian parliament did indeed call on the French to reinstate the rightful government in Beirut. But in an address to the house, Foreign Minister Jamil Mardam hinted at Syrian criticism of the Lebanese leadership, implying that Syrian inaction was justified. He threw doubt on the logic of, as well as on the necessity for, the Lebanese steps and added that the French mandate had in any case 'become more theoretical than real'. It had reached 'such a degree of weakness' that it was no longer any danger to 'an established independence'.[50] Damascus thus seemed content to let the Lebanese pull the chestnuts out of the fire: not until two months after the Lebanese crisis had been resolved did parliament pass a law amending the Syrians' constitution along the lines Beirut had sketched for them.[51]

Arab pressures against the French were reinforced by US reservations over the French measures in Lebanon. Washington threatened to take steps against the Free French in response to events in Beirut.[52]

Eventually, however, it was British intervention which put an end to the crisis. The basic impetus in London came from the long-standing policy of supporting Lebanese and Syrian independence; the underlying British assumption was that only such support could assure tranquillity in the Levant and gain the cooperation of the peoples there. But it must be kept in mind that the way this overall policy was applied, most especially during 1943, bore the unmistakable mark of Spears's direct and personal influence and of his obsessive anti-French views.

When Spears learned of the French measures, he seems to have felt that they were a dire threat to all he had tried to achieve in the Levant. His reports and memoranda to the Foreign Office and to Casey reveal the depth of his hostility towards the French. During the twelve days leading up to the crisis, he sent no fewer than 360 cables to London and Cairo. He did not mince words in giving vent to his sentiments and suspicions and tried as best he could to convince addressees of the need for strong and immediate action against the French. To press the point upon them, he made every effort to depict the situation in Lebanon as being on the point of an explosion, adding that only British intervention could prevent the worst. At one point, for instance, he mentioned the possibility that volunteers from Palestine and Syria might infiltrate into Lebanon and take up arms against the French. He reported Iraq's intention of intervening by the force of arms and finally gave it as his opinion that certain Lebanese quarters were prepared to use force, unless the crisis was quickly resolved by other means. Directly or indirectly, he pictured himself as the staunch defender of law and order in Lebanon. According to his own report, he told Far'un, in reply to a question, that he objected to the use of force on the part of the Lebanese; to engage in violence would cost Lebanon the sympathy of the 'civilized world'.[53]

Reports from other British officials in the region took a quieter line. Holmes, the general commanding British forces in the Levant, for instance, reported on 12 November 1943 that Beirut was quiet and that earlier reports (undoubtedly a reference to the dispatches from Spears) had been much exaggerated. He added that, so far, nothing had happened that was likely to endanger the British lines of communication in the Levant, or otherwise affect vital British military interests there.[54] The Foreign Office does not seem to have taken Spears's reports too literally. A memorandum dated 17 November stated that it was hard to object to the French measures since their aim was to maintain the status quo while the war was going on. It added, however, that the arrests of members of the government were too severe a step.[55] Spears was incensed; in his memoirs he complained that the Foreign Office did not really feel strongly about what the French were perpetrating in Lebanon.[56] But this time the British War Cabinet adopted the view of the Foreign Office rather than of Spears; its instruction to Casey enjoined him to remember 'that the Lebanese Government were not without blame, and that if the French had not taken such precipitate and unjustified action, we might have thought it right to support the French against the attitude adopted by the Lebanese'.[57]

Yet the British could not ignore for any length of time the potential menace events in Lebanon posed to the peace and quiet of the Levant and the Middle East as a whole. Nor could they disregard their impact on the future of Anglo-French relations. Harold Macmillan noted in his diaries: 'The Lebanon crisis is running absolutely full out … . it worries me greatly … . I feel that Spears is out for trouble and personal glory, and Casey is so weak as to be completely in his pocket.'[58] The sense of apprehension and foreboding is brought out well in an intelligence report written shortly after the crisis and summing up the course of events. Speaking of the situation in mid-November 1943, it stated: 'It was clear that the moment was fast approaching when further delay could no longer be tolerated.' The calm in Lebanon was no more than 'superficial' and 'everyone was waiting … for action to be taken quickly. Moreover, excitement … throughout the Arab world was daily increasing.'[59]

By the middle of November, the British had decided to end the crisis as quickly as was feasible. Yet the British government remained divided on whether to proceed by exerting overt pressure on the French or by applying quiet diplomacy. London soon realized that the job ahead was easier than was first thought, for the French themselves were much more badly divided on what should be their proper course than was apparent to outsiders. Helleu tried to convey the impression that he had acted on clear-cut instructions from Algiers and waved a bunch of cables at journalists in Beirut to make that point, telling them that they contained personal directives from de

Gaulle.[60] But when Catroux arrived in Beirut on 15 November, he totally disavowed Helleu and insisted repeatedly that the latter had acted without proper authority.[61]

The question of whether Helleu followed instructions from de Gaulle or (encouraged by advice from his closest associates) acted on his own initiative is still a moot point today. On the face of it, French documents indicate that de Gaulle gave Helleu to understand that he would back him fully. But Catroux alleged that neither de Gaulle personally nor the Free French Committee knew the details of Helleu's plan of action and were embarrassed by the ensuing complications. When de Gaulle decided, on 13 November, to send Catroux to Lebanon to extricate France from the impasse there, he cabled Helleu as follows: 'The forceful measures which you believed you had to take were perhaps necessary. In any case, I must consider that they were since you took them. You are covered in this respect and we will not disavow you.'[62] His words reveal some doubt and a certain ignorance of the precise circumstances, as well as a resolve not to blame a subordinate.

Helleu seems to have been influenced especially by a group of close advisers of whom Catroux was to say later that they had been in Lebanon for too long, had come to think of the country as a colony, and had failed to understand that circumstances had changed.[63] Other sources corroborate his view. US representatives, for instance, registered their opinion that Helleu was a weak character overly influenced by his advisers.[64]

It must be added that the Lebanese crisis occurred a short time after a reorganization in the Free French Committee. Its membership had been enlarged and de Gaulle's personal authority had been curtailed. A group of more cautious members had joined the committee. The latter did not hesitate to express their reservations concerning Helleu's proceedings and sought a solution not dependent on British intervention.[65] The leading figure in this group was Catroux, who later wrote that the events of November 1943 had been a severe blow to French prestige in the Levant and had done more to undermine the traditional affection of the Lebanese for France than had the French defeat of 1940. He added that Helleu's measures had provided Spears with extra ammunition, had encouraged pan-Arabism and turned the western democracies against France.[66]

Catroux arrived in Beirut determined to resolve the crisis in a manner least likely to hurt French prestige. He hurried to send an emissary to the 'Bashamun government' and visited Khuri in his place of detention in the township of Rashaya. Catroux proposed to Khuri that he would order his release from detention on condition that Khuri dismiss Sulh and appoint another prime minister. Khuri rejected the proposal and also turned down other French suggestions; for instance, to hold new elections. It was perhaps typical of the tense atmosphere of these days that some Lebanese indeed suspected Khuri of being prepared to sacrifice his prime minister. When even his own son (not seeing Sulh next to Khuri when the latter was eventually released) wondered what had befallen Sulh, Khuri upbraided him for as much as thinking that he, Khuri, was capable of such an act of betrayal.[67]

As the crisis dragged on, the British decided to step up their pressure on the French. Acting on instructions from the War Cabinet, Casey came to Beirut on 19 November and handed Catroux an ultimatum, demanding that Helleu be employed elsewhere and that the Lebanese leaders be released by 10 a.m. on 22 November. Failing this, the British would proclaim martial law throughout the country. Catroux reacted with a great deal of bitterness, telling Casey that this was 'another Fashoda'.[68] (The reference was to an incident at a small place of that name on the Upper Nile in 1898, in which Britain and France nearly came to blows over their respective plans to colonize the area; France was compelled to give in.) Yet the French realized that they had no choice but to accept. Their acceptance was made easier by the fact that the British line partly coincided with what Catroux had himself planned to do to end the crisis. Helleu was recalled to Algiers, where he was told of his dismissal; all the measure which he had proclaimed on 11 November were revoked; and, on 22 November, all the Lebanese political detainees were released, returning to Beirut in a triumphal convoy.

They seemed to be received enthusiastically by the Lebanese public. But even if public reactions were not quite balanced, the popular response was significant: the constitutional crisis provided the Lebanese at large with their first opportunity to close ranks and fight for a common cause – and they firmly grasped it. The crucial British role notwithstanding, public responses were another proof of the validity and wide acceptance of the National Pact and, in broader terms, of the national consensus that had emerged round the issue of Lebanese independence.

This may well have been the moment for the leadership to take the process a step further, to transcend the principle of communalism and give greater substance to the supra-communal state and its structures. This was not done. For one thing, the national consensus related to a state maintaining, rather than abolishing or even narrowing, communal structures – a state weak in the exercise of its authority and largely symbolic in character. For another, it is perhaps wrong to consider the 1943 crisis as so momentous an upheaval. For all the tension surrounding it and for all the rivers of ink later spilt over it, it was, in the final analysis, a limited and modest event; a milestone, but not a chasm. Albert Hourani had a point when he called it 'child's play' (see the beginning of this chapter). A US intelligence report opined that with eighteen dead and sixty-six wounded, independence had come cheaply.[69]

PART TWO

# First Steps

## CHAPTER 5

# Between East and West: Lebanon on the International and Regional Scene

The resolution of the November crisis of the Lebanese constitution removed the question mark hitherto placed against the idea of Lebanese independence. Yet independence remained partial, fragile and threatened. French ambitions had not evaporated. Looking back over the past decades with the benefit of hindsight, it seems to us only too obvious that France's historical role in the Levant was about to come to an end. But this was not at all clear to contemporary Lebanese and Syrians. Moreover, it was anticipated that, as the war was nearing its end, the Levant would no longer be of strategic importance to Britain or the USA, and that neither would continue to take an active interest in the region; there would thus be nothing to prevent France from staging a come-back.

If the French threat, such as it was perceived by Lebanese leaders at the time, was the most immediate and urgent, it was not the only foreign menace preoccupying their minds. The problem of how to ensure the country's independent status at a time when a new regional order was emerging loomed equally large. The end of the war would make it necessary to integrate the country into the Arab system without exposing its independence to threats likely to come from new Arab ideologies and power constellations.

The perception of these issues as threatening the country's independence followed from the new concepts the Lebanese elite now held with regard to their state. The National Pact had severed the link with France. As far as Lebanon was concerned it had also relegated Britain and the USA to the sidelines, though perhaps at a distance short enough for them to be still useful as insurance, as it were, against domestic or regional risks. Also, no Lebanese was in doubt that cultural and economic ties with the West needed to be maintained. Politically speaking, however, most Lebanese felt that the role of the West as sole, or even as principal, protector of the country was played out. Khuri's government viewed overly close political ties with the West as an obstacle on the road to Lebanon's assimilation into the Arab world. But the country's integration into the new Arab system was part and parcel of his and his colleagues' 'grand design' intended to ensure two things: Lebanon's independence and Khuri's dominant position in it. The 'grand design' – whether we look at it from the point of view of Lebanon's future ties with Britain and the USA or from the angle of its relations with the Arab states – made it imperative to loosen France's continuing grip on Lebanese affairs.

Lebanon's busy activities in the Arab arena were undertaken not only with an eye to the Sunnis at home where, for Sulh, they served to bolster his standing in the community and, for Khuri, showed that he was the only Maronite leader who could successfully steer a course between East and West; they were also meant to open the growing Arab markets to Lebanese traders, bankers and businessmen. Without a foothold there, Lebanon's prosperity could not be assured and without prosperity it would not be possible to uphold the leadership role of the present elite. Finally, for Beirut to play an active inter-Arab role seemed the only way to evade potential threats emanating from the new regional constellation. One such threat was the desire of many Syrians to absorb Lebanon into their country; another stemmed from the efforts of the Hashemite dynasty (both its Jordanian and its Iraqi branch) to bring about a union of the Fertile Crescent (as Nuri as-Sa'id referred to his scheme) or of Greater Syria (the term used by Amir 'Abdallah of Transjordan). Both plans envisaged the inclusion of Lebanon in a larger Arab entity. Beirut saw them as all the more menacing because they were believed to have British backing. Many Maronites complained that these ominous prospects had been conjured up, rather than mitigated or diverted, by Lebanon's activities on the inter-Arab scene. But the truth is that they were inherent in the new realities of the Middle East emerging as the war drew to its close. This also explained why a western guarantee would no longer suffice to secure the country's independence: Sunni sentiments of belonging to the surrounding Arab Muslim world were too strong for that. At every turn, Sunni attitudes were bound to turn an inter-Arab issue of the kind just mentioned into a dangerous domestic controversy.

Under Khuri, therefore, Lebanese diplomacy endeavoured to devise a system of checks and balances in international and regional relations which would extend into foreign affairs the domestic balance instituted by the National Pact. One such endeavour was to enlist Syria in efforts to make Sunni leaders and the Sunni public at large take a moderate stance and support the present Lebanese government. The Hashemites for their part were 'recruited', as it were, to keep Syria preoccupied by pressing for the above union schemes and thus make Damascus seek Lebanese cooperation as a counter-weight. The Egyptian–Saudi alignment would in turn come in useful, in Lebanese eyes, to restrain the Hashemites and blunt their drive for regional union. The western powers, finally, were to remain present in the wings, not visible enough to complicate Lebanon's inter-Arab moves, but not too far away to prevent them from coming to the country's rescue should there be a serious breakdown in this elaborate system of balances.

The capability of thus playing off potentially dangerous actors against one another was one key to Lebanon's ability to protect its independence against domestic and regional hazards, just as it was a key to the survival of Khuri's government for almost a decade. Initially at least, it was a brilliant success story. True, the international and regional dangers eventually turned out to have been less severe than the Lebanese leadership believed at the time; in many ways, circumstances actually worked in favour of Beirut's role and some of the work that might have fallen on Khuri's shoulders was actually done for him by others. Thus, for example, in setting itself free from the vestiges of French overlordship, Khuri's government could sit back and watch Britain and Syria do the main job. Or again: in striving to counter Hashemite ambitions, Lebanon found Egypt and Saudi Arabia moving ahead of it and exerting their more powerful pressures exactly the way Beirut would have wished them to. Even the British and French military presence in the country (however unwanted it was – particularly that of France) furnished Lebanon with a bargaining counter in determining its place in the new inter-Arab political system. It could be used to make Arab countries (most of all, Syria) suspect that any Arab step unacceptable to Beirut would drive it back into the open arms of France (or the other western powers).

One cannot help feeling that Khuri and his associates transferred to the field of foreign relations the practices and tactics they had honed at home. In any event, the establishment of full independence from France and the integration of Lebanon into the Arab system without compromising its independent status allowed the government to maintain the momentum created during the constitutional crisis. This was most useful in disarming its domestic opponents, whether they were isolationist Maronites or militantly nationalist Sunnis. The obverse side of the coin was that Lebanese leaders acquired the habit of devoting most of their efforts to foreign affairs, at the expense of nation-building and state-constructing.

## Independence from France

The events of November 1943 were the beginning of the end for France in the Levant, yet it took another three years for the last French soldier to leave Lebanon. Until then, the French issue headed Khuri's list of priorities. Three controversial points dominated the conflict: the transfer of the 'common interests' and the assumption of full authority by the Lebanese; the evacuation of the foreign forces; and the matter of the treaty of friendship with France (which would affect the entire gamut of future Franco-Lebanese relations). On each, the government adopted an adamant stand.

The first point was the most urgent and, comparatively speaking, the easiest and was therefore tackled first. Already on 1 October 1943, Lebanon and Syria had come to an agreement on the joint administration of the 'common interests', especially the Syrian Lebanese Bank and the customs union. Such an agreement was vital for the presentation of the Syrian and Lebanese case to the French.[1] Indeed, after the resolution of the November crisis, the French declared themselves ready to negotiate the transfer of the 'common interests', in the hope of thereby easing the way towards the signing of a treaty of friendship.[2] Matters proceeded quickly and, on 23 December 1943, the Syrian and Lebanese governments informed their countries' parliaments that an agreement had been reached. It provided for the transfer of 'common interests' and most of the formal authority for running the two countries' affairs to take place on 1 January 1944. The few areas still remaining under French administration or influence were transferred over the following years.

While cooperative on these points, the French (this time with British backing) refused to hand over to the local governments the so-called 'special forces' (i.e. the local military units), arguing that internal security and the maintenance of stability and order must remain in French hands until the end of the war.[3] France would only consent to place the regular police and the gendarmerie under the authority of Syria and Lebanon. On this issue, as so often before, Spears acted on his own rather than in consultation with London. In the summer of 1944, he brought Anglo-French relations to the brink of crisis when, at his instance, the British military command proposed issuing thousands of rifles to gendarmerie units in Syria and Lebanon.[4] Before this could be carried out, however, both the Foreign Office and the War Office instructed their respective representatives (Spears and General Paget) not to take any action without French consent.[5] Spears reacted by proposing a special consultation in London. Foreign Secretary Anthony Eden wrote to Churchill advocating such a meeting so that 'you and I may once more be able to make our policy clear to him, which is not to undermine the French in the Levant'.[6] (As it soon turned out, these and similar consultations were preparatory steps for Spears's removal from the region.) The upshot was that rifles were not issued to the gendarmerie and the 'special forces' were transferred to the local authorities only when the evacuation of the French forces from Lebanon and Syria was already imminent.

The question of the evacuation of the French forces and the nature of Franco-Lebanese relations (two inseparable issues in the eyes of the French) presented a much tougher challenge. After the November 1943 crisis, the French had realized that they were no longer able to hold on to their authority as the mandatory power. Instead, as we have seen, they pinned their hopes on a special treaty to be signed between the two countries. The idea had first been brought up immediately after Khuri's election. Khuri had rejected it then and had done so again on later occasions.[7] Now, the French made the evacuation of their armed forces from Lebanon conditional on the conclusion of a treaty. Khuri's former argument, to the effect that the Algiers committee was not a proper French government and therefore no partner for treaty discussions, became central to the issue during 1944. However, it lost its validity in August 1944 when the Free French entered Paris. Already on 2 September 1944, General Beynet, the new commander-in-chief of French forces in the Levant and French high commissioner there, came to see Khuri and formally reiterated France's request for a treaty. Khuri rejected the request, this time taking the line that Lebanon was a sovereign state and therefore entitled to refuse to sign a treaty containing pre-set conditions.[8]

The French treaty proposal was, as a matter of policy, backed by Britain. A day before Beynet's meeting with Khuri, Eden had instructed Spears (then in London) to encourage both Lebanon and Syria to sign treaties with France as the only means to attain full independence and subsequently to maintain and protect it.[9] At a meeting on 2 January 1945 with the Lebanese minister in London, Camille Chamoun, Eden told him that Britain had indeed 'recognized Lebanese independence and had guaranteed [it] and was not considering going back on its recognition, yet it wishes to make it perfectly clear that while the Lebanese were Britain's friends, so were the French'.[10]

Eden's instructions notwithstanding, Spears did not conceal his opinion that Britain must not press French treaties on the Levant states. Rather, he thought, London should encourage both Beirut and Damascus to oppose them. At the time of the resolution of the constitutional crisis in November 1943, he had written to the Foreign Office that 'the Levant Governments have never had the least intention of negotiating with the French. To suggest that they should do so now, is to show how little the depth of feeling aroused by recent events has been understood.' For all their restraint, he went on, the Lebanese had not forgotten 'the outrages perpetrated upon their leaders or the murder of their children. For us to press them to discuss a treaty now with the perpetrators of those crimes would strike them as callous and unseemly.'[11]

At the meeting with Eden already referred to, Spears sharply attacked the French, telling the foreign secretary that for Britain to put pressure on Syria and Lebanon to sign the treaties was an action devoid of all logic. He went on to remind Eden that it had been the French who had let the Germans into the Levant at the beginning of the war, adding that they might do so again.[12] In subsequent notes from Beirut he went on to argue against the idea of the treaties so forcefully that no Lebanese diplomat could have done better.[13] (He had indeed informed the Foreign Office at the end of 1943 that since, unlike France, Lebanon had no diplomatic representative in London, he had taken it upon himself to fill that role.)[14] Nor did Spears seem to hesitate in stating his position in conversations with regional leaders. The latter came away from meetings with him reinforced in their opposition to the treaties and confident that he had meant to reassure them that Britain would once again back them against France.[15]

It is of course impossible to be sure whether Lebanon and Syria would have signed treaties with France if Spears had not made such vigorous efforts to set them against it. The Lebanese, by their own testimony, might have come round, had they felt that London insisted on treaties being signed. Lebanese Foreign Minister Salim Taqla, for instance, told British representatives at a meeting in Beirut in September 1944 that if the British really wanted the treaties, neither the Lebanese government nor the Chamber of Deputies would be able to refuse.[16] Even more noteworthy are Khuri's words at a meeting with Sa'dallah al-Jabiri and Jamil al-Mardam, respectively Syria's prime minister and foreign minister. The meeting, it will be recalled, had been convened to coordinate positions with regard to the forthcoming talks with France. Salma Mardam later wrote: 'The issue of a treaty with France was raised and discussed at length.' Mardam spoke of the 'incapacity' of the Free French Committee to negotiate treaties. But Khuri did not dismiss the possibility offhand; he said that 'if a treaty had to be concluded, it would have to be inspired by the … letters attached to the Franco-Syrian and Franco-Lebanese treaties of 1936. Mardam Bey replied that it would be best not to be constrained by any agreements.'[17]

Taking all the evidence together, the attitude of Britain (as represented by Spears) seems to have had less weight with the Lebanese than that of the Syrian leaders. The latter were constrained in their decisions by strong anti-French sentiments among the Syrian public at large. While it is certainly true that Lebanon could not have flown in the face of Syria on an issue so central to both, yet, in the last analysis, rather than persuasion it was the force of common interests and identical historical circumstances which caused the two countries to take the same line. After the events of May 1945 (see below), the question of the treaties no longer figured on the agenda of either side.

Spears's opposition to regional treaties with France exacerbated the tensions already existing between him and the Foreign Office, and between him and Eden in particular. While Eden continued to favour the conclusion of treaties, Spears gave the local leaders to understand that British policy was not all that cut and dried and that pronouncements from London might as well be ignored. Eventually, Eden reached the conclusion that Spears had gone too far and, with considerable effort, convinced Churchill (for so long Spears's staunch defender) to dismiss him. In November 1944 Eden had already given Spears a hint to that effect. Spears thereupon wrote to Churchill, asking to be kept in his post until the end of the war;[18] but Churchill turned him down, his reply including a reference to Spears's 'Franco-phobia'.[19] On 23 November 1944, Spears was notified that Terence Shone (then British minister in Cairo) had been appointed to replace him on 15 December.[20] The Foreign Office softened the blow by announcing, on 5 December, that Spears's replacement did not imply any change in British policy. And indeed, Shone's opinions did not differ substantially from Spears's, attesting to fairly uniform attitudes among British men on the spot (as distinct from opinions in London) on France's future standing in the Levant.[21]

The French, in mounting their campaign in favour of the treaty, did not solely rely on support from London, but attempted to enlist Francophile sections of the Lebanese public, mainly from among supporters of Edde. But these had emerged weakened from the November 1943 crisis and were unable to make their weight felt on the domestic scene. By contrast, the Maronite church under patriarch 'Arida now gave firm support to the French. 'Arida ignored his own tense personal relations with the French representatives. Nor did he allow his support of the anti-French faction during the November 1943 crisis to prevent him from proclaiming his support for Lebanon's historical ties with France. On 29 May 1945, he convened a meeting of Latin and Uniate church leaders at his seat in Bkirke, at which he spoke in support of full independence and cooperation with neighbouring Arab countries, but also advocated signing a treaty which would, he said, remove all misunderstandings between Lebanon and France.[22] 'Arida may have taken this line in response to the rapid (too rapid, as far as he was concerned) rapprochement between Lebanon and the Arab states. (The Alexandria protocol, for instance, containing an annex regarding Lebanon's place in the projected Arab League, had been signed in October 1944; see below.) But we may perhaps also detect in his words the signs of his disappointment with Khuri's policies and with the insignificant and marginal role to which Khuri and his government had relegated the church. In any event, the personal and political alliance between 'Arida and Khuri that had existed since the early 1940s had come to an end; they had become bitter rivals.

It seems, however, that the Maronite church establishment was not united in its support of 'Arida. The Maronite archbishop of Beirut, Mubarak, for instance, warned the Bkirke convention against a treaty with France, mainly because of the hostile response this would elicit from the Lebanese Sunnis and throughout the Arab world. Instead, he suggested, Lebanon should seek a joint guarantee for its independence from all the great powers acting together. According to a French report, 'Arida replied that Mubarak's proposal presupposed appealing to the communists and to Protestant powers, while he wished the country to turn to its traditional Catholic protector.[23]

Overall, the influence of the Maronite church, and of 'Arida personally, was on the decline and was not to recover the weight it had once possessed. This accounts for Khuri's ability to ignore 'Arida (sometimes demonstratively so) and explains why the church's advocacy of a Franco-Lebanese treaty received little public attention. The only support it found came from certain Maronite church circles holding rather extreme views. True, reservations about the current inter-Arab policies of the government were fairly widely felt among Maronites, but the objectors did not therefore opt for a treaty with France.

The French had to face a challenge of a different sort from the outside. New actors were appearing on the scene. The USA had become a vigorous defender of Lebanese independence and was strongly opposed to any treaty obligations towards France or to any other way of maintaining France's special standing in the Levant. On 19 September 1944, the USA recognized Lebanon as a fully independent state, having previously turned down a French appeal to delay doing so until both Lebanon and Syria had recognized France's special status there.[24] The American recognition came only a short while after the original French demand for the treaties had been submitted in Beirut and Damascus (cf. above). US attitudes were shaped to a considerable extent by the personal views of Wadsworth, the US consul in Beirut, later to be his country's first minister in the Levant. Together with Spears, he played an important role in encouraging the Lebanese government to resist the French demands and contributed a great deal to the emergence of an anti-French policy in Washington.[25] The Soviet Union, too, began to evince an interest in regional affairs. On 19 July 1944, the USSR recognized the independence of Lebanon and on 20 October 1944, the first Soviet minister presented his papers to President Khuri.[26] Both the USA and the USSR were active in ensuring that Lebanon and Syria were invited to the founding conference of the United Nations at San Francisco in March 1945 – despite French opposition, quietly supported by Britain. France argued that neither Lebanon nor Syria had declared war on the Axis powers and were therefore not entitled to figure among the founders of the UN. The Lebanese and Syrian governments replied that they had refrained from declaring war, because Britain had asked them to do so.[27]

The establishment of the Arab League constituted another constraint which France would henceforth have to take into consideration. Indeed, some Lebanese politicians and officials, among them the Lebanese minister in London, Chamoun, used the Alexandria Protocol and the League Charter (signed in March 1945) to assert that the idea of a treaty with France could no longer be entertained. But such arguments prompted some Maronite circles to assert that the country was replacing its former dependence on France by an exaggerated dependence on the Arab countries. As Mubarak put it: 'Lebanon has been independent for 14 centuries and will thus refuse to accept any change in its status. Therefore, neither the Alexandria Protocol nor the clarifications given concerning it, nor the Lebanese representative in London [Chamoun], nor any of our neighbors – none of these will succeed in taking away our freedom.'[28]

Since the Lebanese government itself claimed that neither the establishment of the League nor its own inter-Arab policies affected the country's full independence, Lebanese representatives soon stopped using such arguments. Khuri himself called them 'nonsense',[29] and Foreign Minister Taqla told French officials that the Alexandria Protocol did not limit Beirut's political freedom of action.[30]

Towards the end of 1944, relations between France and Lebanon (as well as between France and Syria) had thus reached a state of deadlock. A crisis was clearly looming; it broke in May 1945, as soon as the war in Europe had ended. The French immediately saw the hand of Britain behind it. A French report asserted that the crisis had been 'clearly inevitable' since the end of 1944, but that it was only in May 1945 that 'the British gave the Syrian leaders freedom of action against France. It would have broken out earlier had England wanted it to.'[31]

In actual fact, two other factors seem to have been more important. One was the Syrian government whose attitudes exacerbated relations at a time when clashes between the population and the French forces in Syria were escalating. For our purposes here, it is immaterial whether Damascus acted deliberately or was simply powerless to prevent such an escalation. The other was the more forward, more vigorous policy of the French who felt that the end of the war and the rehabilitation of France in Europe had given them much greater freedom of action than they had hitherto enjoyed.

Unlike 1943, when the Lebanese were in the van and the Syrians were watching from the sidelines, in 1945 it was Syria which led the anti-French action, leaving Lebanon some distance behind. The immediate event triggering the outbreak was the arrival of French reinforcements in Lebanon in May 1945. For some time, the Lebanese, backed by Syria, had been demanding to be given prior notification of the arrival of any French unit in the country. The principal object of their demand was to obtain advance warning of the deployment of Senegalese troops who were especially hated because of the conspicuous role they had played in the constitutional crisis of 1943. The Lebanese had also been demanding that the French should not unilaterally increase the overall strength of the French forces in the country. They argued that now that the war in Europe was over there was no possible reason for sending extra troops to the region, and warned of the consequences of the deployment of additional French forces in the Levant. Britain, though perhaps not quite as decided on the matter, backed the Lebanese; London had been alerted in April 1945 when it became known that de Gaulle had ordered the dispatch of reinforcements to the Levant.

On 8 May 1945, the French destroyer *Montolan* entered Beirut harbour, carrying 850 soldiers – most of them Senegalese. French officials spoke of a routine rotation. Indeed, the ship sailed the following day, taking some 500 soldiers with it. But on 17 May, another French naval unit, the *Jeanne d'Arc*, landed 555 men in Beirut. Demonstrations immediately started in Beirut and continued even after the ship had sailed, on 20 May, with a contingent of home-bound French soldiers on board.[32]

Soon afterwards, though perhaps not in direct connection with the troop movements, Beynet submitted to Beirut and Damascus what amounted to an ultimatum, demanding the signing of treaties along the lines of those drafted in 1936. The treaties were to provide for cultural and economic links between France and the Levant states, for the grant of bases for the French army and navy on Levant territory, and finally for the 'special forces' to remain under French control even after their formal transfer to the authority of the local governments. Tension mounted immediately, in Syria more so than in

Lebanon; a general strike was proclaimed throughout Syria and violent clashes involving French forces and Syrian crowds occurred in towns and cities throughout the country. The French lost effective control of Damascus and other Syrian cities. When the riots peaked on 29 and 30 May, the French bombed and shelled Damascus, killing some 800 people. Severe damage was caused to government buildings, most of all to the building of the Syrian parliament.[33]

Lebanese reactions, both official and public, were restrained. The Lebanese government published a statement deploring the bloody events in Syria, registering its protest against them, and warning of the possible consequences in Lebanon. But it also noted with satisfaction that law and order were being maintained in Lebanon, due to the restraint and discipline displayed by the Lebanese. That, the government asserted, was the way they had chosen to demonstrate their solidarity with the Syrian government and people.[34] Khuri summoned the British minister and asked for Britain's diplomatic intervention with a view to maintaining the present calm in Lebanon.[35] The Lebanese leaders were obviously unwilling to see violent clashes spill over into their own country, nor, for all we know, did the public at large feel any differently. Lebanese militancy had its limits, even if independence was at stake – as had been borne out by the events of November 1943.

Whatever the differences with regard to the use of force, when it came to rejecting the French demands Damascus and Beirut were united. The point is worth stressing in the light of contemporary diplomatic assessments – preserved mostly in French, but also in some British documents – that it was primarily Syrian pressure which stood in the way of the Lebanese agreeing to a treaty with France. If Syria could be neutralized, these diplomats felt, Lebanon could be expected to become more forthcoming.[36] Diplomats also noted the apprehensions of the Lebanese government concerning the likely reaction of the country's Sunnis, should such a treaty be signed. They pointed to the negative influence of the government reshuffle which had taken place in Beirut in January 1945, when 'Abd al-Hamid Karami had replaced Sulh as prime minister. Karami had for long been known as anti-French. Sulh himself had become more strongly anti-French; now that he was no longer restrained by being an incumbent but was able to speak with the freedom of an opposition spokesman, his statements were even more likely to make negotiations difficult.[37] But the Lebanese government needed no encouragement from any quarter to object to the treaty: dissociation from France was part and parcel of Khuri's basic policy as it was of his and his ministers' world-view. Syrian pressure as well as anxiety about local Sunni reaction played their part, but it was a minor one. With or without them, a treaty with France was no longer on the cards.

Even though Lebanon remained calm during May, it was obvious that, if the crisis turned out to be prolonged, the country's tranquillity would not last. Shone wrote to London that Foreign Minister Taqla, whom he called 'the strongest personality in [the] Government,' seemed 'genuinely interested in confining action to the diplomatic plane'. The prime minister, he went on, was violently anti-French, but 'irresolute'. He and his associates (mostly Muslims) would

> like to force the issue but are uncertain how much support they could command amongst Christians. In general, although extreme Christians are still obsessed by [the] advantages of French protection, hostility to the French is more widespread than at any time since November 1943. If [the] situation worsens it seems certain that [the] Government will either have to adopt [a] policy of aligning themselves with [the] Syrians in resistance to France or will have to give way to [a] more extreme group who will do so.[38]

Things did not reach that pass. As in 1943, British intervention brought the crisis to an end. On 31 May 1945, the commander-in-chief of the British forces in the Middle East was instructed to order the French troops back to their bases and to use all the means at his disposal to restore order and tranquillity throughout the Levant. Simultaneously, Churchill sent a note to de Gaulle saying:

> In view of the grave situation which has arisen between your troops and the Levant State, and the severe fighting which has broken out, we have, with profound regret, ordered the Commander-in-chief, Middle East, to intervene to prevent the further effusion of blood in the interests of the security of the whole Middle East which involves communications for the war against Japan ... In order to avoid a collision between British and French forces, we request you immediately to order the French troops to cease fire and to withdraw to their barracks. Once firing has ceased and order has been restored, we shall be prepared to begin tripartite discussions here in London.[39]

Because of some technical hitch, the note reached de Gaulle only after the British ultimatum had already been delivered to the French commanders in the Levant – a fact which increased de Gaulle's resentment. On 2 June, he convened a press conference at which he sharply attacked Britain for the role it had played in the Levant ever since 1941.[40] On the spot in the Levant, however, France had no choice but to accept the British demands and thereby terminate the crisis. The way it ended was a severe blow to France's standing in the region; henceforth the question of the final evacuation of all French forces from the Levant was merely a matter of time. Yet it took more than a year of hard Anglo-French bargaining to agree on the modalities of the withdrawal, as the French made desperate attempts to salvage something of their traditional status.

An agreement in principle between Britain and France on the evacuation was arrived at on 13 December 1945, but it was no more than a declaration of intent. It set no date for the withdrawal; rather, it called on Britain, France and the Levant states to negotiate the precise arrangements which were to

govern it. The Levant states rejected the agreement and the Lebanese Ministry
of Foreign Affairs listed its objections and reservations in a note to the
Foreign Office. It began by expressing regret that the Lebanese government
had not been consulted beforehand: 'Had they been consulted, they would
have been able to make suggestions for the elimination of a large number
of ambiguities which may in the future give rise to serious misunderstandings.'[41]

The two Levant states now decided to pin their hopes on the United
Nations. On 4 February 1946, they submitted a joint complaint to the UN
Security Council protesting against the failure to set a date for the evacuation
of foreign troops from their two countries. This was a rebuff to Britain
which had regarded itself as the proper mediator in the dispute.[42] Moreover,
the complaint contradicted numerous Lebanese statements to the effect that
Beirut did not object to the presence of British troops in the country. In
July 1945, for instance, Khuri had told British representatives that unless
some British uniforms remained visible in Lebanon, the country's joy at the
withdrawal of the French would not be complete. When asked to comment
on a statement by the Lebanese foreign minister, Far'un, demanding the
evacuation of *all* foreign forces, Khuri reacted furiously, saying that he
personally was not interested in the departure of the British forces.[43] Even
if there is room for doubt whether Khuri really thought in terms of a
prolonged British military presence in Lebanon, it is clear that he did not
want the British to withdraw before all French forces had been evacuated.[44]

The UN Security Council discussed the issue in mid-February 1946. The
USA submitted a compromise proposal acknowledging the need for a speedy
withdrawal of all foreign forces; but it left the date to be set by further
negotiations between the sides concerned. At these contacts, the logistics of
the evacuation were to be fully considered. The draft resolution was vetoed
by the USSR because it had not been consulted in preparing it. But Britain
and France announced that they would observe its clauses just as if it had
been formally adopted.[45]

The final step was taken on 14 March 1946, when Britain and France
agreed on the imminent withdrawal of their troops from the Levant. The
rest was done quickly; Britain agreed for the evacuation of its forces to be
completed by the end of June. Talks with France ran into a hitch over the
question of the venue. The French proposed to meet in Paris. This was
inconvenient for the Lebanese because, apart from Sulh, their delegation also
included Hamid Franjiyya and Yusuf Salim, foreign minister and minister of
the interior respectively. Chamoun, the minister in London, suggested holding
the talks in Beirut, with the participation of Britain and Syria.[46] He was
perhaps acting on the advice of Spears who continued to pull strings even
after his retirement and to act out his anti-French convictions. When the
Lebanese delegates proceeded to Paris regardless, Spears attacked them
personally. In letters to 'friends' in Lebanon, including Khuri, he claimed

they were not suitable to conduct the negotiations and accused them of not really believing in their mission. He added that he had been personally disappointed by Sulh who on the fateful day when his country's destiny was in the balance at the Security Council had found nothing better to do than to hunt for a present for his wife.[47] Khuri preferred to ignore the letter; in his memoirs he wrote that he had made up his mind not to let Spears's Francophobia influence his own political decisions.[48]

The Paris talks were soon concluded: on 25 March, it was agreed that France would withdraw the bulk of its forces by 1 August; the rest would leave Lebanon by 31 December 1946. The evacuation marked the end of France's historic role in the Levant; its weight as a great power would not again be felt in Lebanon.

## Lebanon on the Inter-Arab Scene

The core of Lebanese policy towards, and within, the Arab world was encapsulated in the tenets of the National Pact of 1943. However, in terms of practical policies rather than overall principles, we may trace the beginnings of Lebanon's inter-Arab activity to an even earlier date: to June 1942, when Khuri and the Syrian Prime Minister Jamil al-Mardam met with the then Egyptian premier, Nahhas Pasha. True, their meeting was primarily intended to promote the personal political fortunes of the three participants. At the same time, however, it also marks an important stage in the emergence and consolidation of Khuri's concept of bringing about the integration of his country into the Arab world without imperilling its independence. Apart from Syrian and Egyptian support for Khuri's election campaign, one of the results of the meeting was broad Arab support for Lebanon during the constitutional crisis of the following year.

Syrian involvement in Lebanese affairs had been a permanent fact of life ever since the establishment of the first Lebanese state in 1920. But Egyptian involvement, soon to be followed by that of Iraq, Transjordan and Saudi Arabia, resulted from the emergence of an inter-Arab political system during the final years of the Second World War – a constellation not previously found in such a form. Since in most respects its development served Lebanon's interest, Khuri and Sulh did not oppose it; at times, they even actively encouraged it. In the long run, however, it became a burden and sometimes turned into a menace to the country's domestic stability.

Towards the end of 1943, inter-Arab contacts intensified in an endeavour to respond to the new realities at a time when the war was clearly drawing to its close. The Hashemite rulers of Iraq and Transjordan were seeking broader Arab legitimation for the union schemes they sought to realize ('Greater Syria', as proposed by Amir 'Abdallah of Transjordan, or the 'Fertile Crescent' plan, as proposed by Nuri al-Sa'id from Baghdad). Against them were ranged Egypt and (with even greater fervour) Saudi Arabia. Both were interested in promoting inter-Arab cooperation, but opposed any change in the existing political and territorial status quo. Such changes, they felt, would only serve the interests of their Hashemite rivals. Both Lebanon and Syria had a vital role in these contacts: both were the objects of Hashemite designs and were liable to be submerged in one or the other of the projected union schemes. In retrospect, the Hashemite plans are easily seen for what they were: unrealistic ideas going beyond the bounds of practical politics. But at the time, in the eyes of the newly independent Levant states, they loomed threateningly. Seen from Beirut, the Greater Syria scheme looked the more dangerous; it came from closer by than the Iraqi scheme and was promoted by the Hashemite amir (soon to be king) in person, while the latter was the particular cause of Nuri al-Sa'id – not himself a member of the Hashemite family. 'Abdallah's image as a forceful personality, as well as the widely-held (though erroneous) assumption that his scheme had British backing, added to this perception.[49] What seemed most dubious to Lebanon's leaders was 'Abdallah's suggestion that the Christians of Mt Lebanon (though not those elsewhere in the country) should enjoy an autonomous or even independent status, provided they dropped their opposition to his plan. As 'Abdallah himself explained:

> Lebanon had a framework of its own already in the Ottoman period, especially in all that concerned Little Lebanon. The Arabs are not interested in upsetting this framework. Therefore, the right of Lebanon to exist in such a framework will not be affected when Arab unity is realized, except for the four districts that were taken from Syria and added to Lebanon in the move to set up Greater Lebanon.[50]

Khuri's main worry was that in order to further his schemes, Transjordan might try and enlist his rivals within the Maronite community, first and foremost Edde and his supporters. As we have seen, Edde had called for the constitution of a Little Lebanon in Mt Lebanon alone – an idea capable of meshing easily with the Greater Syria scheme. The atmosphere of distrust and suspicion then prevalent in Lebanon regarding such plans is illustrated by the following example. In the summer of 1946, Edde went to Paris for a vacation; but Beirut rumours had it that he had gone there to seek contacts with 'Abdallah and also intended to meet British Foreign Secretary Ernest Bevin to win him over to the idea of setting up a Little Lebanon as a step towards forming Greater Syria. (Bevin happened to be in Paris in connection with the UN General Assembly.) The Lebanese government hurriedly demanded clarifications from Britain, only to be informed that there had been no change in British policy regarding London's support of Lebanese independence.[51]

Syria joined Egypt and Saudi Arabia in their resolute opposition to 'Abdallah's scheme. Syrian President Shukri al-Quwatli declared in the summer of 1945: 'The Greater Syrian plan is an imperialistic scheme and the efforts

[now] being made to carry it out are no more than part of a well-planned move to realize a design decided upon long ago.'[52] 'Abdallah's attempts to seek support within Lebanon failed; the Maronites remained at best indifferent, while the Sunnis were plainly hostile to his plan. (Their reactions attested to the low regard Arab nationalists everywhere had for the Hashemites at that time.) To cite an example: during his tenure as prime minister, in October 1945, Sami al-Sulh responded to 'Abdallah's urging to proceed with the establishment of Greater Syria by saying, 'Lebanon has joined the Arab League on condition that it maintain its sovereignty and independence, and as far as we are concerned the Greater Syrian plan is therefore not a subject for discussion.'[53] Similarly, in November 1948, Riyad al-Sulh told the Chamber of Deputies: 'We shall not accept anything that harms our independence, whether by the establishment of Greater Syria or by means of any other plan.'[54] During the same debate, 'Abdallah al-Yafi said: 'As a Lebanese-Muslim-Sunni deputy … I wish to make it clear that we in Lebanon – whether Christians or Muslims – are satisfied with the existing situation and do not wish to change it.'[55]

A more delicate and complex issue was the matter of Lebanese policy towards Syria. This was not purely an issue of foreign policy; Syria's strong influence among Lebanese Sunnis constantly made relations with Damascus a domestic question of the first rank. During the preparatory talks, held late in 1943 and early in 1944 to lay the groundwork for the establishment of the Arab League, Syria took positions which aroused Lebanese apprehensions. In October 1943, for instance, when Nahhas Pasha met the Syrian delegation, its leader, Prime Minister Jabiri, took a rather ambiguous line towards Lebanon. Jabiri was quoted as saying that, in his opinion, 'the great majority of the inhabitants of Lebanon, both Christians and Muslims, are unconditionally interested in forming part of Syria. This is especially true of the areas added to Lebanon at the end of the first world war.' Jabiri went on to say:

> The Lebanese are now experiencing a feeling of relief and comfort, but it is us who provide the source for these sentiments, because they are being brought forth by the hope for a union [with Syria]. But we suspect that the leaders of Lebanon are seeking security in the arms of France, and will thereby allow the latter to regain a renewed foothold in the region, after the war has removed the ground from under their feet there. For this reason we have recognized Lebanese independence and have given it our support – on condition that they, like ourselves, will demand the consummation of full sovereignty and will follow in our footsteps, adopting an Arab character [for their state]. [He added:] We have always demanded that the fabric of relations between Lebanon and Syria should revert to what is natural to it, that is to say that the ties between ourselves and Lebanon be based on ties of unity, or, alternatively, that the districts torn away from Syria be reunited with it and that Lebanon revert to what it had been before [i.e. prior to the First World War].[56]

The views Jabiri presented in this conversation were part of a broader picture: Syria publicly supported the cause of Arab unity, meant to include the other parts of the Fertile Crescent. This must give pause to the researcher of the period. Syria was, after all, no less hostile than Lebanon to the Hashemite schemes and, just like Beirut, Damascus considered them a danger to its independence. It much preferred the status quo over any scheme likely to upset it. If, all the same, the Syrians presented themselves as the standard-bearers of Arab unity, we may follow Y. Porath in assuming that this was primarily intended for internal consumption. As he points out, this was easy to do in light of Syria's knowledge that the firm Egyptian and Saudi resistance, as well as Iraq's hesitancy, had already removed such a course from the realm of practical politics. It was therefore safe to clamour for Arab unity; the danger of being taken at one's word was close to nil.[57]

In practical terms, therefore, these matters did not stand in the way of normal, even close, relations between Lebanon and Syria. Such relations did indeed exist – at least until 1949 (see Chapter 10). Until 1946, moreover, the need to present a united front against France contributed a great deal to the stability of bilateral ties. So did the necessity of cooperating to oppose the Hashemites and their schemes. The personal friendship linking the leaders of both countries added another element. So, finally, did Syria's domestic weakness which would have precluded any drastic action on the broader Arab scene. Only the consecutive military *coups d'état* in 1949 turned Syria from a dormant source of possible trouble into an effective threat to Lebanon.

Whatever the state of relations with Syria, there was greater safety for Lebanon in relying on Egypt and Saudi Arabia to counter the Hashemites. On 5 January 1944, the Lebanese delegation to the preliminary talks on the founding of the Arab League came to Cairo. Its leader, Prime Minister Riyad al-Sulh, told his Egyptian interlocutors that much as Lebanon favoured close cooperation with Syria and the other Arab states, this could only come about if his country's independence and sovereignty were ensured.[58] It will be recalled that this position now put forward by the Muslim prime minister coincided precisely with that stated by Christian presidential candidate Khuri in his talks with Nahhas and Mardam back in 1942 – a remarkable piece of evidence attesting to the Christian–Muslim consensus on this issue.

In April 1944, Sulh complemented his Cairo visit by a trip to Saudi Arabia. King Ibn Sa'ud was equally sympathetic to what Sulh had to say and used the occasion of his visit to proclaim Saudi Arabia's recognition of Lebanon in its present borders.[59]

The formal preparatory conference on the League – and thus on the future character of inter-Arab relations – was convened by Nahhas Pasha and opened in Alexandria on 25 September 1944. Again it was Sulh who represented Lebanon. In his address, he said that he and his political allies who, in the past, had supported union with Syria and had opposed the Lebanese state in its present form, were now supporting it. They would battle to preserve it against any side trying to harm it, for Lebanon had now become an Arab state.[60] The conference ended with the adoption of resolutions on the charter of the future Arab League. The document containing them became known as the Alexandria Protocol. At the suggestion of Syria, it included a special clause concerning Lebanon which called for the respect of Lebanon's independence and sovereignty in its current boundaries.[61]

The special clause demonstrated the participants' understanding for, and sympathy with, Lebanon's particular requirements. It none the less elicited a considerable amount of criticism from Lebanese Christian quarters. This is exemplified by a passage from Yusuf Salim's account of the conference. Salim, then Lebanese minister in Cairo and an active participant in the debates, related that Khuri's *chef de cabinet*, Musa Mubarak (a member of the delegation), refused to sign the protocol. It required special instructions from Beirut, given by means of a telephone call by Khuri himself, to make him do so.[62]

The next stage in the process of Lebanon's integration into the Arab world was marked by the signing of the League Charter on 23 March 1945. Its final wording had been worked out by a sub-committee sitting from 14 February till 3 March. Its Lebanese member was Foreign Minister Far'un. As we have seen above, Karami had shortly before replaced Sulh as prime minister. Karami came to his office with the reputation of a confirmed Arab nationalist. As prime minister, he proved colourless and weak. Unlike his predecessor, he did not usually take a strong personal stand on inter-Arab affairs. This allowed Far'un to set the tone in this regard. Under his leadership, the Lebanese delegation challenged every word capable of being interpreted as limiting the country's independence. He objected, for instance, to the establishment of a body for compulsory arbitration in disputes between member-states. He insisted that the League as a body should not be empowered to take an explicit stand on any political issue, since doing so might be considered an obligation binding on all members. The League, Far'un said, should not be allowed to become a 'super-state' possessing greater weight than its constituent member-states.[63] With overt Saudi and tacit Egyptian backing, Far'un's suggestions were almost all written into the final text of the charter. The League emerged bereft of all practical authority. As Sulh had proposed (or demanded) a year earlier, the League became a body whose 'most important goal ... was to safeguard the complete independence of each Arab country'.[64] The only Lebanese proposal to be turned down was that for a clause forbidding any two member-states to come to an agreement between themselves which might be considered 'unfriendly' by a third member.

In addition, Lebanon did not conceal its apprehensions regarding a tendency on the part of certain Arab politicians – among them League Secretary-General 'Abd al-Rahman 'Azzam – to underline the League's Islamic character. Khuri told British representatives that he, as a Christian head of state, would be embarrassed by any such accent. Moreover, this would encourage the radical elements in the Christian camp, such as the patriarch and those close to him who, he added, never missed an opportunity to condemn him for having 'sold out' the Lebanese Christians.[65] His words deserve special attention because they were uttered in the belief that Britain had an important say in the establishment of the League and in determining the contents of the charter.

The protocol and the charter were thus not so much documents promoting Arab unity as a set of rules to maintain the existing fragmentation of the Arab world. They attested to the inability of the Arab states to create a system of close ties and mutual cooperation. They reflected their lowest common denominator and as such there was nothing in them to endanger Lebanon's independence. On the contrary, the perpetuation of the existing divisions had its obvious advantages, both for bolstering Lebanon's inter-Arab importance and for consolidating the standing of its current leadership at home and abroad. The Arab rift between the Hashemites and the Egyptian–Saudi axis was of undoubted benefit to Beirut. Khuri regarded it as a guarantee of sorts for the preservation of the status quo, whether in the inter-Arab arena or with regard to Lebanon's standing in it. For Sulh, it was yet another opportunity to demonstrate his abilities as arbiter and mediator – a role useful for enhancing his reputation in domestic and inter-Arab politics.

Khuri's foreign policy, and in particular his inter-Arab policy, became a model which most subsequent Lebanese governments imitated. What made it a successful pattern for emulation was the triple balance it contrived to strike: the domestic balance; the inter-Arab equilibrium; and a balance between the great powers. The ability to translate the domestic balance into foreign policy terms vividly attests to Khuri's sophisticated powers of political manoeuvre. Yet it must be remembered that in the early years of his incumbency the regional and international challenges to Lebanon were, in actual fact, not nearly as severe as Khuri's perceptions depicted them. It was only in the early 1950s that they assumed proportions powerful enough to erode his presidency.

CHAPTER 6

# Domestic Challenges,
# 1943–47

Until the completion of the French evacuation in 1946, Khuri and his colleagues perceived foreign policy challenges as more immediate and more momentous than the domestic contests waiting for them in the wings. From that belief, they devoted most of their energies to matters abroad; but that did not mean that they were indifferent to the personal political benefits to be derived from quick and highly visible results in this field. Successive achievements in foreign affairs did much to sustain and consolidate Khuri's regime. But as we shall see later, the events of 1948 were to turn concentration on external issues from a boon into a grievous burden. The evacuation of the French had removed a major issue from the agenda; within two years, its place was taken by the consequences of the Arab defeat in Palestine. The former had brought Lebanon spectacular success; the reverberations of the latter were altogether negative.

All the while, however, the real key to Lebanon's future lay hidden away in domestic affairs. The pivotal question was how to adapt the internal political system, with its deep roots reaching back to Ottoman times, to the requirements of independent statehood. For Khuri and his associates, though, their own political survival had higher priority. The National Pact had consecrated the traditional 'Lebanese way', and thus incorporated the defects of the old order into the new. This blocked the emergence of an efficient and functional administration; worse, it inhibited the various components of the population in their incipient identification with the new state. In the short term, a fairly stable equilibrium was thus ensured, but this was only made possible by sacrificing the prospects of stability in the long run.

We may ask ourselves whether Khuri and his government could have acted otherwise. Arab countries close by (Syria, Iraq, to some extent Jordan) had set an example of instituting central, and centralizing, governing bodies and had shown how useful they were for the consolidation of newly independent states. This could have been done in Lebanon, too – even within the existing patterns – thereby reinforcing long-term stability, enhancing the sense of statehood and broadening the state's field of action in social and economic affairs. Persistent, if gradual, efforts to mitigate the effects of the 'Lebanese way' might have circumscribed the harmful effects of communalism. Above all, it might have been possible to create a broadly acceptable mechanism for the periodic review of the National Pact and for bringing it up to date in accordance with changing circumstances (for instance, with demographic changes affecting the numerical composition of the population). Lebanese history had, after all, amply demonstrated that no single formula for communal coexistence was capable of answering the needs of the country for an extended period of time. Unless periodically adjusted by agreement, it was bound to be overturned by other means, quite possibly including violence.

Regardless of their public image as a strong and stable leadership, the president and the Cabinet nevertheless preferred to overlook the requirements of the domestic scene and refrained from any corrective action. They were, after all, themselves the products of 'the Lebanese system', had made their way to the top by playing according to its rules, and were mentally unprepared and politically ill-suited to change or amend it. Indeed, Khuri's aim in these early years was therefore to ensure his own political survival. To do so, he followed a double-barrelled approach: within his own community, he took action against Edde and his followers; *vis-à-vis* the other communities, most of all the Sunnis, he endeavoured to bolster his leadership standing.

As we have seen, Edde had been opposed to the Lebanese state such as it had emerged during the struggle for independence, but first and foremost he was Khuri's chief personal rival in his own community. The achievement of independence from France and of Lebanon's integration into the Arab world had pushed Edde and his associates into a corner and had rendered many of their arguments outmoded and irrelevant. Edde's camp was not only weakening but had also begun to resign itself to the present realities. More than that: many of its members had started seeking ways to join the new order. Edde's conduct at the time of the November 1943 crisis seemed to be the exception proving the rule rather than an indication of his basic attitudes. Since the beginning of the 1940s or even since the late 1930s, these had started shifting to the middle ground. Like Khuri himself, Edde had sought allies among the Sunni leadership. After 1943, he and his faction were no longer a real threat to the government, let alone to the new Lebanese state. Khuri's relentless struggle against him seems therefore to have been motivated by political calculations. He was out to neutralize the man who had been in the past, still was at present, and might again be in future, his greatest personal rival. There was an element of vengefulness in Khuri's attitude: he wanted to revenge himself on Edde for his actions in November 1943 and more generally for having successfully blocked Khuri's way ever since the 1920s. But Khuri was to find out quite soon that the main danger did not come from Edde but rather from people within his own camp, notably from Chamoun. Those who wanted to replace him as president after, as was expected, he vacated his post in 1949 were not the old rivals but men presently close to him. Yet the period between the crisis of 1943 and up to the final evacuation of the French at the end of 1946 was marked by the contest between Khuri and Edde – a contest riddled by frequent crises.

## Edde's Expulsion from the Chamber of Deputies

The events of November 1943 had left Edde extremely vulnerable. As soon as the actual crisis was over, Khuri's followers clamoured for Edde's dismissal from the Chamber. On 1 December 1943, Hamid Faranjiyya submitted a draft law stipulating punishment for those who had conspired against the constitution and the state (that is, Edde and his associates).[1] Among those calling for punishment were some of Khuri's closest allies, headed by Arslan and Far'un – a fact attesting to Khuri's own active, if discreet, role in the matter. There is some evidence that the British covertly encouraged action against Edde.[2]

As against them, the majority of the Maronite leadership, with patriarch 'Arida at their head, rallied to Edde's defence. The archbishop of Beirut, Mubarak, as well as Pierre al-Jumayyil, the leader of the Phalanges, though by now supporters of independent Lebanon, joined them over this issue. Even Chamoun appeared reserved. To account for their attitude, one can assume that they regarded the matter as an internal Maronite issue which should have been decided in a closed Maronite forum rather than being trotted out in the Chamber in front of the representatives of all communities. Some considered it a purely personal vendetta between Khuri and Edde which need not lead to the formation of an anti-Edde camp within the community. Chamoun in particular had in the past been personally close to Edde and had often enjoyed the latter's support, their basic differences of opinion notwithstanding. Now, he felt, was the time to reciprocate. Jumayyil, by contrast, seems to have hoped to fill the void which the elimination of Edde from Maronite communal politics was bound to create. To do so smoothly, he would need Edde's blessing.

The French, too, came out in defence of Edde, hoping that their old-time ally would still be useful to them some day in the future. Assuming that Spears was behind the campaign against Edde, they turned to London, asking the government to restrain him. And indeed the Foreign Office told Spears that steps against Edde would unduly embarrass the French and that, in any case, punitive measures should not be taken against a person simply because he belonged to the political opposition.[3]

Rather surprisingly, Riyad al-Sulh joined the ranks of those opposed to measures against Edde. He made use of the prime minister's prerogatives to delay the debate in the Chamber.[4] No doubt, Sulh acted from gratitude for the friendship Edde had shown him for so many years. But cool-headed political calculation also played its part. For one thing, Khuri's insistence on remaining behind the scenes suggested to Sulh that he was expected to do Khuri's dirty work for him. This would have brought the wrath of Edde's supporters and sympathizers upon him – quite unnecessarily so, as Sulh saw it. In addition, there is room for doubt whether Sulh thought it wise to add to Khuri's strength by removing the latter's chief Maronite rival from the scene. Moreover, he probably felt the issue was an internal Maronite quarrel, best left to the Maronites to settle themselves. In broader terms, Sulh presumably did not think it proper for the government as such to meddle in internal community affairs, let alone in an issue so intensely personal. This, he felt, would set a dangerous precedent which might one day be used against himself, too.

We find these considerations clearly reflected in a conversation held in late December 1943 between Khuri and Furlonge which points up Khuri's personal engagement in the drive against Edde. Furlonge reported to Spears:

> I asked him what were the Government's intentions as regards Edde. He said that he personally thought that this snake ought to be scotched, at least by being expelled from the Chamber, since his continued presence there would constitute a perpetual focus for intrigue; but Riyad [al-Sulh] seemed imbued with the idea of not making enemies and the other members of the Government were irresolute ... He himself could not press the point, as, in view of his well known and longstanding feud with Edde, this would savour of vindictiveness, but he wished someone would push Riyad into taking action.[5]

The last phrase can only be interpreted as an indirect appeal to Britain actively to back Khuri. He himself later gave what is perhaps the best account of the political complexities of the moment when he wrote in his memoirs:

> The entanglement was complete, as happens often after a grave shake-up has occurred in a small state where everybody knows everybody else and where relations are based on family ties and personal friendships – a small state where the desire for personal revenge is conspicuous, but perhaps not any less so the desire to appease and to emerge [from the problem] with a friendly understanding. In such a situation, relations between people of whose existence one would [otherwise] hardly have been aware [suddenly] become important.[6]

Eventually, a compromise solution was found. On 31 March 1944, the Chamber passed a motion for the expulsion of Edde from the house, but without taking any further measures against him. The formula had been offered by Far'un and Emile Lahhud and the voting was thirty-five in favour and eight against.[7] All Khuri had to do personally was to reply to the French when they appealed to him to leave Edde otherwise unharmed; he told them that Edde was now a private citizen and his future would be determined solely by his own actions.[8]

Edde's political career was now widely considered to be over. The label

Khuri had succeeded in marking him with – viz. that of an enemy of Lebanese independence – was enough to prevent him from finding allies anywhere outside the Maronite community. Without such allies, he would find his way back into active politics barred. Edde nevertheless managed to salvage some of his former prestige among the Maronites. In the late 1940s, Edde's sons would lead his old supporters back into the hub of Lebanese political action.[9]

## The Incident of 27 April 1944

The 27 April incident occurred against the background of three by-elections to the Chamber, held to fill the seats vacated by Khuri's elevation to the presidency, by Edde's expulsion, and by the death of Wahib Taraya Ja'ja. The former two held seats allocated to Mt Lebanon, the latter a seat to Northern Lebanon. The elections to replace Khuri had been scheduled to take place on 14 November 1943, but the November 1943 crisis intervened and they were postponed until 20 April 1944.

The two by-elections in Mt Lebanon passed quietly. Both the new deputies, Farid al-Khazin and Khalil Abu Jawda, belonged to Khuri's Constitutional Bloc, were known to be his supporters and, in turn, to be supported by him. Both won by large majorities.[10] Government influence certainly had something to do with the outcome; nevertheless, the results clearly indicated a shift in popular sympathy away from Edde and towards Khuri.

It was the by-election in Northern Lebanon which provided the surprise. Three candidates competed to fill the vacant seat there. One was Yusuf Karam from Zagharta, from a family of Maronite notables whose members had, a century earlier, taken a prominent – or, according to local lore, a heroic – part in the Druse–Maronite armed clashes of that period. Yusuf Karam had long been known to be close to the French mandatory authorities, was still considered their ally, and was counted among Edde's political supporters. – His competitors were Nadra 'Isa al-Khuri (supported by the president) and Hasib Taraya Ja'ja, the brother of the deceased incumbent. The latter had the support of Prime Minister Sulh.[11]

In 1943, Nadra 'Isa al-Khuri had run opposite Karami and Faranjiyya on a list considered pro-French. He had lost, but the support he now received from Khuri encouraged him to try again.[12] It soon became clear that this time, too, his chances were low. Khuri persuaded him to drop out of the race in return for an 'appropriate' monetary compensation. Sulh for his part tried to persuade Karam to act likewise, but the latter turned him down.[13]

The Ja'ja–Karam race into which the elections had thus turned was now thought of as a straight contest between a government candidate (Ja'ja) and an anti-government figure (Karam). The government's prestige was therefore at stake. More than that: since Karam was considered pro-French, the local contest took on the coloration of an Anglo-French confrontation. As so

often, the French accused the British of meddling in the elections in favour
of the government candidate. French reports spoke, for instance, of attempts
by Spears to enlist patriarch 'Arida on Ja'ja's side. They accused the British
political officer in Tripoli of having told local notables that, if they wanted
order and stability in their area, they should support the government
candidate.[14] But the Anglo-French tug-of-war proved rather irrelevant to the
actual campaign. The supporters of the two candidates did not divide according to their pro-French or pro-British sympathies. Equally beside the point
was the government theory that Karam's backers were Maronite isolationists
whom Edde (with French backing) was urging to act against the country's
independence.

To get closer to the actual considerations guiding the main actors we must
look at the attitudes of some of the pivotal figures of the regime. Far'un,
for instance, one of the pillars of Khuri's presidency, was among the more
conspicuous supporters of Karam. Originally, Far'un had supported Nadra
'Isa al-Khuri; when the latter dropped out, he had two reasons for refusing
to transfer his support to Ja'ja: he was angry with President Khuri for having
abandoned Nadra 'Isa; and he held it against Ja'ja that he was a 'protégé' of
Sulh whom, at that time, Far'un considered as a bitter political rival. He
therefore backed Karam and gave him substantial financial support. The
means thus placed at Karam's disposal had a great deal to do with his
eventual victory.[15]

Two other Maronite notables from the north, both defenders of Lebanese
independence and backers of the government during the constitutional crisis,
also refused to support the government candidate. They were Yusuf Istafan
and Hamid Faranjiyya. In public, they remained neutral; in private, they quietly
backed Karam. Their primary motive seems to have been their resentment
over government interference in the northern district which they considered
the jurisdiction of the local notables, themselves included. In their view, any
intervention from the centre meant setting a dangerous precedent. They also
had personal reasons to oppose Ja'ja.[16] Finally, 'Abd al-Hamid Karami, who
had great influence over northern Muslim voters, was reluctant to back Ja'ja.
When both Khuri and Sulh appealed to him to do so, he replied that the
choice of Ja'ja was an internal Christian affair.[17] Moreover, his competition
with Sulh over their respective positions in the Sunni leadership was sharp
enough to make him act against Sulh's advice for that reason alone.

Far'un's backing and the thunderous silence of the northern notables who
had declined to come out for Ja'ja combined to give Karam a resounding
victory.[18] His success was seen as a grievous blow to the prestige of the
Beirut government who had invested such efforts to bring in Ja'ja. Government figures quickly came to speak of the outcome as a victory for the
enemies of Lebanese independence. Khuri wrote in his memoirs:

The results had hardly become known when the enemies of the era of independence already hurried to proclaim their victory [and] fraudulently depicted the results as a victory by the supporters of imperialism over the supporters of Lebanon. Those who presumed to speak in the name of the Christians were quick to proclaim that the resurrection of the dead was at hand and began organizing popular demonstrations for Karam's entry into the Chamber.[19]

On 27 April, Karam came to Beirut to be sworn in. As was customary, he arrived accompanied by a crowd of supporters, estimated at between 5,000 and 6,000 persons. Some carried the old mandatory flag of Lebanon, some the French flag. The crowd soon blocked access to the Chamber building and then tried to force their way into it. In the mêlée, an officer from a French unit stationed nearby tried to hoist the French flag over the gates of the building. He was shot and wounded. French soldiers thereupon opened fire on the Lebanese police unit present there. Four people were killed and twenty wounded.[20]

The Lebanese government reacted sharply, blaming the French for the incident. Before the session during which the incident had occurred was over, Sulh had used it to attack the 'traitors' responsible for it, promising that they would be dealt with 'with an iron fist'.[21] Minister of the Interior Chamoun lost no time in stating that there had been a French conspiracy. The demonstrators, he added, had been brought to the scene in French trucks and many French soldiers had taken part in the event. Without being provoked, they had then opened fire on the Lebanese police.[22]

On closer scrutiny, there can be no doubt that the incident was a local and limited occurrence, not at all a conspiracy to bring down the government. The available evidence shows that neither the French nor Edde and his men were involved. That very day Karam himself avowed his support for the government and his commitment to Lebanon's independence.[23] The course of Karam's career during the following years showed that he accepted Lebanese independence as an accomplished fact (much like Edde did, too). Integration into the new establishment was their only option. During the next few years, Karam would cooperate with Karami and Far'un in their political struggle against Sulh – a struggle comprehensible only against the background of an independent state.

It is hard to say whether the government leaders really believed in a conspiracy or whether – as happened so often – they merely exploited a narrow local affair for the best tactical advantage they could extract from it. There may have been some truth in both versions: the government was still sufficiently unsure of itself to believe that France would want to make its weight felt in Lebanon; but the incident was also a lever to maintain the useful momentum created by the November 1943 crisis. It must be remembered that Sulh's cabinet was at the time running into difficulties and therefore in need of such props.

Immediately after the incident, the government ordered mass arrests to be carried out among Edde's followers – although they knew, or should have known, that Edde had no part in the event. Some eighty people were detained.[24] The French denied any connection with the April occurrences, though they admitted half-heartedly that some of their soldiers stationed near the building might have taken part in them on their own initiative. They deplored the arrests carried out among Edde's men – their Lebanese sympathizers – and expressed concern about the renewed threats now being made against Edde.[25] The French Foreign Ministry stated that High Commissioner Beynet had been authorized to 'deal' with the situation. This caused some apprehension among the Lebanese leaders and there were rumours that the French were planning a coup. Sulh went to see Spears to ask him to intervene. The Foreign Office asked Spears to caution Beynet not to take any steps liable to create tension in the region. Beynet replied that France had no intention of doing any such thing. He denied that there had been any French conspiracy, and when Spears suggested that an investigation be launched, he agreed unhesitatingly. He even conceded that some Frenchmen might be too hot-headed to understand the policy he, Beynet, was trying to apply.[26]

Initially, Spears seems to have believed that the French were indeed behind the incident. On the day it happened, he took the unprecedented step of attending the meeting of the Lebanese cabinet – ostensibly to calm down the ministers, but actually to strengthen their hand against the renewed threat against them.[27] In his first report, written two days after the event, he adopted most of the views held by the Lebanese. He stated, for instance, that the government had expressly asked for Karam not to be accompanied to the Chamber by an armed crowd. He added that the exchange of fire had occurred after a French officer had tried to hang a French flag on the gates of the Chamber's building.[28] Later, however, Spears dismissed the idea that there had been a deliberate and organized French plot to bring down the Lebanese president and cabinet. What had happened, he concluded, was that some subaltern French figures, together with their Maronite followers, had tried to make a show of strength and that Beynet had nothing to do with it. In a summary written about a month later, he said:

> My own theory about the incident of April 27th is that it was meant to be no more than a demonstration against the Government and an attempt to see how much ground the Government had lost and the Edde party, as the symbol of French influence, had regained. There seems to be enough evidence to show that the Sûreté Générale had a large hand in the affair and it is at least probable that Emil Edde himself and his principal supporters had a hand in it, but rather cooled off after Karam had proclaimed his allegiance to Riyad Sulh. I do not believe it was a deliberate attempt to overthrow the Government by violence. In fact it was rather in the nature of a ballon d'essai.[29]

Spears went on to mention that the person in charge of foreign affairs for the FCNL (French Committee of National Liberation) in Algiers, Massigli, had warned the British minster to Algiers, Duff Cooper, that the French might again act against the Lebanese government in a way similar to the November 1943 crisis. Spears called it 'curious' that such thinking was present in the highest official quarters rather than being confined to 'French hotheads here'.[30] Nevertheless, he took these warnings seriously enough to recommend to the Lebanese leaders that they tone down their anti-French pronouncements and stop blaming France for the incident. During a conversation with Sulh, Spears told him that few people in Lebanon believed the government version of the incident. When Khuri, at a meeting with him, claimed that the event had been planned by Edde's supporters, together with French reactionary circles who wanted nothing more than to set Christians against Muslims, Spears suggested that Khuri stop blaming Edde and take no further steps against him.[31]

The Lebanese leaders took Spears's advice. Sulh said that his statement in the Chamber had been intended only to call on the house to shoulder its responsibility and that he had not meant to blame anyone for the incident. He went to the length of apologizing to the French for the things he had said, adding that Chamoun had misled both the government and Spears, with the intention of creating a new crisis in the country's relations with France. He also told French representatives that he was about to demote Chamoun: he was in touch with the British about appointing him minister in London in order to remove him from the Beirut scene.[32]

## Government Reshuffles

Next to the struggle against the vestiges of French influence, the main concern of Khuri was to consolidate his standing in the eyes of the elites of the various communities. This was especially true of the Sunni notables, his closest collaborators since the institution of independence. His ability to do so was predicated on one vital condition: to appear willing and capable of maintaining the 1943 status quo. It was a task that taxed all of Khuri's political talents. His principal weapon was his prerogative to appoint and dismiss cabinets; more particularly, to pick, or drop, the Sunni leader who would head them as prime minister. For the entire length of his incumbency, Khuri made ample use of the political opportunities this privilege offered him.

Between 1943 and 1947, Lebanon had seven cabinets under four prime ministers: Riyad al-Sulh, 'Abd al-Hamid Karami, Sami al-Sulh and Sa'di al-Manala. Their average incumbency lasted seven months. From the first, each premier and each cabinet minister devoted their best energies primarily to their own political survival. There were three principal threats they had to fend off: the constant intervention of the president in cabinet business and his ceaseless attempts to undermine the premier's authority; the endless rivalries of other Sunni leaders who themselves aspired to the premiership; and the relentless pressures from notables of all communities for a share of the benefits which were in the ministers' gift. These might go to themselves or serve to oblige their kinsmen. If their expectations were disappointed, a campaign of vengeance and retaliation would ensue.

These dangers flowed naturally from the concept politicians held of the task of the president and the ministers, particularly of the prime minister. For Khuri, the prime ministership was a means to ensure the loyalty of the Sunni elite. As 'king-maker', he made sure that the internal rivalry in the Sunni community did not abate, or that – the worst case possible – a Sunni coalition against him should come into being. This meant replacing the heads of government at fairly short intervals; a prolonged incumbency would have allowed the prime minister to build up too efficient a power base. It would also have prevented the president from holding out hope of satisfying some other leader's ambitions, thereby keeping him loyal until that day arrived and then to cash in on his gratitude. The Sunni leaders for their part thought of the prime minister as a springboard for themselves. Membership of this circle was meant to offer them benefits, some of which they could pass on to their associates or followers in the community, thus enhancing their own prestige among them. Finally, the elites of all communities held the government responsible for the equitable sharing in government largesse by them all.

This being so, it cannot come as a surprise that, on the whole, the Lebanese cabinets failed properly to transact government business. But since that was in any case not what they were primarily expected to do – at least not by their fellows in the elite – efficiency or the lack of it had little to do with either their appointment or their dismissal. What determined their fate were changes in the balance of power between them and the president, the prime minister, and their common or separate Sunni rivals. It should be added that the premiers and ministers, though superbly familiar with the ins and outs of the country's political system in which they had made their way up, came to their positions with no prior experience of administering a government department. They lacked the conceptual equipment and the practical skills required to be at the helm of a young state during the inevitable difficulties of its early years.

The country's first prime minister, Riyad al-Sulh, held office from 25 September 1943 till 9 January 1945, heading two governments. He was called back on 14 December 1946 to head the cabinet which was to prepare for the general elections of April 1947. When first appointed, he came to his post with a great deal of public credit, with the image of a forceful and energetic personality, and with massive support from the Sunni community. In his first cabinet, Sulh served also as finance minister. Chamoun was minister of the interior and of post and telegraph; 'Adil 'Usayran (Shi'i) was minister of food supplies and of the national economy; Salim Taqla (Greek Catholic) was minister of foreign affairs and of public works; the Amir Majid Arsalan (Druse) was minister of defence and of health.[33] Of special note was the presence in the cabinet (as minister of justice and of education) of Greek Orthodox Habib Abu Shahla, a close associate of Edde. He owed his appointment to Sulh's desire to create the broadest possible basis for the cabinet (and perhaps also to his wish not to burn his bridges where Edde was concerned).[34]

Sulh's speech presenting the cabinet to the Chamber was at the time seen as a programmatic declaration affirming the principles of the National Pact.[35] Relations with France and ties with the Arab world were the two main concerns of the cabinet. Domestic affairs were of no great interest to Sulh, nor did he possess the qualifications to deal with them effectively. Khuri admitted as much already in December 1943 when he told Furlonge (according to the latter's report) that the 'Government had two weak spots in Riyad al-Sulh's lack of interest in administration and 'Adil 'Usayran's quarrelsomeness and indiscretion'. Riyad, he went on, had dealt 'brilliantly' with the French, but was 'incapable of studying a dossier or indeed of sitting in an office chair for more than an hour at a time, so that his administrative decisions were always snap ones taken without proper consideration; he was also too much concerned to placate possible adversaries'.[36]

Spears explained Sulh's difficulties by pointing out that he had spent a political life-time in opposition and now found it hard to adjust to administrative duties. As a result, urgent matters of state went unattended. Moreover, Sulh and Interior Minister Chamoun spent much of their time quarrelling with each other.[37] A lengthy assessment of the cabinet and its ministers, composed by Furlonge in May 1944, showed that the passage of time did not improve things. He said that after eight months in office, the government was 'bound to become increasingly shaky, since Ministers will have exhausted the immediate benefits they could confer on their followers'. Ambitious deputies were likely to feel that their turn had come. All previous governments, he added, had 'laid themselves open to criticism by the defectiveness of their internal administration', once a similar period had elapsed. That was no less true of the present cabinet.[38]

The one figure concerned with administrative reform was Interior Minister Chamoun. With the support of the British, he established a reputation for being a reformer, even a revolutionary. Whether he did so because that was an image useful to his career, or because he held a genuine political vision of this kind is hard to say. In any event, it was a reputation valuable for influencing public opinion and perhaps also for winning friends among western representatives. But it quickly placed him on a collision course with the rest of the establishment which, as we have seen, was devoted to the preservation of the status quo. His outspoken criticism of the way Khuri, Sulh and the other ministers were functioning led, in June 1944, to his removal from the cabinet (and his appointment as minister to Britain).[39] Chamoun's place as representative of the Maronite community was occupied by Faranjiyya who became finance minister; Sulh himself took over the Ministry of the Interior. In agreeing to appoint Faranjiyya, Sulh seems to have been influenced by the need to include a representative from Northern Lebanon in the cabinet. But the choice was also useful to weaken, even to break, the alliance between Faranjiyya and Karami and to draw some of Faranjiyya's supporters over into Sulh's camp.

Chamoun's removal was the prelude to a broader government reshuffle by which Sulh hoped to refurbish his public image and reinforce the other ministers' dependence on him. Supply Minister 'Usayran, under criticism for the continued shortages he had been expected to relieve, was next in line. More important, though, was the fact that his very presence in the cabinet prevented Ahmad al-As'ad from supporting it. Like Chamoun, 'Usayran was offered diplomatic employment (there was talk of his appointment to Washington), but he refused and thereby dragged the entire cabinet into a crisis.[40]

Western diplomats may, however, have overrated the influence of administrative flaws and of public criticism on the fate of the cabinet. Its difficulties stemmed mainly from the unstable equilibrium between the president, the prime minister, the other ministers, and the Chamber. What threatened Sulh's standing right from the start was: (1) the struggle against him on the part of other Sunni leaders, principally Karami; (2) the president's too frequent interference in cabinet business and his tendency to undermine Sulh's authority so as to bolster his own; (3) Sulh's failure to secure a firm basis of support among the elites of other communities – elites who tended to take a short-term view of politics and to seek personal benefits and immediate career advantages. Among the notables, Far'un was most conspicuous in his opposition to Sulh. The two became caught in a bitter quarrel over the appointments of Far'un's allies to important posts and over their respective shares in positions of power.

Things came to a head in June 1944 when Karami and Far'un succeeded in bringing together a temporary anti-Sulh alliance – an enterprise in which they were tacitly and covertly supported by Khuri.[41] Khuri later described the anti-Sulh coalition in his memoirs, but failed to mention his own part. He wrote:

> Riyad al-Sulh's foreign policy was well received in all nationalist quarters, and certainly had the support of the entire Chamber. But the same cannot be said of his domestic policy. Some of his political enemies – mostly from his own community and from among those who were contenders for the premiership – were lying in ambush for Riyad. Among them was 'Abd al-Hamid al-Karami, Sa'ib Salam, 'Abdallah al-Yafi and Sa'di al-Manala. All these were assisted by Henri Far'un. Together, they formed a [new] political party under the name of Independence Party (*Hizb al-Istiqlal*). But they refrained from choosing a leader for it, because they did not want to expose the dispute between ... Karami and those who actually backed this political move and took a leading part in it. They were wary of publicly opposing Riyad so as not to bring the anger of the public upon themselves – least of all from among the country's Muslim quarters who were giving ample support to Riyad.[42]

Sulh reacted by reshuffling his cabinet with a view to attracting greater support in the Chamber and among the public at large. He added Faranjiyya to the cabinet in order to broaden his own support in the Chamber, and he dropped 'Usayran in order to appease his rival al-As'ad. Following these changes, Sulh won a vote of confidence in the Chamber, with forty-four deputies voting in favour and ten against.[43]

The reshuffle gave Sulh a breathing space but, towards the end of 1944, relations between him and Khuri soured again, among other things over the matter of administrative appointments for the latter's protégés. A British report from January 1945 stated that Khuri had never got rid 'of a tendency to promote the interests of his former Party, the Constitutionalists', but now found Sulh 'disinclined' to help him do so. Sulh had always wanted to placate 'friends and enemies alike' and did not wish 'to abandon this line in favour of the President's relatives and friends. Relations between them had consequently become strained.'[44]

Khuri may have wished, at that juncture, to allow another Sunni leader to take over the premiership and thereby gain that person's loyalty (as well as giving others hope for the future). Moreover, appointing a new prime minister would have given him the advantage of appearing as mediator and arbiter among Sunnis eager for promotion. Whatever his precise reasons, he used his presidential standing to strengthen Sulh's rivals in the Sunni elite as well as his opponents in the Chamber. He also enlisted some Maronite quarters against him. The French archives contain transcripts of Khuri's telephone conversations monitored by French intelligence which point to his contacts with Phalanges leader Pierre al-Jumayyil, at the time one of the sharpest critics of Lebanon's foreign, and especially inter-Arab, policy. Jumayyil was wont to blame Sulh for what he considered a harmful line. The archives show that some of his attacks against Sulh were made with Khuri's knowledge, some even at his request.[45]

The elections to the position of speaker of the Chamber, held in October 1944, gave a clear indication of the weakening of Sulh's position in the house. His favourite was Sabri Hamada, the Shi'i 'feudal boss' of the Biqa' who had been speaker during the preceding session and who was believed to be the front-runner. But his opponent, Yusuf Salim, a Greek Catholic from Southern Lebanon, was able to recruit a large number of National Bloc deputies (i.e. followers of Edde) on his side. These were joined by some of Sulh's Sunni rivals, for instance 'Abdallah al-Yafi, and also by 'Usayran who was seeking revenge for his removal from the cabinet. It was only by an intense personal effort that Sulh succeeded in overcoming the resistance of this grouping. Eventually Hamada was elected by thirty-five against fifteen votes.[46] There is another noteworthy aspect of this event: the mere possibility of a Greek Catholic running for the office of speaker, even though under the National Pact this position was reserved for a Shi'i, attests to the internal weakness of the Shi'i community. It also shows that, in 1944 (just a year after the formulation of the National Pact), there was as yet no universal commitment to its stipulations.

In December 1944, Defence Minister Majid Arslan resigned from the government. He had been one of the leaders of the Constitutional Bloc and was a close associate of Khuri's. Khuri may have urged him to resign, but Arslan also had personal reasons for doing so. His resignation struck a heavy blow at the prestige of the cabinet – heavy enough for Sulh to offer his own resignation on 7 January 1945.[47] The immediate background, though, was a motion in the Chamber to repeal the press censorship law. A British report spoke of a 'group of deputies, who with the President's connivance, began organizing opposition to Riyad al-Sulh in the Chamber. It came to a head over ... a motion for the abolition of internal press censorship.' Sulh was altogether opposed to the idea, arguing that without censorship newspapers could easily be 'suborned by the French and the Edde group'. When Sulh found that the bill was supported not only by the opposition but also by many deputies normally siding with the government, 'he undoubtedly felt that the Chamber had at last got beyond his control'.[48]

Sulh's resignation led to a brisk struggle over his succession. The main contenders were Karami, Yafi, Sami al-Sulh and Sa'ib Salam. Karami was 'number-two' after Sulh in the Sunni community and, at that time, commanded a great deal of support in the Chamber, because of an ad hoc alliance with Far'un. He had also gained much public sympathy because of an attempt on his life: on 13 December 1944, on his way home to Tripoli he narrowly escaped an ambush, probably manned by members of the Muqaddam family, his chief local rivals with whom he had a blood feud. Sami al-Sulh had turned to Maronite Patriarch 'Arida and sought his endorsement. Salam was widely thought of as too young and inexperienced. Beirutis tended to believe that Khuri's preferred candidate was Yafi who was known for his good connections with the French and might be useful in bringing the negotiations with them to a conclusion.[49]

Eventually, it was Karami who secured the appointment. One thing in his favour was the support he could count on in the Chamber. Another was that Khuri must have felt that a man who had been a confirmed opponent of the Lebanese political entity for so long could not but bolster its independence by now accepting the premiership. Yet another consideration was that it would be useful, during the concluding phase of the negotiations with France, to have a prime minister capable of mustering a majority among the Sunnis in all circumstances (even if concessions had to be made to the French). Finally, Khuri expected to benefit from increasing the tension between those two old Sunni rivals, Sulh and Karami.[50]

Karami's government was in power from 9 January until 22 August 1945. In his speech presenting the cabinet, Karami spoke of his commitment to the independence of Lebanon in its present boundaries. He stressed the need for the greatest cooperation with the Arab states which, he added, were as interested in the country's independence as was Lebanon itself. Like his predecessor, he promised to place administrative reform at the top of his agenda. In international and inter-Arab affairs, he would follow the lines of the outgoing cabinet.[51] However, observers did not look forward to any particular achievement from the new government and the British did not expect it to last very long.[52] Already in November 1944, after an altercation between Sulh and Karami in the Chamber, Furlonge had written of Karami's 'lack of education and complete ignorance of administration' and had described him as 'a failing man ... no longer capable of fulfilling the task of Premiership'. He also noted that Karami's influence in the north, 'though still great', was less than it used to be.[53]

Karami quickly turned out to be a weak and colourless prime minister. In particular, he proved unable to make his weight felt in inter-Arab relations – the area which had, so to speak, been Sulh's home turf. He left Arab affairs to Far'un and took no active part in the contacts leading to the establishment of the Arab League. Neither did he exercise much influence over the course of the negotiations with the French. For a few months, however, he enjoyed freedom of action to an extent such as other Lebanese premiers hardly ever experienced. This was the result of a nervous breakdown suffered by Khuri which necessitated his treatment abroad. The breakdown resulted from prolonged and painful treatment he had received after breaking his hand on 15 December 1944 while on vacation, as well as from his shock over the death of his old friend and ally Salim Taqla on 11 January 1945.[54] Khuri was taken incognito to Tiberias and from there to Haifa where he received medical treatment for several months.[55] Rumours in Beirut threw doubt on the prospect of his eventual resumption of duties, even though Khuri did some work in Haifa, consulting with other government figures and meeting western diplomats. The latter talks reinforced rather than dispersed such doubts. The Belgian chargé d'affaires, for instance, reported that the signs of the breakdown were clearly discernible and that Khuri had started crying several times during their talk.[56]

Khuri recovered, and returned to Lebanon and to the presidency on 31 March 1945. British Minister Shone came away from their meeting in April firmly convinced that Khuri was well, though still a little tired. Shone added, however, that Khuri was not a very strong man at the best of times.[57] Khuri's return put an end to Karami's unwonted freedom and did not make life easier for him. Neither did Riyad al-Sulh's relentless scheming against him. Sulh kept trying to reduce Karami's support in the Chamber and criticized him on the subject of inter-Arab and Franco-Lebanese affairs – the two areas in which Karami was weakest. His verbal attacks were meant to impress first of all the Sunni community. He held up Karami's conduct of the negotiations with the French as hesitant and accused him of yielding too much. Karami often complained of the burden Sulh's criticism placed on his shoulders and charged him with ingratitude; he himself had given Sulh loyal support during his tenure, but Sulh did not requite him similarly.[58]

Karami was none the less given some extra breathing space by the French

demand for a treaty with Lebanon. During the ensuing confrontation, Khuri
thought it best to seek a reconciliation – even if a temporary one – between
Karami and Sulh. He feared that continuing public quarrels would cause
both to take up more extreme positions. As a result, Lebanon might find
itself too deeply implicated in the parallel Franco-Syrian tensions. In his
memoirs, he explained: 'I succeeded with difficulty in defending the cabinet
in front of the deputies and to tone down Karami's anger against them.
Thus we passed this phase, too, with a great deal of effort, acting from a
wish to ensure stability.'[59] But as soon as the crisis was over, in May 1945,
Khuri had no further need to hold down tensions within the Sunni community. On the contrary, what was now required, Khuri felt, was to restore
a proper balance among the Sunni leaders – an aim best achieved by cutting
short Karami's incumbency. As a result, Karami soon found the ground
crumbling under his cabinet.

In June 1945, Riyad al-Sulh succeeded in mustering a majority for himself
in the Chamber. The deputies now siding with him demanded that an
extraordinary session be held to vote the Karami cabinet out of office and
replace it with a broader government of national unity. Sulh stepped up his
attacks against Karami, arguing that the latter had failed to display sufficient
solidarity with Syria during the May 1945 crisis. Khuri decided that the time
had come to abandon Karami to his fate. He recalled the Chamber from its
recess ahead of time – a step understood to imply the withdrawal of
presidential confidence in the cabinet and to afford the Chamber a ready
opportunity for a vote of no-confidence. Khuri expected Karami to resign
before a vote was taken and to vacate his position calmly.[60] He wrote later:
'I acted quietly behind the scenes to make it possible for the government to
win the vote, so that the prime minister could [then] withdraw with dignity,
being [a man] easy to take offence.'[61] On 15 August 1945, the Chamber, by
a vote of thirty-four against nine, did indeed express confidence in the
cabinet. (No Lebanese government was ever brought down by a vote of no-
confidence; all resigned as a result of deals struck behind the scenes.) When
the vote was taken Far'un voted against the government and Karami himself
abstained.[62] But Karami refused to leave the scene quietly, as Khuri had
expected him to do. He did resign on 16 August, but openly accused Khuri
of having brought about his downfall in order to block the domestic reforms
he, Karami, had wished to carry out. He spoke of himself as an old man
no longer suited to fill the post of prime minister, but added quickly that he
would still be available, if recalled.[63] The circumstances of Karami's resignation are noteworthy, because he was the first, and for a while the only, Sunni
who refused to do as Khuri bid him, viz. to serve as prime minister for a
few months, allow his authority to be attenuated by the president's, and
eventually withdraw without protest, waiting to be called again. Moreover,
instead of blaming his Sunni rivals for the fall of his cabinet (and thereby
adding strength to the president's image as arbiter of Sunni affairs), he

attacked Khuri personally, and criticized his entire way of governing and his attitude towards the premiership.

The next government was formed by Sami al-Sulh on 22 August 1945 and survived until 22 May 1946. Sami al-Sulh's strength lay in his political and personal weakness. True, British and other western observers considered his weakness, alongside his lack of administrative skills, as his main defect and as the principal cause of the cabinet's inactivity.[64] But in Khuri's eyes, these were Sami's greatest assets. It was his weakness which made it possible for him to hold office with the approval – or at least the tacit consent – of both Riyad al-Sulh and Karami, his two great rivals in the Sunni elite. Sami's incumbency enabled them to achieve what they wanted most: to keep each other out of office. Karami even went to the length of allowing some of his strongest supporters, chief among them Sa'di al-Manala, to join Sami's cabinet.

We have noted earlier that Karami's strength in the Chamber resulted from his alliance with Far'un and his close ties with the Shi'i leaders As'ad and Hamada. He now formalized these links by establishing the Independence Party (Hizb al-Istiqlal). Apart from the commitment to the country's independence implied in the choice of its name, the party advocated closer relations with the Arab states, but programmatic proclamations were not its real *raison d'être*. As soon as Karami had resigned (and had come to realize that his relations with Far'un were no longer close), he set up a new group, the Reform Bloc (Kutlat al-Islah). He enlisted various notables to join it, among them Karam, Muhammad al-'Abud, and Kamal Junbalat.[65] Karami now decided to use this bloc not only to reinforce his strength in the Chamber but also to continue his personal struggle against Khuri. As it turned out, though, it was nearly always Sami al-Sulh who suffered from his attacks, rather than Khuri whom they were intended to hurt. Already in January 1946, Sulh's government appeared shaky. The immediate background to the renewed tension was Karami's demand for a novel law introducing smaller, single-seat constituencies. Karami threatened that if this was not done, he would bring Sulh's government down, precipitating the entire country into a crisis. Khuri promised Karami to consider his proposal, but had obviously not the slightest intention of adopting it. He found that Karami's own supporters were not enthusiastic about it either. He turned to the Egyptian chargé d'affaires and to the British legation, asking them to intercede with Karami. He argued that at that particular juncture in the negotiations with France, a government crisis would only benefit the French. Under British and Egyptian pressure, Karami desisted from threatening the government and accepted as sufficient Khuri's promise to 'study' the proposal.[66]

The next crisis erupted in March 1946, soon after the agreement on the evacuation of French troops was reached. At Khuri's request, Riyad al-Sulh had been included in the negotiating team. Khuri meant this to be some sort of compensation for Sulh for not having been appointed prime minister after Karami's resignation, but also considered it a safeguard to ensure broad acceptance of the resulting accord. However, the success of the agreement, and the credit Sulh was able to take for it, were such that they provided him with new leverage to seek Sami al-Sulh's ouster and his own return to the premiership. (The competition between the two cousins, Sami and Riyad, can be traced back to the 1943 elections, or even before.)[67] During the negotiations, Riyad had succeeded in gaining the support of two other members of the delegation, Interior Minister Yusuf Salim and Foreign Minister Faranjiyya. While still in Paris, Salim announced that he was about to resign from the cabinet, stating that it had constantly interfered in the course of the talks and had prevented the delegation from functioning properly. At the same time he admitted that he was 'not interested in going down' with what he called Sami al-Sulh's 'sinking ship'.[68] Beirut rumours had it that Faranjiyya, too, was about to resign so that the cabinet was in danger of falling apart.[69]

Sami al-Sulh tried to find other notables to replace Salim and Faranjiyya; his candidates were Philippe Taqla (Greek Catholic) and Yusuf Istafan (Maronite). Philippe was the son of Salim and had been elected to the Chamber on his father's death in March 1945, after a sharp contest with Phalanges candidate Elias Rababi. He might not have won, had it not been for government support.[70] But this created new complications: Taqla made it a condition for his joining the cabinet that Arsalan, a political ally of his, should be recalled to the cabinet with him. But the cabinet already included one Druse, Jamil Talhuq, and the appointment of a second was bound to be seen as an infringement of the communal balance. Istafan's appointment, too, ran into difficulties: Karami's supporters objected to his appointment because of the local rivalries between them in northern Lebanon, from where they both came. It was feared that if Taqla and Istafan were appointed, Manala – a pillar of the group of Karami's supporters in the house – might resign.

Even so, Khuri was in no hurry to dismiss a prime minister as amenable to his own policies as Sami al-Sulh. Besides, the present sharp competition between Karami and Far'un on the one hand, and Riyad al-Sulh on the other, would have made it extremely difficult for Khuri to form a new government. Better to keep Sami al-Sulh in power for the time being.[71] Khuri therefore personally urged Taqla to agree to join the cabinet without setting conditions. Eventually, in April 1946, Taqla declared himself ready to do so. Faranjiyya for his part, having in the meantime returned from Paris, agreed to stay on in the cabinet. Their decision was influenced by what transpired concerning the publication in the press of a letter Spears had sent them in Paris. The letter was critical of their conduct of the negotiations and they suspected Sulh of having leaked it. However, when they returned home they found that the source of the leak had been Sa'ib Salam and that they had no special reason to be angry with Sami al-Sulh.[72]

This was no more than a short respite. Soon afterwards, Karami – on whose good-will the government depended in no small measure – decided that the time had come to bring it down. In mid-May 1946, ministers Manala, As'ad and Talhuq, all allied with Karami, decided to resign. Sami al-Sulh grew tired of the unceasing in-fighting and, on 22 May, he tendered his own resignation. Like Karami, he preferred to ignore the power struggles within the Sunni community and explained his departure by a reference to those 'who acted behind the scenes'[73] – an unmistakable allusion to Khuri and his role in bringing him down.

Since it was a coalition centred round Karami which had caused the cabinet's downfall, Khuri turned to Karami to form a new government, but stipulated that it should be a broad government including a wide spectrum of central figures, such as Riyad al-Sulh, Far'un and Chamoun. Karami accepted Khuri's condition, but countered by one of his own: reforms of the state machinery, especially the changes he wished to introduce in the electoral law (see above), must go forward. Khuri turned him down, arguing that there was no backing for the reforms in the Chamber, not even among Karami's own followers. Karami's candidacy was thus quickly aborted. It seems probable that Karami himself was not keen to return to office, remembering only too well how he had fared during his recent tenure. Khuri, too, may have approached Karami primarily in order to take the wind out of his sails, cause him to tone down his demands, and turn him away from the pursuit of reform.[74]

There was, however, at that moment no other leading candidate to command a majority in the Chamber: Yafi had the Constitutional Bloc against him because of old quarrels between them; Sa'ib Salam was unwelcome to the Sunni elite because he seemed to be gathering strength too quickly for their liking; and Riyad al-Sulh's choice was opposed by Karami and Far'un. Eventually, Khuri turned to Manala who, having the backing of Karami, was expected to muster enough votes.[75] Manala (from Tripoli) was a weak character with little political backing in his own right and owed his political advancement to Karami. A British report spoke of him as not being particularly intelligent.[76] A US legation paper stated that Manala had 'many of the ambitions of the weak'. Such weak persons, it went on, like to 'try their hands at the games of the strong, intensely enjoying the temporary glory and at peace with their conscience when they fail, in the knowledge that they were not made for great things'.[77]

Manala's government, shaped in his own image, was devoid of any forceful figure. The only exception was Sa'ib Salam, the minister of the interior. Salam soon gained saliency by his firm handling of a wave of strikes in public services which threatened to paralyse the country during the early months of his incumbency. The background to the strikes was the economic distress caused by the early stages of the evacuation of the French forces. Manala refused to negotiate with the workers as long as the strike was on, and on several occasions had some of the ringleaders arrested. This raised his prestige in Khuri's eyes and gained him the respect of western diplomats

who suspected the communists of having fostered the social protest movement.[78] On the other hand, Salam's salient position elicited the hostility of
other Sunni leaders (who would later combine against him at the time of the
1947 elections).

The politician who eventually paid the price for Manala's weak stance was
the speaker of the Chamber, the Shi'i deputy Sabri Hamada. When the 1946
session opened on 22 October, he was replaced by Habib Abu Shahla, a
Greek Orthodox from Beirut, who was voted in by twenty-nine deputies;
Hamada had received only twenty-two votes. He owed his defeat to Riyad al-
Sulh who was now taking his revenge for Hamada's having joined Karami's
camp. In ordinary circumstances, the authority of the prime minister would
have been sufficient to give the post of speaker to the candidate he himself
preferred, just as Sulh had done on an earlier occasion. But Manala lacked
the drive and political skill to do so. Hamada's defeat (a contravention of the
National Pact) drew forth a wave of protests on the part of the Shi'is. They
raised the counter-demand of having one of their number appointed prime
minister. Hamada himself proposed a law abolishing the communal principle
in politics.[79]

From the start, Manala had been no more than a compromise candidate,
chosen because none of the foremost Sunni leaders was, at the time, in a
position to form a cabinet. His government fell towards the end of 1946,
largely because of the approach of the general elections due to be held
shortly. Their advent made most communal elites eager for the formation of
a strong government in which they would have a share and which would
oversee the elections in a manner likely to ensure their own re-election. Most
of all, Khuri was keen to pack the next Chamber with his own supporters
and thus ensure a second presidential term for himself. To make this possible,
Khuri needed a strong personality to take over the premiership, a man who
could make the elections appear fair and proper. Only Riyad al-Sulh was held
capable of filling that role. The British minister, for his part, assumed that
Khuri, having been able to resolve the issue of the French forces, was now
primarily motivated by fear of his old rival Edde. He wrote that 'the latter's
visit to Paris ... and reports that he had been in touch with British personalities, caused [Khuri] great uneasiness. This was further increased by the
decision of Edde's party to modify their previous ... hostility to the Arab
League in the hope of gaining the support of the Christian Nationalists.'
Khuri realized that this narrowed the gap between the attitudes of his and
of Edde's Christian followers. He also suspected that Edde had been 'offering
full cooperation with the British authorities'. Riyad al-Sulh's appointment as
prime minister, the minister went on, had 'allayed' Khuri's fears and he now
seemed to face 'the coming elections with more equanimity'.[80]

Despite the long-standing hostility between the two men, Far'un had now
joined Sulh's camp, reasoning that he would need Sulh's support during the
forthcoming elections. But their new-found alliance altered the balance of

power in the Chamber and left Manala without sufficient support. In consequence, Manala resigned on 14 December 1946.

Riyad al-Sulh's government, formed primarily in order to oversee the elections scheduled for mid-1947, was set up immediately. It included several of the most prominent community leaders, among them Yafi, Chamoun (now back from London), Far'un, Arsalan and Junbalat. As so often before, the Shi'is were underrepresented, having only a single minister in the cabinet: Hamada, who had become minister of the interior. The Druse, by contrast, gained two cabinet seats: at Khuri's request, Junbalat joined the cabinet, in addition to his co-religionist Arsalan. Khuri advanced Junbalat in order to detach him from his old alliance with Edde and ensure his loyalty to himself in the future. He was aware how important the backing of the Junbalat family had been for Edde's victory in Mt Lebanon in 1943, and was determined to make sure that in 1947 they would support the Constitutional Bloc. With the same aim in view, he worked for a reconciliation between Junbalat and Arsalan, competitors for first place in their community. (Their relations in the recent past had become extremely strained as a result of an altercation between them in the Chamber in May 1946, which ended in fisticuffs and in Junbalat's removal from the session.)[81]

Within two weeks of the entry into office of Sulh's cabinet, the last French soldier left Lebanon. For the first time in its history, Lebanon had no foreign overlord. No outsider could be blamed for the country's problems or for the failure to deal with them appropriately. Many Lebanese realized that the government had now assumed a role Lebanon had not experienced before. *Al-Hayat* newspaper summed up the new feeling in a leading article entitled: 'The Hour of Domestic Effort Has Come'. It said in part:

> In the past, those in charge justified their reluctance to undertake domestic reforms by reference to their being busy with foreign affairs, but the debate about the details of the evacuation is now over; those in charge are now obliged to hurry and carry out the hoped-for reforms. If they want to wait until the [agreed upon] evacuation is actually completed, they risk being evacuated themselves: from their seats of power … We want the government to draw their conclusion from [existing] realities and to understand that the [present] situation of Lebanon is the result of the way they have neglected domestic issues ever since the beginning of independence.[82]

Such expectations notwithstanding, the pivotal event of the period immediately following the French evacuation was not the institution of reforms; rather, as the preceding months had foreshadowed and as the events of March 1947 were to prove, it was the further entrenchment of Khuri's position as the unquestioned master of Lebanese politics and the ultimate guide of its destinies.

# PART THREE

# Peak and Decline

CHAPTER 7

# At the Peak of Power: The 1947 General Elections; Khuri Elected for a Second Term

Khuri's first six years were his best. His government had considerable achievements to its credit, especially in foreign affairs, achievements conspicuous enough to obscure its weaknesses in administering the country. These were also the years which gave Khuri the highest political standing he was ever to achieve. Towards the end of his first term, he had assured a superior position for himself; had relegated most of his rivals to the side-lines; had gained the loyalty of most Sunni leaders and made some of them altogether dependent on himself; and had obtained the support of most of the notables of the other communities. All this is most convincingly attested to by his success, in 1948, in ensuring his re-election for another six years in total defiance of the language, and even more so of the spirit, of the constitution. His re-election was predicated on placing a substantial majority of his supporters in the Chamber through the general elections scheduled for May 1947.

Yet, paradoxically, the high point of his success and power was also the beginning of his decline. The peak he reached was tantamount to an infringement of the balance which lay at the core of the Lebanese political system. Gradually, Khuri became a menace to all other leading elements in the country. This was true first of all of his colleagues in the Maronite elite who saw their own chances of occupying the presidency recede into the future. But it also applied to the Sunni leadership who watched how the (Sunni) prime minister changed, in front of their eyes, from a full, power-sharing partner into a junior figure dependent on the president. Inevitably, then, all those placed in the shadow by Khuri's success gradually began to make common cause against him. Eventually, they were to succeed in bringing him down.

The late 1940s were thus not only the years during which Khuri's powers peaked, but also the period in which cracks began appearing in the support he used to enjoy on the part of the communal elites. This was most particularly true of the Sunni and Maronite communities. It was at this time that an incipient but potentially effective opposition began to coalesce against him. To begin with, this opposition remained limited in scope, but in the late

1940s the government begun running into difficulties. These became first apparent in foreign affairs, as a result of the 1948 war in Palestine and the 1949 crisis in Lebanon's relations with Syria. Both chains of events turned Arab and regional affairs from assets useful to Khuri into heavy liabilities. Domestic difficulties came in the wake of foreign problems. In the long run, both were to contribute to Khuri's eventual undoing.

## The 1947 General Elections

Balloting for the general elections took place on 25 May 1947.[1] They were the first elections to be held in independent Lebanon and the first carried out without interference from foreign powers.

During the run-up, several unsuccessful attempts, mostly backed by Far'un, had been made to change the electoral system. Many politicians considered the existing election law one of the major handicaps of the political system. Far'un, however, did not suggest any radical treatment but merely proposed to enlarge the membership of the Chamber from fifty-five to seventy-seven. His motives had to do with his experiences during the 1943 elections, when he had entered the Chamber on Hamada's list for the Biqa' region. He had had to pay Hamada a large sum of money for the privilege of being included in his list. Having quarrelled with him for most of the four years since then, he feared that Hamada might now demand even more money, or, worse, refuse outright to have him on his list. Most particularly, there had been bad blood between them since Far'un's attempt, in October 1946, to prevent Hamada's re-election as speaker. Far'un would therefore have preferred to run in a different electoral region, preferably in the Beirut constituency where he had good relations with the Sunni leaders. The problem was, however, that his community, the Greek Catholics, had no representative in the capital. Hence his proposal to enlarge the Chamber. This would have made it possible to add a Greek Catholic to the number of Beiruti deputies and thereby to solve his personal problem.[2]

Far'un's proposal was initially supported by Khuri and Sulh who hoped that the enlargement of the Chamber would give them greater political elbow-room and allow them to satisfy a larger number of notables by their inclusion in it. But Chamoun and Junbalat (both members of the cabinet at the time) were opposed to the idea. Since Khuri wanted their support and was reluctant to injure their prestige, he struck the proposal from the agenda. Publicly, Chamoun and Junbalat argued that Far'un's amendment, rather than improve things, would make matters worse. But their actual reason seems to have been the apprehension that their rivals rather than their allies would gain from it. In particular, they feared the rise of Salim al-Khuri (see below). Khuri himself apparently had second thoughts, anticipating that an undue proportion of the extra seats might go to Edde's Mt Lebanon list.[3] The electoral system of 1947 did not, therefore, differ from the one applied in

1943. Not surprisingly, this resulted in a Chamber made up almost entirely of Khuri's supporters. Taking the electoral districts one by one, we find the following.

SOUTHERN LEBANON  The Shi'i list which had figured in 1943, but had already disintegrated soon afterwards, now formally split into two: one headed by 'Usayran, the other by As'ad. The former was based on the 'Usayran and the Khalil families; the latter was supported by the Zuwayn family. As'ad's standing with the Shi'i population of the south was stronger than 'Usayran's and his list had the advantage of Khuri's overt support. It received a large majority of the votes. 'Usayran himself was the only person voted in from his list. Sulh had intended to run on 'Usayran's list, but Khuri feared Sulh would thus fail to enter the Chamber and not be able to support him there. He therefore brought about a reconciliation between Sulh and As'ad, over-coming the tense relations which had developed between the two. Sulh then ran on both lists and won.[4]

THE BIQA'  Here, in the second Shi'i stronghold, too, the local 'feudal boss', Hamada, remained supreme. His victory was assured by an alliance between his family and the Haydars (also Shi'is) who ranked second after them. Furthermore, Hamada exploited his standing as minister of the interior to further the interests of the list. The only issue to arouse some interest was the matter of the Greek Catholic member running on Hamada's list. In 1943, Far'un had gained that community's seat. Though Far'un was an experienced and very wealthy politician, Hamada's standing in the region was such that he could do as he liked. As we have seen, Far'un had wanted to enlarge the Chamber, detach himself from his dependence on local Biqa' politics (i.e. on Hamada), and run in Beirut. Having failed, he was forced to ingratiate himself with Hamada once more. But, to Far'un's surprise, Hamada's grudge against Far'un was such that he preferred another Greek Catholic, Georges Saqaf. It was only through the personal intervention of Khuri that Far'un was, after all, placed on Hamada's list.[5] Far'un had to disburse a considerable amount of money and Saqaf was compensated by being placed on As'ad's list in Southern Lebanon. As'ad's original Greek Catholic candidate, Yusuf Salim, was dropped.[6]

BEIRUT  In 1943, the winning list had owed its success to an alliance of Beiruti Sunni notables, led by Sami al-Sulh and Yafi. Much the same alliance – running under the name the 'Popular List' – still figured in the 1947 elections, except that Sulh and Yafi had meanwhile grown suspicious of Sa'ib Salam's growing power and preferred not to include him. In addition, Far'un, for long involved in quarrels with Salam, seems to have urged the two to keep him out. So apparently had Riyad al-Sulh who wanted to make room for his ally Husayn al-'Uwayni. The Sulh–Yafi list included Abu Shahla as the

Greek Orthodox candidate, Ra'uf Abi Lama' as its Maronite member, and Musa Furayj as the representative of the various smaller Christian denominations. The list became known as the 'Government List' because of the unconcealed official support it enjoyed. Having been excluded, Salam put together an independent list. So did another Sunni notable, Amin Bayhum. He, too, had failed to get himself included on Sulh–Yafi list.[7] Bayhum called his grouping the 'Democratic List' and included one of the leaders of the Lebanese communists, Mustafa al-'Aris, as well as Alfred Naqqash.[8]

On balloting day, the Sulh–Yafi list emerged with a clear majority, proving once again how thoroughly the Sunni elite controlled the Beiruti electorate. Khuri commented on this in his memoirs, writing:

> In Beirut, the government list gained an easy victory, but some of the ballot officials tried to make it bigger. They noted the names ... on the rolls of those who had not voted and put in ballot slips in their stead to make the government list stronger. Their illegal acts aroused an unnecessary scandal, but did not substantially affect the election results.[9]

The other two lists, by contrast, did not get even a single candidate elected.

NORTHERN LEBANON  The 1943 elections had been won by a Sunni–Maronite alliance headed by Karami and Faranjiyya. But their group had fallen apart soon afterwards. Over the intervening years, Karami and Faranjiyya had become bitter political rivals, largely because Faranjiyya had started to cooperate with Karami's opponent, Riyad al-Sulh. There had also been splits between Karami and other local Sunni notables, such as Sulayman al-'Ali and Muhammad al-'Abud. As the 1947 elections approached, the latter two linked up with Karami's traditional Tripoli enemies, the families of Jisr and Muqaddam, and formed a joint list to run against Karami. Most local Maronite notables joined in as well. These included Faranjiyya as well as Nadra 'Isa al-Khuri.[10] Eventually, after much heart-searching, Karam joined them as well. He would apparently have preferred to continue as Karami's ally, but lack of funds to conduct his campaign and his reading of the changes on the local political map persuaded him otherwise.[11] The anti-Karami list thus gathered a great deal of electoral strength, putting a question mark against the chances of any grouping formed to oppose it.

These developments came at a difficult time for Karami. He was of advanced age and in ill-health, visibly approaching the end of his career (even of his life). His prestige had suffered because of his recent poor political performance, both on the national and the regional scene. His premiership had resounded to his discredit, particularly among his supporters. He had failed to make good use of the broad support he had in the Chamber (stemming in no small measure from the hostility many deputies harboured for Riyad al-Sulh). Instead of drawing on their support, his conduct had alienated them and driven them into the arms of Sulh. He had not only omitted to build up friendly relations with Khuri but eventually came out against him. He had thus made an enemy of him, even though Khuri's original inclination had been to keep Karami at his side as a counter-weight to Riyad al-Sulh. Simultaneously, Karami's family was in trouble in its traditional stronghold of Tripoli. Karami's brother, Mustafa, the mayor of Tripoli, was involved in a corruption scandal. This added to the strength of the rival Jisr and Muqaddam families. As a result, even the party of the National Call (al-Nida' al-Qawmi), founded and run by members of the Sulh family who had not played much of a role in Tripoli before, now gained a foothold there, exploiting popular doubts about the continued commitment of the Karamis to the cause of pan-Arabism. People had become doubtful when Karami, to advance his own career, had gone to the length of seeking the cooperation of Maronite leaders, even of Edde's men, in the Chamber. Karami's supporters set up a Party of National Youth (Hizb al-Shabbab al-Qawmi), but made little or no progress promoting it.[12]

Local tension peaked when, on 4 March 1947, Fawzi al-Qa'uqji returned to his native city of Tripoli from exile in Germany. Qa'uqji had become well-known through his involvement in the 1936–38 Arab revolt in Palestine and in Rashid 'Ali al-Kaylani's rebellion in Iraq in 1941. His reception soon turned into a violent clash between supporters of the Muqaddam family and of Karami. Eighteen people were killed and forty-eight wounded. Among the fatal casualties was Nafidh Muqaddam, a prominent member of the family. He was not armed when he was shot, and his death appalled the Tripoli population.[13] The president and the cabinet could not remain indifferent in the face of such events and perhaps also wished to exploit them to strengthen the hand of the central government in Tripoli. The president promptly dismissed the governor of Northern Lebanon, 'Abd al-'Aziz Shihab, who had been known as a supporter of the Muqaddams. He was replaced by Nur al-Din al-Rifa'i, a known supporter of Karami and even more so of Far'un. However, in order to be seen as acting even-handedly, the government also dismissed Mayor Mustafa Karami.[14]

Karami had long hesitated to gather his supporters and to put together a list of his own. Had he done so in time, he might have been able to frustrate the efforts of his rivals to rally against him. Now the action taken by the government gave him the necessary impetus. He declared that, because of the state of his health, he had no intention of running for office.[15] This was widely considered a tactical move meant to force the government into supporting him and to elicit local protestations of support.[16] But one cannot exclude the possibility that he actually did wish to withdraw and now saw a chance to do so without losing face.

The president and the prime minister seem to have believed that it was preferable to have Karami in the Chamber; being a deputy caused him to moderate his views and desist from the sharp attacks against Khuri and Sulh in which he had indulged lately. But they were in two minds. They could not ignore the local momentum which had developed against him, nor did they overlook the chance it offered them to weaken him even further. They sent emissaries (most prominent among them Far'un) to Tripoli to promise Karami electoral success, but made this conditional on his running on a list headed by one of his rivals. Karami found this unacceptable. He eventually put an end to these contacts by announcing that his decision to withdraw was final.[17] This opened the way for the victory of his rivals who indeed netted all the seats of the district. Defeated, Karami stepped up his attacks against the government. For a while he led a grouping which threw doubt on the propriety of the balloting. But his career was over. He died of cancer on 21 November 1950.

MT LEBANON    As in 1943, the 1947 election campaign in Mt Lebanon was stormy. The area was considered especially vital for the future of the government, being the largest electoral district, with the largest number of deputies, and the one with the largest Maronite population. Edde, the victor of 1943 (see Chapter 2), still had some residual influence there. In the intervening years, he had worked to improve relations with the Sunni notables. Even Karami had from time to time sought the help of Edde's men in the Chamber in his struggles with Khuri. Early in 1947, Edde announced his intention to run again. He hinted that he had a great deal to say about his role during the November 1943 crisis, but that freedom of speech in Lebanon had not yet reached the degree making it possible to conduct a real debate on these matters.[18]

Edde's seriousness in planning his return to the political arena was attested to by his attempts to improve relations with the British. His first step was to send his son Raymond to the British legation to obtain their advice on whether he could sue Spears's wife for having called him a quisling in her memoirs and accusing him of growing hashish. Legation staff expressed regret at the expressions chosen by Lady Spears, but added that the British government did not wish to be involved in a dispute of this kind.[19] This served as a prelude to a second conversation, with the participation of Emile Edde himself, at which the elections issue came up. The British report stated that Edde 'said that his opponents were always stressing that the British were opposed to him ... Monsieur Edde continued that he was sure that the British were neutral as regards the elections ... and expressed the hope that His Majesty's Minister would do something to counter such propaganda.'[20]

We noted earlier that Edde's various attempts to place himself in the mainstream of Lebanese politics came under the heading of 'too little and too late'; mainly, 'too late'. The November 1943 crisis had placed an indelible stain on his reputation, regardless of whether it was placed there by his conduct or by the hostility of his rivals (chief among them President Khuri). The name he had made for himself as an enemy of Arabism was equally harmful and equally lasting. Together, they barred his way into the political system of independent Lebanon and in particular obstructed any cooperation with Sunni leaders. It was only after Edde's death in 1949 that Sunni notables were ready gradually to end their boycott of his camp.

However, in Mt Lebanon the real threat to Khuri's government did not come from Edde; it came from the direction of Chamoun and Junbalat. On his return, in March 1947, from his mission to London, Chamoun had been appointed to Sulh's cabinet. But even as a minister, he did not conceal his long-lasting criticism of Khuri, mainly with regard to the latter's failure to introduce far-reaching political, administrative and social reforms. Neither did he hide his ambition to replace Khuri as president after what was then still regarded as the end of his incumbency in 1949. He considered the general elections as a preliminary test of strength for the presidential contest. The US minister reported that Chamoun believed that

> the country's salvation was essentially dependent on the return to Parliament of only the 'best and worthiest' elements. His train of thoughts ... had been set by a number of factors some of which were (a) the innocent and/or calculated advice and criticism of his British friends, (b) his own growing ambition highly excited by the nearness with which he had missed the Presidency in 1943, (c) his genuine desire to 'reform the commonwealth'.[21]

Junbalat had entered the Chamber in 1943 on Edde's list and had been a prominent supporter and associate of his ever since. In choosing his line, he had been guided by his mother Nazira who, until her death in 1951, was the dominant figure in the Junbalat family.[22] In 1943, he had opposed Khuri's election to the presidency as well as the constitutional amendment, but over the years he had adapted his views to the prevailing realities. He had become an enthusiastic partisan of independence and had even become a convert to pan-Arabism. But he remained a bitter critic of the National Pact and of the political system it had consecrated. This reflected, at least in part, a genuine interest in reforms, inculcated in him by Chamoun, but it also expressed his protest against the 'demotion' of the Druse community as a whole, in comparison to the status it had enjoyed before the creation of Greater Lebanon. But his struggle both against the 'Lebanese system' and against Khuri who represented it more than anyone else, also had a great deal to do with Junbalat's personal ambition to become recognized as the unquestioned leader of the Druse, and perhaps to play a leadership role at the national level as well. Until then, the main target of his struggle had been his rival for the Druse leadership, Majid Arsalan – an old ally of Khuri's. Nevertheless, Khuri was aware of the standing of the Junbalats in their community and when Sulh formed a cabinet in December 1946 to supervise the forthcoming elections, he had asked Kamal Junbalat to join it. He had hoped that his appointment would cause Junbalat to moderate his criticism of the regime and would later ensure his support for Khuri's re-election. It soon turned out that the president had deluded himself.

On the eve of the election, rumours began to circulate that Chamoun and
Junbalat, together with Pierre al-Jumayyil, would set up a list of their own to
run against Khuri's Constitutional Bloc. Edde and some of his associates were
also expected to figure on the new list. Jumayyil's relations with the government had been tense ever since he had accused it of intervening in favour of
Taqla and against Jumayyil's candidate, Rababi, in a by-election in the Biqa' in
1945.[23] Eventually, however, Khuri succeeded in regaining Jumayyil's support
and the latter decided not to run at all in Mt Lebanon.[24] Khuri's next success
came when he managed to persuade Chamoun and Junbalat to drop their idea
of putting together an independent list. Instead, they consented to run on the
list of the Constitutional Bloc. Quite possibly, their ostensible intention of
forming a separate list had never been more than a move to strengthen their
hand in bargaining with Khuri. If so, their tactics had worked: Khuri now
granted them the right to veto other names on the bloc's list in Mt Lebanon.
The two explained that all they wanted was to see higher standards applied
in the choice of candidates – standards of the kind they thought proper for
reform-minded people like themselves. But there can be no doubt that they
exercised their right primarily to demonstrate their control of the district's
candidates; this, they anticipated, would be useful indeed in the coming
struggles in the Chamber.[25]

Not surprisingly, the first name to fall victim to their veto power was that
of Khuri's brother Salim. Under the aegis of the president, he had become
the sole arbiter of political affairs in Mt Lebanon and was known as 'Sultan
Salim'. His domain was called 'the State of Furn al-Shubak' (*Dawlat Furn al-
Shubak*) after the name of the east Beirut quarter from where he exercised
control. (In the days of the *Mutasarrifiyya*, the quarter had belonged to Mt
Lebanon.)[26] He now aspired to enter national politics through membership
of the Chamber. Chamoun and Junbalat were determined to keep him out;
they considered him the symbol of everything distasteful to them in the
'Lebanese system'. Moreover, his election would weaken their own standing
and compromise Chamoun's chances of reaching the presidency. This gave
Khuri the unenviable alternative of dropping his brother or losing two
potential supporters whom he needed to bolster his national and local
standing as well as to augment his chances of re-election. He resolved to
drop his brother, later describing his decision as 'an act of sacrifice'.[27] He
also allowed the veto to remove two other supporters of his: Emile Lahhud
and Bahij Taqi al-Din.[28]

Salim al-Khuri did not appear especially shaken and immediately announced
that he would run on a separate list – possibly with his brother's tacit
agreement, possibly as a protest against his sacrifice. It is important to
remember the sort of relationship existing between the two brothers – with
Salim rather than Bishara setting the tone for most of the time – in order
to understand the antecedents of Khuri's eventual fall from power. We have
had occasion before to point out that Khuri lacked charisma, had a funda-

mentally weak character, and did not have much of a following personally loyal to him. He compensated for his weaknesses by his masterly understanding of the innermost workings of Lebanese politics and his supreme skill in mounting political manoeuvres. These frequently enabled him to neutralize political actors more forceful than himself. The Lebanese system was such that it often enabled him to turn his weakness to advantage: it made it easier for other notables to cooperate with him, since they had no cause to think of him as a menace to themselves. This they did, quite enthusiastically, for many years. What Bishara lacked, Salim was able to supply. Starting from nothing, he built up a firm power base, ostensibly for the Khuri family, in fact for himself.[29] There is not enough evidence to judge conclusively what Bishara's attitude towards Salim was. Did he back his brother? Did he use his services to get certain things settled in Mt Lebanon without having to dirty his own hands in local, or later in national, horse-trading? Or did he find himself helpless in the face of Salim's unscrupulous proceedings? In the short run, Salim obviously served Bishara's interests; in the long run, he became a liability, because those who suffered from Salim's high-handedness blamed Bishara and turned to him to complain. Together, they ended up creating the widespread suspicion that the Khuri family was concentrating more power in its hands than was compatible with the Lebanese system of checks and balances.

To return to Mt Lebanon, the upshot was that there were three lists running there: the Constitutional Bloc list headed by Chamoun and Junbalat; Salim al-Khuri's list; and that of Edde. Some observers had expected the competition between the first two lists to benefit Edde, but the election results showed them to have been mistaken: no one from among Edde's followers gained a seat. Chamoun and Junbalat received a large majority and most of their candidates were elected. If there was a surprise, it was that Salim al-Khuri succeeded in getting himself elected and even in taking his most prominent allies, Lahhud and Taqi al-Din, with him to the Chamber.[30]

Salim did not, however, take his seat; the legality of his elections was contested and he reacted to the suspicions raised against him by resigning from the Chamber. He also resented the subsequent appointment of his rival Chamoun as minister of the interior in Riyad al-Sulh's new government (formed quickly after the elections, in June 1947). Possibly, Bishara prevailed upon Salim to resign because of the widespread criticism against the way the election campaign in Mt Lebanon had been conducted – criticism which might be harmful to Bishara in his quest for re-election. The Chamber initially failed to confirm Salim's resignation by the required two-thirds majority, but Salim refused to attend and, in mid-1948, the Chamber finally resolved to accept his withdrawal.[31]

The election results were thought of as a sweeping victory for Khuri's government and for him personally. The coalition of notables which had formed around him and which had his support during the elections had won forty-nine out of fifty-five seats, giving him much more than the two-thirds he needed for a second presidential term. But a shadow was cast on his success by the severe criticism of the methods he had employed to secure it. The attack was led by the losers, notably Edde's followers in Mt Lebanon and some unsuccessful candidates from Beirut.[32] They were joined by Karami, even though he had not run in the elections (see above). Among the winners, Chamoun and Junbalat were equally critical. In fact, they had already protested against the meddling of government officials in favour of Salim al-Khuri while the campaign was still on. On balloting day, when there were delays in counting the votes and in publishing the results, they clamoured to invalidate the ballot in several polling stations, claiming that there had been fraudulent practices. They even threatened to resign from the government, unless their claims were recognized.[33] But if that had been done, there would have been similar claims in other electoral districts as well. Khuri went out of his way to make the two withdraw their charges, promising to appoint a neutral arbitrator to look into the matter. This was duly done, but the arbitrator decided that, even though Chamoun and Junbalat had a point, it was impossible to invalidate only a few ballots: the choice was between cancelling the entire elections in Mt Lebanon, or else accepting the results as they were. Khuri turned down the former alternative out of hand. Junbalat refused to accept the arbitration result and, on 30 May 1947, resigned from the government. He pronounced the existing Chamber illegal, since the ballot had been 'fraudulent', and demanded new elections.[34] Chamoun for his part accepted the result, withdrew his resignation, and defended the legality of the elections at a special press conference convened for the purpose. He was promptly included in Sulh's new government.[35] Chamoun seems to have hoped to be elected president instead of Khuri; to do so, he needed the good-will of the deputies which would not be forthcoming as long as he threw doubt on the propriety of their election.

A particularly scathing attack against the election process came from the Maronite archbishop of Beirut, Mubarak. As we have seen, he had initially been one of the most enthusiastic Maronite supporters of independence. He had gone to the length of comparing Khuri's suffering in French detention to the suffering of Jesus and had proclaimed that providence was standing at Khuri's side.[36] Now he sounded a different note and openly expressed his anger at the government's failure to intervene in favour of several candidates close to him personally. But there seem to have been other, graver reasons for his sudden attacks on Khuri. He resented his pan-Arab policies, took offence at being personally ignored by him, and found his new stance useful for strengthening his own standing in the church and the community. In a letter to Khuri, written in April 1947, he wrote:

> Archbishop Mubarak, the faithful friend, is today in a state of deep despair. As a person who took a substantial part in building up Lebanese independence – more

than anyone else in the present period – he senses the lack of the security, justice, happiness and serenity which the Lebanese people are entitled to. All he sees is anarchy taking root everywhere; it finds expression in corruption and injustice practiced in the courts; it exists in the robbery and larceny committed by those ruling the state ... From a sense of honor and in order to clear my conscience I call on you to resign as president of Lebanon and to cease running the affairs of the state; if you do not do so, your fate will be like the fate of Nero.[37]

Critics of the conduct of the elections had a point: polling in Lebanon had never been a model of democratic practice. Buying votes and forging ballot results were frequent occurrences. The most recurrent and pernicious practice was the automatic *en bloc* vote of entire population sectors in rural areas, acting on instructions from their 'feudal bosses'. But the 1947 elections differed from past (and future) ones. The fact that they were the first ballot held without foreign interference had raised expectations with regard to their propriety which Khuri's government found difficult to meet. Khuri and Sulh perceived it as being in their interests to influence the outcome, and their control of the political system made government intervention in the balloting a great deal more effective than it had been in the past.

Western diplomats in Beirut, as their reports make clear, mostly sided with Khuri's critics. A US dispatch reported a conversation with the head of Lebanese military intelligence who told US legation staff that Khuri had instructed the commander-in-chief of the Lebanese army, Fu'ad Shihab, to prevent opposition supporters from reaching the polling stations.[38] But it is worth quoting the relevant passage from Khuri's memoirs, expressing what may be a more balanced view.

It is a mistake to think that the government is capable of putting together lists of candidates as it wishes; it has to consider the real strength of the [proposed] candidates as well as the overall circumstances in the state and in the various electoral districts. Nonetheless, the government can exercise considerable influence, particularly if it understands how to utilize the prevalent mood and adapt itself to trends in public opinion. After all, the Lebanese are accustomed to expect more of their rulers than is in their power to do and are quick to involve them in the elections ... A Lebanese asks the government to keep neutral only after he has despaired of securing its support. As long as he is on good terms with it, he usually asks for its full support.[39]

Overall, then, it would seem that (much like in 1943) the 1947 elections, though partly influenced by government interference, did reflect the country's political realities. They attested to the broad support Khuri and his government were, at the time, still enjoying among the communal elites. Both aspects are well brought out in a British report summing up the outcome:

As a whole, the elections were undoubtedly an unedifying spectacle – apart from irregularities and Government pressure, the free use of money by prospective candidates – Government and Opposition alike – to buy off their opponents during the pre-electoral period created the worst impression, although it must in fairness be added that the inadequacy of the ... Electoral Law ... was to a great extent responsible. On the credit side it should be recorded that although the campaign was tense, it was marred by little loss of life, extremist elements, including the Communists, were unsuccessful ( ... the wearing of uniforms by such para-military organizations as the Phalangists was made illegal) and the regime at the critical juncture in the country's history was firmly re-established thus ensuring a continuity of policy. Moreover, it is admitted even by the Opposition that 80 per cent of the new Chamber would be re-elected if the elections were repeated.[40]

Whichever view one adopts, critics of the 1947 elections supplied Khuri's rivals with a banner to rally round. They set off a public campaign against his regime the vehemence of which enabled them to set aside their existing ideological differences. The election results, though producing a Chamber of the kind he wanted, added to the number of Khuri's opponents in the various communities. Among its resentful victims were Junbalat, 'Usayran, Mubarak and others. The limits of Khuri's ability to keep pleasing all the notables were becoming visible. Until then, he had secured their loyalty by conferring benefits on their friends. In 1947, for the first time, he had to be selective, satisfying many, perhaps most, of the notables, but making enemies of others. The formation of the lists in Southern Lebanon and Mt Lebanon and the conduct of the campaign there were salient examples of this trend: local disputes left Khuri no choice but to range himself on one side and alienate the other. In Southern Lebanon he decided to support As'ad, but thereby inevitably added 'Usayran to the list of his opponents. Worse, 'Usayran was now able to make his struggle for local superiority look like an act of resistance to the government as a whole. In 1947, such cases were, so to speak, ripples on an otherwise rather smooth surface; but they foreshadowed the complications which were soon to make life hard for Khuri and eventually to bring him down.

For the time being, Khuri's enemies lacked the cohesion, the well-defined goals and, above all, the consolidated leadership required to conduct a meaningful struggle. That was to change in the early 1950s. But for now, opposition was still disorganized. Thus the attempt, late in May 1947, to organize a general strike, just fizzled out. True, Karami succeeded in setting up a new political body capable of acting as an umbrella organization for several opposition groups: the so-called National Liberation Committee (Hay'at al-Tahrir al-Qawmi). Bayhum, Mubarak and Alfred Naqqash joined in. Together, they called for the dissolution of the Chamber and for new elections. But Edde's camp, as well as Junbalat (whom Karami offered the deputy leadership) refused to join Karami. In June 1947, two mass rallies were held by opponents of Khuri's: in Tripoli by Karami and in Beirut by Mubarak. A third rally, planned for July at Sufar, was banned by the government which sent out army units and had the surroundings proclaimed a 'closed area'.

Mubarak called for civil disobedience, but was reprimanded by the patriarch and withdrew his appeal. The organizers thereupon cancelled the event.[41]

Short-lived though it was, Mubarak's appeal attested to the violent character the opposition to Khuri was beginning to acquire. Generally speaking, the government was reluctant to use strong-arm methods against those threatening violence. Hesitation was in keeping with its overall character, nor did the 'Lebanese system' as such lend itself to the use of forceful measures. But its reaction to the planned rally at Sufar seems to show that the government understood the menace of spreading violence. The new mood found expression in the first attempt at a coup to overthrow the regime. A hapless, unimportant affair in itself, the attempt was mounted in February 1948 by Nihad Arsalan, brother and rival of the Druse leader Majid Arsalan. Nihad seems to have been of unstable character. In 1947, he had originally run on Edde's list, but had withdrawn during the election campaign. He then joined Karami's Liberation Committee and was later to claim that Karami was behind his coup attempt.[42] Be this as it may, on 2 February 1948 Nihad and his men attacked a police station at Sufar – an attack meant to signal the beginning of a nation-wide uprising. One policeman was killed, but the rest succeeded in defending the station and eventually repulsed the attackers. That put an end to the whole undertaking. Nihad took refuge in the Druse Mountain area of Syria, but as a result of mediation on the part of Druse leaders there, he returned to Lebanon at the end of July and gave himself up to the authorities. He was arrested, but in September of the same year, he was released and all charges against him were dropped.[43]

## Khuri's Re-election for a Second Term

Khuri's first term as president was due to end on 21 September 1949. This would have meant the termination of his eventful and eminent political career which, after prolonged struggles, had carried him to the peak of power. The Lebanese constitution contained a clause expressly barring a president from holding office for more than one term. No Lebanese politician had done more than Khuri – the leader of the party he had chosen to call the Constitutional Bloc – to have the constitution accepted. Nobody was more committed than he to preserve the system of balances which lay at its core and which had provided the foundation on which independent Lebanon was built. At the time of the 1943 presidential elections, Khuri had used the above paragraph as a weapon against his competitor Edde.

All the above notwithstanding, almost right from the start Khuri had cast about for possibilities of prolonging his incumbency. Sami al-Sulh, for instance, wrote in his memoirs that in 1945 Khuri had asked him what he thought of the matter and that he advised Khuri to retire after a single term and take a vacation in Switzerland.[44] In his own memoirs, Khuri himself listed a number of reasons for wanting a second term: he pointed to the

Syrian president Quwatli's re-election, arguing that Lebanon should respond similarly; he stressed the climate of crisis which had taken hold of the country as a result of the 1948 war in Palestine; finally, he added that he was only acting in response to the pressure of others whom he could not turn down.[45] But, to his credit, his memoirs leave no doubt that his personal desire for prolonged power was his principal motive. He wrote:

> A person must be an angel or a prophet in order to refuse to prolong his tenure of office. In all modesty: I am neither an angel nor a prophet but an ordinary human and God is my witness that I did not seek this [prolonged tenure], but the flag of the struggle for renewing [my] incumbency was carried by important deputies in the Chamber whom I could not refuse.[46]

Pinkerton, the US minister in Beirut, had this to say about Khuri's intentions: 'His intimates, including his relatives, admit that he loves the pomp and prestige of his office, and would hate to give them up to retire to the obscurity of a pensioned President such as Naqqash, Edde or the late Petro Trad. Presidents are quickly forgotten in Lebanon.'[47]

It was on the eve of the 1947 elections that Khuri finally decided to seek a second term. The presidency was, after all, in the gift of the Chamber and it was that self-same body which had the authority (by a majority of two-thirds) to pass the necessary amendment to the constitution. It was with this in mind that Khuri conducted the election campaign. The same thought had guided him, late in 1946, in appointing Riyad al-Sulh to head a cabinet including the strongest figures on the Lebanese political scene, among them Chamoun and Junbalat. Again the same considerations had led him to support Far'un's proposal to enlarge the Chamber (though he later withdrew his support). They prompted him to conduct the election campaign the way he did. And they might conceivably have had something to do with his decision to allow Sa'ada to return from Syria (see Chapters 9 and 10). As we have seen, the outcome of the elections gave Khuri a majority of more than two-thirds in the Chamber. All he had to do now was to wait for a propitious moment to act. This was soon provided by the outbreak of the war in Palestine. Khuri and Sulh led their country into war with considerable enthusiasm stemming from political considerations of their own (to be set out fully in the following chapter). The outbreak of war quickly caused a public mood favourable to the extension of Khuri's tenure; in light of the challenges of wartime, both Christians and Muslims came to think of the president as the right man in the right place. Christians came to think of him as the one leader capable of diverting an upheaval and ensuring continued stability, precisely by virtue of the position he had carved out himself in inter-Arab affairs as well as among the country's Sunnis. The latter for their part saw him as the man most likely to continue along the path of Lebanon's integration into the Arab world and thus of keeping Beirut involved in the Palestine issue. It was a characteristic sign of such sentiments that, from the end of 1947 onwards, Khuri's most ardent rival, 'Abd al-Hamid Karami, stopped criticizing him. He remained opposed to Khuri's re-election, but stated that the Palestine issue must override domestic considerations.[48]

The broad support Khuri now received from most of the notables as well as from the politically aware sectors of the public at large points to a national consensus on two issues: the desire to see Lebanon maintain its independence on the basis of the National Pact; and the recognition that Khuri's presidency was the best possible guarantee for the pact's continued application and thus for Lebanon's stability. Typically, a leading article in *Al-Hayat* wrote of Khuri that he had an 'advantage over his competitors because he has maintained the policy of equilibrium and reconciliation between the communities – a policy which forms the basis of Lebanon's independence ... Renewing his incumbency thus implies a promise that this policy will continue [to be applied] for the benefit of all ... inhabitants.'[49]

The British and US ministers, both habitually critical of Khuri, now praised his decision to seek re-election. The US minister pointed to 'widespread opposition to, and dissatisfaction with, the Lebanese Government', but immediately added that it was 'equally certain that the majority of people are afraid to substitute any of the present leaders for ... Khouri'. The president, he went on, was the only Christian leader who had 'the support of a substantial margin' of the Muslim electorate. In a crisis, he was the only figure 'with an assured control of all elements of the electorate', regardless of community.[50] His British colleague wrote that Khuri's re-election 'will do much to create stability of Government ... and will definitely remove one possible cause of internal friction, namely the inevitable intrigue which precedes a presidential election ... From a short term view, therefore, the President's reelection will do some good.' Whether administrative reforms would be undertaken during the second term was another question. 'In the long run, the absolute need for internal administrative reform must outweigh any short term advantages which may be obtained from temporary stability.' He added that reform laws had already been drafted in accordance with Khouri's election promises. Some of them might reach the Chamber, 'but time alone will show'.[51]

As soon as Khuri had convinced himself that the right moment had come, he lost no time. Already on 9 April 1948, more than a year before the end of his first term, he caused the Chamber to pass a special law allowing him to be elected for a second term, in light of the country's special circumstances and in recognition of his personal merits in achieving Lebanon's independence. Forty-six deputies (80 per cent of the house) voted in favour. The presidential elections themselves took place the following month, on 27 May 1948. Khuri was re-elected unanimously by all deputies present; nine members of the house stayed away from the session, first and foremost his two chief opponents, Chamoun and Junbalat. Other absentees were Karam, Sulayman al-'Ali and Nasuh al-Fadil.[52] Almost a year later, in September 1949, when his first term actually expired, Khuri was sworn in a second time as president.

His re-election offered him a chance to revive the flagging fortunes of his regime. He carried out a cabinet reshuffle; had a new press law passed which was described as more liberal than the old one; let fresh blood into the civil service, mounted an anti-corruption campaign and dismissed 179 officials. The creation of an upper house was considered with a view to making room for more notables in the political establishment, and a revision of the electoral law was mooted,[53] but nothing came of these ideas. Khuri also tried to establish a dialogue with his principal rivals, justifying his approach by wartime exigencies. He met with Karami and (as a special gesture of regard) visited Junbalat at his home in Mukhtara to congratulate him on his wedding.[54] With the aid of a British go-between, he received Chamoun at the presidential office.[55] Yet he did not conceal his suspicion that British representatives were backing Chamoun in his oppositional stance towards him; he argued that it was no coincidence that the reforms suggested to him by both Chamoun and the British were so similar. (The US minister also noted these similarities.)[56] In their conversations with Khuri, the British categorically denied any such connection. But in response to an appeal from Khuri, they urged Chamoun to tone down his criticism of the president. The British minister reported in December 1948 that during a meeting with Chamoun, he 'took the opportunity of pointing out the dangers involved in precipitate action by the Opposition and advised him to make further attempts to secure reforms by normal means'. Chamoun answered that in the absence of a properly functioning 'parliamentary machine ... fundamental changes of Government could only be achieved by violence or by British pressure'. But he agreed nevertheless to try and collaborate with the president, 'if only the latter would give some indication that he was prepared to go some way to meet him'. The minister added that he 'found [Chamoun], though far from optimistic, at least more reasonable and moderate' than in August 1947. Chamoun, he wrote, now understood that reforms could only be gradual, and no longer insisted on the immediate dissolution of the Chamber.[57]

And yet, the peak of Khuri's personal strength also marked the first beginning of his decline. The political power he had concentrated in his hands was becoming incompatible with the equilibrium on which the country's political system had been built and which kept it functioning. Rumours of his intention eventually to secure a third term or even be elected life-time president reinforced the unsettling effect. Facts and rumours were interpreted as signalling the diminution of the prime minister's standing in his capacity of chief representative of the Sunni community. Among the Maronites, they were felt to be tantamount to a demotion of rival leaders inasmuch as they themselves aspired to the presidency. The notables of the other communities also began resenting the excessive power of a single leader.

Of greater moment was Chamoun's move into the opposition camp, made in consequence of Khuri's re-election. Since the beginning of Khuri's first term, Chamoun had not concealed his ambition to succeed him. Yet, however unwillingly, he had cooperated with Khuri and his cabinet. He had accepted a ministerial appointment in the first post-independence cabinet, but had remained sharply critical of the president. This led in 1944 to his 'honourable exile' to diplomatic post in Britain. Having returned home, he was 'exiled' again in 1947 and became his country's representative to the UN in New York and later in Geneva. When he learned that, in his absence, Khuri had secured a second term for himself, he finally changed sides. He returned home in April 1948 and the following month resigned from the government (of which he had continued to be a member throughout his years of diplomatic activity). He wrote a personal letter to Khuri scathingly critical of the corruption which characterized the regime and of the constitutional amendment Khuri had caused the Chamber to pass for his own personal benefit. He concluded with an appeal to all like-minded patriotic quarters in the country to cooperate with him in his struggle against Khuri.[58]

Khuri's opponents still had a long way to go before they could offer a political alternative, let alone pose a threat, to his government. Within a year, two of his foremost rivals died: Edde succumbed to a heart attack on 27 September 1949, aged sixty-four; Karami died of cancer on 23 October 1950. Chamoun remained ill and inactive for quite some time. In the short run, this made life easier for Khuri. But in the long run, Edde's and Karami's deaths removed a barrier which had prevented their respective followers from making common cause against Khuri. Edde especially had been a controversial figure with whom other politicians found it hard to deal. His two sons, Raymond and Pierre, were very different types. Already in August 1950, Edde's party, the National Bloc (now led by them) participated in a convention of anti-Khuri figures, and from then on cooperated fully with Chamoun and Junbalat in their struggle against the president.

It now became evident that Khuri had failed to turn the period of the domestic truce to his advantage by breaking or dividing his opponents. He had, for instance, refused to arrange a state funeral for Edde. He later justified his refusal by saying that the family had not officially advised the authorities of Edde's death and had asked that government figures should not take part in their mourning.[59] But the failure to pay due respect to the departed leader was widely and sharply criticized. The funeral, attended by more than 100,000 people, turned into a show of strength by the opposition. Many participants were former enemies of Edde who now wished to turn over a new page with regard to his two sons, and at the same time display their opposition to Khuri.[60] Even the British minister was critical of Khuri's behaviour at this juncture, observing 'that it may prove beyond ... Khuri to bring himself to rise above village politics and to think and act in manner worthy of ... the highest office'. He added that

the announcement of the 'new' cabinet, coming as it did on top of the President's ineptitude in regard to the death of a former incumbent in his high office, are not auspicious auguries for the next six years. However, the pressure of events in this and neighboring countries may eventually force ... Khuri to realize that even a small and unimportant country such as this cannot in these days be run like a petty family business for the benefit of an insignificant minority.[61]

It is noteworthy that during the years here reviewed, the voice of the Maronite church establishment was hardly heard (with the salient exception of Mubarak; see above). This was helpful to Khuri since, had the church spoken more often or more loudly, its basic opposition to Khuri would have become more evident. The silence of the clerical establishment can be accounted for by pointing to three partly inter-dependent reasons: erosion of the standing of the church as a result of the foundation of Greater Lebanon (see Introduction); the ill-health of patriarch 'Arida, now in his eighties; and (most importantly for our context) the struggle between the Vatican and the patriarchate over control of the church. Attempts by Rome to subject the Maronite church more firmly to its rule had gone on for centuries. But their dispute had sharpened recently when 'Arida was made patriarch against the express wishes of the Vatican. Beginning in the 1940s, Rome had exploited 'Arida's old age and infirmity and, with the help of opponents of his from within the church, had interfered more brusquely in church affairs, bypassing its titular head. This created a community of interests between the Vatican and the Lebanese presidency. Indeed, whether through the Lebanese minister at the Vatican, Charles al-Hilu, or through the agency of political allies or relatives of his among the Maronite clergy, Khuri tried over and over again to enlist the Vatican in his struggle against the patriarchate.

On 18 May 1948, the Vatican appointed an Apostolic Commission whose three members were to supervise the Maronite church because, as Rome claimed, the patriarch was no longer capable of performing his duties. Two of the commission's members were close to Khuri: Bishop Boulus Ma'ushi of Tyre and Archbishop 'Abdallah al-Khuri (a cousin of the president). Their membership gave rise to the suspicion that Khuri had acted behind the scenes to have the commission appointed.[62] Suspicions grew firmer when, in 1950, the Vatican instructed Mubarak, archbishop of Beirut and Khuri's ferocious opponent, to come to Rome for a vacation because of his political activities against Khuri and his letter to him on the Palestine question (see above). Vacationing in Rome seems to have had a sobering effect on him: when he returned home, he did not resume his attacks against Khuri. But Rome was not satisfied; early in 1952, Mubarak was forced to resign because of what he described as prolonged interference in the affairs of his archbishopric on the part of the Vatican.[63]

At the time we are speaking of, a consolidated domestic opposition capable of concerted action against Khuri did not come into existence. But his government was exposed to shocks and challenges from abroad: the war in Palestine, the crisis in relations with Syria, and the confrontation with the PPS. Together, they put an end to the safe and stable years of his rule.

## CHAPTER 8

# The 1948 War in Palestine

The war in Palestine broke out at a time when Khuri was at the peak of his power. Entering the war was expected to add two important achievements, both bound to reinforce his position even more: domestically, by providing a suitable foil for his re-election to the presidency; in Arab affairs, to provide the culmination of the pan-Arab policy he had pursued consistently since Lebanon's independence. So far, this policy had given him continual success; now it was to bring him nothing but misfortune. The Arab armies were defeated; the inter-Arab system became paralysed; public opinion in most Arab countries turned vehemently against the existing regimes which it blamed for the defeat; and Palestinian refugees streamed into neighbouring countries, many of them into Lebanon. These were blows to the prestige of the Lebanese regime from which it found it hard to recover. Inter-Arab relations turned from a source of strength into a menace to Lebanon's stability and eventually to its very existence.

Lebanon's entry into war stemmed from its Arab policy over the preceding five years – a policy which was one of the cornerstones of its independence. Therefore, when the dynamics of the inter-Arab system propelled the other Arab countries into war, Lebanon had virtually no choice but to follow suit. Yet it would appear that the country did not join the wartime coalition unwillingly nor did its leaders do so against their inner convictions. On the contrary, going to war suited the leaders' personal political interests. This accounts for the complacency, even the enthusiasm, with which they took the decision to do so, and for the important part they played in the all-Arab resolutions leading to war. Most salient in this respect was the personal role of Riyad al-Sulh. Against this background, Lebanon's entry into the 1948 war should be made the subject of renewed consideration.

## Lebanon and the Palestine Question: Historical Background

The Palestine question began to preoccupy the Arab countries in the 1930s and soon became the dominant issue of public debate. In Lebanon, the Sunnis adopted the prevalent Arab attitudes, and in particular those of Syria, against Zionism and against a Jewish state in Palestine. Lebanon, they held, must join the rest of the Arab states in fighting for the rights of the Palestinian Arabs. True, some Sunni leaders did business with Jews in Palestine and some, for instance the Salam family, were involved in the sale of land to Jews.[1] But as the moment of truth arrived, their commitment to the Arab cause overrode other considerations and they did not hesitate to join the dominant Arab trend.

The attitude of the Shi'i and the Druse leaders, on the face of it, differed from Sunni opinion. Their policy was guided by expediency. They displayed no emotional involvement or ideological commitment, nor were they constrained by the public opinion of their communities. More than that: there were friendly ties between Jewish settlements in northern Palestine and Shi'i villages in southern Lebanon. Both sides had been cooperating with each other for many years. Shi'i and Druse leaders, among them Ahmad al-As'ad, Sabri Hamada and Majid Arsalan, maintained various business ties with the Jewish population in Palestine almost until the outbreak of the war. They were involved in deals for the sale of land to Jews and helpful in smuggling arms and Jewish immigrants into Palestine.[2] Nevertheless, once war was close, they rallied to the official line of their country's government. For them, this was a reaffirmation of their recognition of independent Lebanon – the state which had made room for them in its official establishment and had thereby contributed greatly to the maintenance of their personal positions within their own communities. Now was the time for them to show respect for a major foreign policy decision taken by the central authorities in Beirut. Moreover, like other Middle Eastern minorities (for instance the 'Alawis) the Shi'is and the Druse had come to the conclusion that the existence of minorities in Lebanon and elsewhere in the Arab world had now become contingent on their adopting a pan-Arab stance – at the very least as a matter of lip-service. Hence their readiness to fall into line with the prevalent pan-Arab, anti-Zionist concepts, at first by means of verbal pronouncements and eventually by their actions.[3]

By contrast, the Maronite outlook differed sharply from Sunni, Shi'i and Druse attitudes. Some Maronites, particularly from among the community's intellectuals, publicly advocated cooperation with the Zionists; for instance, the Association of Young Phoenicians led by Naqqash and the poet Charles Corm. Their views on Zionism were an extension of their basic claim that Lebanon was the 'national home' of the Maronites and as such should be altogether separate from the Arab world.[4] Even within the mainstream establishment of the community there were important figures – such as Edde, patriarch 'Arida, archbishop Mubarak and their respective followers – who for years maintained regular contacts with representatives of the Jewish population of Palestine. In their conversations with them, at least in those held in private, they did not hesitate to point to the community of interests existing between the two communities and to speak in support of the foundation of a Jewish state. But it was to become clear that these contacts had only limited significance; the Lebanese interlocutors aimed at exploiting their ties with Jewish – and, later, with Israeli – representatives to enhance their own standing within the Maronite community. Even those who harboured some genuine sympathy for the Jewish cause were unwilling to say so in public and incapable of putting their sentiments into practice.

This trend is best illustrated by reviewing the long series of meetings by Jewish Agency officials with patriarch 'Arida and with Edde (then Lebanon's president) which started in the 1930s. The Agency representatives sought political cooperation between the Maronite leadership and the Jews in Palestine and support for the establishment of a Jewish state. Edde for his part sought the assistance of the Jewish Agency in his negotiations with France on the issue of a treaty between Lebanon and France. While the Agency officials displayed considerable enthusiasm, Edde was cautious in the extreme. He expressed his (presumably genuine) sympathy, but remained noncommittal towards the practical side of Zionism. True, Edde and other Maronite leaders had proposals for a Maronite–Zionist alliance and discussed the possibility of encouraging Jewish settlement in southern Lebanon so as to counter the percentage growth of the Lebanese Muslim population; but all these were vague ideas, not considered binding and with no concrete intentions to back them up. Edde and other Lebanese participants in the talks seem to have been perfectly aware that, beyond certain tactical considerations, their basic interests lay in achieving an understanding with the Muslims of Lebanon and with the Arab Middle East. The differences between Khuri and Edde in this regard, sharp as they were, could not negate the underlying similarity of views. Edde was glad to receive promises of Jewish Agency support for the Lebanese side in the talks with France and seems to have believed that the Agency was capable of influencing the then French prime minister, Léon Blum (himself Jewish), but refused adamantly to come to some practical agreement with the Agency. The talks thus ended in deadlock.[5]

Zionist–Maronite contacts were renewed after the entry, in 1941, of allied forces into Lebanon. Now, the main interlocutor on the Lebanese side was patriarch 'Arida. At least in their early stage, the renewed contacts were undertaken with French blessing. In 1944, the Agency went to the length of proposing to the French a joint plan meant to harm the public image of Spears, the enemy of both France and the Zionists, in the hope of having him removed from the region.[6]

## The 1946 Agreement between the Maronite Church and the Jewish Agency

The talks culminated, on 30 March 1946, in the conclusion of a Maronite–Jewish agreement. It was signed on behalf of 'Arida by one of his close associates, Tawfiq 'Awad, and on behalf of Haim Weizman, head of the

Jewish Agency, by Joseph Bernard (later Dov Yosef), then deputy head of
the Agency's political department. It outlined modalities for closer ties and
cooperation between the Maronites of Lebanon and the Jewish population
in Palestine, on the basis of mutual recognition of the national rights and
aspirations of both sides. One clause spoke of the Agency's recognition of
Lebanon's Christian character and contained the assurance that the Jewish
population did not claim any part of Lebanon's territory. For its part, the
Maronite church affirmed its support of free Jewish immigration into Palestine and of the establishment of a Jewish state there.

The agreement was not made public in Lebanon. It soon transpired that
'Arida was not able (and perhaps not really willing) to turn it into a matter
of practical politics. His associates were later to claim that he had not
authorized 'Awad to sign the agreement. Contacts between 'Arida and Agency
representatives continued for some time, mainly at the initiative of the Agency,
but then petered out.[7] The agreement turned into a dead letter.

'Arida's readiness to enter into such an agreement must be understood
against a broader background. His old age (and possible senility), his struggle
for survival against rivals in his community and against the Vatican, and
finally his inability to resign himself to the loss of the hegemony of the
church – all these played their part and combined to produce confused and
self-defeating policy choices on his part. Intended to reinforce his standing,
they often had the opposite effect. The convoluted story of his relations
with the French, his initial support of and subsequent opposition against
Khuri, his contacts with various Muslim circles, his communications with the
British were all parts of the same web of ties which included the agreement
with the Agency.[8]

True, back in the 1930s, 'Arida had privately expressed himself in favour
of Jewish settlement in Palestine, but he consistently avoided acknowledging
his views in public or giving them practical effect. In 1937, for instance,
though requested to do so by Agency officials, he refused to testify in favour
of the Zionist position before the Peel Commission on the future of
Palestine. He refused again in 1947 and 1948 when, respectively, the UN
Special Committee on Palestine and the Anglo-American Committee were
sitting.[9] It is more than doubtful, therefore, that 'Arida's private utterances
reflected much of a real desire for friendship with the Jewish body politic
emerging in Lebanon's proximity. What he most probably wanted to gain
was Jewish support in the various struggles he anticipated, but without placing
himself or the church under any obligation towards the Zionist movement,
let alone making pro-Zionism an integral part of his policies. The March
1946 agreement was just another step taken in the same context. A noted
researcher of this episode has appropriately called it 'desperate diplomacy'.[10]
But the despair, or, to put it more cautiously, the malaise, was 'Arida's, not
that of the Maronite community. And even for 'Arida personally, this kind
of diplomacy was a *cri de coeur* rather than a well-thought-out policy.

Archbishop Mubarak, too, held talks with Jewish Agency representatives and later with Israeli officials. Unlike 'Arida, he frequently spoke in public of his pro-Zionist attitudes. In August 1947, he sent a letter to the UN Special Committee on Palestine, expressing support for the establishment of a Jewish national home in Palestine. A closer look at his language reveals, however, that the burden of his argument was to promote the cause of the Maronites rather than that of the Jews. 'There are many reasons,' he wrote, 'social, religious and humanitarian, which make it compulsory to set up two states for two minorities, a Christian homeland in Lebanon, such as has always existed, and a Jewish homeland in Palestine. It would be well for the two states to be geographically contiguous and to cooperate economically. This will turn them into a cultural bridge between east and west.' He concluded by saying: 'Lebanon wishes for freedom for the Jews in Palestine just as it wishes for freedom and independence for itself.'[11]

Just like 'Arida's, Mubarak's approach stemmed from Lebanese domestic interests, even from internal considerations concerning the Maronite community. Mubarak had originally sided with 'Arida over the question of independence from France during the November 1943 crisis in which he had taken Khuri's side. Then, against the background of the 1947 elections, Mubarak had fallen out with Khuri, and it was the latter dispute which seemed to account for his pro-Zionist turn. He expected his pro-Zionist line to bring him political dividends within the Maronite community, but soon found that he had miscalculated. His letter to the UN Committee was leaked to the Lebanese press by a gleeful government and the newspapers made much of it. All political quarters as well as spokesmen of all the communities condemned it, first and foremost being the political leadership of the Maronites.[12] 'Arida refused to censure Mubarak, but also refrained from backing him. Instead, he issued a vague appeal to the general public 'to stand like one man behind the truth of the Palestine issue'.[13] Mubarak made no further attempt to give vent to his views on the question. Whether consistent or not, his sentiments did not prevent him from cooperating with Muslim and even with pan-Arab personalities when it came to opposing Khuri. His most prominent Muslim ally was Karami with whom he associated himself immediately after the 1947 elections. His above letter notwithstanding, he had other things to say to the public at large.

These and various other Maronite–Jewish contacts of the 1940s not only failed to create a commitment to the Zionist cause, they were all – unlike the talks with government leaders a decade earlier – meetings with figures whose standing in their community and their country was declining. The debate on the future 'Arab face' of Lebanon had, as we have seen, already been decided much earlier. The decision had gone against them; Lebanon had opted for the Arab world and thus, inevitably, for the Arab cause in Palestine.

The various contacts described above cannot obscure the fact that for the entire period between the achievement of independence in 1943 and the outbreak of civil war in 1975, there was a Maronite consensus that Lebanon must adapt itself to the all-Arab (usually meaning the Syrian or even the Egyptian) line on Palestine, and accept Arab League resolutions. This was what the National Pact had envisaged, and this was the only way for a Maronite leader to gain Sunni backing at home and Arab support abroad; and these in turn were the keys to his own leadership position. This being so, the establishment of a Jewish state in Palestine could only be a source of concern and anxiety to them: it threatened that delicate fabric of inter-communal relations which they had laboured so hard to bring about; there was the suspicion that certain Maronite quarters might cooperate with Israel and thus undo the ties holding Christian and Muslim Lebanon together and dissociate the country from the Arab world; moreover, there was the fear that Israel would turn into a powerful economic competitor of Lebanon. Ultimately there was the apprehension that Israel might become a regional power strong enough to threaten Lebanon's territorial integrity or even its independence. The new state was thought likely to harbour designs on southern Lebanon and its water resources.

All this was brought out well in official statements made by Maronite leaders, but it can also be found in statements made privately to western diplomats. To illustrate: in the summer of 1948, Khuri told the UN mediator, Count Bernadotte, that he attributed great importance to the future of Galilee because of the Zionist danger to Lebanon. In his memoirs, Khuri stated that he told Bernadotte:

> Everyone with eyes to see is aware of the existence of hidden thoughts about the creation of a Zionist state ... to be linked with Christian and 'Alawi states [further north]. The problem is that merely uttering such thoughts is bound to harm the Muslims and even the Christians of Lebanon who regard cooperation with their Muslim brothers ... as vital for the quiet and stability of the Arab East.[14]

At a meeting with US Minister Pinkerton in November 1948, and speaking under the influence of the fighting then going on in Galilee and spreading into southern Lebanon, Khuri expressed fear of Israeli intentions towards Lebanon and asked the US to intervene in order to block Israeli attacks.[15] In 1951, in a conversation with the British minister, Chapman Andrews, he voiced similar concerns and asked that Britain 'keep Israel in check'.[16] Earlier, in November 1950, Foreign Minister Taqla had warned British representatives of Israel's intention to annex the Litany River region. He had added that such a step might cause extremist Maronite circles to ally themselves with Israel, thus bringing about the disintegration of Lebanon.[17]

The assessment of many Lebanese was perhaps best set forth by Michel Chiha himself, when he told a US diplomat that Lebanon would like to live, and trade, with a moderate Israeli state, but that the present rate of Jewish immigration convinced many Lebanese that Israel was bent on expansion.

Lebanon could not make any plans for the future while it watched Jewish hands stretching out further and further towards it.[18] Chiha's articles in the newspaper he edited, *Le Jour*, were anti-Zionist[19] (according to an Israeli official, even anti-Semitic).[20] But once the state was set up, he adopted a tone of acquiescence, though he continued to express fears about Israel's intentions.

Chiha then met Israeli representatives in Paris in 1949. He told them that he was not anti-Israeli or anti-Semitic, expressed his hope for good relations between Israel and Lebanon and even hinted that Israel might eventually replace France as the western country defending Lebanon. He none the less impressed his Israeli interlocutors as being greatly afraid of Israeli expansionist designs. They tried to allay his apprehensions and felt that they had a certain degree of success. They took up Chiha's hint about a western protector, arguing that Israel's very existence could relieve Lebanon of the need to look for a patron.[21] But the meeting had no practical results, either for Israel's relations with the Lebanese state or with its Christians or the Maronite community. Personally, Chiha seems to have been prepared to come to terms with the existence of Israel and did not share Muslim or Arab-nationalist hostility towards it. But he had, after all, been one of the founding fathers of the Greater Lebanon concept and was thus unable to fly in the face of Muslim opinion.

The same was, as a matter of course, true of any Maronite leader with aspirations for the presidency or other high office. Pierre al-Jumayyil and Chamoun, for instance, both conformed to the same pattern. Chamoun was Lebanon's UN representative during the debates on Palestine and stood out for the venom of his anti-Israeli statements. He persisted in these attitudes after his return home when he accused the president of inaction over Palestine.[22] Such attitudes, he judged, would serve him well in his struggle against Khuri.

## The Road to War

As the foregoing section makes clear, Khuri's overall Arab policy subsumed Lebanon's conformity with Arab resolutions on Palestine. Already on 2 November 1944, Lebanese public figures formed a body called the Association of Lebanese Parties for the Struggle against Zionism (Ittihad al-Ahzab al-Lubnaniyya liMukafahat al-Sahyuniyya), composed of almost all parties and political organizations.[23] The Chamber of Deputies began devoting a steadily increasing share of its time to the Palestine issue. In 1945, Lebanon followed Arab League resolutions and issued anti-Zionist regulations, such as a ban on the sale to Jews of land owned by Lebanese in Palestine, and a boycott of goods produced by Jews in Palestine.[24] However, Beirut traders and farmers in southern Lebanon were unwilling to lose their Jewish clients and did not, initially, take the new regulations very seriously. Local Druse and Shi'i leaders kept smuggling arms and immigrants into Jewish areas of Palestine in defiance of the rules and regulations.[25]

When the UN Special Committee on Palestine published its recommendations in October 1947, a general strike was proclaimed throughout Lebanon. After the UN partition resolution of 29 November 1947, there was a series of anti-Zionist demonstrations, mostly in Muslim residential quarters in the big cities. Some bombs were thrown into Beirut's Jewish quarter as well as at the US legation and the headquarters of the Communist Party (whose patron, the USSR, had voted for partition).[26] A few days later, the Sunni mufti of Lebanon declared that the partition resolution justified, indeed made it mandatory, to wage a *Jihad* against the emergence of a Jewish state in Palestine. The government began registering volunteers for fighting in Palestine; within a month, 3,000 men had enrolled.[27]

The years 1947–48 were thus the period when the Lebanese public was pulled into the warlike maelstrom that was taking hold of the Arab countries. Rather than leading his country, Khuri, it seemed, was dragged along by events. And indeed, the partition resolution and the developments following it between November 1947 and May 1948 cut the ground from under the feet of those Arab leaders who had hoped to reach an acceptable solution without all-out war. They had pinned their hopes on international intervention or else on the ability of the Arab irregulars to turn the tide in Palestine before actual war broke out. Neither hope had materialized.

Moreover, King 'Abdallah's territorial aspirations, King Faruq's personal ambitions, the weakness of the regimes in Syria and Iraq, and more than anything else Arab popular pressure – all combined to create a warlike momentum which led the Arab states, including Lebanon, into belligerency.[28] But Lebanon did not enter the war against its will. The evidence we possess suggests that the extraordinary activity of Khuri and Sulh in the inter-Arab councils leading to the outbreak of hostilities, as well as their ultimate decision to make their country go to war, were deliberate policy choices. They stemmed from an assessment that a warlike policy would benefit their personal political interests.

Khuri expected wartime exigencies to further his chances of re-election, and especially win him greater support among the Sunni population. Moreover, he probably thought of going to war as no more than the logical extension of the pan-Arab policy he had pursued so consistently and which, in his judgement, was in his country's best interests. In a convincing-sounding passage of his memoirs, he wrote of the decision to enter the war: 'At that time, we did not know how ill-prepared and ill-equipped the Arab armies were ... and we tended to ignore the strength and organization of the Zionist gangs and their intention to conquer all of Palestine.'[29] His words bear witness to the fundamental mistake he and Sulh were making; both seem to have genuinely believed that the war would go well, that they need not involve Lebanon too heavily in the fighting, and that they would keep the situation under strict control. Eventually, they would reap the full domestic and inter-Arab benefits bound to accrue to them from warlike success. Things were to take a different course.

Sulh's role in steering Lebanon into the war was more prominent than Khuri's, though, according to the latter's own testimony, their steps were fully coordinated.[30] For his part, Sulh too needed an external event to strengthen his alliance with Khuri and to justify his help in the latter's re-election. He expected the war in Palestine to bolster his standing much like the struggle against the French had done during most of the 1940s.[31] He also seems to have hoped that his involvement in the Palestine issue at the inter-Arab level would allow him to emerge from the war as an all-Arab leader of the first rank. He had, after all, had a promising taste of such prominence during his premiership of 1943–44.

During the first months of 1948, Sulh travelled tirelessly from one Arab meeting to another, trying, together with his Syrian colleague Mardam, to bridge gaps between Arab leaders and to bring about full Arab cooperation on Palestine. He devoted particular efforts to achieving a reconciliation between the Hashemite rulers of Jordan and Iraq on the one hand, and Faruq and Ibn Sa'ud on the other. Khuri wrote later: 'Lebanon played an important role in enlisting Arab governments for the rescue of Palestine from the claws of the Zionists ... Riyad, in full coordination with myself, tirelessly devoted all his energies to this matter. This made me love him all the more, increased my esteem for his properties, and turned him into a real statesman.'[32] One may doubt how far Sulh's shuttling between Cairo, Baghdad and Amman made a real difference to the course of events. There were, after all, broader Arab interests at work, and at least King 'Abdallah and King Faruq were headed for war anyway. But Sulh's relentless activities are worthy of note: they attest to his and Khuri's determination not to let their country miss an opportunity to achieve the honour and glory they believed to be in its grasp.

## The Course of Hostilities

From 15 May, the day the war began, until 4 June 1948, the day the first truce came into effect, Beirut was optimistic. An Arab victory still seemed certain. Under the original overall Arab plan, the Lebanese army had been given the mission of advancing from Ra's al-Naqura in the direction of Acre and Haifa, while Syrian units were to advance from Bint Jubayl in the direction of Safed, Nazareth and Afulah. But because of King 'Abdallah's objections, the point of departure of the Syrian troops was shifted from Bint Jubayl (on Lebanese territory) to Tsemah on the Syrian–Palestinian border. In consequence, the Lebanese thrust was now to begin near Malkiyya (in central Galilee), reach the Yizra'l Valley and then push towards Haifa.[33] This was an ambitious undertaking and one may well doubt the resolve of the Lebanese leadership to carry it out. They did indeed want war, but they wanted it to be strictly circumscribed, and intended to remain in full control of all moves.

Indeed, when the war started, Lebanese units did not cross into Palestine. It was Qa'uqji's Army of Deliverance (Jaysh al-Inkaz) which involved itself in fighting in Galiliee. Qa'uqji's men took Malkiyya and Quds at the western edge of northern Galilee, soon to be stopped by Israeli troops. At the time the Israelis believed that they were fighting the Lebanese army.[34] Thus, when the initiative passed to the Israeli side, on 29 October Israeli forces mounted an offensive on the northern front, during the course of which it seized northern and central Galilee and occupied a narrow strip of territory in southern Lebanon (containing fourteen villages).[35] To the surprise of the Israeli units, the inhabitants, particularly the Maronites, showed little opposition to their advance. According to Israeli military reports, Lebanese from neighbouring villages came to ask the Israeli officers to occupy their villages, too, and even spoke of enlisting in the Israeli army. Some Ministry of Defence officials were rather enthusiastic about such possibilities, but the Foreign Ministry refused to go along with the idea.[36]

The reversal of the fortunes of war along the Lebanese–Israeli frontier caused grave apprehension in Beirut, reviving old fears of Israeli intentions. Lebanon hurriedly asked for Syrian military assistance and simultaneously appealed to Britain and the USA to restrain Israel.[37] The military reverses came at a most inconvenient time for Khuri and his government: the opposition had resumed, and was even stepping up, its attacks on the leadership, taking as its point of departure what it called the government's sins of omission in conducting the war. Opposition figures accused the government of having added its share to the overall Arab defeat. One of the high moments of this confrontation was the clash between Sulh and Chamoun in the Chamber. In a conversation with the US minister, Khuri conceded that the Israeli offensive had caused great embarrassment to his government. The minister (using cable style) reported on Khuri's hesitation to turn to the UN Security Council with regard to the invasion of Lebanese territory by Israel

> because Lebanese Government has not officially announced to its people that such invasion has actually taken place and some officials have publicly denied it. To present it formally at this time would be highly embarrassing and might even result in overthrow of Riyad al-Sulh's Government although President's position appears secure. To admit that Jews have been able to invade Lebanon would cause loss of face.[38]

## From War to Armistice

In the light of the new situation at the front, Khuri and Sulh began seeking for ways to end the hostilities and to enlist other Arab leaders to take up the same quest. They applauded Egypt for having been the first Arab state to enter into publicly acknowledged negotiations with Israel.[39] But they did not hesitate to open secret channels of their own to sound out Israeli representatives about the prospects of an armistice. Such contacts were first established during the UN General Assembly in Paris towards the end of 1948.

Prime Minister Sulh himself headed the Lebanese delegation to the General Assembly. Before it opened, he had adopted an intransigent stand and called on the Arab states to resume the war and simultaneously to recommend that the UN revoke the partition resolution. This, he asserted, would allow Jews and Arabs in Palestine to live together just as Muslims and Christians were living together in Lebanon.[40] But his militant public stance was no more than a cover for his country's efforts to achieve an armistice. The news of the Israeli offensive in Galilee and the entry of Israeli units into southern Lebanon reached Sulh in Paris and reinforced his desire to end the hostilities.

The UN General Assembly provided good opportunities for Israeli–Arab contacts of various kinds, whether for political exchanges or for the purpose of intelligence-gathering. Sulh's meetings were no exception. On the Israeli side, Eliyahu Sasson was the main figure in these meetings. He reported directly to Prime Minister Ben-Gurion. The latter referred to Sasson's reports to him in his diary (in an entry dated 9 November 1948), saying that Sulh would

> work for us. Lebanon has no territorial demands or chances [of putting forward such demands], the war is already weighing down on them, but they cannot proceed alone and would therefore prefer for all [the Arabs] to proceed together. Riyad al-Sulh cannot expect promotion – he has risen as high as a Muslim can in Lebanon. Outside Lebanon, he has nothing to expect; his only ambition is to be influential in the [Arab] League.[41]

These lines suggest that some kind of agreement – possibly no more than a personal understanding – was reached between Sasson and Sulh, but they also allow us to draw a broader conclusion: much like King 'Abdallah, or like some figures in King Faruq's entourage, or, at a later date, the new Syrian leader Husni al-Za'im, Sulh did not reject the idea of settling the Arab–Israeli dispute by peaceful means.

This impression is reinforced by some internal correspondence of the Israeli Foreign Ministry. The ministry's representative in Paris, Tuvia Arazi, wrote to Sasson:

> I hope you have received my cable concerning Riyad. It is a pity that you have not yet advised me of his final response and whether it is possible for the evacuation [of Lebanese territory held by Israeli troops] to begin at the time of Riyad's return to Beirut. If it is true that we are ready to evacuate the villages, as B[en] G[urion] has told [UN mediator Ralph] Bunche, and that we are going to carry out [the evacuation], it would be well to coordinate this with his journey and [then] we could gain something in exchange for the evacuation. As I wrote

to you … . Riyad is ready to have the evacuation carried out through [chief of UN observers] General Riley who would invite an officer of ours and a Lebanese officer. Riyad feels that we are evading giving an answer.[42]

Despite Ben-Gurion's words about Sulh's readiness to 'work for' Israel, there is no definite evidence of an understanding with Sulh. The above entry in Ben-Gurion's diary is the only clue we have. Furthermore, there would have been no political logic on Sulh's side for entering into clearly defined obligations of such a nature. Doing so would have contradicted his entire world-view and his whole long political record up to that point. It would have demolished his position in the eyes of the Muslim public in Lebanon as well as in the eyes of the rest of the Arab world. Ben-Gurion recognized this when he wrote that Sulh could not rise any higher at home and the only prospects he had were of a leading role on the all-Arab scene.[43] This remark also shows that for the Israeli prime minister, Sulh and perhaps other Lebanese Sunni leaders were not actors in their own right but rather pieces on a larger board on which a game with the entire Arab world, or at least its principal countries, was being played out.

Despite the Israeli assessment reflected in the above quotes from the diary and from the Foreign Ministry correspondence, it should be emphasized that on the Lebanese side, Sulh's approach to the Arab–Israeli dispute and the prospects of its resolution did not differ much from that of other Lebanese leaders, including Khuri's. Their approach was complex; one component was a deep-seated suspicion of, and hostility towards, the new Jewish state, because of the threat it was perceived to pose to Lebanon's territorial integrity, its economy, its inter-communal balance, and the basic concepts around which the state had been erected. Another aspect was Lebanon's unswerving adherence to the all-Arab line and its unwillingness to go out on a limb by pursuing an independent policy on the Palestine issue or towards Israel. But neither consideration precluded the search for a possible Israeli–Lebanese settlement, provided it formed part of a broader Israeli–Arab accommodation.

However, in terms of immediate policy goals for late 1948, Khuri and Sulh focused on three points: (1) the termination of hostilities in Palestine. Sulh made this his urgent and personal concern, and Sasson's above report should probably be understood in the context of Sulh's search for an armistice or a state of non-belligerency. However, recognition of Israel or a formal peace with it was another matter entirely. (2) Originally, the Lebanese seem to have had hopes for territorial gains in northern Israel or, alternatively, for the establishment of a demilitarized zone there, to form a buffer between the two states. But after the Israeli occupation of Lebanese villages, Beirut's main effort was directed at achieving their evacuation and the restoration of the old border. (3) A solution of the problem of the Palestinian refugees whose inrush was beginning to place a heavy burden on Lebanon.

Khuri's conversation, at the end of November 1948, with US Minister Pinkerton illustrates these points. Pinkerton reported: 'In discussing Zionist intrusion into Lebanon ... Khuri was anxious that any request ... for intervention of US Government be considered unofficial. He did not at this time wish to be placed in the position of entering into formal negotiations concerning any phase of the Palestine problem.' Khuri mentioned current plans for setting up 'neutral zones' in the Negev and said 'if they could be made equally applicable to Galilee he would be content. He hoped US Government would use its influence in [UN] S[ecurity] C[ouncil] to that end.' Khuri added that 'Arab Palestine policy would have to be dictated by Arab League and he was afraid that no individual Arab State would be willing to take lead in suggesting any agreement with Israel. This is particularly true of Lebanon which must avoid charge that it is less Arab than other states as Christians of Lebanon have shown little interest in pursuing war in Palestine.'[44]

The matter of Lebanese territorial acquisitions recurred in a later report from Sasson to the Israeli Foreign Ministry. Writing from Lausanne in May 1949, he mentioned Lebanese soundings about a possible meeting between the Lebanese and Israeli foreign ministers. He added that, as compensation for coming to an agreement with Israel, Lebanon expected to annex some parts of Galilee. Similarly, the Lebanese held, Egypt should be allowed to annex the parts of southern Palestine it had occupied earlier.[45]

There is, however, no mistaking the fact that the readiness in principle for a peaceful resolution of the Arab–Israeli conflict, such as was mooted by Lebanese leaders in private conversations with western diplomats, was always contingent on an Arab consensus on this point. For this reason alone, it remained a vague, general postulate, not to be translated into practical politics. The only point on which Beirut took the lead – even then acting with the extreme caution typical of the country – was the quest for a cessation of hostilities. Beyond that, no Lebanese leader would go. And we must assume that none possessed either the resolve or the ability to pursue a settlement with anything like the drive Lebanon had displayed in the opposite direction only a year or so earlier. No western diplomatic source as much as hints at such a possibility. Sulh was much too committed to his pan-Arab course, too much of a captive of the Sunni public mood and a hostage of his own past record, to be the man to initiate an overall settlement with Israel. Sasson (interested as he must have been in giving his own mission a broader aspect and in giving his reports an optimistic note) allowed himself to be impressed by the ostensible seriousness of Sulh's intentions, but the latter was doing no more than create the right atmosphere for a speedy armistice. The fact that the Lebanese press mentioned these contacts points in the same direction;[46] had they been more serious, the government would have prevented the press from reporting them.

By the end of 1948, the Arab front, both militarily and politically speaking, was on the point of collapse. Against this background, the only aim the Lebanese now had was to regain their territory up to the international border. For this purpose, they were ready to enter into official contacts with Israeli representatives, but still considered themselves subject to an all-Arab consensus. Therefore, when UN mediator Bunche invited them on 31 January 1949 to join the Rhodes armistice negotiations, the Lebanese government delayed its answer. Only after the Egyptian–Israeli armistice was signed on 24 February was Lebanon willing to reply in the affirmative.[47] Even then, the government first made sure that Syria would not object to Beirut's participation in the Rhodes talks. Syrian Prime Minister Khalid al-'Azm visited Beirut at the end of February and expressed his consent. Khuri wrote: 'Syria cannot accept the invitation of the UN mediator to open negotiations with Israel ... because Syrian public opinion is opposed to such a step.' But he added: 'Lebanon [however] is entitled to conduct such negotiations itself.'[48]

Accordingly, armistice negotiations between Lebanon and Israel began on 1 March 1949. With characteristic caution, Lebanon demanded that they be attended by military men only and insisted on their taking place at the border crossing point of Ra's al-Naqura rather than at Rhodes (where the Egyptian armistice had been negotiated and signed). Both demands were meant to underline that the talks were purely military contacts devoid of political consequences. The Israeli side at Ra's al-Naqura insisted on a linkage between the negotiations with Lebanon and those with Syria (which had not yet started); in return for the evacuation of the fourteen Lebanese villages, Israel demanded a Syrian withdrawal from certain areas the Syrian army had occupied in Israel. Israel justified this by recalling that Lebanon and Syria had coordinated their attack on Israel in the early stages of the war and that Syrian troops had mounted their attack from Lebanese territory.[49] Eventually Israel dropped its demand. The armistice was signed on 23 March and one of its clauses stipulated Israel's withdrawal from southern Lebanon.

There followed a long period of calm along the Lebanese–Israeli border. More than that: a dialogue was kept up and a certain measure of cooperation maintained, primarily with a view to maintaining a quiet frontier. Police and army officers from both sides met from time to time. The contacts culminated in a meeting of the two chiefs-of-staff on 23 March 1952. Measures to prevent infiltration, smuggling and other violations were agreed upon. Lebanon consented to the continued emigration of Lebanese Jews to Israel.[50] But the Lebanese would not, and could not, go beyond such matters. Khuri and his associates remained suspicious and distrustful of Israel. This was attested to by their attitude at the time of the only really serious incident between the two countries: on 14 July 1950, a Lebanese passenger plane on its way from East Jerusalem to Beirut mistakenly veered from its route and crossed into Israel. An Israeli air force plane intercepted it and fired on it, killing two passengers and wounding eight. The incident caused a panic in Beirut severe enough for the government to ask the USA to guarantee Israel's full observance of the armistice. (A UN investigation found both sides equally responsible.)[51]

The Arab defeat in Palestine had a deleterious effect on the standing of Khuri and his government, even to the point of posing a threat to the country's long-term stability. For one thing, the Lebanese watched other Arab populations turn against their governments as a result of the defeat, eventually bringing down some of them. Such a chain reaction could not fail to affect them as well. Secondly, the war produced a deep rift in the Arab League, primarily between Jordan and Egypt, and virtually paralysed it. This removed an important prop from under the Lebanese regime, the League having been considered capable of neutralizing both domestic and inter-Arab threats to Lebanon's stability, integrity or independence. Thirdly, it gave added strength to the domestic opposition against Khuri and provided it with a series of handy and telling arguments against him. Fourthly, Lebanon now bordered on a new state which many of its leaders thought of as a political, military and economic threat. The fact that secessionist quarters in Lebanon maintained good relations with Israel was also perceived as menacing Lebanon's cohesiveness and internal balance, as well as its proper relations with other Arab states. Another factor was the heavy economic burden placed on the government by the influx of some 120,000 Palestinian refugees. Besides being hungry and homeless, they were a resentful and unruly element; moreover, their very presence altered the communal balance since the majority of them were Sunni Muslims. Other economic damage was done by the sheer magnitude of wartime expenses as well as by economic dislocations caused by the war. Southern Lebanon, for instance, lost its traditional markets in Palestine. Finally, the war may have widened the gulf that was opening between Khuri and Sulh. The latter's long-standing and direct involvement in the Palestine issue now made him an easy target for criticism. He was quoted as having said to those close to him: 'The Arab defeat in Palestine in 1948 strengthened Khuri in comparison with myself, because the defeat in Palestine was my personal defeat and caused my position in Lebanon to collapse.'[52] If Sulh did indeed express himself like that, he ignored (perhaps momentarily) the equally heavy harm done to Khuri by the events in Palestine.

## Israel and the Maronites: First Contacts

We have just now pointed to Lebanese suspicions that Israel might make common cause with the more isolationist quarters in the Maronite community and encourage them in putting their conceptual and ideological aims into practice. Documentary evidence released during the last decade, particularly from Israeli archives, allows us to judge how far these suspicions were justified. We find that during the first years after the establishment of the State of Israel contacts with Maronites continued, much along the lines of the pre-1948 contacts reviewed earlier in this chapter. They gave rise to the view that Israel was pursuing an activist policy in Lebanon, a policy intended to encourage isolationist elements to step up their struggle against the existing Lebanese regime and perhaps to replace it.[53] But a closer study of the documents reveals that rather than constituting a meaningful Israeli–Maronite dialogue the various meetings failed to acquire any real significance.

Beginning in 1948, Israeli officials stepped in more or less at the point at which Jewish Agency representatives had left off. Meetings took place at three levels: with Edde in 1948; with representatives of Archbishop Mubarak in 1949; and with Phalanges leader Rababi from 1948 till 1951.

The contacts with Edde took place in Paris (where he was vacationing) during May–July 1948. The Israeli side wished to discuss a plan for 'concrete action by the Lebanese opposition against the government, especially in the light of a possible situation in which parts of southern Lebanon would be occupied by the Israeli Defense Forces'. Edde replied that the opposition (including himself) lacked real strength and were not capable of taking serious action to change the domestic situation.[54] Nevertheless, he asked for a meeting with the Israeli President Haim Weizman whom he said he had known for years. He also sought Israeli help in gaining US support for the Lebanese opposition.[55]

A scrutiny of the Israeli reports on the conversations with Edde leaves the reader in doubt whether they had, or were even intended to have, any operative significance. They were held because Edde (not unlike other Arab leaders, among the confirmed anti-Zionists) was ready to meet the Israeli interlocutors; they were useful for creating a desirable atmosphere, even if they lacked purpose.[56] Edde himself – visibly at the end of his political career – had little hope for a useful result and said so to the Israelis he met. Edde's own efforts to rebuild his position were directed towards the British and the Hashemites rather than the Israelis. Edde was attracted by Amir (later, King) 'Abdallah's plan for a Greater Syria in which the Maronites would enjoy autonomous status in Mt Lebanon. This was in a way a revival of the 'Little Lebanon' concept. During this period, Edde met frequently with the Transjordanian minister in Beirut; in December 1947, a delegation of his party (the National Bloc) visited Amman.[57] 'Abdallah was helpful to Edde in his efforts to reach a closer understanding with Britain, telling British diplomats that they were wrong to ignore the National Bloc.[58] After Edde's death in September 1949, his two sons joined the Lebanese mainstream and adopted the consensual attitude on Palestine, even though this meant abandoning some of their father's pivotal ideas.

Three representatives of archbishop Mubarak visited Israel in February 1949, presumably for business; but while there, they also contacted Israeli officials, including a Foreign Ministry representative, S. Ya'ari. They told him that Mubarak 'wishes to learn the attitude of the Israeli government toward a *coup* in Lebanon'. One of the three, Tawfiq Sam'an, who was introduced as Mubarak's personal emissary, claimed that Edde and Pierre al-Jumayyil were partners to the plan. Ya'ari replied that Israel would 'welcome any attempt on the part of the Christians of Lebanon to set themselves free from the pan-Arab leaders, but could not express an opinion on the [present] proposal until it had a precise plan of action [stating] how the Christians intended to carry out the *coup*, what forces they had their disposal and what assistance they were asking for from Israel'. Ya'ari enquired about the relations between Mubarak and other Christian parties, such as the National Bloc and the Phalanges. He recommended that Mubarak consult other, like-minded leaders, 'especially men of the Phalanges, and tell them to prepare a plan of action'.[59]

No great importance should be attributed to the whole affair, documented in a single, one-page document in the Israeli Foreign Ministry archives. For one thing, the visitors were emissaries; Mubarak himself made no contact with Israelis. The envoys presented letters of 'accreditation', but Ya'ari observed that at least two of the three came for black market deals. The third, Sam'an, claimed to be a close associate of Mubarak's and to have been sent by him personally in order to establish contacts with Israeli officials. But Ya'ari spoke of him as a 'wealthy man', conveying the impression that he assumed him to have business reasons for coming to Israel.[60] Furthermore, talk of a coup did not imply operative or concrete ideas. An actual coup seemed out of the question in the light of both the situation in Lebanon at the time, and in Mubarak's known political vagaries. There is ample room for doubt concerning Mubarak's intentions, even concerning his actual role in sending the emissaries; he probably intended no more than to sound out Israel about rendering him some (unspecified) assistance at some (unspecified) point in the future. Like Edde, Mubarak was nearing the end of his career which was brought about a few years later (in 1952) by his dispute with the Vatican.

Finally, relations with the Phalanges were maintained from late in 1948 till 1951 through contacts with Rababi. Officials of the American Zionist Federation had earlier been in touch with the Maronite bishop Yusuf 'Awad, a resident of the USA who had at times received financial assistance from them.[61] Towards the end of 1948, 'Awad informed his Zionist contacts of the presence in the USA of a delegation from the Phalanges headed by Rababi. 'Awad added that its members had told him of their organization's preparations for a military uprising intended 'to bring down the government and seize power in Lebanon'; but to do so they required 'tangible help'. He recommended that Israeli officials meet the delegation and offer the Phalanges assistance.[62]

A series of meetings ensued, partly in the USA, partly in Europe. Rababi gave a greatly exaggerated account of the strength of the Phalanges, claiming that it numbered 50–60,000 men. Once in power, he added, a Phalanges regime would establish diplomatic relations with Israel. But in order to proceed, the movement needed a grant of $100,000, required for funding its political activities and for the purchase of weapons.[63] The Israeli officials were hesitant. They assured Rababi that they valued the contacts with the Phalanges, agreed that Rababi was thinking in terms of a 'far-reaching realignment in the structure of the entire Middle East', but avoided committing themselves to his plans. They handed over a much smaller sum than Rababi had in mind, more in the nature of a reimbursement for expenses incurred or payment for information received.[64]

The Israeli Foreign Ministry considered Rababi's proposals and decided to turn them down. They favoured maintaining contact with the Phalanges in the hope that something positive might in time emerge, but did not see any such prospects at present. The foreign minister, Moshe Sharett, as well as his professional advisers preferred to keep the matter on the back burner. The ministry's research branch gave it as its opinion that the Phalanges could not be expected to 'bring about a change in Lebanon's attitude toward Israel'. A small sum, however, might be useful in maintaining their good-will.[65] (Rababi constantly reverted to the theme of monetary assistance, including help for the 1951 elections campaign of the Phalanges. He later claimed that the campaign had cost his movement $100,00, hinting that Israel should refund the Phalanges.)[66] Lack of seriousness on the part of Rababi and hesitancy on the part of Israel eventually caused the meetings to come to an end.

It should be recalled that, unlike Edde or Mubarak, the leader of the Phalanges, Pierre al-Jumayyil, belonged to the mainstream of Lebanese politics and therefore shared the Lebanese consensus regarding Israel. Personally, Jumayyil was not an ardent anti-Zionist, but the Phalanges were well aligned with the prevalent attitudes. They joined the Association of Lebanese Parties for the Struggle against Zionism and supported government policy on the issue of Israel. The Phalanges organ Al-'Amal, edited by none other than Rababi, abounded with anti-Israeli material. Jumayyil toured the Syrian–Israeli frontier as a guest of the Syrian army in June 1949.[67]

Israeli contacts with the Phalanges were restricted to meetings with a single person. There is no evidence that Rababi's steps were backed by others in the Phalanges or sanctioned by Jumayyil. A decade later, when Jumayyil himself sought the help of the head of Beirut's Jewish community to establish new contacts with Israel, he did indeed recall Rababi's talks but discounted them by adding that he was now looking for 'more serious' contacts with a 'different purpose'.[68]

It should also be remembered that seeking aid (including monetary aid) from abroad was a conditioned reflex for many Lebanese politicians before, during and after the period here reviewed. As a rule, such requests were not meant to commit the Lebanese side, and foreign partners who expected a political dividend were usually disappointed. The Israeli Foreign Ministry seems to have understood this very well and did not attribute much significance to the Rababi talks.

It should be pointed out that, rather than being launched by Israel, the talks had been initiated by the 1948 wartime emergency council of the American Zionist Federation. Presumably seeking reasons to perpetuate its existence after the end of the war, the council had pursued the contacts with the Phalanges with considerable enthusiasm. Foreign Minister Sharett observed that the council tended to 'overstate the importance' of the contacts and to 'exaggerate the chances' of the Phalanges achieving results. Nevertheless, he added, their reports should be studied carefully for the 'kernels of truth' they might contain.[69]

The ministry's professional staff were even more sceptical: they not only discounted Rababi's claims as to the military strength of his organization but doubted its overall capacity to take action for the realization of its ideas.[70] A scrutiny of the reports on the talks leaves the reader with the impression that the Israeli side related to Rababi most of all as a source of intelligence on Lebanon. Sums given to him were for expenses incurred and for encouraging future services. No political investment seems to have been intended.[71]

It is instructive to consider a later exchange of notes between Sharett and Ben-Gurion, during the years when the former was prime minister and the latter was out of office (1953–55). Ben-Gurion wrote to Sharett about the possibility of encouraging a military coup in Lebanon which would create a state to be run by the Christians and ready to cooperate with Israel. Sharett was resolutely opposed to the idea.[72] It should be added that Ben-Gurion had consistently thought along such lines since the late 1920s, but had never translated them into a clear plan of action. From its inception in 1948, the Israeli Foreign Ministry had as consistently opposed such schemes (and similar ones elsewhere), and had clung to a line of political realism. The ministry's basic attitude is perhaps best summed up by quoting the words of one of its senior officials at the time, Y. Shim'oni, who wrote:

> The ties with the Maronites in Lebanon did not create a Lebanese–Maronite 'orientation' as a comprehensive political concept ... [They] remained something separate and marginal, since it was clear to the Zionist leadership and its representatives in the Arab arena that Lebanon, weak as it was in its state of communal fragmentation, could not be a reliable ally in the context of the broader Arab world; that the Maronites did not really control Lebanon; that the Maronites themselves were disunited; and that even confirmed friends in Lebanon were not fully to be relied upon at a time of crisis.[73]

CHAPTER 9

# The Syrian–Lebanese
# Crisis

Lebanon's ties with Syria occupied a special place in Beirut's overall relations with the Arab world. At times, they became the pivotal issue of Lebanon's entire foreign policy. This was particularly true of the first years of independence. During these years, a considerable part of the Lebanese public looked to Syria as a model for ideological and political emulation. These were primarily the people who, in the past, had wanted union with Syria. Though they had renounced that aspiration, or had relegated it to an uncertain and perhaps distant future, they continued to think of close relations with Syria as a vital Lebanese interest. In Syria, their counterparts were major sections in the population who, in their hearts, continued to regard Lebanon as a rightful part of Syria, torn off from the fatherland by French imperialism. Both quarters aroused suspicions in the minds of pro-independence Lebanese leaders who felt compelled to monitor developments in Damascus with close and constant attention. In a different context, good relations with Syria were necessary for Beirut to block Hashemite union schemes intended to embrace both Syria and Lebanon. Finally, for quite some time after independence, the two countries still constituted a single economic area, just as they had done under the French mandate. Syria was both an important market for Lebanese products and re-exports and a vital transit route for trade with other Arab countries. Close neighbourly ties with Damascus became a cornerstone of Lebanese foreign policy because the country's leaders knew that its independence, its internal stability and its prosperity were all in some degree dependent on Syrian good-will. Moreover, the maintenance of the good personal relations which both Khuri and Sulh had fostered with Syrian leaders was an important component of their (and their government's) standing in the eyes of the Sunni community.

Lebanese–Syrian relations during the 1940s were in the nature of an alliance founded on common political and economic interests between the two governments, the two ruling elites and among the individuals then in power in Beirut and Damascus. Both countries were facing similar challenges: the vicissitudes of early independence; the issue of the evacuation of French troops and the need to establish a new kind of relationship with the West; the necessity to protect their independence from the pressures of the newly emerging inter-Arab system and the union schemes of the Hashemites; and the quest for internal stability. In Lebanon, moreover, the Sunni—Maronite alliance depended in large measure on close and proper relations with Syria. On the face of it, its size and population, its function as Lebanon's conduit to the rest of the Arab states and its leverage with the Lebanese Sunni population should have given Syria considerable influence. But this was neutralized by Syria's domestic weakness, by Lebanon's economic edge, and by the then widely current assumption that Lebanon still enjoyed the protection of the West or that its independence was guaranteed by it.

The personal friendship linking Syrian President Quwatli and Prime Minister Mardam with Khuri and Sulh (as well as with other Lebanese leaders) was an important element in shaping the two countries' overall relations. Some Lebanese politicians complained that the Syrians had greater influence with Khuri than the Lebanese cabinet or Chamber.[1] In addition, several members of the Sunni elite had close family ties with Syrian notables. Sulh was married to a niece of Sa'dallah al-Jabiri and Yafi's wife was a cousin of Khalid al-'Azm. Such links of kinship were useful for enhancing mutual confidence in the two capitals and helped to mitigate the many differences of opinions that came to the fore during the 1940s, mainly over economic issues but also over political questions. The latter often emerged because public opinion in the two countries tended to exercise contradictory pressures on their respective governments.

One precondition for the maintenance of good relations was domestic stability in Syria, i.e. continued rule by the 'old guard' who knew the Lebanese leaders well and were personally friendly with them. But domestic stability, never Syria's strong suit, suffered a grievous blow as a result of the 1948 war. The old problem of outside Arab interference in Syria's internal affairs became much more acute: Iraq and Jordan proposing regional union schemes were trying to recruit local helpers; so did Egypt and Saudi Arabia opposing such schemes. More than that, war and defeat sharpened old domestic conflicts: social tensions, disputes between religious communities, and the contradictory interests of the country's various geographical regions. The old elite which had run Syria's affairs since independence was clearly on the point of collapse.

## Husni al-Za'im's Military Coup

On 31 March 1949, the Syrian chief-of-staff, Husni al-Za'im, seized power in the first of several military coups which Syria was to experience over the following years. For all we know, he had no military or political plans with regard to Lebanon but he knew little about the Lebanese leadership and had no way of judging their reactions. As we shall see presently, both sides soon came to think of each other as enemies. His regime lasted only 137 days before he was brought down by another military takeover. But his short rule caused great, and partly irreversible, damage to Lebanese–Syrian relations.

The Lebanese view of events in Damascus was negative, even hostile, right from the start. Beirut delayed recognizing Za'im's regime for about a month, but refrained from making any official statement. The Lebanese press, however, particularly those newspapers close to Sulh, had no such constraints. They attacked Za'im and affirmed their support for former president Quwatli and his government.[2] They expressed distaste at the very idea of a military takeover, regretted the fall from power of the Syrian figures with whom they had been familiar, and suspected Za'im of seeking contacts with the Lebanese opposition and of pursuing inter-Arab policies deleterious to Lebanon's standing in the Arab world. No wonder then that Za'im came to regard Sulh as a personal foe who threatened his standing at a time when he was struggling to consolidate his regime. He soon convinced himself that Sulh wanted him dead.

At the outset, Za'im had tried to reassure Lebanon. The communiqué announcing his takeover and explaining its aims contained a passage reading: 'As to our Lebanese sister [state], we support the continuation of the existing status quo and respect its independence. We hope that it will be possible to resolve in the near future all the bilateral problems on the agenda which have not found a solution so far.'[3] But in the light of the hostile reception his regime received in Lebanon, he soon changed his tune. On 4 April 1949, he sent a personal note to Khuri reading:

> I have to inform you that the attitude taken by your prime minister [Sulh] with regard to our liberation movement is inappropriate and dangerous. To our regret many details of his proceedings have been brought to our notice and these are bound to aggravate relations between our two sisterly states which are linked by close ties and common interests of long standing; I am concerned that his actions may have undesirable results ... I am asking you to take it upon yourself to look into this matter closely and attentively and to act in order to make relations between the two states revert to what they were before.[4]

Later the same month, Za'im began speaking of Sulh's intention to have him assassinated as part of a plot being hatched by Sulh and the former Syrian defence minister, Ahmad al-Sharabati, now a refugee in Lebanon.[5]

Za'im was an unstable and impulsive character and his suspicions of Sulh soon became an obsession. When the British minister in Beirut met Khuri and Sulh in April 1949, Khuri told him of a visit to Damascus by Lebanese Foreign Minister Faranjiyya two days earlier. Faranjiyya had reported that he found it difficult to talk to Za'im on any subject for longer than just a few minutes, because the latter kept bringing in files to prove that Sulh, or someone else in Lebanon, was planning to have him killed. Khuri also mentioned that on 14 April Za'im had sent Hasan Jabara (Syria's delegate to the Council for Common Interests) to see him so as to expedite the matter of Lebanon's recognition of the new Syrian regime. Jabra had also asked Khuri to restrain Sulh, adding that he had been charged by Za'im to tell Khuri that, for all Za'im's desire for friendly relations with Lebanon, he would not be able to cooperate with Sulh. Later the same day, however, Jabra was instructed over the telephone from Damascus to see Sulh and tell him of Za'im's hopes for future cooperation between the two men.[6]

On the Lebanese side, distrust mounted because of certain contacts which Za'im now developed with domestic anti-Khuri opposition quarters and as a result of some of his inter-Arab moves. Yet there is room for doubt as to whether Za'im really posed a threat to Lebanon or its rulers. His primary concern, after all, was the stability of his own regime. The steps he took in inter-Arab politics as well as in Lebanese affairs were meant to serve that purpose. He does not seem to have sought foreign adventures nor the inclusion in Syria of Lebanon. He had no record of pan-Arab convictions and was probably the first Syrian ruler to place his country's interests above its commitment to the Arab cause. This is borne out by his contacts with Israel.[7] Moreover, he was clearly under the influence of the western powers, especially of the USA. In regional affairs, he was careful to take Arab, particularly Egyptian and Saudi, sensibilities into consideration. None of this left room for an actively anti-Lebanese policy.

Nevertheless, the vehement attacks against him in the Lebanese press troubled Za'im. Even more so did the fact that several of the Syrian leaders he had removed from power had found refuge in Lebanon. There, he believed, they were plotting to bring him down, enjoying Sulh's active help. Such perceptions caused him to react sharply; he tried to counter Lebanese 'plots' by aiding Khuri's domestic rivals. Things were made worse by Za'im's habitually erratic behaviour and his impulsive and at times showy conduct which often conveyed a sense of menace even where none was intended. Little wonder, then, that Syrian—Lebanese relations soon became tense.

As a result of Za'im's approaches, some of Khuri's and Sulh's opponents began expressing support for the new regime in Syria. Karami, Junbalat, Chamoun, and even Sami al-Sulh made pilgrimages to Damascus, receiving promises from Za'im to back them in their struggle against the Lebanese regime which was now cast in the role of their common enemy. Following his visit to Damascus in mid-April, Chamoun told British diplomats that he was convinced that Khuri would not serve out his second term. Karami said that Za'im's promises to the Lebanese opposition had included the supply of arms and army personnel.[8]

In addition, Za'im was in touch, through a variety of conduits, with the PPS and its leader Sa'ada whom he offered asylum in Syria. This created mounting tension between the PPS and the Lebanese government and sharpened Lebanon's sense of being threatened by Za'im. Yet it was soon to became apparent how hollow this threat was: when it came to the crunch,

Za'im extradited Sa'ada to Lebanon. (For a full account of the PPS and its activities at the time, see the following chapter.)

A second cause of Lebanese concern was Za'im's hectic activity in inter-Arab affairs. Lebanese leaders had become accustomed to think of all-Arab affairs as their own particular forte and as a source of strength. Now Za'im threatened to turn them into a hostile sphere. Initially, Beirut suspected that Za'im was on the point of joining Iraq and Jordan in merging the Fertile Crescent or Greater Syria region into a single state whose very existence would pose a danger to Lebanon. The enthusiastic welcome Za'im's regime had found in Baghdad and Amman evoked Lebanese concern and roused the suspicion that Iraq and Jordan had been involved in the coup from the start. Khuri noted in his memoirs: 'Even if it is ... a takeover carried out in the domestic context, it stands to reason that the Hashemites in Baghdad and Amman, with the British in the wings, will exploit it for their own purposes.'[9]

The near-panic of the Lebanese leadership is reflected in a conversation Khuri had with British Minister Houstoun Boswall in mid-April 1949. Khuri opened by admitting that events in Damascus had caused him great concern. Lebanon, he went on, had always been at pains to maintain close relations with Syria. This had been made possible because Quwatli had accepted the 1943 National Pact. But Quwatli's fall from power had created a new situation. In what sounded like a cry of panic, he went on to say that if Iraq was ready to respect the pact, he (Khuri) would be ready to cooperate with Baghdad even in the realization of the Fertile Crescent union scheme. He added that Sulh would soon visit Baghdad and that he himself was on the point of sending a friendly message to 'Abdallah.[10]

Khuri's profession of readiness to accept the Fertile Crescent scheme must of course be taken with a pinch of salt. He was addressing the representative of a power who, so he believed, had backed Za'im or was at least likely to exploit his rise to power to advance British–Hashemite interests. He was trying to sound out the minister as to Britain's intention and to convey a message of good-will likely to remove the threat he thought Za'im was posing. Simultaneously, Foreign Minister Faranjiyya called in the ministers of all the great powers in order to express Lebanon's concern over the rise of Za'im.[11] At the same time, Beirut was trying to enlist Egypt and Saudi Arabia, its traditional allies in opposing Hashemite union schemes, on its side. In a personal note to King Ibn Sa'ud, Khuri asked him to reaffirm his country's commitment to Lebanon's independence.[12] Also in April, Lebanon's representative at the UN, Charles Malik, asked for a meeting with the Israeli representative, Tuviya Arazi. Malik may have acted on his personal initiative rather than on instructions from Beirut. Even so, his step reflects the sense of stress prevalent in the Lebanese establishment. He asked Arazi about Israel's attitude towards Za'im and towards a possible Syrian–Iraqi–Jordanian union. Arazi replied that Israel would support the continued existence of a separate Syrian state and Malik did not conceal his relief and satisfaction.[13]

It did not take long, however, for Za'im to change track and dissociate himself from the Baghdad–Amman axis. This did not allay Lebanon's fears. What now troubled Beirut was Egypt's apparent backing of Za'im. Soon after his takeover, he had met a delegation of Egyptian army officers in Damascus and, on 21 April 1949, he himself visited Cairo. Later, it became apparent that Cairo's aim had been to stop Za'im from getting too close to the Hashemites. Egyptian diplomacy did indeed have a moderating influence on Za'im and was thus helpful to Lebanon; Beirut need not have worried.

Za'im's actual aims regarding Lebanon seem to have been rather modest. First, he wanted to deter Beirut, and Sulh personally, from acting against the new Syrian regime. After a while, as a result of Syrian pressure, the Lebanese press toned down its attacks on Za'im.[14] Secondly, Za'im wished Lebanon formally to recognize his regime. But Beirut preferred to wait until the great powers and the principal Arab states, especially Egypt, had granted it their recognition. Once this was done, Lebanon followed suit (on 23 April 1949).[15] Lebanese–Syrian tension immediately abated somewhat. The next day Sulh visited Damascus and was received by Za'im. The latter spoke of Syria's desire for better mutual relations, particularly in the economic field. He concluded by attacking the Hashemite rulers who, he told Sulh, were a menace to Syria and Lebanon alike.[16]

Mutual suspicions had already accumulated to such an extent, however, that they could not be totally removed. Bilateral relations remained under a cloud. An incident on 9 May 1949 revived both countries' misgivings and quickly escalated into a crisis: a Syrian army intelligence detachment led by Captain Tabara entered southern Lebanon in broad daylight and killed a Lebanese citizen whom the Syrians suspected of spying for Israel. Beirut was not only conscious of the severe infringement of Lebanese sovereignty implied by this act, but also thought it signalled Syria's intention to liquidate Syrian political refugees in Lebanon. The detachment was captured. When Za'im demanded its prompt release, Lebanon refused. Za'im then closed the Syrian–Lebanese border and prohibited the movement of goods from Lebanon into Syria.[17] The Syrian media immediately joined the fray. A commentary over Radio Damascus blamed Lebanon for the outbreak of the crisis and spoke of 'a small group in Lebanon who endeavor to drive a wedge between sister states and who make efforts to distance Lebanon from every [joint] Arab action'. The commentator went on to say that this group was making spurious claims to represent Lebanese public opinion, when in actual fact 'the Lebanese people follow with indignation the artificial struggle [conducted by this group] over the question of Lebanese sovereignty. After all, the maintenance of Lebanese sovereignty is closely linked with the maintenance of Syria's sovereignty.'[18]

Lebanon appealed for help to Egypt and Saudi Arabia and by their mediation the crisis was resolved. The border was reopened and Syria and

Lebanon agreed to arbitration regarding the incident. The arbitration panel found that Syria had indeed violated Lebanese sovereignty, but that, in the circumstances, it had been morally and politically justified in doing so.[19]

Reviewing the sequence of events, one is led to conclude that, once again, the crisis was psychological rather than substantive. It is hard to assume that the dispatch of the intelligence detachment was to be the opening shot of broader anti-Lebanese designs on the part of Za'im. Rather, it was his rashness and lack of forethought that led him to encroach on a matter as delicate and sensitive as the issue of Lebanese sovereignty. The ensuing crisis did not reflect the significance of the actual incident; rather, it attested to the overall weight of suspicion and enmity which had accumulated on both sides since Za'im took up power. This accounts for the unwonted toughness of the Lebanese reaction in refusing to release the Syrian soldiers. Za'im for his part overreacted in a manner characteristic of him, but he, too, was careful not to let the crisis slip out of control and sought ways and means to resolve it. He decided to send his foreign minister, 'Adil Arsalan, to Beirut to meet his Lebanese counterpart Faranjiyya. It was at their meeting on 22 May 1949 that inter-Arab arbitration was agreed upon. The following day, two Syrian emissaries personally informed Khuri of Za'im's consent to the arbitration plan.[20]

The matter did not rest there. On 3 June, another Syrian detachment penetrated into southern Lebanon, probably to capture and punish Lebanese citizens who had helped in the capture of the soldiers involved in the earlier incident. The detachment was stopped by Lebanese army units and, this time, Za'im hurried to announce that his men had entered Lebanese territory by mistake. He then took offence at Beirut's vehemently hostile reaction and renewed the ban on the transit of goods across the border.[21]

A month later, on 24 June 1949, Za'im finally made a more determined attempt to clear the air. He met Khuri and Sulh at Shtura (in Lebanon). The date was significant: the following day, a plebiscite was due to be held in Syria to confirm Za'im in the presidency. At Shatura, Za'im endeavoured to allay Lebanese suspicions. Khuri later quoted from the protocol of the meeting: 'Za'im stated that the purpose of the meeting was to set the minds of Lebanon's leaders at rest and to declare before them his goodwill [and] his respect for the independence and sovereignty of Lebanon and his readiness to act for the maintenance of the good fraternal relations existing between the two states.' Za'im apologized for the two border incidents, stressing that they had taken place without his knowledge, and expressing the hope that 'nothing liable to impair the friendship between the two sister states will occur in the future'. He concluded by saying that his principal aim at this critical juncture was to strengthen the Syrian army as a means to consolidate the Syrian state. None of his actions should cause apprehension in Lebanon nor be construed as being directed against it.[22]

And yet only a few days later, when the PPS crisis broke out (see next chapter), the sorry state of Lebanese–Syrian relations became apparent again. With his usual lack of prudence, Za'im had encouraged PPS leader Sa'ada in his struggle against the Lebanese regime. When this led to a confrontation, Za'im reacted aggressively to the point of hysteria, only to recoil quickly and eventually extradite Sa'ada.

On 14 August 1949, Za'im was overthrown and put to death by Sami al-Hinawi. Beirut did not conceal its satisfaction at this turn of events,[23] but it soon became clear that the new ruler was no friendlier towards Lebanon. Having deteriorated under Za'im, relations between Beirut and Damascus remained tense under Hinawi.

## The Dissolution of the Customs Union

As we have seen, Lebanon and Syria continued to constitute a single economic area after independence, just as they had done before. The principal instrument for ensuring this was their customs union. At the time of the negotiations with France, the union had suited Syrian interests in underlining the Syrian–Lebanese community of interests. Later, it had sustained the hopes of those who kept thinking in terms of Lebanon's eventual 'return' to Syria. In Lebanon, economic interest in the union easily prevailed over the feeling that it detracted somewhat from the paraphernalia of independence. Transit trade with and through Syria was too central to Lebanon's prosperity to allow doubts on the subject. So were imports from Syria, especially of grain and other foodstuffs.

A series of agreements had formalized economic relations between the two countries. They regulated the transfer of the so-called 'common interests' (see Chapter 5) from France to Syria and Lebanon and laid down that 56 per cent of the revenue from them and from customs dues should go to Syria, the rest to Lebanon.

Beginning in the late 1940s, Syria had moved towards a more closely government-controlled economy. Protectionist policies began to be applied to economic branches thought capable of advancing the country towards economic independence. These included farming by more modern methods as well as some industries. Protective customs rates were set to allow them to compete with foreign products. Work was started on a port at Ladhiqiyya in order better to integrate the surrounding 'Alawi areas into the overall Syrian economy as well as to lessen dependence on the Lebanese ports. This ran counter to Lebanon's interests, according to which Beirut was to be the principal port of entry for the entire eastern Mediterranean. Overall, the new Syrian policies contrasted starkly with the Lebanese free-market and free-trade economy. Lebanon's economic elite wielded both political and economic power and a free economy lay at the core of their 'concept of Lebanon', of its character and essence, and of its future course as they saw it.[24]

The scene was thus set for an eruption of discord between Beirut and

Damascus on all aspects of economic policy. The main bone of contention was Syria's demand to set higher customs rates for imports. This was intended to improve Syria's foreign trade balance, prevent the flight of capital to Beirut (quickened by political instability in Syria), keep the value of its currency high and, finally, secure a good price for Syrian wheat.[25] Such policies also accorded with the nationalist and anti-western sentiments now shaping the Syrian public mood. They were illustrated by Syria's attitude during the negotiations regarding the laying of the oil pipe-line from Saudi Arabia to the Mediterranean (the Tapline). Its principal beneficiaries were the Lebanese who would receive handsome royalties and for whom the refinery to be built at Tripoli would provide thousands of new jobs. They therefore hurried to conclude the matter, signing an agreement with the American company in August 1946. But the Syrians held out for better terms. In any case the prevalent anti-western atmosphere would have rendered it difficult to sign an agreement. Lebanon was forced to wait. It was only in 1949, under Za'im, that Syria too came to an agreement with Tapline. As usual, Za'im was motivated by seeking advantage for Syria rather than by consideration for the all-Arab point of view. (In the meantime, Beirut had already informed Tapline that it would agree to the pipeline passing through Jordan and Palestine rather than through Syria.)[26]

Another example was provided by Franco-Lebanese and Franco-Syrian monetary agreements which were supposed to take care of a number of financial and economic loose ends left over from before independence. Negotiations were fully coordinated between Beirut and Damascus, but at the last moment Syria demurred. Damascus criticized Beirut for not waiting for Syria and threatened to dissolve the customs union and proclaim an economic boycott against Lebanon.[27] Under the shadow of the war in Palestine, the dispute was patched up, some issues being resolved, others postponed. The status quo remained in force. Some time later, the Syrians signed an agreement with France which differed but little from the Franco-Lebanese one. Henceforth, though, the future of the customs union was in doubt.

As with all other aspects of Syrian–Lebanese relations, economic links were also affected by the rise of Za'im. On 5 June 1949, Za'im handed the Lebanese an ultimatum demanding that they choose between three options: (1) full economic union with Syria; (2) complete economic separation; or (3) new arrangements for bilateral economic ties in accordance with Syria's demands. A month later, under pressure from France and Egypt, Za'im withdrew his demands and concluded an interim agreement with Lebanon stipulating that further discussions were to be postponed. (The agreement may have been part of a broader deal, with another clause providing for Sa'ada's extradition.)[28]

Za'im's downfall raised hopes in Beirut that the economic differences between the two countries could now be settled by businesslike negotiations, as had happened in the past. But this was not to be. The new Syrian regime did not revert to the friendly ways of Quwatli. The new strongman, Adib al-Shishakli (who had replaced Sami al-Hinawi shortly after the latter's assumption of power) was known to be a sympathizer of the PPS. Khalid al-'Azm, Shishakli's prime minister when the crucial decisions were taken in Damascus, was an old personal enemy of Sulh. The mutual suspicions bred under Za'im remained very much alive under Shishakli. Moreover, steady relations depended on political stability in both capitals, but Damascus had now entered a long period of volatile politics. The new leaders were only too susceptible to the push and pull of radical pan-Arab and anti-western crowd sentiments. The two countries found they were following greatly divergent courses, first on economic policies, later on foreign policies as well.

On 7 March 1950, Syria presented Lebanon with another ultimatum which again offered Beirut the choice between full economic union or economic separation. As they usually did in such circumstances, the Lebanese asked for extra time to consider the issue, hoping to arrive at a temporary compromise solution to tide them over the immediate crisis. But Syria did not respond and, on 15 March, announced the dissolution of the customs union. Limitations were placed on the movement of goods from Lebanon into Syria and customs houses were put up on the border.[29]

There were indeed substantive issues involved in the economic dispute. Nevertheless, Syria's decision seemed hasty and one cannot fail to notice the contrast between the high-handed methods now being used in Damascus and the traditional tolerance and patience prevalent in the past. The personal hostility between the two prime ministers had much to do with the harshness of the present methods.[30] In a section of his memoirs dealing with the economic crisis, 'Azm accused Sulh of placing his personal political prestige higher than the maintenance of the customs union. Sulh, he went on, was so accustomed to getting his way with the Syrians that he rejected the ultimatum in the expectation that, this time too, the Syrians would not go through with it.[31]

The Lebanese, too, did not act in their accustomed manner. In rejecting the Syrian ultimatum, they seemed to have invited the dissolution of the customs union. There had already been some earlier indications pointing in the same direction. In her *The Merchant Republic of Lebanon*, Carolyn Gates concluded that the preservation of the existing economic relations with Syria had become too costly an option for the Lebanese, because it would have placed limitations on their free economy. For reasons already referred to above, a free-market economy was vital to them. If they wished to preserve it, they had no choice other than rejecting the Syrian demands.[32] Moreover, Lebanon's leaders took heart comparing the strength of Lebanon's economy with Syria's economic weakness. The international backing they knew they enjoyed encouraged them. They remembered the heavy blows Za'im had directed at them, but also recalled that they had known how to parry them.

In short, they had learnt that, in order to steer their own course, they could defy Syria with comparative impunity.

Overall, economic separation from Syria caused some damage to the Lebanese economy. Syria had been Lebanon's most important supplier of agricultural produce. Moreover, the closure of the southern borders as a result of the war in Palestine had left Lebanon with Syria as its only land bridge with the rest of the Arab world. The effects of the rift with Syria were most strongly felt in Tripoli where trade with Syria dominated economic life. The town had long been resentful of the development of Beirut as the country's major port. With its large Sunni majority, it had always been in the van of demands for union with Syria. In October 1950, a three-day strike was proclaimed in Tripoli in protest against the economic distress caused by the new relationship with Syria. But the strike also had a local political background which, in the final analysis, may have counted for more than its ostensible cause. This had to do with the local power struggles which had revived after the death of 'Abd al-Hamid Karami. 'Abd al-Hamid's son Rashid was now trying to make his way into the inner circles of local and national power; opposite him, his uncle Mustafa, a former mayor of Tripoli, claimed first place for himself. And Mustafa was of the opinion that vehement pan-Arab and pro-Syrian attitudes were likely to further his cause.[33]

For all the difficulties it now had to undergo, the Lebanese economy soon demonstrated its inherent strength in admirable fashion. Except for certain branches of industry and agriculture, the crisis left no lasting marks. The average income remained what it had been; customs revenue did not diminish; and banking prospered spectacularly during these years. Newly-developed business with Jordan, Iraq and the Persian Gulf area made up for the Syrian trade (which diminished but certainly did not cease). A considerable share of Syria's foreign trade continued passing through Beirut.[34] In the long run, the economic separation from Syria added an important tier to Lebanon's sovereignty and independence. In the absence of the former close economic ties, Syria was now less capable than before of exercising domestic pressure from within Lebanon. Previously pro-Syrian circles in Lebanon were now deterred by the perpetual instability in Damascus. In February 1950, Kamil Muruwwa, editor of *Al-Hayat* and a well-known advocate of pan-Arab ideas, published an editorial under the heading: 'Syria, the Sick Man'. He wrote: 'The Syrian state exists on paper only and is torn between competing blocs and contradictory intentions. [These are being] pursued with daring and resolution, but daring and resolution do not derive from any clear concept ... Everybody sinks like in a sea, and Syria goes down with them.'[35]

The deterioration in Syrian–Lebanese relations was not only, perhaps not even primarily, a matter of economics. More significant was the loss of friendly support from Damascus, following the fall from power of the group of old political allies there, headed by Quwatli. Their attitude had contributed to the maintenance of Lebanon's perpetually precarious domestic equilibrium and of its delicately balanced foreign policy. Their overthrow affected the high morale and self-confidence with which Khuri and his government wished to inspire their country's political public. The crisis in relations with Syria may have been a blessing in the long run, but in the short run it soon added a heavy burden to Khuri's already difficult position.

## CHAPTER 10

# The Confrontation with
# the PPS, 1947–49

On 8 July 1949, at 4 a.m., Antun Sa'ada, leader of the Syrian Nationalist Party or Parti Populaire Syrien (PPS) was executed after a summary trial before a Lebanese military court. He had been charged with an attempt to carry out a military coup and to seize power in Lebanon. But his execution must be seen against a broader background; it allowed the Lebanese regime to put an end to the menace Sa'ada's movement had long posed to the government, to the country's stability and perhaps to its very existence. Sa'ada's death did not have the expected results; rather than calm down the Lebanese scene, its reverberations added greatly to Khuri's difficulties at home and abroad. Its most dire consequence was the assassination, in July 1951, of Riyad al-Sulh by members of Sa'ada's movement avenging their leader's death.

In studies of the period, the PPS and its leaders are usually spoken of as operating outside the Lebanese political system, determined to undermine and, in due course, to overturn it. The eventual confrontation between the PPS and the regime is therefore mostly described as an inevitable ideological clash between two incompatible world-views. The claim by Khuri's government that Sa'ada had planned to bring down the regime (a claim supported only by evidence obtained from Sa'ada's men after the event)[1] was accepted unquestioningly by the Lebanese public. It seemed to fit Sa'ada's aims and concepts perfectly and provided justification for forcible action against the party and the execution of its leader.

A careful scrutiny of the evidence we now possess leads to different conclusions. The confrontation with the PPS should rather be viewed as one move among many to ensure the survival of the existing Lebanese regime in its struggle against domestic and foreign enemies. Sa'ada was no more than a marginal figure in this contest. At most times, he seems to have been a mere instrument used by one side or the other. Until the eve of the final confrontation, the Lebanese regarded the PPS as an odd but legitimate part of the country's politics (much as they regarded the communists and several other smaller political groupings). For many years, establishment figures did

176

not hesitate to cooperate with the PPS. After Sa'ada's return home in 1947, Khuri's rivals – among them Chamoun, Junbalat and even the Edde family – sought contact with him. Hostile to Khuri as they were, these men were part and parcel of the Lebanese system and were committed to its perpetuation. Cooperating with Sa'ada did not, in their view, imply a desire to subvert it. Moreover, the threat to Lebanon, or more precisely to the Lebanese regime, did not so much derive from the PPS ideology even though its programme did negate the existence of a separate Lebanese state; rather, it stemmed from the wish of Khuri's opponents – whether domestic or, in Za'im's time, Syrian – to turn Sa'ada into an instrument to serve their own purposes. The sharpening of the struggle between Khuri and his domestic opponents, and the widening of the gulf between Lebanon and Syria after the advent of Za'im, in turn exacerbated the confrontation between the regime and the PPS.

Rather than being the villain of the piece, Sa'ada thus was to some extent a victim of circumstances. The weakness of the Lebanese regime, its irritability, the panic to which it was then becoming subject – all these had as much to do with Sa'ada's trial and execution as his own actions. Yet he was no innocent victim: he entered in the confrontation with open eyes and willingly allowed Khuri's rivals to exploit him. Moreover, he did not hesitate to challenge publicly the Lebanese political system and to question the right of the Lebanese state to exist. In doing so, he hastened his own end.

Antun Sa'ada, a Greek Orthodox, was born on 1 March 1904 in Shuwayr in the Matan region of Mt Lebanon. His father left Lebanon before the First World War, first for Egypt, later for South America. After the death of his mother in 1920, Antun joined his father in Brazil where the latter published a periodical called *Al-Majalla*. Antun helped with editing it. In 1928, the younger Sa'ada returned to the Levant, first living in Damascus (where he joined the staff of the daily *Al-Ayyam*), but shortly afterwards moving back to Lebanon. He made ends meet by giving private lessons, then secured a position as instructor of German at the American University of Beirut.[2] On 18 November 1932, Sa'ada founded the PPS as an instrument to propagate the ideological concepts that he had started developing while in Brazil.[3] From its inception, the party's paraphernalia, structure and methods of organization had certain fascist characteristics. Sa'ada had members call him 'the leader' (Za'im) and salute each other with a raised hand and with the words: 'Long live the leader.' A bolt of lightning was chosen as the movement's emblem. Its hymn opened with the words 'Syria, Syria above all'.[4] While his models cannot be mistaken, there is no evidence that Sa'ada or members of his party had any formal contacts with either the Nazis or the fascist party or, later, with the Axis powers.

Sa'ada set out his ideological tenets in a long series of writings, notably in his books *The Basic Principles* [of the PPS] (*Al-Mubadi' al-Aasasiyya*), first published in 1932, and *The Genesis of Nations* (*Nushu' al-Umam*), published in

1937. The core of his doctrine was the belief in the existence of a Syrian (as distinct from an Arab) nation. He wrote:

> The Syrian nation is the product of the unity of the Syrian people, who have inhabited the area throughout its long history. All the peoples who inhabited Syria were in the end capable of dissolving into one harmonious organic unity, constituting the Syrian nation – all, that is, except the Jews, who retained 'alien and exclusive racial loyalties' and could not be integrated in the Syrian nation.[5]

This followed from Sa'ada's definition of a nation. It was 'a group of people living together in a definite region of the world, separated from other regions by natural boundaries, and bound together by common material and spiritual interests and a common destiny [and] whose interaction with it [the region] through the course of evolution brands it with peculiarities and qualities which distinguish it from other groups'.[6]

Hence the importance Sa'ada attributed to defining the boundaries of the Syrian fatherland, i.e. of that 'geographical environment in which the Syrian nation evolved'. They went much beyond the scope usually ascribed to Syria, extending

> from the Taurus Range in the north-west and the Zagros Mountains in the north-east to the Suez Canal and the Red Sea in the south and includes the Sinai Peninsula and the Gulf of Aqaba, and from the Syrian Sea (Mediterranean) in the west, including the island of Cyprus, to the arch of the Arabian desert and Persian Gulf in the east. (This region is also called the Syrian Fertile Crescent, the island of Cyprus being its star.)[7]

Originally, Cyprus, Iraq and the corner of western Iran did not figure as parts of Syria; they were added in the last and definitive edition of the *Basic Principles* in 1947.[8]

Being an Arab had no inherent importance as far as PPS doctrine was concerned. According to Sa'ada, neither a common language nor religion was sufficient to constitute a nation. The Syrians were a nation; the Arabs were not. Rather, they were divided into a number of nations, of which Syria was one. In time, however, he took a less dismissive view of Arabism, but still claimed that Syria was superior to other Arab nations. The Arab movement which he expected to come into existence would, he thought, be basically Muslim, would drive off Christian Arabs and would not cooperate with Christians. The various Arab nations might eventually arrive at a measure of political cooperation, but this, he argued, could happen only when each of them had realized its own unique and separate character. Then, an all-Arab front could come into being – to be led, as a matter of course, by Syria.[9]

Blending politics and religion was harmful to the existence of nations. Sa'ada asserted that state and religion must be separate; the state must be secular. 'Every Syrian', he wrote, 'has the right to hold any religious belief he wants ... But he should always remember that his correlative duty is to be a true social nationalist, true to his nation and his country.'[10] He himself was a sceptic. According to *Nushu' al-Umam*, Sa'ada's conclusion was that there was no such thing as revealed religion and that 'religious beliefs belonged to a stage when science was not yet sufficiently developed to explain the mysteries of life'.[11]

Sa'ada thought of his party as the elite cadre foreordained to lead the Syrian nation towards its destiny. To do so, it might have to take power by violent means. He asserted:

This elite group would lead the people, in justice and love, to realize its being and free it from all its evils and its nightmares. After assuring a deep spiritual unity ... and only then, the populace will be able and hence allowed to rule itself. Otherwise, elections are a mere farce ... Consequently, the rulers of the Syrian state should not be politicians but worthy individuals who are viewed by the people as their true and capable leaders ... whom they would support trustfully and obediently.[12]

It is worth noting that Sa'ada was not the first to speak in terms of a Syrian nation. Such ideas first came to the fore towards the mid-nineteenth century following the *Tanzimat* (the Ottoman reforms) among Christian intellectuals. To some extent, Sa'ada was influenced by Henri Lammens, whose book *La Syrie* was published in 1921, as well as by Philip Hitti's *Suriyya wal-Suriyyun min Nafidhat al-Ta'rikh* (Syria and the Syrians in History) which appeared in 1926. His being a Greek Orthodox had much to do with the formation of his world-view. Members of his community were dispersed throughout the Middle East and were everywhere dependent on the good graces of the Muslim majority in whose midst they were living. For that reason, they did not develop a nationalism of their own as the Maronites had done; rather, wherever they were, they searched for a common denominator transcending religion and capable of uniting them and their Muslim neighbours, whether as Arabs or, as in Sa'ada's case, as Syrians. They rejected the Maronite idea of National Home for the Christians.

Within a few years of being formed, the PPS had attracted several thousand followers throughout Syria and Lebanon. Most were Greek Orthodox, some were Druse. Originally, the party was a clandestine movement, using the appellation *al-Sharika al-Tijariyya al-Suriyya* (The Syrian Trading Company) as a code-name, but its rapid growth made covert operation impractical. In November 1935, apparently acting on information supplied by an insider, the French uncovered the organization and started making life difficult for its members. Sa'ada was arrested several times, being detained for several months on each occasion. The party's activities were at times banned, at times subjected to various limitations.[13]

Unlike the French, the Lebanese authorities at first tolerated the PPS. President Edde and Prime Minister Ahdab disregarded the fact that the party's doctrine negated the existence of a separate Lebanese entity. They successfully intervened with the French for the release of most of the PPS detainees and, until the late 1930s, allowed the party to operate freely in Lebanon. To justify their leniency (or, at times, even their outright support, including grants of money), they could point to solemn assurances Sa'ada had given them. Party doctrine notwithstanding, he vowed to them that he did not mean to harm Lebanon or work for a union with Syria. All he wanted to do, he pledged, was to promote the idea of Syrian nationalism.[14] French intelligence reports, however, pointed to the political interests underlying the attitudes of both Edde and Ahdab: they wished to turn the PPS into servile instruments of their own policies. Edde wanted to exploit it for his struggle against pan-Arabism, making use of the anti-Arab element in the PPS ideology; Ahdab hoped to use it in his contest with Sulh and other Sunni leaders.[15]

Two conclusions can be drawn from Sa'ada's relations with the Lebanese regime in the later half of the 1930s. First, Sa'ada was prepared to play a role within the system, relying on the practice of political pluralism so cardinal to it. This need not come as a surprise; at the time, other groupings too were negating a separate Lebanon, yet operated within the existing system and were considered a legitimate part of it. Suffice it to recall Karami's appeal for the 'return' to Syria of Lebanon, or parts of it; or Edde's advocacy of a smaller Lebanon. Second, Sa'ada tended to take part in struggles not primarily concerning himself or the PPS. He would eventually pay a high price for this inclination. He may have felt that this was a useful way of advancing the fortunes of his party, but mainly it seems to have been the result of political immaturity. Lebanese politicians more experienced than himself were quick to exploit it.

In 1938, Sa'ada went on a fund-raising trip among Syrian emigrants in South America. The deteriorating relations between himself and the French authorities and his fear of being arrested once again may have made his departure more urgent. On his way to South America, he stopped over in Italy and Germany. This aroused French suspicions of Sa'ada's possible cooperation with the Axis. There was nothing to substantiate them. To be on the safe side, the French banned the PPS as soon as war broke out and arrested many of its functionaries. Sa'ada was not allowed back into the Levant.[16]

On the eve of the entry of the allies in the Levant states, French High Commissioner Dentz released most of the PPS detainees. He did so in response to appeals from a number of Lebanese notables, among them dignitaries of the Maronite church like archbishop Karam of Mt Lebanon, Sunni clerics like the mufti of Lebanon, and several politicians. Among the latter was Chamoun, who was later to become the principal Lebanese ally of the PPS.[17] Whatever the specific political interests of each of them, their lobbying for the PPS reinforces our above conclusion: the PPS was felt to be a legitimate component of the Lebanese system.

Once the allies were in control, the PPS started moving towards the centre of the Lebanese political scene, taking its stand within the bounds of the Lebanese consensus such as it was at the time. Led by Sa'ada's deputy, Ni'mat Thabit, it supported the struggle for independence from France and backed Khuri during the November 1943 crisis (see Chapter 4). The party developed a more distinctly Lebanese orientation, allowing the emphasis on union with Syria to taper off. This was reflected in the new name it adopted: Al-Hizb al-Qawmi (National Party), dropping the word 'Syrian' from the former name. In May 1944, the government officially allowed the party to resume its activities. The cabinet had been urged to do so by Chamoun (then minister of the interior) whom the PPS had backed in the 1943 elections.[18]

In the circumstances then prevailing, the French suspected that the British were backing the PPS. They were led to think so by (among other things) the similarity between the concept of Syrian unity propounded by the PPS, and the Hashemite Greater Syrian scheme.[19] Later, French as well as US sources reported that British pressure had led to the government giving permission for Sa'ada to return to Lebanon. He travelled on the same special plane that brought Qa'uqji home, both arriving on 2 March 1947. A US intelligence report spoke of Lebanese 'uneasiness over the return of these two exiled leaders and their simultaneous arrival. It places a militant aspect on the National Syrian Party.' Their plane also carried the assistant British military attaché, leading to 'conjecture that the British have arranged the move for if a coup d'etat were planned to set up a Greater Syria, no better medium could be found'.[20] This is, however, not borne out by British sources. These show that contacts with the PPS were maintained merely for information-gathering, much like contacts with a multitude of other political groupings.[21]

The Lebanese authorities had allowed Sa'ada to return only after his followers had promised that their leader would not threaten the regime. Some politicians, though, had positively wanted him back. Chamoun has already been mentioned. Junbalat and Far'un, both then members of the cabinet, also favoured Sa'ada's return. They (and, for that matter, Khuri too) wished to exploit the party's influence for their own purposes, being aware of its growing number of sympathizers, especially in the Mt Lebanon area. This was important against the background of the upcoming elections. While still abroad, Sa'ada had promised that his men in Mt Lebanon would cast their votes for Khuri's Constitutional Bloc.[22]

Changes in the party's attitudes which had occurred during Sa'ada's absence were not to the latter's liking. He felt that they connoted a retreat from the party's original precepts and that his position as leader was being eroded.[23] On his very first day home, he publicly reaffirmed his adherence to the old tenets of the PPS, first and foremost the principle that the existence of the Lebanese state had no ethnic, geographical or economic justification.[24] His words attracted much attention and within twenty-four hours he was summoned to be interrogated by the General Security Service in order to explain his statement. He refused to present himself and fled into hiding. An arrest warrant was then issued against him.[25] But Sa'ada did not seek a head-on confrontation. As usual with him, he first used strident rhetoric (probably for internal party consumption), then immediately tried to allay tension and to convince the authorities that no threat against them had been intended. From his hide-away, he sent a letter to General Security, asserting that his arrival statement had not been intended as an attack on the Lebanese entity.[26] More than that: in a press interview he averred that he now accepted Lebanon's separate existence as justified, at least in part, on political and religious grounds. But, he added, he continued to believe that the Lebanese formed part of the Syrian nation. Interestingly, he also told the interviewer that he had considered running for the Chamber, but had had second thoughts, being afraid of electoral fraud.[27] This clearly pointed in the direction of acceptance of Lebanese realities and of operating within their framework, at least in the short run. The realization that this was the case probably stopped the authorities from arresting him, even though the location of his hide-out was an open secret. The public soon lost interest in Sa'ada. The warrant of arrest was revoked in September 1947 and, following another solemn declaration that he respected the Lebanese authorities, his file was closed.[28]

Being no longer under pressure, Sa'ada started rebuilding his position within the PPS and returning its doctrine to its pristine state. He changed the party's name once again, now calling it the Nationalist Socialist Party, reflecting his increased interest in socialist tenets.[29] He purged the cadres of members (including deputy leader Thabit and Ma'mun Ilyas and As'ad al-Ashqar) whom he accused of having deviated from the party's principles by recognizing the existence of a Lebanese nation. He also used the occasion to rid himself of two members, Fa'iz Sa'igh and Ghassan Tuwayni, who, he thought, might become a threat to his leadership.[30]

Sa'ada's alliance with Chamoun and Junbalat – Khuri's principal opponents – caused a change for the worse in the government's attitude towards him. Sa'ada had proved useful to his allies when he backed their campaign against Sulh over the conduct of the war in Palestine.[31] At the time, Sa'ada published a series of articles in the newspaper *Kull Shay'*, arguing that the defeat in Palestine was proof of the failure of the pan-Arab doctrine.[32] The outcome of the war seems to have brought more people, including many Sunnis, into the ranks of the PPS. The editor of *Kull Shay'*, Muhammad Ba'albaki who had been a well-known Arab nationalist and supporter of Sulh, now joined the PPS. We find hints that his 'desertion' caused Sulh to turn against the party.[33] It remains doubtful whether Sulh saw in Sa'ada a real competitor for power within the Sunni community. But his attacks on the war issue and his cooperation with the opposition leaders had now stamped him as an enemy of both Sulh and Khuri.

The Lebanese regime soon came to think of itself as facing a common front formed by Za'im in Syria, its traditional rivals at home and its new adversary, Sa'ada. Za'im's takeover in Syria a few months later marked a turning point in the history of the PPS and further worsened the government's stance towards it. Khuri noted in his memoirs that some time after Za'im's takeover, 'we received information on the PPS's intention to engage in violence on a large scale, intended to develop into a domestic revolt for the overthrow [of the regime]. The authorized bodies in Lebanon also received information on contacts between the party and extremist opposition elements, inspired from abroad, with the aim of setting Lebanon ablaze.'[34]

It is against this background that, in the summer of 1949, the government decided to take action against the PPS. It was a decision taken from a position of weakness, from an overall sense of being threatened by Za'im, and from a belief that the PPS was turning into a tangible menace to the existence of Lebanon. Yet Sa'ada was no more than a pawn on a chessboard on which a larger game was being played. True, he had chosen the road of confrontation, but he may not have understood what course events were now bound to take. He may have deluded himself that, as in the past, the Lebanese government would recoil from serious action; or else he may have believed in the promises given him by Za'im as well as by Chamoun and Junbalat.

Other parties in Lebanon had not shared the forbearance towards the PPS characteristic of the government in the past. The communists always considered it a fascist movement and had been hostile to it all along. So had the Phalanges who saw themselves as the guardians of Lebanon's independence. But the tension between them and the PPS was not merely a matter of ideology; differences in ideology also existed between the PPS and Edde's National Bloc and between it and the Arab nationalists, yet they did not lead to a comparable degree of enmity. Between the communists, the Phalanges and the PPS, rivalry became more acute because all three appealed to the same target population: the Christian lower-middle classes and, in the case of the Phalanges, the Maronite lower-middle classes. This caused them to state their ideological differences more stridently, to attack each other vehemently, and eventually to engage in violence against each other.

Violence peaked on 9 June 1949 in a clash in Beirut between men of the PPS and the Phalanges. It started with a Phalanges meeting at a local coffee shop situated opposite a building to which the editorial offices of the PPS organ *Al-Jil al-Jadid* had recently been moved. When cries 'Long live Syria, long live Sa'ada' were heard from the building, the Phalanges members felt provoked and a violent clash ensued. Soon several hundred men were involved. Shots were fired and several persons were killed. The incident ended with the Phalanges burning down the building occupied by *Al-Jil al-Jadid*.[35]

The reasons for the incident are not altogether clear. There is no evidence of its having been planned in advance by either side. That did not prevent Sa'ada from claiming immediately that the government, and Sulh personally, had plotted against his party.[36] The rank and file believed him as a matter of course, and his allies, among them Chamoun and Junbalat, added that Lebanese security had cleared the area ahead of time to make it easier for the Phalanges to attack.[37] These charges were echoed in western diplomatic reports and eventually made their way into several studies of the period.[38]

They were not devoid of logic: the government may well have wanted to exploit the tension between the Phalanges and the PPS in order to work for the elimination of the latter. But it must be remembered that the Phalanges, though generally cooperating with Khuri, were opponents of Sulh. So were the leaders of the PPS who, ever since the advent of Za'im, had blamed Sulh for conspiring against them. At that particular time, the Phalanges were also critical of Khuri, accusing him of having used the government to throw its weight against their candidates in Beirut in the 1947 elections (and even once before, in the 1945 by-elections in the Biqa'). Moreover, in the wake of the June incident, the government had some fifty Phalanges men arrested.[39] The regime's relations with the Phalanges became even more tense after a second major incident, which occurred on 18 July 1949, this time involving the Phalanges and a group of communist port workers in Beirut. The workers apparently shouted hostile slogans when passing the Phalanges headquarters situated near the port. Trigger-happy Phalanges guards at the building opened fire and wounded two of the workers. Police appeared on the scene, broke into the building and conducted a search. A large number of weapons were found. (This was the second such find: earlier, Phalanges men had been caught carrying explosives intended, so the security forces claimed, for use against the director-general of the Ministry of the Interior; the Phalanges had accused him of acting against them during the recent elections.)[40] On 10 June, the government had banned the PPS; now, on 19 July (the day following the port area incident), it issued a decree disbanding *all* para-military organizations, including the Phalanges. In actual fact, however, the decree was carried out only with regard to the PPS.[41]

On balance, then, it does not seem that the government stood behind the June incident. Rather, the Phalanges had their own reasons for taking action; being engaged in a 'battle' with both the communists and the PPS for control of the streets of Beirut, they hoped to deliver a decisive blow. (For a major clash between Phalanges and communists, see below.) But even if the government was not, in fact, behind the incident, it was quick to exploit it. The cabinet convened the same night and, after a session lasting into the small hours of the following morning, decided to proclaim the PPS an illegal organization. Large-scale arrests of PPS men were carried out immediately. Arms were discovered at its headquarters and official sources claimed to have seized documents attesting its intention of bringing down the government. Other documents allegedly exposed prolonged PPS contacts with the Axis powers during the Second World War and with Britain and the USA later on. The PPS was also accused of having been in touch with Israel. Ten thousand Lebanese lira were set aside as a reward for information leading to the capture of Sa'ada. Sa'ada fled to Syria, into the open arms of Za'im.[42]

Throughout June, the security forces continued pursuing PPS men. From his refuge in Syria, Sa'ada reacted by stepping up his attacks on the government; he now started calling for a popular uprising against the regime. In doing so, he may have relied on promises from Za'im to assist him with arms, money and men.[43]

A series of armed clashes between government forces and PPS men followed. On 2 July 1949, a group of PPS members attacked two Lebanese gendarmerie posts in the Biqa', killing one policeman and wounding two. The following day, Sa'ada appealed to all PPS sympathizers in the army, police and gendarmerie to consider themselves forthwith as 'recruits in the ranks of the nationalist socialist revolution of Lebanon and therefore to disregard orders from the despots ruling Lebanon'. They were to proceed at the earliest possible moment to 'the area about to be occupied by the nationalist forces'.[44] On 4 July, gendarmerie units raided the important PPS stronghold at Bashmun and arrested a large number of party followers. In response, Sa'ada proclaimed a general rebellion. Two days later, a group of PPS members crossed from Syria into southern Lebanon, aided by a Syrian intelligence unit, and attacked the police stations at Mashghara and Rashaya. The attacks failed, possibly because of prior warning obtained by the Lebanese. Some of the attackers were captured by the Lebanese army; the rest escaped back into Syria.[45]

The government now came to feel that a veritable military uprising was in the offing. Za'im's overt support for Sa'ada, and his conjectured covert support for other opponents of the regime, contributed a great deal to darken the atmosphere.[46] Khuri had this to say about the situation:

> We soon knew about Sa'ada's finding refuge in Damascus, from where he is directing his supporters, enjoying Za'im's patronage. I called Sulh to discuss the situation and we both expressed anxiety over the security of our country, as well as astonishment at the policy of Za'im who, all of a sudden and with no reason at all, began showing an attitude of estrangement and hostility toward Lebanon, in total contrast to his [earlier] declarations of respect for the links with us.

Khuri added that both the prime minister's office and the army headquarters had received news of PPS plans to attack government buildings and assassinate political figures.[47]

An additional worry for the Lebanese government was the attitude of Britain towards the PPS. For a while it was believed in Beirut that Britain was backing Sa'ada. A British report drafted soon after the June incident referred to the reasons for these conjectures. It stated:

> One of the aims of the P.P.S. was the creation of a Greater Syria ... It was also violently anti-communist. It is perhaps for these reasons that the Party was popularly supposed to enjoy British support. It is unfortunately true that two of the Lebanese staff of the Information Section of this Legation are among

those arrested [in the wake of the incident]. They were dismissed for engaging in local political activities as soon as enquiry had established that they played an active role in the work of the Party.[48]

The Lebanese found confirmation of their suspicions in broadcasts transmitted by the British-run Radio Near East. One commentary, for instance, contrasted Za'im's struggle against 'Levantinism' with Lebanese domestic intrigues and political horse-trading. Sa'ada might indeed be seeking a dictatorial regime, the commentary went on, but the Lebanese government had used the incident to create an artificial crisis, because that was useful for deflecting public opinion from the country's internal disruption.[49] The actual evidence we have suggests, however, that there was no truth in the rumours: the few contacts Britain had maintained with the PPS in the early 1940s were gradually discontinued and had ceased altogether by the time Sa'ada returned to Lebanon.

Altogether, it is more than doubtful whether Sa'ada posed an actual threat to Lebanon. There seems to have been no real plan for an uprising. Testimony to the contrary by Sa'ada's followers (given after the event) was based mainly on hearsay.[50] It is also doubtful whether Za'im – his promises to Sa'ada notwithstanding – possessed the resources to help Sa'ada carry out a coup. Patrick Seale described his moves as a 'quixotic enterprise'.[51] Khuri used the word *I'tida'at* ('attacks') to head the relevant section of his memoirs, but studiously avoided the word 'coup'.[52] Indeed, the memoirs of actors on the scene as well as contemporary diplomatic reports show that the sporadic PPS attacks against isolated targets in outlying areas could not possibly have brought about the downfall of the regime.

Moreover, Za'im's speedy abandonment of Sa'ada throws light on the real nature of the alliance between the two, and on Za'im's actual intentions. Za'im thought of Sa'ada as a bargaining chip in the running fight he was conducting with the Lebanese leadership, and in particular with Sulh whom he suspected of working against him in Syria itself. For this purpose, it was useful to encourage and support Sa'ada. But Za'im's real objective was Syria. As we have seen, his policy towards Lebanon was essentially defensive rather than offensive. When he eventually reached an accommodation with Khuri and Sulh at his meeting with them in June 1949, the subject of the PPS seems to have come up (among other things) and an understanding may have been reached about it.[53] In any event, some PPS members construed the events of July 1949 as pointing to the existence of a plan jointly concocted by Za'im and the Lebanese leaders to liquidate Sa'ada. They alleged that Za'im gave the PPS defective weapons, informed the Lebanese of its operational plans, and finally delivered Sa'ada into the hands of his enemies.[54] There is no proof for their version; rather, it would appear that Sa'ada did not correctly interpret Za'im's resounding rhetoric nor the latter's promises. Quite possibly, Za'im himself was not fully aware of where his words were bound to lead. Therefore, when he realized the depth of the crisis, which he had not wanted and for which he was ill-prepared, he preferred to extradite Sa'ada.

Many explanations have been offered for his decision to do so. There are references to Saudi and Egyptian pressure; others speak of pressure from the western powers to whom Lebanon had appealed for help.[55] Za'im's own prime minister, Muhsin al-Barazi, a brother-in-law of Sulh's, was likewise engaged in bringing about an improvement in Syrian–Lebanese relations. According to one account, Sulh bribed Barazi to apply pressure for the extradition of Sa'ada.[56] All this enabled Za'im to justify his action by saying that the combination of pressures had left him no other choice.[57] In actual fact, no such pressures were necessary: extradition stemmed from the inherent logic of the situation. Za'im had struck a deal with Khuri and Sulh of which Sa'ada's extradition was one part. The other was the economic agreement signed between the two countries a few days later (see preceding chapter).[58]

On the evening of 6 July 1949, Sa'ada was handed over to two Lebanese officers – the chief of police, Amir Farid Shihab, and the commander of the gendarmerie, Nur al-Din al-Rifa'i – who brought him to Beirut. Za'im hurried to declare that there had been no extradition at all: Sa'ada, he alleged, had been arrested on Lebanese territory.[59] The Lebanese authorities imposed a black-out on the story, forbidding local newspapers to publish a full account. A British legation press survey stated that 'despite official silence (the result of a promise to Za'im), the rumour soon circulated that it was the Syrian government which had handed him [Sa'ada] over'. An editor who printed this story was sentenced to three months' imprisonment. A French-language paper likewise printed the story, but left blank spaces for the words 'Damascus' and 'Syria', thereby escaping prosecution.[60]

Sa'ada was immediately placed before a military court and given a summary trial lasting about twenty-four hours. He was charged with a long series of criminal acts, including high treason, an attempted uprising and cooperation with Israel. Evidence on the last point was given by one Muhammad Jamil Yunis, in charge of the party branch in Acre, who testified that Sa'ada had instructed him to collect information on Arab armies and pass it on to the Israelis. This caused much astonishment, since Sa'ada was known as an extreme anti-Zionist. Despite Yunis's testimony, the sentence made no mention of this point.[61] Sa'ada denied all the charges, but repeated in court that in his view Lebanon was not a state but a district of Syria, and that the Lebanese were not a people but formed part of the Syrian nation. On 7 July, he was convicted and sentenced to death. President Khuri refused to mitigate his sentence; so did a special amnesty committee. The following morning, he was placed before a firing squad; he refused to have his eyes covered. His last words were: 'Thank you.'[62] From among the sixty-eight party members tried with him, twelve were sentenced to death. Of these, six were executed; the others had their sentences commuted to life imprisonment.

Immediately after Sa'ada's execution, the government published a lengthy special announcement. It recalled the permission given to Sa'ada to return home from South America, resume his political activities and publish his newspapers 'even though he believed neither in Lebanese patriotism nor in Arabism. The Lebanese government did so from a desire to make freedom of political convictions possible.' But surveillance had revealed that Sa'ada's party had 'devoted its energy to undermining the foundations of the Lebanese political structure and to prepare a *coup* against it. Thanks to the vigilance of the security personnel and their commanders, these criminals have been arrested during the last few days and the security of all Lebanese has thus been ensured. The party's leader, Sa'ada, has been tried and has received the punishment due to him.'[63]

Sa'ada's death elicited harsh reactions in Lebanon. Carrying out an execution for a political crime – the first such case in the country's history – was seen as a blatant contravention of the Lebanese tradition of pluralism and tolerance. To illustrate: *Al-Hayat* wrote that 'the Lebanese government has turned its conflict with the PPS into a private quarrel, prosecuting, sentencing and carrying out an execution while keeping the Lebanese people uninvolved and at a distance ... yet now it appeals to the people and expects it to support what [the government] has done.'[64] Among many protesters, Junbalat stood out: having been politically close to Sa'ada, he tried to intervene in his favour. Despite the loss of face involved, he asked Khuri for an interview at which he proposed postponing the trial until the public atmosphere had calmed down. When he sensed that Khuri was resolved to go ahead anyway, he said defiantly that Sa'ada should not be tried any more than archbishop Mubarak and Nihad Arsalan; both had called for uprisings but were left untouched.[65]

Such reactions, as well as various attempts made by PPS members to take revenge for the death of their leader, caused Khuri to deny any responsibility for Sa'ada's trial and disclaim any involvement in his execution. In his memoirs, he depicts his own role as altogether passive, saying that Sulh alone had conducted the whole affair, informing him only at the very last moment. He relates how Sulh woke him up at 2.30 a.m. on 7 July 1949, telling him over the phone that 'Sa'ada has been seized and is being held at the base camp of the gendarmerie. I was greatly surprised ... for as far as I knew Sa'ada was at Damascus enjoying Za'im's protection.'[66]

As against this, people close to Sulh painted a very different picture. They asserted that Sulh had been against the death sentence; it was only under pressure from Khuri that he had given consent for the execution to be carried out.[67] 'Azm noted in his memoirs that Sulh later admitted to his friends that this had been a mistake, made solely in order not to spite Khuri. It was, Sulh conceded, one of the three major mistakes of his career (the other two being his support for Khuri's re-election as president and his consent to the dissolution of the customs union with Syria).[68] But 'Azm's convoluted relations with Sulh should caution us not to take his version too literally.

Viewing the picture as a whole, there can be no doubt that Sulh was the prime mover in the series of events ending with Sa'ada's death. He had thought of him as an instrument in the hands of Za'im, the man he hated most. But then, if Za'im and Sa'ada posed a threat to anyone in Lebanon, it was to Khuri rather than to Sulh. Moreover, Khuri was in control of the army and the security services who in turn were in charge of Sa'ada's extradition, trial and execution. Therefore, he must have had at least as much of a say in the matter as Sulh. It is thus extremely difficult to accept Khuri's claim that Sulh informed him only at such a late date of a matter so important to both their careers and to their country.

Sa'ada's death added a group of bitter enemies to the old opponents of the Lebanese regime; even with their party disbanded, his former followers continued to act against Khuri, many from Syria, some from within Lebanon. They mobilized their strength to back Junbalat and Edde against the president. In 1951, for example, during the run-off elections in Mt Lebanon, they helped Pierre Edde to beat government candidate Pierre al-Jumayyil. The following year, they participated in the struggle which ended with Khuri's downfall (see Chapter 13). More significantly, they engaged in a series of terrorist acts against their political enemies. In August 1949, PPS men were involved in the fall and execution of Za'im and Barazi. On 9 March 1950, a young Druse party member, Tawfiq Hamdan, tried to assassinate Sulh in Beirut, but failed.[69] On 16 July 1951, other party members succeeded: Sulh was mortally wounded during a visit to Amman. Others killed Yusuf Sharbil, the presiding judge of the military court that had sentenced Sa'ada. Khuri escaped a similar fate; according to statements by PPS men, he was spared because he was responsible only in a lesser degree for Sa'ada's death.[70]

Sa'ada's execution was a blow from which his party found it difficult to recover. Most of its activities were transferred to Syria. In 1955, however, when members of the party assassinated the Syrian deputy chief-of-staff and commander of the air force, 'Adnan al-Maliki, all political groupings in Syria combined to put an end to PPS operations there. The party's centre of activities was transferred back to Lebanon. During the crisis of 1958, it backed its old ally Chamoun. In 1961, its men participated in a coup attempt; in the wake of its failure, the Lebanese government again banned party activities for several years. Over time, the party's ideology changed, though its men kept professing their commitment to Sa'ada and his ideas. Beginning in the early 1970s, its revised doctrines led the PPS to support the Syrian regime under Hafiz al-Asad. In their view, he was the successor to Sa'ada's ideas and as such would eventually establish a Greater Syrian state.[71]

PART FOUR

# The Downfall

## CHAPTER 11

# Khuri and Sulh: A Parting of the Ways

General elections were due in the spring of 1951, but in 1950 expectations for new power constellations were already running high. In particular, Khuri's brother Salim had great hopes. He had used the past few years to entrench his position and now felt ready to form an independent power base in the new Chamber, so that he would no longer have to rely on the good graces of his brother. Some of Khuri's opponents too had high hopes, expecting to use to their advantage the increased power they had gathered since the 1947 elections. They did not believe themselves capable of replacing the regime; in their view, the new elections were too likely to be a replay of 1947 to make that possible. But they believed that Khuri and the government had learned the lessons of the past. The widespread criticism of the practices employed during the last elections would, they expected, force Khuri to apply fairer and more democratic methods this time round.

In July 1950, the British minister wrote to London:

> When everyone in the country ... knows that personal ambition is the domin-ating motive in the mind of nearly every member of the Government, efficiency and progress are not to be expected. If the Lebanon were a democratic country in more than name, there could be little doubt about the issue of the elections; the present administration, which has enjoyed and abused power for a good many years now, would go. As it is, the people are so apathetic and the President ... and ... Sulh so astute that ... it is as likely as not that the Prime Minister and the same clique will still be in the saddle ... after the elections; but they will have to raise enough dust to conceal their electoral methods, as I doubt whether even the docile Lebanese could stand for a repetition of the blatant trickery employed in May 1947.[1]

It was precisely this demand for fairer and more democratic elections which provided Khuri and the politicians close to him with the excuse to remove Sulh from his position of power. They demanded that a politically neutral government be appointed to supervise the elections. But it was evident that fairer election practices were not the end Khuri had in mind when he supported a move to unseat the man who had been a close and loyal ally for so many years. Rather, the reason must be sought, at least partly, in Khuri's desire to improve his own standing with the Sunni community at a time when elections were approaching and his opponents were stepping up their activities. Reopening the race for the premiership among the leading Sunni notables would allow Khuri to regain some of the manipulative power he derived from his constitutional right to appoint and dismiss prime ministers – a right he seemed to have forgone during Sulh's four-year tenure. Reviving the competition for the premiership would ensure him the support of all those Sunni notables who felt they might yet make it to the top. More than that: by thus suddenly making his leading Sunni opponents beholden to his personal good-will, Khuri would also neutralize the remaining ones and render it obvious that they had no alternative to offer. Despite their claims to the contrary, he would prove once again that he was the only politician capable of ensuring Sunni–Maronite cooperation and thus safeguarding the foundations of Lebanon's independence.

Khuri himself hinted at this line of argument in his memoirs. 'Various political and psychological elements', he wrote, had led to Sulh's removal, and Khuri himself fully backed the step.

> I came to an agreement with my friend [Sulh] that for the purpose of conducting the elections a neutral government should be formed under Hajj Husayn al-'Uwayni; next 'Adballah al-Yafi was to be appointed prime minister and after him Sa'ib Salam, so that each Sunni [leader] should bear his part in shouldering the burden [of the premiership]. We also agreed that after that, Riyad al-Sulh should return to power, so that I would end my presidency the way I had started it – together with him.[2]

But Khuri went on to say that, even though Sulh had at first agreed to the arrangement he went back on his word when it came to the point of carrying it out. As a result, relations between the two deteriorated markedly.[3]

The rift now developing between the two men was deeper and more complex than Khuri's memoirs would lead one to suppose. Its main element was the constant strengthening of the power of the president (and, lately, of the position of his family). This had become a great deal more noticeable during Khuri's second term. It is significant that, for all we know, Khuri's own role in creating the rift was secondary; the salient figure here was his brother Salim who pushed Bishara al-Khuri into a confrontation with Sulh. He did so from a well calculated design to promote the Khuri family's political interests and, above all, his own. It was Salim who made Bishara perceive Sulh as an obstacle to his political future, in view of the latter's unchallenged standing at home and, even more so, his strong stance in the Arab world. Sulh's entrenched power now seemed more dangerous to the Khuri than the opposition led by Chamoun and Junbalat.

Acting out his views, Salim opened a relentless campaign against Sulh which ended with the latter's dismissal from the premiership. In the short term, Salim got what he wanted: Sulh's removal opened the way for him and Bishara to become the unquestioned masters of the Lebanese political scene. But in the long run, the result was highly detrimental. Once opened, the gulf could not be bridged again. Sulh's assassination a short time afterwards left an open wound: relations with the Sulh family never returned to what they had been before, and in some ways that was true for the rest of the Sunni leadership as well.

The rift was not quite sudden, though; it had its antecedents. Already a year before the start of the 1951 election campaign there had been signs of tension between Sulh and Salim al-Khuri. The Khuris and Sulh, both having public appointments and other spoils of office in their gift, quarrelled over who the beneficiaries were to be. With Salim's greed for power constantly becoming more visible, Sulh was at pains to advance his own associates all the more vigorously.

Towards the end of May 1950, the Party of the National Call (Hizb al-Nida' al-Qawmi), a grouping controlled by the Sulh family, arranged for a reception in honour of the visiting Iraqi politician Salih Jabir. During the ceremony, the Lebanese folk poet 'Umar al-Za'ni recited a variation on a well-known popular song to which he gave the heading 'Renew His Tenure' – a hint at Khuri's recent re-election for a second term. It contained the following lines:

> Renew [his tenure], and don't you worry, there is nothing left for him to take;
> He has had his bellyful and has no worries, and his son, too, got what he wanted;
> He has no ambition left; he renewed, and don't you worry; His wife has had
> plenty of travel, the dollars have satisfied his appetite.[4]

At other times, that might have gone unnoticed, but now the government had become more sensitive. In his memoirs, Khuri mentioned the event as 'the first cloud on the horizon', harbinger of the storm about to break.[5] Sulh ordered the poet arrested; he was tried and sentenced to six months' imprisonment. Beirut rumours had it that Sulh himself had been behind the affair, wishing to harm Khuri's image or at least to warn the Khuri family not to harm his own.[6] The Khuris shared that view.

The following month, a new political scandal preoccupied the public. The editor of *Al-Sayyad* newspaper, Sa'id Fariha, was summoned to a police interrogation following the publication in his paper of an article critical of the president. The summons was sent out at the personal instructions of the commander of the police force, a man close to Salim al-Khuri, and without the knowledge of Sulh. Fariha for his part was a political ally of Sulh. At that time, in addition to being prime minister, Sulh was also minister of the interior and thus formally in charge of the police. Furious, Sulh immediately demanded the police commander's dismissal. But the latter's protector, Salim al-Khuri, threatened to bring his supporters into Beirut for a demonstration against Sulh. The commander of the gendarmerie, another protégé of Salim's, added to the tension by stating that if Salim's men rallied for a demonstration, he for his part could not guarantee public order. Sulh then threatened to call out his own supporters for a counter-demonstration. Next, he ordered the arrest of the editor of Salim al-Khuri's own newspaper, *Nida' al-Watan*, for publishing an article against himself (Sulh), ostensibly as a reply to the original article in *Al-Sayyad* and to Za'ni's song. President Khuri did not, at this point, wish to become too deeply involved in the quarrel between his prime minister, Sulh, and his brother Salim. He thought of both of them as vital elements for his continued rule and wanted to paper things over. He therefore stepped in with a view to finding a solution. After some debate it was decided to send the police commander on a month's vacation. When he returned, he found that control of the police had been transferred from the ministry of the interior to the prime minister's office. Sulh had taken this step because the director-general of the ministry of the interior who shared in supervising the police was an ally of Salim al-Khuri's; but once under the supervision of the prime minister's office, the police would be under Sulh's sole and full control. The commander refused to resume his duties under these altered circumstances and went off for another month of vacationing. Only in September 1950 did he take up his command again.[7]

These incidents – no more than the tip of the iceberg – led Salim al-Khuri in mid-1950 to try and bring matters to a head. He hoped that another Sunni leader would prove more pliable in the office of prime minister and that it would then be easier to use the elections as a lever for perpetuating the Khuris' grip on power. Salim began putting pressure on the ministers belonging to the Constitutional Bloc, first and foremost Taqla and Arsalan, to persuade them to resign and thus bring down the cabinet as a whole. But the two hesitated; moreover, Bishara al-Khuri was not yet ready to drop Sulh. He restrained Salim as well as his allies in the cabinet and the Chamber and, for the time being, prevented Sulh's fall from power.[8]

Even though Salim had failed, his very attempt demonstrated to what an extent Bishara al-Khuri's position was now endangered by the ambitions of his brother. For the first time, a gap became discernible between the political interests of the two brothers. Bishara was losing control of Salim's activities and was to pay a high price for allowing this to happen.

At the beginning of 1951, with the elections drawing closer, Salim renewed his efforts to bring Sulh down. This time, he succeeded in persuading his brother to cooperate with him and, indeed, at the end of a prolonged campaign of pressures, Sulh agreed to resign – undoubtedly in the expectation that, once the elections were over, he would be recalled to the premiership. On 21 February 1951, 'Uwayni formed a new government in which two senior administrative officials (Boulos Fayd and Edward Nun) were appointed ministers – an earnest of the Cabinet's neutral stance. Its main task was to ensure fair and (no less important) quiet elections. But many Lebanese pointed to the fact that the cabinet was in fact entirely under the control of the president. 'Uwayni was a personal friend of Khuri's; so was Fayd who was, moreover, a business associate of Khuri's younger brother Riyad. Nun was married to another Khuri kinsman, Fu'ad al-Khuri. His ministerial appointment was to compensate Fu'ad for having been dropped from the list of the Constitutional Bloc at the time of the previous elections.[9]

## The Elections of May 1951

Bishara al-Khuri's main electoral aim was to maintain the coalition of notables who had supported him during the last four years by ensuring seats for them or their allies in the new Chamber. Salim for his part hoped to emerge as the most powerful figure in the Chamber.

In 1950, Far'un had succeeded in his old ambition of having the Chamber enlarged. A new law set the number of deputies at seventy-seven (up from fifty-five). The various communities all had their proportionate share in the increase. In Beirut, there was now, for the first time, room for a Greek Catholic candidate, and Far'un was preparing to run there. From his point of view, this was greatly preferable to running on Hamada's list in the Biq'a, as he had had to do in the past. It will be recalled that he had to pay Hamada a large sum for this privilege.[10] The new electoral law also subdivided those constituencies large enough to send more than fifteen deputies to the Chamber. The number fifteen was not coincidental: it was chosen because this way the new law would not touch the constituency of Southern Lebanon (with fourteen deputies) – the traditional stronghold of feudal bosses. Applying the new law there would, for instance, have deprived As'ad of his local predominance. But As'ad was a salient supporter of the government, so this would never do. As it was, the only two constituencies to be affected were Mt Lebanon and Northern Lebanon. The former was divided into four electoral districts: Kisrawan, Matn-Ba'abda, Shuf and 'Aley; the latter into the districts of Tripoli, Zagharta-Batrun and 'Akkar. By and large, these two constituencies used to favour anti-government candidates. The redivision would weaken them, because they would now find it more difficult to rally enough voters in each separate district to carry all its seats.[11]

The election campaign was turbulent. The public at large was conscious of a lack of law and order and felt a pervasive sense of insecurity. There had been several incidents of reckless firing into the air and these were expected to presage worse. At the end of 1950, the Prophet's birthday happened to fall on a date close to Christmas. At the celebrations, Sunnis – by now aware of the attempt to remove Sulh from power – vented their anger by firing revolvers and setting off explosives. The British minister wrote that the 'dynamite explosions and continuous revolver shooting were reminiscent of London under bombardment'. The incidents, he added, were thought to have been a 'demonstration of strength by Sulh'.[12] The Christians, mostly supporters of Salim al-Khuri, 'retaliated' on Christmas Eve by using similar means.[13]

Similar incidents kept occurring. On 25 February 1951, shots were fired into the air in Tripoli to mark the announcement by a local notable of his decision to run in the elections. Two days later, 500 followers of As'ad came to Beirut airport to meet his son on his return from abroad; they welcomed the event with several volleys. Police arrested several people found firing their weapons. When As'ad intervened to secure their release, Prime Minister 'Uwayni threatened to resign.[14]

The gravest incident occurred closer to the date of the elections, on 18 March 1951, in the Shuf mountain area. A group of armed Druse, on their way to a rally their leader Junbalat was holding in Jabal Baruk, clashed with a gendarmerie unit who were trying to stop them. A gendarmerie officer and four Druse were killed; seven gendarmerie men and twelve Druse were wounded.[15] Junbalat was quick to blame the gendarmerie. Moreover, he accused Salim al-Khuri of exploiting his influence over the gendarmerie commanders to make them work against his, Junbalat's, party.[16] The following day Prime Minister 'Uwayni made a forceful speech over Radio Beirut, saying that he would apply the full force of the law against anyone guilty of unlawful behaviour, even if he was a close associate of his own.[17] Within the next few days, the police arrested sixty-five of Junbalat's followers and threatened to arrest several hundred more from among those involved in the incident.[18]

The elections were held in two rounds, on 15 and 22 April 1951. There were 273 candidates competing for seventy-seven seats. Voters' participation was about 50 per cent – considered fair in Lebanon (where women got the franchise only in 1953).[19] On the eve of ballot day, the president and the prime minister appealed for fair elections.[20] Indeed, the ballot proceeded quietly. The US minister noted that the president had 'proved to be a moderating influence on such leaders as have consulted him. He has not dictated the choice of candidates nor has he interfered with the freedom of the elections.'[21] His British colleague later summed up the situation as follows: 'There are glimmerings of a new sense of responsibility in the conduct of public affairs and a growing realization that independence not only carries privileges but demands standards of public service as well. The 1951 elections, although hardly a model of probity ... were nevertheless conducted ... with a greater measure of honesty than was the case in 1947.'[22]

A dissenting view was presented by the British *Economist* which found that 'corruption has greatly increased'. The country's 'true prosperity ... has been jeopardized'. There was much gambling, illegal trade and drug traffic. Communist activities were increasing, 'Yet the Lebanon could easily lead the Middle East in social reforms.' British advisers were needed to carry out a 'much discussed scheme for increasing the country's resources and regaining its social services'.[23] The article caused a minor crisis in Anglo-Lebanese relations. Khuri professed himself deeply hurt. The British legation told London of their dismay at the article's contents and at the moment chosen to publish it. They went on to criticize it as unbalanced.[24] Khuri, though, was not easily appeased. When *Al-Nahar*, a newspaper close to Junbalat, published a translation of the article, it was closed for eight months and its editor fined 800 Lebanese lira.[25]

In retrospect, the 1951 elections did not differ much from earlier ballots. 'Uwayni made considerable efforts to ensure their fairness and was widely praised for doing so, even by opponents, but the overall pattern was that known from earlier occasions. Khuri was no less involved than previously, though he acted behind the scenes rather than in the public eye. By contrast, Salim al-Khuri intervened overtly. Their joint involvement brought back much the same coalition of notables Khuri had gathered round himself earlier. But then the political realities such as they were in the constituencies pointed that way in any case. The return of the old guard was particularly noticeable in Beirut, the Biqa' and Southern Lebanon. The successful candidates there were supporters of Khuri but, as always, their main loyalty was to their own political and personal interests, and their devotion to the president was contingent on it.

In Southern Lebanon, all fourteen men on As'ad's list were elected. As before, Sulh ran on As'ads list as well as on the list of As'ad's competitor 'Usayran. Sulh was elected, 'Usayran himself did not win a seat.[26] In the Biqa', as had been expected, Hamada won seats for all the eleven candidates on his list. Several candidates, mostly Christians led by Jean Saqaf (Greek Catholic) had refused to accept Hamada's terms and financial demands and had formed a list of their own. They were amply financed by Far'un, but lost all the same.[27] In Beirut, a joint list of all important Sunni leaders (including Yafi, Sami al-Sulh, Salam and 'Umar Bayhum) won a major victory. Several Christians had joined their list: Far'un, Abu Shahla, Charles al-Hilu, and a Phalanges candidate, Yusuf Shadir. This was the first time since 1943 that the Sunni leadership of Beirut was able to close ranks and form a single list, even including Salam whose growing strength was beginning to scare Yafi and Sulh. Far'un had laboured hard to produce a joint list, fearing that he himself would not otherwise be able to enter the Chamber as a member from Beirut. Moreover, he wanted it to form the core of a coalition for future confrontations with Sulh and Salim al-Khuri. Opposite this so-called 'Grand List' there ran a 'Popular List' headed by Muhi al-Din al-Nasuli, editor of the newspaper *Bayrut* and an associate of Sulh's. Several members of the Sulh family ran on it, but Riyad al-Sulh's strong political and financial support for it could not prevent its defeat.[28]

Mt Lebanon was Khuri's traditional stronghold, but also the home ground of his adversaries Chamoun, Junbalat and the Eddes. In all the area's new electoral districts, the two factions fought hard. Khuri's Constitutional Bloc received fourteen from among the total of twenty-three seats of the four districts combined – a victory, but not an overwhelming one. In the Shuf district, for instance, the Constitutional Bloc won four seats as against five going to the opposition.[29] An interesting sidelight on the elections in Mt

Lebanon was provided by an attempt by Khuri to win over the sons of Emile Edde: Raymond and Pierre. Khuri may have acted from a wish to promote an historical reconciliation between old rivals, but also wanted to prevent the Edde brothers from joining Chamoun. He probably thought that the two were too young to pose a menace and might be won over by an offer pointing the way to positions of power. After contacts lasting over a year, he eventually offered them half the seats on the Constitutional Bloc's list. But this ran counter to Salim's ambition to become the unquestioned leader of the area. He refused to sacrifice his prospects for the sake of his brother's (as he had been forced to do in the past) and sabotaged the deal. In actual fact, Raymond's reluctance to go along with Khuri's proposal might have caused it to fall through in any event.[30]

In the Matn (alone among the four Mt Lebanon districts), a second round was necessary. The contest there was between government-backed Phalanges leader Pierre al-Jumayyil, and Pierre Edde. Jumayyil first ran as an independent candidate, but Salim al-Khuri persuaded him to run on the Constitutional Bloc list for the second round. The Eddes and the Jumayyils had been bitter rivals since the death of Emile Edde. They personally and their two movements, the National Bloc and the Phalanges respectively, were all trying to fill the political void left behind by the demise of the elder Edde. Moreover, each grouping presented itself as the only authentic guardian of the Maronites' true interests. As so often in Lebanon, their competition turned violent. On 23 August 1950, a group of Phalanges members broke into the offices of the National Bloc. On 1 September, an explosive charge was placed opposite Raymond Edde's home.[31]

To return to the elections: in order to ensure Jumayyil's success, Salim al-Khuri compelled two Constitutional Bloc candidates, Na'im Wadi' and Khalil Abu Jawda, who had done better than Jumayyil in the first round, to withdraw from the second round. They did so, but Wadi' secretly instructed his followers to vote for Pierre Edde; most of Abu Jawda's backers stayed away from the polling booths. Moreover, the Constitutional Bloc's Druse backers (including Arsalan) refused to support Jumayyil and voted for Edde instead.[32] In addition, Edde gathered Muslim and Greek Orthodox votes. Also, Junbalat persuaded the PPS to support him.[33] Edde won by a very small margin (9,907 to 9,760). Even so, his victory caused some surprise: after all, Jumayyil had government backing and the Phalanges had done well in other places. Edde apparently owed his success to Druse, Muslim and Greek Orthodox rather than to Maronite voters, most of whom supported the Phalanges.[34]

Northern Lebanon had also been subdivided (see above) and each of the new districts had its own distinctive features. In the 'Akkar district, an anti-government local boss, Sulayman al-'Ali, carried all seats, thoroughly defeating his government-backed opponent. In Tripoli, Karami family candidates, headed by 'Abd al-Hamid's son, Rashid Karami, won all seats, wiping out their defeat of 1947. They had been opposed by their perpetual local rivals, the Muqaddam family. The main contest for the leadership of the list, however, between Rashid Karami and his uncle Mustafa, the town's mayor, had taken place some time before. Rashid, considered the more moderate of the two, had government backing and won the internecine struggle. Mustafa had strong pan-Arab convictions and the authorities suspected him of wanting to turn Tripoli into a stronghold of anti-regime forces.[35] Finally, in Zagharta-Batrun the anti-Faranjiyya coalition headed by Yusuf Istifan won a clear majority, although Faranjiyya himself was elected, the only member of his list. Faranjiyya accused Khuri of being responsible for his defeat.[36]

Overall, the election results favoured Khuri and gave him greater strength in the new Chamber than he had had in the last. But the real winner was Salim al-Khuri. He now dominated the Constitutional Bloc members from Mt Lebanon, had allied himself with As'ad and Hamada who were the bosses of the Biqa' and the south, and had arrived at an understanding (at least a temporary one) with Far'un who controlled the majority of members from Beirut. This meant that he was now capable of rallying an absolute majority in the house and thus of influencing the composition and policy of future cabinets. His chief opponents in the Chamber were Chamoun, Junbalat and Edde, in turn supported by Faranjiyya. They now formed the Socialist National Front which served as their umbrella organization until Khuri's downfall.

If Salim was the principal winner, Riyad al-Sulh was the main loser. He lost overall control of the Chamber which now passed to his various opponents, led by his old rivals Salim al-Khuri and Far'un. Khuri could thus afford to dispense with Sulh's services. His brother pressed for the appointment of another Sunni to the premiership and in May 1951, acting on the joint advice of Salim and Far'un, Khuri named 'Abdallah al-Yafi prime minister.

## The Assassination of Riyad al-Sulh

During the election campaign and until the appointment of Yafi's cabinet, Khuri and especially Sulh preferred not to make a public issue of the tension between them. Sulh still hoped to become prime minister after the elections. Once he realized that his hope had been in vain, he dropped his former restraint and sharply attacked Yafi and his government, both in person and through the medium of people close to him. Nor did he hesitate to attack Khuri whom he held responsible for leaving him in the political wilderness.

In order to compensate himself for his loss of standing at home, Sulh turned to inter-Arab activities – an area which had brought him ample dividends in the past. He may have hoped that, as once before, building up his reputation on the broader Arab scene would eventually also gain him the premiership at home. From among his old Syrian friends most were now in exile and were therefore politically useless. He turned to King 'Abdallah with whom he had not been on close terms in the past but who might now prove helpful. Khuri was suspicious of this new-found alliance. In his memoirs, he denied feeling threatened by it and attributed Sulh's new approach to his personal distress.[37] But he was unlikely to overlook the possible consequences of Sulh's forming close ties with the Arab leader who was then the principal proponent of the Greater Syria scheme and who, to that end, wanted to see Lebanon reduced to the Mt Lebanon area.[38]

As we have seen in the preceding chapter, it was at the conclusion of a round of talks with King 'Abdallah that Sulh was assassinated; PPS men shot and gravely wounded him as he was about to take off from Amman airport on 16 July 1951. He died soon afterwards. Two of his assassins were killed in hot pursuit. Both were Christians, one a Lebanese, the other a Palestinian. A third, the driver of the group, was able to escape.[39] In Lebanon, most people believed that the killers had acted at the behest of Syria; two of them had arrived from Syria, and the PPS was known to act there freely.[40] The strong-man in Damascus, Shishakli, was blamed personally; he was a sympathizer of the PPS, a political enemy of Sulh, and likely to gain from instability in Lebanon. The Lebanese press repeatedly accused him of the ultimate responsibility for the murder. So did some of the politicians of the day in their memoirs, for instance Sami al-Sulh. He wrote that shortly before the assassination, he visited Shishakli and asked him to restrain the PPS in Syria and thereby prevent them from taking action against Riyad al-Sulh. According to Sami's account, Shishakli promised to do so, but observed that Riyad would do well not to travel much.[41] It must, however, be noted that, even though Syrian backing was a possibility, we do not possess documentary evidence for it.[42]

Sulh's violent death came as a shock to the Lebanese. As soon as the news was broadcast, a wave of violence erupted in Beirut. Muslim crowds enforced a business strike. Traders, mostly Christians, who were not quick enough to close their premises were attacked and one was shot to death. The security forces intervened and succeeded in restoring order, but by next morning there were four dead and substantial damage had been done to property.[43] The government blamed criminal elements for having exploited the situation, but it seems more likely that the outburst was the result of accumulated economic and social distress among urban, particularly Beiruti, Sunnis.[44]

Khuri's position became most difficult. The Sulh family began charging him with indirect responsibility for Sulh's death; removing him from power, they argued, had exposed him to his enemies. Khuri was aware that he might be next on the PPS hit-list, but he attended Sulh's funeral and eulogized him. During the funeral procession, several people tried to break through towards him and Sulh's daughters looked at him (as he put it in his memoirs) 'with eyes full of evil, as if I was a criminal'.[45] In his memoirs, Khuri tried to clear himself and described his relations with Sulh as correct. He adds that, shortly before Sulh's trip to Amman, he asked Fu'ad Shihab, the army chief of staff,

to tell him that once two or three other Sunnis had held the premiership, he
(Sulh) would be appointed again. According to Khuri, Sulh welcomed this
assurance and promised that, as soon as he was back from Jordan, he would
mend his fences with Khuri.[46]

The Lebanese public, however, had a different picture of the situation.
They felt that a gulf had opened between the families of the Sulhs and the
Khuris and found confirmation for their view in the events surrounding the
by-elections held to fill Sulh's vacant seat. Several members of the Sulh
family competed among themselves for the seat in the Chamber, assuming
that whoever would eventually be chosen by the family was assured of victory.
Among the aspirants was a son of Sami's and another Sulh backed by Riyad's
widow. Eventually, a third figure, Kazim al-Sulh, was nominated.

The by-elections were set for 8 September 1951. Kazim al-Sulh was running
opposite Salah al-Bizri, the mayor of Sidon who had the backing of the
regional 'feudal' boss, As'ad. The Sulhs asked Khuri to work for their
candidate, but the president refused, arguing that he had to remain neutral.
The Sulhs interpreted his reply as indicating support of Bizri. Khuri later
explained in his memoirs that he refrained from backing Kazim al-Sulh
because he knew that Bizri had much stronger local support.[47] He was right;
in the elections of April 1951, Sulh had won only because he had the support
of many Shi'is in the south whom As'ad had mobilized for him. Even then,
the Sunni vote had tended to go to Nazih al-Bizri (another member of the
same family who had then run against Sulh). To prevent a second defeat, the
Bizris now fielded Salah who got on better with As'ad and eventually won
his support. Again the Shi'i voters, taking their cue from As'ad, decided the
vote and gave Bizri a sweeping victory (17,975 to 4,909).[48] The extent of
As'ad's influence was reflected in the results: in Kazim's home town, Sidon,
he received more votes than Bizri (1,294 to 1,189); in As'ad's home village,
Tayba, all votes went to Bizri (354 to 0).[49] Local realities were such that, even
if Khuri had intervened, the results might not have been much different; but
the outcome added to the bad feeling between the Sulhs and the Khuris.

Sulh's death shook Khuri's confidence and seemed to conjure up the
beginning of the end for him. The assassination followed the pattern of a
blood feud. It frightened Khuri physically because he was another potential
victim of the same feud, since many in Lebanon believed he had inspired
the murder. Further Syrian action intended to destabilize Lebanon was also
possible. To make things worse, King 'Abdallah was murdered a few days
later. Even though his assassination was not connected with Sulh's, it gave
rise to a feeling that a series of political murders had begun and that violence
and instability were about to engulf the Arab states.

Furthermore, for Khuri (though not for his brother Salim), Sulh had long
been an important political asset. He had absorbed much of the personal
and political criticism levelled at Khuri and his government. This was true,
for instance, of reactions to the defeat in Palestine, to Sa'ada's execution,

and to the dissolution of the customs union with Syria. Now, there was no other Muslim personality of the same calibre; now, whatever criticism was voiced hurt Khuri alone. More than that: Sulh had been Khuri's partner in devising the National Pact and had consistently rallied the Muslim community to the cause of independent Lebanon. No successor with similar qualities and of like prestige was in sight. Finally, by the force of his personality Sulh had been able to balance the president's power and check the domineering ambitions of the Khuri family, especially Salim's. Khuri himself and his associates may not have been able fully to appreciate the value of the service he thus rendered them. Sulh's dismissal and subsequent death removed such obstacles, weakened the delicate balance underlying Lebanese politics, opened the way for the Khuris to entrench themselves in power and thereby hastened their end.

Khuri's loss of self-confidence (which he tried hard to conceal from the public) is attested to by his appeal to the British minister to guarantee Lebanon's independence (and, by implication, his own continued rule). In his report, the minister noted that Khuri had looked tense. He had warned of the dangers inherent in the tension and instability engendered by the recent assassinations. In what the minister interpreted as a hint regarding the domestic Lebanese situation, Khuri had stressed the need to maintain the status quo; any change might turn out to be dangerous.[50] Khuri made a similar appeal to Saudi Arabia, asking King Ibn Sa'ud to exercise his influence for the preservation of stability and for calming down the public mood.[51]

Personal difficulties apart, Khuri now also came up against political adversity. Domestic and regional constraints prevented Lebanon from drawing closer to the West, as its inclination and its basic interests would have prescribed. Inter-Arab relations, formerly a source of strength, had turned into a menace. The instability left behind in many Arab countries by the war in Palestine spilt over into Lebanon. The paralysis which had taken hold of the Arab League as a consequence of inter-Arab disputes deprived Lebanon of an instrument for containing Syrian and other Arab pressures. Moreover, it was Sulh who had been the Lebanese leader most influential in all-Arab affairs. Neither his successor Yafi nor any other Sunni then actively engaged in politics had the skill and charisma to take his place. Compared with Sulh's time, Lebanon now played a much reduced role on the Arab scene. On the first anniversary of his death, an *Al-Hayat* editorial stated plaintively: 'Arab delegations no longer arrive in Lebanon, and Beirut has turned into a village of dark alleys.' It went on: 'The blood vessel that linked Lebanon with the Arab capitals is gone.' Those coming in its stead had 'lost their way and forgotten their faith'.[52]

As regards Syria, Za'im's fall had not improved relations with Beirut. Tensions, it turned out, had deeper roots in Damascus than just the personal enmity of Za'im and 'Azm towards Sulh. The differences in economic outlook and policy have already been discussed. The even more fundamental question of Syrian acceptance of Lebanese independence was still felt to be unresolved. This was brought out, for instance, by Khuri's request in July 1951 (i.e. during 'Azm's premiership) for Syria and Lebanon to exchange ambassadors in order to formalize their relations, and even more so by 'Azm's refusal to do so.[53] When Shishakli finally seized power overtly in Syria, on 29 November 1951, he was at first considered a strong, and therefore dangerous, ruler heading a stable regime. In fact, much like his predecessor, he had to grapple with the problem of legitimacy and to struggle hard for greater stability. He blamed his troubles, at least in part, on the Syrian expatriates in Lebanon and indirectly on the Lebanese regime which had offered them refuge but had, in his view, failed to rein in their activities. Shishakli was known as a sympathizer of the PPS and was thus suspected in Lebanon of having had a hand in Sulh's assassination. Beirut therefore perceived him as a danger to the Lebanese regime and as a source of encouragement for its domestic opponents.

Of even greater moment for Khuri was the incipient loss of influence over his traditional bases of power. His opponents gained strength; the press and the public mood turned against him; and eventually the elites of notables of all communities, who had been loyal to him for so long, began withdrawing their support. This was to prove decisive in bringing about the end of his regime.

## CHAPTER 12

# Rift with the West

Lebanon's attainment of full independence (and Khuri's basic policy to that end) implied severing its historic ties with France and a deliberate waiving of that country's guarantee of protection. Instead, Beirut made a determined effort to integrate Lebanon into the Arab political system; but that did not mean that it considered the Arab world as the only source of assuring its independence and security. On the contrary, the country's leaders were aware that, alongside its many advantages, an Arab orientation also posed certain dangers. These needed to be contained by close links with the West which would be tantamount to a western commitment to Lebanon's independence and territorial integrity. After all, the president and government knew very well to what extent the British presence in the Levant had enabled them to sever ties with France. Britain, and in some measure the USA, thus replaced France though, unlike the latter, they were to remain in the background. At the same time, they were assumed to be ready to intervene vigorously at times of acute crisis.

During the 1940s, as we have seen, Lebanese leaders turned to Britain for help and reassurance whenever they were threatened – or thought they were. This was true both of domestic and of external threats. True, Lebanon's trust in Britain was not beyond doubt; London's ties with the Hashemite rulers and its presumed backing for their union schemes were disquieting to Beirut and placed certain limits on its relations with Britain. Overall, Lebanon built up a delicately balanced web of diplomatic ties in which western and Arab cross-currents offset each other. But conflicting inter-Arab pressures were also balanced: Egypt and Saudi Arabia, for instance, countered Hashemite unionist ambitions.

Towards the end of the 1940s, the USA gradually turned into the predominant western power in the region. Lebanese leaders do not seem to have grasped the full impact and the possible dangers of this process until, in the early 1950s, they rather suddenly found themselves at a low point in US–Lebanese relations. This low resulted from the US policy of adopting a rather forward, activist stance in the Middle East – a region of which it then had little intimate knowledge and whose particular interests it did not always assess correctly. By insisting on regional security arrangements, Washington was asking a price for continued good relations which Lebanon found too high to pay. As against this, integration into the Arab world was likewise exacting a high price, particularly through its reverberations on the domestic scene. Khuri's sweeping charge (in his memoirs) that US intervention in Lebanese home affairs brought about the downfall of his regime should be rejected.[1] But it remains true that matters were aggravated by personal differences in outlook, and the resulting mutual distrust between Khuri and Harold Brink Minor (who represented the USA in Beirut during Khuri's final years in office).

Studies based on recently released documentary materials have brought to light a layer of US activities in the Middle East that was previously unknown: involvement in Za'im's coup in Syria; the fostering of closer ties with Jamal 'Abd al-Nasir; and covert attempts to bring about an Israeli–Arab settlement.[2] They attest to the rapid growth of US interests in the region. These centred on the Persian Gulf oil fields and their access routes, but were sustained by an underlying concept of the region's role in global strategy and in a new world order. Internal instability and Soviet penetration were Washington's main worries. The activities of Middle Eastern communist parties, quite insignificant in themselves at that time, nurtured suspicions of the Soviet Union. US attitudes towards Britain were equivocal: its decline as a regional power elicited regret since it removed a western prop, but also caused some satisfaction because Britain's negative, colonialist image was considered onerous for regional relations with the West as a whole. The Arab–Israeli conflict was seen in Washington as one of the main reasons for the anti-western (and thus often pro-Soviet) stance of many Arab countries. The latter's internal political, social and economic crisis – largely occasioned, so Washington believed, by the absence of democratic regimes – was thought to provide fertile soil for communist influence. All these factors needed to be overcome in order to draw the region into the western security sphere. Domestic ills would be cured by new and (genuine or self-professed) progressive regimes who would sweep away the colonial legacy of corruption and inefficiency and carry out radical reforms.

Most studies of US regional policy during these years pay scant attention to Lebanon. Until the civil war of 1958, Lebanon was regarded as an oasis of stability, firmly planted in the western camp, and as rather irrelevant to the overall dynamics of the Arab world. As such, it was thought to be marginal to the main US diplomatic effort in the region. But documentary evidence from US archives, as well as previously published Arabic sources, paints a different picture. It shows that a certain measure of US involvement in Lebanese internal affairs existed well before the 1958 crisis. The failure of the West to draw Lebanon into regional defence schemes and the failure of the Khuri regime to produce a better and cleaner administration (thereby, in the US view, inviting Soviet penetration) engendered a certain negative, not

ile, attitude towards Khuri's Lebanon in Washington. It needs to
gain that Khuri's downfall was not engineered by the USA but
rom domestic developments. It is also true that the main focus of
Middle Eastern policies lay elsewhere. Nevertheless, there is no denying
the fact that US relations with Lebanon provide an additional angle from
which to view Washington's overall regional diplomacy. They reflect the US
obsession with Soviet influence and attest to an inclination to assess Lebanon's
political, social and economic realities with purely western eyes. They also
illustrate the discrepancy between the political concepts laid down in Washington and their interpretation and implementation by the men on the spot.

## The Emergence of American Interests in Lebanon

The broadening of US interests in Lebanon became visible soon after the
end of the Second World War. In August 1947, the British minister noted
that, despite Britain's 'virtually predominant position', it was 'now being asked
whether the Americans, almost overnight, are taking over this position'. He
reassured London by saying that:

> In general ... the Arabs are in a vague way suspicious of American policy, not
> only because of its pro-Zionist tendencies, but also because it smacks of 'dollar
> imperialism'. And in spite of difficulties in Palestine and Egypt there is a wide-
> spread feeling that the Arabs cannot do better than continue their association
> with His Majesty's Government ... who have shown understanding and sym-
> pathy for Arab aspirations.

He added that the Americans were aware of Britain's 'long experience of
Arabs and aptitude for Arab affairs' which they for their part did not 'show
much sign of acquiring ... Likewise, the danger of the Arab Governments
playing them off against us ... cannot have escaped them.'[3] Comparative US
inexperience in Arab affairs was often cited subsequently as a cause of many
of the problems posed by US policies in the region.

Economic, cultural and educational US activities went back to the nineteenth century. The shift to markedly political interests occurred during the
Second World War. After the allied landings in North Africa in 1942, major
American forces began operating in the Mediterranean theatre of war. It was
then that US regional policy, as briefly sketched above, started to take shape.
One of its elements was described (with a note of implicit criticism) in the
following words of Elie Kedourie:

> Roosevelt and many other influential political figures, as well as high officials in
> the State Department and foreign service officers, believed that the British (and
> French) Imperial positions had, somehow or another, sooner or later, to be
> liquidated, and the people ruled by Imperial Powers helped to independence.
> So far as one can tell from available evidence, neither Roosevelt nor other
> prominent U.S. political figures gave any thought to the consequences in

international politics of weakening or crippling friendly Imperial Powers or, more specifically, to what bearing the policy they favored would have on the formidable problem of dealing with the Soviet Union (but this was probably not seen as a problem, let alone a formidable one).[4]

Lebanon was soon assigned its specific place in the evolving regional policy. The US consul-general in Beirut, George Wadsworth, wrote to the head of the Near Eastern and African Division in the State Department in Washington: 'If we are to play a major role in world politics ... we must do so regionally and not primarily by long-range propaganda from Washington. And in this region ... Lebanon-Syria would seem to be the most inviting spot to cut our teeth.' He mentioned the good prospects of Lebanon achieving higher living standards and went on: 'As American cultural and material investment increases, as it seems bound to do, [Lebanon could become] a vital focus of American influence based on mutual interest rather than special privilege.'[5]

The expectation that Lebanon might turn into a strategic stronghold for the USA flowed from the recognition of its geo-political position as well as from the conviction that the country was firmly pro-western in its inclinations. This came to the fore in planning the Saudi Mediterranean oil pipeline (Tapline) and in the debate about the placement of its western terminal. Comparing seven possible outlets, the US petroleum attaché proposed choosing Tripoli, but noted that to make this choice the USA must 'see to it that Syria and Lebanon become wholly independent, with no foreign troops within their territory, and that no foreign country have a preferred political or economic position or treaty with them'.[6] The report, it should be noted, was drafted at a time when French and British troops were still stationed in Lebanon. It did not take long for the attaché's conditions to be fulfilled.

The outbreak of the Cold War added to the force of such arguments. A memorandum of the US Coordination Committee of the Departments of State, War and the Navy laid down that:

> [I]t is in the national interest of the U.S. to maintain and develop its friendly relations with Lebanon. The war has emphasized the strategic importance of the country, with its important port, air bases, railways and oil pipe-line terminal. The commercial and military value of Near Eastern oil reserve[s], the deterioration of Britain's strength, the emergent interest of the Soviet Union ... emphasize the importance to the U.S. of a politically stable and economically prosperous Lebanon.[7]

US policy-makers understood very well that Lebanon was not the key to the Middle East and that countries such as Syria and Egypt were closer to centre-stage; but Washington still considered it worthwhile to foster close relations with Beirut. All the more so, as no major effort needed to be invested there, given the country's (and especially the Christians') natural pro-western orientation and the public awareness of the need for western protection.

During the late 1940s, the USA pursued three immediate policy goals with regard to Lebanon:

1. Concluding the Tapline accord. The relevant agreement was signed on 10 August 1946 and ratified by the Lebanese Chamber of Deputies on 12 February 1947.

2. Rendering Lebanon economic assistance under Point Four of the Truman Doctrine of 12 March 1947. Point Four spoke of help to such recipient countries as would use it to fight off Communism. Negotiations proceeded slowly, partly because Beirut found it difficult to prepare appropriate plans on the scale suggested (over $30 million for 1950 alone), but also because Lebanon was worried about the political implications of joining the scheme.[8] To the disappointment of the USA, the final agreement was signed only on 4 December 1951, four and a half years after Point Four aid was first proposed.

3. The conclusion of a treaty of friendship and commerce. This was first proposed by Washington in 1946. But Lebanon was reluctant to commit itself so strongly to the USA and made counter-proposals of a more modest nature. These in turn were not acceptable to the USA.

US hopes for a breakthrough were thus foiled, with Lebanon placing a stronger emphasis on forming ties with the Arab world than with the USA. This had already been implied in the principles underlying the National Pact, but Washington blamed Khuri and his government for the hesitant progress of US–Lebanese links. There seem to have been more sides to Lebanon's reluctance than only consideration for the Sunni community at home and for the neighbouring Arab countries abroad. Khuri and his political allies were apparently slow to realize to what extent their world was changing and to grasp the significance of Britain's decline and the rise of the USA. US diplomats did not make things easier for the Lebanese; they did not, for instance, consult Britain over their steps in the region, thus failing to take advantage of Britain's greater experience of the Middle East. The proposal for a US–Lebanese treaty of friendship became known to the British minister by a slip of the tongue of a US diplomat. When he hurried to the Lebanese Foreign Ministry, he was amazed to learn that a US draft for the treaty had been under consideration for quite some time, but neither the ministry nor the US legation was ready to give him more detailed information. All the US minister was ready to tell him was that this was a standard treaty the USA had signed with many countries. The State Department replied similarly to a British enquiry in Washington. Only in 1947, a year or so later, did the director-general of the Lebanese Foreign Ministry hand an unmarked copy of the draft to the British, adding that he hoped Britain would sign a similar treaty with Beirut. The Foreign Office reacted by warning its minister in Beirut not to intervene.[9] US support for Israel did not seem to bother the Lebanese too much. True, in October 1950, the US minister complained that

US policies on Israel elicited hostile reactions in Lebanon,[10] but in the very same report he indicated that this was not a major consideration in shaping Lebanon's attitude towards the USA. Lebanese anger on this point, he went on to say, did not run deep, certainly not among the country's leaders.

## The Middle East Command Scheme

From the end of 1950, western efforts in the Middle East revolved round a plan to establish a regional defence command in which the Middle Eastern countries (including Lebanon) would take part alongside the western powers. Its purpose was to coordinate the defence of the region against possible Soviet aggression. The idea had originated with the British who soon enlisted the USA to promote it with them. During 1951, British and US officials and senior officers visited various Middle Eastern capitals in an effort to persuade local leaders to join the command. Lebanon's turn came in February, when General Robertson, C-in-C British forces in the Middle East, visited Beirut. The British minister there was not pleased. He told his US counterpart that he had objected to the visit 'at this time because … [it] would only cause much talk and he believed nothing would come of it'.[11] He later explained that he had feared negative reactions from Lebanese public opinion, but conceded that, in the event, the public response was more positive than he had expected.[12] Two months later, the US assistant secretary of state for the Near East and Africa, George McGee, came to Lebanon for the same purpose. A formal proposal for Middle Eastern states to join the command was submitted on 13 October 1951.

Lebanon seemed a natural candidate for membership; not only was its basic orientation pro-western, but the scheme also had advantages in the regional context by offering the country protection against regional threats, whether from Za'im's Syria, from Hashemite aspirations, or from Israel. Indeed, when, on 25 May 1950, Britain, France and the USA issued the so-called Tripartite Declaration which laid down principles for upholding the security and territorial integrity of Middle Eastern states, Lebanon welcomed it. Even though the declaration had little or no operational significance, Beirut still chose to view it as an expression of western commitment to its separate existence.[13]

In the past, official Lebanese quarters had themselves suggested more than once that Britain or the USA sign a defence treaty with Beirut. It cannot be determined with certainty how serious these proposals were; they usually came against the background of some particular regional predicament or crisis. Quite possibly, if western representatives had responded to the Lebanese initiatives, Beirut itself might – for reasons already touched upon above – have recoiled from following them through. Yet making such suggestions attested to a basic appreciation by Lebanon of the advantages a contractual relationship with the West would have conferred upon them.

The first explicit move of this kind had come in December 1947 when Prime Minister Sulh spoke to the Iraqi regent 'Abd al-Ilah (considered to be close to the British government) about the possibility of Lebanon finding its place in a regional defence scheme under British leadership.[14] In November 1948, Khuri, probably under the impact of the defeat in Palestine, reverted to the same idea in a conversation with the British minister.[15] In both instances, the British reaction was cool. An explanation for London's hesitant attitude may be found in the words addressed to Sulh by Foreign Secretary Ernest Bevin when they met in October 1948. The first secretary in the Lebanese legation in Paris informed E. Sasson, of the Israeli Foreign Ministry, of the meeting. According to him, Bevin had recognized that the tense international atmosphere made a defence agreement necessary, but had said that Britain would first have to consult France and obtain its agreement. Furthermore, London would want to wait until there was a settlement of the Palestine question, otherwise public opinion in Lebanon and Syria was likely to repudiate the proposed treaty, as had happened in Iraq. (The reference was to the 1948 Treaty of Portsmouth – a revised version of the former Anglo-Iraqi treaty – which had had to be abandoned by Baghdad under heavy popular pressure.) Also, Bevin went on, Britain needed first to settle its dispute with Egypt. Finally, Britain considered it necessary to strengthen the Arab League and enable it to prevent inter-Arab disputes. This would make it possible for the Arabs to turn to economic development as well as to the task of strengthening their armies. The USA, he concluded, shared the last two aims and was ready to step in with aid along the lines of the Marshall Plan.[16]

Yet another Lebanese attempt with the same aim in view was made in November 1950 when Foreign Minister Taqla, in a meeting with British representatives, pointed to the need for guarantees to protect Lebanon from Israel as well as from the advocates of Greater Syria. Again, Britain remained non-committal.[17]

As we have seen before, Lebanese leaders were slow to grasp the new ascendancy of the USA. Only in August 1950, about a year after being rebuffed by Britain, did Beirut finally turn to Washington and even then it did so in an informal and tentative way. The appeal was made by Minister Malik in a conversation with McGee. According to the latter's report, Malik dwelt on the difference between 'old-fashioned imperialism and exploitation and firm but friendly [western] guidance' and said that 'the Near East States clearly needed western tutelage'. Soviet objections, he asserted, should be ignored. He then went on to say that the USA, Britain and France should set up 'a defense structure in the general area of the Near East'. A 'Mediterranean Pact' should come into being, allying all the littoral countries of that sea with the USA and Britain. Lebanon would welcome the idea, Egypt 'would be interested' and Syria 'receptive'. Special arrangements would be required to include Israel. Iraq and Saudi Arabia, though not adjacent to the

Mediterranean, should be allowed to join. McGee replied that 'in our strategic thinking we looked first to the threat. The threat to the ME would take the form of a Soviet thrust from the north and east (via Iran, Iraq and Turkey). It was most unlikely that Lebanon would be threatened from the Mediterranean ... The defense of the Near East should take place in the mountains of Turkey and Iraq. It is for this reason that we conceived of the Arab States and Israel as a strategic entity.' He added that Mediterranean countries further to the west had 'nothing in common with Iraq, Syria and Saudi Arabia in defense matters'.[18]

McGee's coolness towards Malik may have had something to do with US disappointment with Lebanon over the proposed treaty of friendship and other matters. It also most probably stemmed from a recognition that it was Egypt rather than Lebanon which held the key to western negotiations with the Arabs. Moreover, it was not entirely clear how far Malik represented the views of his government when putting forward such ideas. More than once in the past he had been more markedly pro-western than most of his country's establishment. Twice, Beirut had failed to back his votes or statements at the UN demonstrating his commitment to the western cause.[19] In speaking to McGee, he may likewise have acted without explicit authority. But his appeal no doubt reflected a sense of distress over the state of the Middle East then shared by many Lebanese who would have drawn similar conclusions from the situation.

When the proposal for forming a Middle East Command was submitted by the western powers in October 1951, Lebanon's leaders held back. In private, both Muslim and Christian political figures expressed their support; in public they refused to do so. They feared hostile expressions of public opinion, particularly from the Sunni community; and they were aware that Beirut would not be able to stand up to inter-Arab pressures against the scheme. They preferred to join the rest of the Arab world in rejecting the idea.

Arab opposition to the plan was being marshalled by Egypt. In November 1951, Prime Minister Nahas Pasha sent an emissary to Beirut who pointedly reminded Khuri of the support Nahas had given him in 1943. In addition, Cairo, going over the head of the government, directly appealed to Lebanese (particularly Sunni) public opinion by organizing or encouraging pro-Egyptian rallies and demonstrations. Especially notable was a demonstration by students of the American University of Beirut, on 28 October 1951, organized among others by the late Riyad al-Sulh's seventeen-year-old daughter 'Aliya. Among the participants was the brother of Justice Minister Rashid Karami, both sons of the late 'Abd al-Hamid Karami. When the university's president decided to expel six students for having joined the demonstration, all the students went on strike, compelling him to readmit the six.[20] On 30 November 1951, the Chamber reacted to the pressure from Cairo (echoed by Damascus and other Arab capitals) by adopting a resolution supporting Egypt in the struggle for its national goals.[21]

A month earlier, on 29 October, Khuri had convened a special session of ministers, together with past prime ministers and former senior members of the Cabinet as well as the present and past speakers of the Chamber (among them figures now in the opposition). Jointly, they resolved to turn down the scheme for a Middle East Command. The broad participation was meant to underscore the search for a comprehensive consensus. Most speakers gave it as their opinion that Lebanon would benefit from membership in the command, but the sense of the meeting was that Beirut must follow the lead of the other Arab states.[22] That sealed the fate of the proposal, as far as Lebanon was concerned.

The West was disappointed with Lebanon's negative decision; relations with Khuri and his government became more reserved. Western diplomats began to feel impatient with the government's inability to make a commitment to the West. In October 1951, for instance, the US chargé d'affaires, John B. Bruins, wrote to the State Department giving a list of US complaints against Lebanon: the issue of the treaty of friendship, Point Four aid (for both see above), refusal to let the Voice of America put up a transmitter in Lebanon, and down to minor points like the rejection of degrees from the American University of Beirut as a sufficient qualification for entering the Lebanese civil service. He recommended using the allocation of Mutual Security Program funds as a bargaining counter 'to attain at least some ... [US] aims in Lebanon'. Washington, he added, should not be 'squeamish about the use of *quid pro quo* ... the Lebanese will have greater respect for us if we use it and very little ... if we do not'.[23]

About a month later, US Minister H. Minor struck a more strongly critical note, writing that the Lebanese position on the Middle East Command was 'hardening' and that Lebanese cooperation with the West 'will be difficult until [the] Egyptian affair is settled'. He went on to say that it was not clear whether public opinion was pushing the government into a pro-Egyptian policy or whether the government was exploiting public opinion to promote its own chosen policy. He expressed concern that the government might 'progressively lose control', as had happened elsewhere in the Middle East. He 'found significance' in a remark made by Sa'ib Salam, then a member of the Chamber, in what Minor described as 'a moment of emotion'. Salam had said: 'I think we are now (rpt now) in a position to dictate terms to you and if I were responsible ... I would make them hard.'[24]

## The Issue of Communism

In American eyes, the suspicions engendered by Beirut's refusal to join the Middle East Command were aggravated by fear of growing communist influence in Lebanon, or even of a communist takeover. In retrospect, it is clear that there was no room for such apprehensions, but at the time they were a potent ingredient of western attitudes towards Lebanon. The

Communist Party in the Levant had been founded in the mid-1920s. It was suppressed by the French mandatory authorities and, in 1939, was declared illegal. After the entry of the allies in 1941, the party's life became easier; the French relied on its traditional anti-British stance and on Moscow's instructions for it to cooperate with the French.[25] But in 1943, the party joined the opponents of French rule and from then on remained consistently anti-French. In December 1946, the Levant party split into a Syrian and a Lebanese one. Its supporters in Lebanon numbered several thousands, at most 10,000, mostly from among the educated class and from among the liberal professions. Most were Christians, with Greek Orthodox and Armenians in the van. However, it won broader sympathies by its approach to social and economic questions as well as by establishing the first Lebanese trade unions.[26] In the final analysis, however, communist ideology ran counter to the basic beliefs held by the great majority of Lebanese. Moreover, Soviet support for the partition of Palestine hurt the party's chances in Lebanon, even though the party itself issued an appeal for the defence of Palestine against Anglo-American and Zionist plots.[27]

Bruins's assessment in his report to Washington in October 1951 was that communism 'appears to have comparatively little appeal to the general public, despite the fact that Lebanon lacks a substantial middle class'.[28] By contrast, a US intelligence report of June 1948 stated that 'a significant basic factor in Lebanon is the strength and growth of communism ... in the past few years. It is in Lebanon that the Communists have achieved the best organized and most effective organization in the Near East, which serves as a propaganda base for neighboring countries.'[29] Against this background, western diplomats occasionally made representations to the Lebanese government to ban or take other effective measures against the Communist Party.[30]

Such requests were largely ignored by the Lebanese government. Lebanese leaders seem to have understood better than western representatives how unlikely communist ideology or party activity were to strike a responsive chord in the country. They did not feel that the party's existence endangered the stability of their regime. In their eyes, it was just another small piece in the Lebanese political mosaic, no less legitimate than any other. And indeed, the party accepted the ground rules of Lebanese politics and took part in the elections in accordance with them – though with scant success. Some of its leaders were not above exploiting family influence or patron–client relationships for electoral gain – just as everybody else did. To illustrate: Mustafa al-'Aris, one of the salient personalities in the party, who ran for the Chamber in Beirut in 1947, got his name placed on a list of several well-known Sunni and Christian notables. He did not get elected.

Lebanese government leaders felt that taking too vigorous action against the Communist Party would be tantamount to a denial of the country's fundamental pluralism; it would undermine rather than advance stability. They had before their eyes the example of the PPS, a body much more dangerous to them than the Communist Party. Applying strong-arm methods against it had conjured up greater perils than the exercise of tolerance would have done.

Such attitudes are well reflected in a conversation between Prime Minister Yafi and the US chargé d'affaires in Beirut in late 1951. The American diplomat pointed to the danger of communism, adding that the main source of communist influence was the gulf between rich and poor and the lack of social awareness in the country. He asserted that nothing was being done to improve the lot of the lowest classes. Yafi's reply was that in rural Lebanon there was no real poverty since most people owned their own plot of land and made a living from it, even though a modest one. In the cities, the family protected the individual; besides, religious and other social institutions looked after the poor. Hence, Yafi went on, Lebanon offered no fertile ground for communism.[31]

If at all, the government responded to pressures urging anti-communist steps upon it only to the extent that similar measures were being taken in other Arab states. When, late in 1947, it declared the party illegal because of Soviet policy on Palestine, it only fell in line with the rest of the Arab world. Despite the ban, the party continued to be active. In November 1948, 'Aris was arrested after about one hundred communists had protested in a violent demonstration against a UNESCO congress held in Beirut. The police raided the offices of trade unions controlled by the communists. (The government were piqued by the demonstrations because they considered the holding of the congress in Beirut a special achievement.)[32] These measures against the party did not prevent it from registering a notable success two years later when it gathered signatures for a petition for peace and against nuclear armament. Among the signatories were patriarch 'Arida, Chamoun, Yafi, Faranjiyya and Sami al-Sulh.[33]

Also in 1950, in a partial response to western representations, the government announced that the General Security Service had been authorized to fight communism and foreign espionage and that the press had been forbidden to mention communist activities. But at a meeting with US diplomats, the head of the service stated that he was 'somewhat discouraged at … higher authorities … not permitting him to proceed more actively against Communists'. He then suggested that the US withhold Point Four aid in order to enforce Lebanese compliance. The US representatives replied that assistance should not be used for bargaining; its object was 'to combat communism constructively by raising the standard of living in Lebanon'.[34]

Lebanese arguments discounting the menace of communism were not received well in the West. Diplomats considered them a sign of the government's blindness to danger and its ineffectiveness. Displeasure at the regime's leniency towards the Communist Party now combined with overall western scepticism regarding Khuri's administration and its functioning. This outlook was doubtlessly shaped by applying western standards to a political entity whose unique characteristics were of a different kind and whose nature was ill understood by western diplomats. The Lebanese themselves viewed their state in a different light and did not conceive of their government as an instrument for changing the existing political, social and economic patterns; on the contrary, they felt that the regime drew its legitimacy from its resolve to maintain and uphold the 'Lebanese system' as the only viable basis of the state.

## The Need for Reform

The western view remained that the overall helplessness of the government was responsible for the 'upsurge' of communism. A certain coldness began to make itself felt in western assessments. In 1950, US Minister Pinkerton wrote to the Department of State that Lebanon was 'democratic only in form. Actually it is oligarchic [and] corrupt ... It has no sense of social responsibility and the interests of the population as a whole count for very little with the ruling clique.' But he immediately conceded that there existed 'no person or group ... who could be expected to be more honest'. The problem therefore was 'to teach, guide and influence the present group and hope for a gradual improvement'.[35] In keeping with such attitudes, the USA now began pressuring the government to carry out reforms.

The need for reform was cogently argued in a set of policy guidelines laid down in a State Department memorandum of January 1951. It summed up Washington's objectives in Beirut as follows: (1) the maintenance of security and stability; (2) the development of mutual trade and of cultural links; (3) 'the enhancement of American prestige'; (4) 'the cultivation of Lebanon's orientation toward the United States and the West at large'. One of America's 'principal immediate objectives' was to 'prevent the USSR from gaining control by force or subversion of Lebanon's important strategic assets, particularly its harbors ... its developing aviation facilities' and its present and projected oil facilities at the terminals of the pipe-lines from Iraq and Saudi Arabia. The memorandum concluded that the problem was not a lack of pro-western sympathies but the need to foster 'more representative, effective and honest government. While recognizing that improvements ... must emanate primarily from within the country itself, we should avail ourselves of every favorable opportunity to induce the Lebanese to make these improvements.' US and UN technical and training aid should be used 'for establishing better central, urban and provincial government administration. Wherever possible, we should encourage liberal reforms' and direct aid so as to support 'those elements in the Lebanese government willing and able to introduce ... progressive measures as opposed to those seeking their own aggrandizement or enrichment'.[36] The issue of reform developed into an obsession that ended up distorting the US assessment of Khuri's regime. The uncritical application of western liberal standards made the Lebanese administration appear nothing short of hopeless. Khuri, his relatives and protégés were cast in the role of the corrupt with the 'reformer' Chamoun and the 'progressive liberal' Junbalat opposite them. US diplomats had high regard for Junbalat, choosing to overlook his socialist leanings.

Only occasionally did some individual diplomat fail to conform to this received wisdom. L. Clayton of the US legation, for instance, noted that Beirut was no more corrupt than Philadelphia and held that, while US interests prescribed extending American influence in the Levant, they did not require imposing morality there.[37] On the whole, British diplomats quickly fell into line with their US colleagues. But Furlonge, who had first come to Lebanon as one of Spears's assistants and who was now head of the Eastern Department at the Foreign Office, averred that criticism of the Lebanese government should largely be dismissed. The Lebanese were experts in 'destructive criticism', he wrote, but there were few in the country who could do better than the present ruling group. In Beirut, he added, even harsh criticism was no proof that the standing of the person criticized was declining. Such voices, however, were rare.[38]

Hostility grew in the early 1950s as East–West tensions mounted and the West became increasingly apprehensive about losing its Middle Eastern strongholds because of the weakness of regional governments. Tragically for Khuri, this was precisely the time when he would have most needed western support. Beginning in 1951, a series of local, regional and international events began opening cracks in the ostensibly still solid façade of the regime. Also, just at this time, the three western powers replaced their representatives in Beirut. The British minister, Houstoun-Boswall, was replaced by Chapman Andrews and the French, Armond de Chayla, by Jean Balay. US Minister Pinkerton was replaced by Harold Brink Minor, a professional diplomat whose previous postings had included Jerusalem (1936–40), Tehran (1940–43) and Athens (1947–51). In between, he had headed the State Department's Division of Near Eastern Affairs.[39]

From the start, Minor inherited a legacy of coldness and reserve towards Khuri. He, and to some extent his British and French colleagues as well, stepped up contacts with the opposition. Soon they were believed to be encouraging it (see following chapter). In a small country like Lebanon, not even the tenor of diplomatic reports could be kept secret for long. As far as we can judge from currently available archival material, neither Minor nor his colleagues had instructions from their superiors to try and topple the Khuri regime. But in a summary of events drafted after Khuri's fall, Minor noted that

> prior to the upheaval, the authors of the anti-Khuri revolt frequently visited this legation. While Legation officers maintained a policy of strictest non-intervention and neutrality, these Lebanese friends were always cautioned against resorting to force or violence. Without fail, they pledged themselves to use only

peaceful and Constitutional means, a pledge which was fulfilled in the historical developments which followed.[40]

The picture of Khuri's regime such as it emerged from Minor's reports was so negative that the State Department felt obliged to remind him that he should display a more balanced attitude. Minor's French and British counterparts also tried from time to time to moderate his views, but more often they took their cue from him (see next chapter).

Minor was probably influenced by the State Department's overall regional policy (which he may have interpreted in his own way). His personal bluntness seems also to have played a role. But what had the greatest impact on him and the other western representatives was that in Lebanon, unlike in other Arab states, there existed an obvious alternative to the current president and government. This opposition could easily be described in terms of a reformist grouping struggling against a corrupt regime with a record of failures. US diplomats were in touch with a comparatively numerous Lebanese intelligentsia critical of their government; they knew what the aggressive local press was writing; and they were aware of the relatively broad freedom of political expression and activity in the country (reflecting both its tradition of pluralism and the weakness of its central government). All this may well have given them the impression that Lebanon was on the verge of an upheaval bound to end with the present opposition taking power.

What they failed to appreciate was that the opposition was as much part and parcel of the 'Lebanese system' as the government. Almost to a man, opposition figures were pursuing their personal interests within that system. Opposition rhetoric notwithstanding, the replacement of Khuri was not intended to change the system but merely to replace the men at the top of the pyramid. The pyramid itself would be left as it was. Chamoun would succeed Khuri as president and several other opposition figures would emerge enjoying stronger bargaining positions. After all, the office-holders as much as their competitors were the creatures of the National Pact. They would not challenge it, nor was their foreign and regional policy likely to be much different from Khuri's. This was not well understood in the embassies.

One way or another, the trust the West had originally placed in Khuri had been lost and the western representatives in Beirut had grown suspicious of him. When the domestic crisis assumed its full proportions in the summer of 1952, the lack of western backing and the (conjectured or actual) encouragement of the opposition by the western embassies were so many more nails in Khuri's coffin.

# CHAPTER 13

# The Overthrow

Late at night on 18 September 1952, President Khuri tendered his resignation, ending a nine-year tenure. The road was open for his rival, Camille Chamoun, to succeed him. It was a sad end to the long career of the man described as, 'in the opinion of many, [Lebanon's] most accomplished politician', the man who had done 'most to achieve Lebanon's independence ... and to establish [its] viability'.[1] Khuri himself later wrote of his time in office that there was 'much that was bitter, little that was sweet'.[2]

Khuri's opponents, especially Chamoun and Junbalat, spoke of his downfall as a 'revolution' precipitated by popular forces. A broad popular consensus had formed, they claimed (and some of the press echoed them), and had proved strong enough to bring down a corrupt and tyrannical regime and to replace it with reformist and liberal elements.[3] Some called it the 'glorious' or 'white' (i.e. bloodless) revolution. In his memoirs, Junbalat dwelt on the 'parliamentary, popular and democratic manner' in which it had been carried out.[4] Such terms seemed to imply that there had been no mere reshuffle at the top nor a coup of the type then fashionable in the Arab world, but a redrawing of the ground rules of the 'Lebanese system'; power had been transferred from the old, traditional leadership to young men of liberal persuasions who were responsive to the desires of the public.

Coming from Khuri's opponents, such formulations were understandable. Surprisingly, they have also been adopted in some historical studies. F. I. Qubain, for example, notes the 'general feeling of revulsion and disgust with the old guard' prevalent all over the Arab world at the time, and goes on to say: 'In Lebanon itself, after several years of corruption, graft and nepotism, the public was hungry for reform.'[5] P. Hitti says similarly that Khuri 'bowed to the people's will'.[6] Western diplomatic reports, too, mostly welcomed Khuri's fall as a revolution brought about by a politically conscious public. US minister, Harold Minor, though cautioning against exaggerated optimism, still wrote that the 'first phase of revolution' had now occurred.[7]

Khuri's resignation, though, was caused by realities much more complex than the revolutionary myth fabricated by his rivals, spread by contemporary observers and taken up by later students of Lebanese history. It would not be enough simply to supplement the older versions with new and additional details of the domestic, inter-Arab and international background. Rather, the story needs to be told anew.

From the beginning of the 1950s, it had become obvious that Khuri was in trouble. The main props on which he had leaned since his advent to power were collapsing like domino pieces. There was much public dis-satisfaction with the regime and, before long, allegations of inefficiency and accusations of corruption were being levelled against the president personally. Public resentment in itself did not bring down the president, but it provided the opposition politicians with the groundswell on which to ride to power. Abroad, Khuri had lost the support of the Syrian government. Arab support had become difficult to mobilize because inter-Arab affairs were then in a state of paralysis. Finally, Khuri had lost the support of the West which had been forthcoming so unstintingly in earlier years.

In combination, the above developments detracted from the legitimacy which Khuri had been able to project for most of the years of his tenure. The elites of notables who had long accepted it wholeheartedly were now the first to question it. These trends were eventually strong enough to force Khuri out, but they did not constitute a revolution: they were carried out from within the existing system by men who had risen, and were operating, within it and who did not change its rules (nor did they wish to). The incoming team differed from Khuri's in its personal composition, but not in its political, social or economic background. Both belonged to the same elite groups.

In their studies, both M. Hudson and K. Salibi acknowledge the systemic nature of the event. The former argues that Khuri's downward slide was initiated by his drift away from his old partner, Riyad al-Sulh. Had it not been for this, he might have survived.[8] The latter, while not ignoring the impact of Sulh's departure from the scene, points to the activities of Cham-oun and Junbalat as major factors.[9] For both, power struggles within the system were the main cause of the president's fall. This was especially true of the Sunni leadership, Khuri's mainstay outside his own community. After an interval, Shi'i and Druse notables followed suit.

Khuri's opponents felt impelled to act because in their view the regime was upsetting the delicate political, social and communal balance which had so far prevented any one element from gaining too much power for itself. Now, by contrast, the president and his family were seen to have acquired a disproportionate share of power, and to have done so at the expense of other components of the Lebanese patchwork. These perceptions had much to do with Khuri's re-election: his entering upon a second term meant that Maronite presidential hopefuls saw their prize recede into the future and that Sunni leaders found their bargaining powers greatly curtailed. Over time, all those who felt hurt by the new imbalance joined forces to bring Khuri down and restore the system's proper equilibrium.

As we have seen, Khuri's election to a second term, while bringing his personal and familial power to a short-lived peak, had coincided with a marked decline in his country's regional and international standing. In the long term, it proved counter-productive in domestic terms as well. The increased authority of the president and his greater ability to interfere in all manner of domestic issues elicited growing disaffection. Even more resentment was called forth by the activities of his brother Salim who had succeeded in turning himself into the *za'im* (local 'boss') of Mt Lebanon. A large group of deputies personally loyal to him gave him considerable weight in the Chamber. He had succeeded in acquiring much influence in several branches of the administration, notably in the police, the gendarmerie and the security services. An additional source of resentment was the growing share in the economy which Khuri, Salim, Khuri's other brothers, his sons, and his associates appropriated for themselves.

Khuri's notion of the presidency had evolved towards a concept of equating it with the state itself. In part, this was a throwback to the days of the emirate and the *Mutasarrifiyya* in Mt Lebanon – the soil from which, in Khuri's opinion, modern Lebanon had sprung and whose leaders were his role models. It was not for nothing that Khuri had the palace of Amir Bashir II (1788–1840) in Dayr al-Qamar restored or that he brought his remains back to Lebanon from Turkey.[10] From another angle, he thought of himself as the creator of modern Lebanon and thus its natural and rightful leader. But he ignored the fact that, as an individual, he lacked vital leadership qualities: he possessed neither personal charisma nor firm resolve. More than that: his new concept of himself contradicted the National Pact which had assigned the president the position of senior representative of the Maronite community, not that of ruler. At the time, few Lebanese would have supported a leader on the strength of his national record rather than his communal and/or familial ties.

Khuri's overall notion of what the presidency should be also informed the 'division of labour' he devised between himself and his family, first and foremost between himself and Salim. Salim became, as it were, Khuri's *alter ego*; the US minister called them 'Jekyll and Hyde'.[11] Salim became the 'fixer' in charge of building the family's power base while Khuri – an excellent manipulator – pulled the strings from behind the scenes. Initially, this arrangement was useful to Khuri; Salim gave him political clout, while he himself could assume the mantle of national leader dealing with essentials and keeping himself above the fray. But beginning in the late 1940s, Salim turned himself into a political figure in his own right, becoming more independent than suited Khuri. A clash of interests soon developed. During the final years, public attention was riveted on the aggrandizement of the Khuri family and public criticism centred on it. The family, its critics clamoured, was turning Lebanon into their private estate. The main target of criticism was 'Sultan' Salim; but a second brother, Fu'ad, and Khuri's sons Michel and Khalil came in for their share, too. Khalil was accused of drug dealing, of involvement in organized betting, and of extorting money from traders in exchange for import and export licences.[12] 'Everybody in Lebanon has turned into a sultan,' *Al-Hayat* wrote. Salim was the ruler of Mt Lebanon, it added, but every region has its own 'Sultan'.[13]

Even though Salim may have been named more often, it was Khuri himself who was the principal butt of public criticism; it was he who was held responsible both for the failures of his government and for the actions of his family. Some held that Lebanon was no worse than other Middle Eastern states.[14] Not everyone agreed. 'Adil Arsalan, for instance, a Syrian politician on close personal terms with Khuri, wrote in his memoirs: 'The extent of corruption and degeneracy in the Lebanese regime defy the imagination. Every government has its defects ... yet the volume of thieving [from public property] and the insolence of the thieves in Lebanon have no parallel.'[15]

Many researchers tend to regard the upsurge of public censure of corruption, nepotism, the failure to create a modern administrative apparatus or to grapple with the essential defects of the 'Lebanese system' as a pivotal element in Khuri's overthrow. This seems exaggerated. But it must, nevertheless, be borne in mind that initially, in the heyday of the struggle for independence from the French, Khuri had enjoyed very broad support from the politically conscious segments of the population. The press was for him, the intelligentsia and the free professions were with him. However, at the time we are speaking of, their support had turned into hostility. The press had changed its tune and now pulled out all the stops against him. True, several newspapers attacked him because they were owned by opposition leaders; but there developed an overall press chorus against the president, voicing resentment, causing old allies to abandon him, and giving western observers the impression that the entire Lebanese public was rallying around Khuri's opponents.

More than by all the above circumstances, Khuri's fall resulted from the chasm that gradually opened up between him and the traditional elites. We can trace two lines in this context: the consolidation of the opposition forces; and the loss of faith in Khuri first on the part of the Sunni notables, then by the notables of other communities.

The first signs of a consolidation of the opposition appeared in the period immediately following the 1947 elections and gathered momentum after Khuri's re-election to a second term. While the 1951 elections did not add to the numerical strength of the opposition in the Chamber, it emerged more cohesive, and united round a single and explicit aim: the downfall of the president. It was led by two politicians who, in the public judgment, were rising stars: Chamoun and Junbalat.

Chamoun's drive for reforms enabled him to acquire support beyond his natural stronghold in Mt Lebanon. In particular, it gave him greater influence among well-educated Lebanese anywhere. It also earned him the backing of western diplomats. His record at the UN and his good personal relations with Arab rulers in Iraq and Syria rendered him acceptable to the Arab world and thus helped him with the Sunni community (especially after Sulh's death put an end to the old personal feud between them). In a similar fashion, Junbalat strove to promote his image as a national rather than a communal leader and to be recognized as such in the rest of the Arab world. In May 1949 he founded the Progressive Socialist Party (PSP) devoted to creating a 'new society' based on 'sound democracy [and] social calm' and committed to the struggle for 'justice, welfare, liberty and peace' and for human rights according to the principles of the UN.[16] Such universalist goals did not, however, do much to gain him broader influence outside the circle of Druse supporters of his family – and these were tied to him by tradition, not ideology. The real head of the family was Junbalat's mother Nazira. It was only after her death in 1949 that he became a leader in his own right. He used his new-found liberty to step up his attacks on Khuri.[17] To do so, he found it useful that he had formed good relations with the PPS and the Edde family. After Emile Edde's death in 1949, the Edde sons and Junbalat set up the National Socialist Bloc as an umbrella organization for opponents of Khuri's of various persuasions.

The new bloc soon attracted a number of political figures who had originally been allies of Khuri but had become disappointed with him and his regime. These included some Maronite notables who expected to gain additional strength by joining the bloc. Notable among them was Hamid Faranjiyya who, like Chamoun, considered himself to have presidential potential. Opposing Khuri would, he assumed, promote his prospects; besides, he sought revenge for his electoral defeat in 1951 which he blamed on Khuri. He argued that the chief defect in Lebanon's politics was that the president was powerful but not accountable, while the prime minister was accountable but comparatively powerless. It was a slogan that soon caught on.[18]

Other opposition figures were less dangerous to Khuri. They had been passed over for ministerial or other appointments, but were not really out to bring him down. Their loyalty could be regained with a comparatively low investment of benefits and promises. Many of these refrained from attacking Khuri, criticizing the prime minister instead. But after May 1951, Salim al-Khuri became their particular target. This trend is well exemplified by the case of Far'un. Originally, he was close to Khuri and one of the pillars of his regime. For years he extended his cooperation to Salim as well. But soon after the formation of Yafi's cabinet in June 1951, a rift became apparent between Far'un and Salim, caused by Salim's keeping Far'un and his political friends removed from positions of influence. Far'un grew sharply critical of the regime and, by implication, of Khuri himself. Some observers claimed that Far'un did so because he aspired to the presidency, even though he was a Greek Catholic rather than a Maronite.[19] This does not seem to have been the case: shortly before his fall, Khuri succeeded in reconciling Far'un. This would indicate that the latter's quarrel was not with the president but with

Salim. Yet the damage Far'un's earlier defection had caused proved, at least in part, to be irreversible.

Another example of this process is afforded by Majid Arsalan, for long a devoted ally of Khuri's. Following the 1951 elections, he resigned from Khuri's Constitutional Bloc after having competed for its leadership against Salim and lost. Arsalan did not conceal his anger at Salim. In consequence, when Yafi's cabinet was formed shortly afterwards, the defence portfolio (which Arsalan considered his traditional fief) was given to Rashid Baydun. Chamoun proposed to Arsalan to set up an anti-Khuri front of Druse leaders, but Arsalan could not bring himself to cooperate with Junbalat, his rival for the leadership of the Druse community.[20] Eventually, when Khuri offered him a cabinet post in Sami al-Sulh's government, he returned to the president's camp. But he remained critical of the government and, indirectly, of Khuri too.

Men like Far'un and Arsalan, however, did not join the opposition in order to bring Khuri down but rather to establish bargaining positions for rejoining him. They took care to criticize the cabinet rather than Khuri himself, but in the early 1950s such distinctions were lost on the Lebanese public. Previously, the presidency and the cabinet had been thought of as clearly distinct institutions, but by now Khuri was seen to dominate the ministers and was therefore held responsible for their actions, as well as for those of 'Sultan' Salim. If, in the early 1940s, criticism of, or opposition to, the prime minister or the cabinet was likely to resound to the president's credit, by now the presidency and the premiership were thought of as more or less the same thing. The best way to criticize the government as a whole now was to attack the president.

Next to the fact that the opposition forces were drawing closer together, Khuri's loss of credibility in the eyes of the Sunni leaders contributed greatly to his downfall. They had come to feel that he was disregarding the balance of power between the Maronite president and the Sunni prime minister – a balance stipulated in the National Pact and essential to the proper working of the political system. The break between Khuri and Sulh (largely Khuri's own doing) and Sulh's subsequent death had removed Khuri's closest Sunni ally from the scene. Unlike Sulh, the new premier, Yafi, installed after the elections, had no large personal following in the Sunni community and was entirely dependent on Khuri for his appointment and on Salim for staying in power. It must be remembered that Salim now dominated the Chamber and that prime ministers needed votes of confidence in the Chamber of Deputies. Yafi's successor, Sami al-Sulh, was in no better position. More than ever before, the Khuri brothers were able to exploit to their own advantage the jealousies between the Sunni notables.

Salim told a US diplomat that 'he trusted none of the Sunni deputies who are eligible for the post of Prime Minister. He believed that they were all similar in their subserviency to Muslim elements who wished to dominate

Lebanon. In order to maintain Christian influence, as well as his own, Sheikh
Selim stated that he is pursuing a policy which envisages a change of Prime
Minister every four or five months.' Yafi, Sa'ib Salam, Sami al-Sulh and Sa'di
al-Manala would 'rotate' in the post.[21] It was only a question of time before
the Sunni leaders decided that they would no longer suffer such an affront
to their dignity.

The decisive phase in the run-up to Khuri's overthrow came when, in the
wake of the Sunni notables, other communal elites started abandoning him.
In the early 1950s, Khuri's ability to manoeuvre between the elites and to
reward or chastize them by granting or withholding benefits had reached a
peak. But it was precisely this which forced him to involve himself ever more
deeply in the internal power struggles of each group of notables. This meant
that he made more enemies than he made friends. The group of disappointed,
and therefore disaffected, notables in each community kept growing. Once
the Sunni elite withdrew its support from the president, notables of other
communities abandoned him, too. Khuri's legitimacy crumbled in the eyes of
the notables from the moment when they no longer perceived him as the
guarantor of stability and equilibrium.

In that sense, a straight line led from the elections of 1951 to Khuri's
resignation in 1952. This is exemplified by the two cabinets which he appointed
during the period. The first, Yafi's government (confirmed by the Chamber
on 19 June 1951), was described as feeble right from the start. Yafi had a
reputation for skill and honesty, but was also considered politically weak.
Nevertheless, the British legation assessed the new cabinet in quite positive
terms:

> In general, the new cabinet can be regarded as satisfactory from our point of
> view. Though Abdullah Yafi is not a great figure, and is generally supposed to
> have been entrusted with the task of forming the government because he could
> be counted on to carry out the policy of his influential party bosses, such as
> Sheikh Selim El-Khouri and Henri Pharaon, he has already shown signs of
> independence, and it would certainly be unfair to regard him as nothing more
> than a yes-man. He is well-disposed to England, will welcome our advice, and
> is very much alive to the dangers of communism.[22]

In his inauguration speech, Yafi promised a number of far-reaching reforms,
including the franchise for women in local elections.[23] But at the Foreign
Office, Furlonge (drawing on his ample personal experience of the country)
dismissed his proposals as the sort of empty promises incoming prime
ministers were wont to make. If Yafi was serious about reform, Furlonge
added, he would not last longer than a few months.[24]

The principal critics of Yafi's government were Chamoun, Faranjiyya and
Pierre Edde, but – for the reasons set out above – their criticism of the
cabinet must be interpreted as chiefly directed against Khuri. To their number
must be added Riyad al-Sulh (see Chapter 11) and Sami al-Sulh who had

himself aspired to the premiership. Hamada, having failed in his contest with his son-in-law As'ad over the office of speaker of the Chamber, also joined the opposition. So did Arsalan, who had been passed over once again when the cabinet was formed.[25] Yafi's most grievous troubles, though, were not caused by his opponents but by the two Khuri brothers on whom he depended, and by their associates. Many observers thought his cabinet would not last because he could not for long satisfy Salim's appetite for appointments, influence and material benefits for his political friends.

The first crisis occurred as early as August 1951, against the background of growing political violence. Much of the violence was initiated by Salim who wanted to deter political opponents, but the ambience created by the use of force told against Khuri rather than the opposition. On 23 August, supporters of Salim threw a bomb at the building of the *Al-Bayraq* newspaper, the organ of the National Bloc led by the Eddes. The partisans of the latter responded the following night by throwing a hand grenade at Salim's house. On 26 August, Salim bussed thousands of his followers to 'Aley for a demonstration of support opposite a vacation home where Khuri was staying. There was much firing in the air, and the Beirut–Damascus highway was blocked for a while. The police, under the command of Salim's protégés, failed to intervene. Salim's conduct was widely criticized – a fact which caused, or at least encouraged, Yafi to stage a government crisis. He threatened to resign in protest against the failure of law-enforcement at 'Aley. It was only under pressure from the president, and after he had been promised that those responsible for law-breaking would be duly punished, that Yafi agreed to carry on.[26]

A more serious crisis occurred towards the end of the year 1951. Yafi told British diplomats that the president kept interfering in cabinet business and pressuring him to appoint his protégés to various posts in the administration. He told them of an associate of Arsalan's who was in prison for murder and other crimes. The president had wanted him released, claiming that 'the poor man had no intentions of killing'.[27] Salim for his part systematically foiled any attempt by Yafi to amend the electoral law or to hold local elections. The summary for 1951 by the British legation said in part:

> There were rumours during the summer parliamentary recess that Sheikh Selim would muster his supporters and seek to overthrow ... Yafi who has no personal following. Owing to presidential intervention [he] received a respite, but as the year closed he expressed his view ... that he could not continue much longer, both by reasons of presidential interference in his work, and the fact that ... Selim was sufficiently powerful to withdraw his parliamentary support whenever it suited his book.[28]

By his struggle for a clean administration, Yafi made numerous enemies among various groups of notables. It must be added, though, that at least in part Yafi's anti-corruption drive was a self-seeking enterprise, intended to eliminate personal adversaries. His general campaign against hashish-growing, conducted with much fanfare, was seen specifically as an act of revenge against Sabri Hamada, the local 'boss' of the Biqa', for his opposition to the government. (The Biqa' was the main area of hashish cultivation.) The president's son Khalil was also thought to grow hashish, so he was considered another target of Yafi's drive.[29] An anti-gambling drive initiated in November 1951 was interpreted as a means to damage Arsalan's standing as well as that of the president's family – both known to be involved in the gambling business.[30]

For one reason or another, Salim decided at about this time finally to withdraw parliamentary support from Yafi. The two agreed, however, that Yafi should continue in office until the new economic agreement with Syria was signed and the new budget passed by the Chamber. This having been done, Yafi resigned on 9 February 1951.[31]

Sunni notables at once began a race for his succession. Khuri seems originally to have preferred Sa'ib Salam because of his record as a strong minister of the interior in 1946. However, he later explained that consultations with various deputies had persuaded him that Sami al-Sulh had the best chance of being confirmed by the Chamber.[32] Undoubtedly, however, the main reason for his choice was that he had Salim's backing. But there were others. A report from the US legation, for instance, referred to a statement by Khuri's son Khalil explaining that 'it was chiefly the Christian–Moslem conflict … as it was focalized in the Riyad al-Sulh assassination that induced … Khuri to name Sami Bey Sulh'. Khalil had added that he expected Sulh to remain in office for several months despite the fact that the president considered him 'incompetent'.[33]

Whatever the specific circumstances, Sulh's appointment was part of Khuri's policy of setting one Sunni leader against the others. The US minister thought that Sa'ib Salam had come to grief because, unlike Sulh, he was 'not sufficiently ambitious'. Sulh was expected to 'condone the "irregularities" which will permit the continuance of the corrupt practices of … Selim, and his top-level coterie. This is fully reflected in the character of the new Cabinet.' The minister added that Khuri had apparently concluded 'that the country can stand a few months more of corruption before popular resentment … reaches the danger point'. Khuri, the minister felt, was 'playing with fire' but was 'prepared to change Prime Ministers at any time when public resentment may threaten serious public disorder'.[34]

On 19 February 1952, the Chamber confirmed Sulh in office by a great majority. Only eight deputies, Faranjiyya and seven followers of the National Socialist Bloc (founded by Chamoun, Junbalat and the Eddes; see above) voted against him. Five of the nine cabinet ministers were supporters of Salim al-Khuri, giving him virtual control of cabinet business. Public opinion greeted the new government with disappointment and with much scepticism regarding its life expectancy.[35]

At that particular time, however, any government would have had a difficult time. There was a series of strikes in vital public services (public transportation, telephones, banks, oil companies and more). There was a feeling that the country was sliding into anarchy. While it is true that the Lebanese economy did well in these years, it was the notables, and mainly the economic elite in Beirut, that were the major – and sometimes the only – beneficiaries of this economic prosperity.[36] It should be mentioned, however, that most trade unions were controlled by notables and, more often than not, strikes were a means to advance their personal interests as well as to make life hard for the president and the prime minister.

One of the more conspicuous strikes was that of the lawyers who protested against a new civil status law. They had demanded that lawsuits concerning marriages, divorces, child custody and inheritance be heard in civil courts; but under pressure from communal leaders, Khuri and Sulh agreed to amend the law and leave these matters in the hands of each community's religious courts. The lawyers' strike lasted eighty-four days, finally being settled in April 1952 by a compromise formula.[37] Another notable event was a consumers' strike against the Beirut electricity company, in protest against high prices. It was organized jointly by the Phalanges and several Muslim organizations who expected political gains from it. Half the city's consumers refused to pay their bills, but eventually here, too, a compromise was arrived at.[38]

The Palestinian refugees who had moved into Lebanon during and after the war were not only an economic burden (having to be fed and sheltered somehow); being mostly Muslims, they also threatened to upset the country's demographic balance, to the numerical disadvantage of the Christians. At the end of the war, their number was estimated at 120,000, but more arrived later via other Arab countries. In 1949, the government decided not to admit any more refugees and to deny entry to those among them who had left the country and wished to return. In 1951, the government turned down a UN proposal to build permanent housing for the refugees, arguing that their fate was still undecided. When unemployment rose in 1952, the cabinet resolved to limit the issue of labour permits to them. But the Muslim community protested vehemently, and the government revoked its decision. All the while, Lebanon endeavoured to find other countries ready to take in the refugees, and tried to obtain western help in transferring them to Syria or Iraq. But when the Syrian ruler Shishakli visited Beirut in April 1952, he suggested Jordan rather than his own country.[39]

In a vote of confidence in May 1952, Sulh received only forty-two affirmative votes in the Chamber, compared with his initial majority of fifty-six. This was the result of Far'un and Salam having withdrawn their support from Sulh as a means of demonstrating their displeasure with Salim al-Khuri. The change was widely considered as a sign of the impending end of the cabinet.[40] Criticism of Khuri became more widespread. Unlike Riyad al-Sulh, Sami had no intention of absorbing public censure in order to shield the president. Khuri later noted in his memoirs that there was

> a new development in the statements of some of the ministers and officials; a code word was being whispered so as to make people think that the presidency was responsible for everything that went on in the state, even when the presidency was not involved at all. If someone reproved an official or a minister for something he had done, he would at once wash his hands of it and point to 'higher quarters', as if saying: this is not our business; the decision was made higher up.[41]

One sign of the times was an unbridled press campaign against Khuri. True, most papers were owned by opponents of his, but there were also some independent newspapers which had initially supported him but now joined the anti-Khuri campaign. Journalists of various persuasions joined forces because they feared that the growing strength of the presidency would spell the end of Lebanon's (comparative) freedom of the press. The regime responded harshly by arresting several editors and closing some papers down for lengthy periods of time.

As in May 1952, the tone was once again set by Junbalat. Now, he published an article against Khuri in *Al-Anba'*, heading it: 'The foreigners brought them in; let the people expel them.' He wrote that Lebanon was being ruled by a 'band' created and installed by the French. Not representing the people, it had 'no public sense of duty and no sympathy with public problems'. Chamoun, for one, had left Khuri's Constitutional Bloc shortly after the 1943 elections, 'because he feared that the government had become the means of illegal personal exploitation and enrichment, despotism and anarchy'. Later, the bloc turned into 'a family band'. The Khuri brothers were working for the 'profit, glory and power' of their family 'as if the state were family property'. They 'had no principles', listened to French advisers, and 'never mentioned the word "independence" until Great Britain taught them to do so'. They sponsored Riyad al-Sulh, a genuine struggler for independence, at a time when they were 'shaking with fear' because they themselves were 'not accustomed to struggle'. The people, however, 'united for the sake of a principle', i.e. for independence.[42]

Junbalat believed that his parliamentary immunity would protect him against government action. But the government immediately suspended *Al-Anba'* and had its editor sentenced to fourteen months' imprisonment and the paper closed down for eight months. Eight other newspapers which also published Junbalat's article were suspended for three months each.[43] Most journalists went out on strike in protest against the sentences and against the use of the emergency regulations under which the convictions had been secured. The affair triggered a wave of sharply critical press reactions. *Al-Nahar*, for instance, accused Khuri of ignoring the will of the people; *Bayrut* spoke of those who made millions at the expense of people.[44]

Apart from facing his adversaries, Khuri was in deep trouble with some of his past and present supporters. Most of these frictions were caused by Salim. In May 1952, *Al-Wujdan* newspaper (owned by Salim al-Khuri) attacked Far'un; in response, a bomb was thrown at the editor's house, wounding several members of his family. Salim's followers reacted the same day and there were exchanges of fire between men from both sides. The following day, supporters of Salim broke into the office of the owner of *Al-Tiyyar* newspaper, a supporter of Far'un's, and beat him up. Next, two editors were abducted, one pro-Far'un, the other pro-Salim (the editor of *Al-Wujdan*). The kidnappers of the latter apparently found temporary refuge in Far'un's house; the police refrained from conducting a search there.[45]

Little wonder, then, that in June 1952, Georges Naqqash, editor of *L'Orient* and a political ally of Khuri's, proposed to set up a military dictatorship, to be headed by Khuri (who may actually have inspired the idea). The army, Naqqash asserted, would put an end to anarchy and corruption. The parliamentary regime had failed to suit itself to Lebanese realities and had thus become the root of all evil. The idea caused a furore. Chiha replied to Naqqash in *Le Jour*, saying that what had brought Lebanon to its current deplorable state was not the system but those who presently ran it; a dictatorship headed by the same people would not achieve anything. *Bayrut* argued that the solution lay in reducing, rather than enlarging, the president's authority.[46]

Throughout the first half of 1952, Khuri tried to win over several of the hard-core opposition figures. To some, he offered ministerial appointments. In one such attempt, he sent his son Khalil to see Raymond Edde and to suggest to him that he forget the past and turn over a new leaf in the relationship between their two families. Edde declared himself interested, but posed conditions with regard to electoral reform which he must have known would not be acceptable.[47] Khuri also tried to draw the PPS closer to him. Ghassan Tuwayni, a PPS supporter in the Chamber, denied that such a move was afoot, but told US diplomats that Khuri was now showing 'a degree of tolerance' towards the PPS, probably from fear of assassination. He added that Khuri was making secret 'overtures' to the PPS, but that the party would not agree 'to the type of reconciliation the President would want'.[48] All this was too little too late; by the early summer of 1952, the gulf separating the regime from its opponents had become unbridgeable. Khuri's adversaries were no longer asking for his regime to be reformed; they wanted to see him replaced.

When Khuri realized that his attempts to fragment the opposition had failed, he tried to rally his remaining supporters more firmly around him. To do so, he started to restrain his brother Salim, perhaps even to erode his position. On 6 June, in a move to restore public confidence, he announced a major reorganization of the police and the gendarmerie. This was taken as a sign that the president was now ready to clip the wings of Salim who had, as noted above, acquired powerful influence over the internal security forces.

The police and the gendarmerie were placed under a single command, headed by a supporter of Far'un.[49] Salim, feeling that his position was being endangered, set up a party of his own, the Constitutional Democratic Union Party (Hizb al-Ittihad al-Dusturi al-Dimuqrati), an ad hoc political alliance comprising twenty-seven of Salim's supporters in the Chamber and also backed by As'ad. Clearly, Salim was flexing his political muscles.[50]

On top of all this, western reservations about Khuri's government (see Chapter 9) now made themselves increasingly felt. This undermined Khuri's self-confidence and encouraged his rivals who tried to recruit western diplomats for their cause. In addition, 'Abd al-Nasir's military coup in Egypt also caused the opposition to take heart (see below). The US minister thought that 'public confidence cannot ... be restored unless the Khuri regime is replaced'. He added the following significant paragraph:

> [The legation] has of course refrained from direct intervention but has kept in close touch with all political elements. Of late we have especially cultivated elements which appear to be working for better gov[ernmen]t and ... this ... has apparently encouraged them. Our line has been to state in a positive sense what America stands for. However, our continued abstention from direct intervention is beginning to be interpreted as foreign support for the present unpopular regime.[51]

Minor frequently cited talks he or legation staff members had with Lebanese opposition figures. A conversation with Gabriel al-Murr may serve as an example. Murr was a Greek Orthodox notable from Mt Lebanon. He had been a supporter of Khuri's and had held several ministerial appointments, but when he failed to get elected in 1951, he joined the opposition. He urged the legation to inform Khuri that he no longer had US support and to counsel him to abandon power. He opined that Khuri would do so willingly. Minor couched his report in terms revealing a remarkable degree of identification with Murr's attitudes. He called him a 'representative of the trend ... among a considerable number of patriotic and well-meaning Lebanese who seem to be honestly seeking western leadership'. A crisis was approaching and the USA might 'have to decide on a course of action'. Inaction would confirm the public view that the West was 'quietly but effectively supporting the present corrupt regime'.[52] The readiness to listen and the sympathy evinced by the US officials cannot but have convinced their Lebanese interlocutors that Washington had abandoned Khuri and would welcome, or at least not obstruct, an attempt to replace him.

Another report from Minor, written on 7 June 1952, also attested to the great impression opposition spokesmen had made on him. He referred again to the 'dissatisfaction with the existing regime, particularly with the so-called "Presidential Clique"' and with the 'blatant corruption' practised by it. Its main exponent, he went on, was Salim al-Khuri. He spoke once more of the 'frustration as to means for correcting the situation': Khuri's term was to run until 1955 and parliamentary elections were due only in 1954. But even then, 'political control' by the 'clique' might prevent any change. What, then, was the alternative? Minor dismissed the possibility of a popular or military uprising as inconsistent with the Lebanese character. Since Khuri had been helped to power by the West in 1943, he thought 'the only remedy is for the Western powers again to intervene to rid the country of this regime and give democracy a chance to work'. To underpin his views, he appended a historical review of how Khuri had attained power. His explanations owed much to Junbalat's and Chamoun's presentation, or misrepresentation, of Lebanese history in the 1940s and culminated in the statement that Spears 'made El-Khuri President'. He concluded by referring to opposition suggestions for the three western powers to 'step in and correct the situation'. He had replied by saying that intervention 'may not be wise' and was in any case 'contrary to the political institutions of the Western democratic nations'. His Lebanese interlocutors had pointed to the recent wartime and post-war intervention in Greece and had insisted that western action in Lebanon would 'have the support of the public and the opposition members of Parliament' and was 'the only possible solution'.[53] The State Department reacted by pointing out that, while 'discreet and impartial contact' with a cross-section of Lebanese leaders was commendable, nothing should be done to give cause for criticism of 'interference in Lebanon's internal affairs ... The Legation should continue to work through the government in power in order to encourage stable, honest and efficient government.' But, the department added, there was 'no certainty that the opposition would establish such an administration'.[54]

The British minister was almost as critical of the regime and as sympathetic with the opposition. In the summer of 1952, he noted that the situation was deteriorating and that the three western representatives were under pressure from the opposition to intervene.[55] He wrote home that he had listened sympathetically to opposition spokesmen, but had pointed to the danger of awakening communism and had not given them any reason to believe that he supported them.[56] Later he reported that he had 'tried discreetly to restrain Mr. Minor from appearing to encourage Opposition elements'. He himself regarded some of the opposition leaders as 'not merely unreliable but undesirable from any point of view'.[57]

Despite their loss of faith in him, the western ministers kept prodding Khuri to take initiatives of his own to amend the situation. At a meeting between the three western ministers (proposed by the State Department), it was decided that they would assure Khuri that the West was not against him and would assist him in promoting reforms. After this had been done, Khuri told the British minister that he had been 'gratified' by Minor's words, 'particularly so because ... American Legation staff ... seemed to be deliberately encouraging the more active Opposition elements'.[58]

Looking back later, Khuri attributed his downfall to western interference in favour of his rivals. He felt that this had been done to punish him for his refusal to go along with the West on the Middle East Command.[59] In light of our present knowledge of the chain of events, this argument cannot be upheld. The hostility of the three ministers was no more than an indirect and contributory cause, though it cannot be ignored altogether. In the eyes of the notables, one aspect of Khuri's image was the belief that he enjoyed western protection. Once this was no longer true, his prestige was diminished. The Lebanon public, schooled in the heritage of the French mandate and the subsequent British role in the area, was quick to interpret even cautious diplomatic contacts with the opposition leaders as full-fledged great-power support for them. They acted accordingly.

The officers' coup in Egypt on 23 July 1952 added to the overall sense of instability and eroded the legitimacy of the 'old guard' everywhere in the Arab world. It taught the Lebanese opposition that the old rules of the game were no longer sacred. Khuri himself noted this in his memoirs, quoting an Arab adage to the effect that 'if the minaret of a mosque in Egypt collapses, Lebanon must be careful not to let the pieces fall on it'.[60] A few days after the event, *Al-Hayat* wrote that corruption was as prevalent in Lebanon as it was in Egypt. That was why the Lebanese 'cheered the Egyptian revolutionaries just as [people] did in Egypt and other Arab states'. In another article, the paper wrote that if Egypt had its King Faruq, Lebanon had dozens of Faruks.[61] An order issued by the prime minister, Sami al-Sulh, in August 1952, though no more than an insignificant curiosity, nevertheless throws light on the reverberations of the coup: it forbade ministers to use titles like Excellency or Bey in their correspondence 'and to use only Mr. as … in democratic countries'.[62]

Events in Egypt caused Khuri to move quickly to replace the cabinet. But in the present situation, this old and proven ploy could no longer pacify his opponents nor please the notables as a group. More than that: Sami al-Sulh refused to resign, unwilling to play the role of sacrificial victim that Khuri had assigned to him. Only a few days before the Egyptian coup, on 17 July 1952, a ceremony was held to mark the first anniversary of Riyad al-Sulh's assassination. It was attended by a large crowd, and the prime minister, the rest of the cabinet, and many opposition leaders were also present. Khuri stayed away, saving himself the irritation of having to listen to the many attacks against him and his government.[63] A month later, the opposition – secretly encouraged by the prime minister – called for a mass rally to meet at Dayr al-Qamar, Chamoun's personal stronghold. The gathering turned into a forceful demonstration of opposition forces; speakers used it to make overt and scathing attacks against Khuri. Faranjiyya, for instance, declared that Khuri had gone back on all his promises for reform; he held him responsible for the prevalent corruption and said that all his efforts were for 'personal and family enrichment'. He went on to say that Khuri was not 'the father of our Independence'; rather, it was the people's movement which had gained Lebanon its independence and 'no one should demand special recognition for having done his duty'. Junbalat accused the heads of the regime of smuggling money abroad and letting their relatives amass millions. 'Usayran, Emile Bustani and a few others called openly for Khuri's overthrow, citing events in Egypt as an example.[64]

By now, Khuri understood that he was growing powerless to influence events. He noted later: 'Whatever step was taken in the face of the growing *elan* of the opposition was like stopping one hole while another was opening up, like healing one wound while another appeared, until it became clear to me that – overtly or covertly – a foreign hand, or more than one, was inciting people against me.'[65] The president was furious at the prime minister for having given permission to hold the Dayr al-Qamar rally. He issued instructions to prevent the press from reporting the speeches made there and tried to prevail on his associates to organize a counter-demonstration in his favour. Sulh for his part ignored the president's anger, presumably enjoying his discomfiture. Only under pressure from some ministers still loyal to Khuri, he announced his intention of lifting the parliamentary immunity of those deputies whose utterances at the rally had gone beyond the permissible.[66]

At this point, the flight into the arms of the opposition by formerly loyal supporters of the regime became conspicuous. Chiha had changed sides as early as the beginning of 1952. Next, the Phalanges began distancing themselves from Khuri; eventually, in August, they combined with Sulh's Party of the National Call and the Muslim National Congress in forming an umbrella body called the Popular Front. While refraining, at this point, from publicly calling for Khuri's removal, they were sharply critical of him and his government. Phalanges leader Jumayyil, speaking in August, seems to have been the first of their number to call overtly for a change of regime.[67] Finally, even the Shi'i leaders, Khuri's traditional allies, broke ranks. The speaker of the Chamber, Ahmad al-As'ad, failed to consult the president before announcing that he would seek re-election at the beginning of the next parliamentary session, something that could not have happened earlier on.[68]

Only now, when it had become clear that the cabinet was about to fall and might drag Khuri down with it, did the president take action. He announced a series of reform measures of the kind he had so far studiously avoided during both his terms. They included, among other things, authorizing the prime minister to issue decrees effective for six months without requiring parliamentary confirmation; amendments of the electoral law; a reorganization of the court system; and the setting up of a Council for Economic Development. The measures were received with much scepticism. A US legation report doubted whether a nine-year-old system could now be changed overnight.[69] Junbalat, speaking for the opposition, declared that the reforms did not even meet its basic demands.[70]

Determined to bring about Sulh's resignation, Khuri decided to convene the Chamber ahead of time so that the prospect of losing a vote of confidence would cause Sulh to step down of his own accord. Eventually, however, the session of the Chamber was postponed again. Just before its new opening date, three ministers resigned in order to increase the pressure on Sulh to do likewise. One of them, Ahmad al-Husayni, sent Khuri an official letter explaining that he was leaving office for health reasons; but the press published another version containing a bitter personal attack against the president.[71]

When the session of the Chamber opened (on 9 September 1952) in the expectation that it would quickly cause the government to fall, Prime Minister Sami al-Sulh turned the tables on Khuri by making a dramatic speech attacking him and his family. He referred to 'complaints against corruption, anarchy and oppression', but insisted that he and the cabinet were not responsible for the situation. Rather, he went on, it had been created by 'ignorance of the law, lack of respect for the authorities, and ... particular interests'. Individuals 'with no regard for the constitution' were working behind the scenes. In hardly veiled terms, he held the Khuri family responsible for the death of Riyad al-Sulh, saying: 'They have danced on the skeletons of the dead; Riyad al-Sulh ... was a victim of their hypocrisy and intrigue ... He sacrificed his head to save theirs.' They had accused others, but it was 'their hands who committed the murder'. He went on to complain of constant interference with cabinet business on the part of 'influential personalities ... without responsibility [who] put their noses into everything' (obviously an allusion to Salim al-Khuri and his associates). 'Judges and police officers must ... serve their interests, to the detriment of justice and law.' These men, he continued, had been fighting the cabinet because it wanted to stop smuggling into Israel, destroy hashish plantations, stop gambling, and unveil the illegal sources of their wealth. 'They fought us because we did not submit to their demands and serve their personal interests [and] ... shut the door in their faces and in those of their sons and relatives.' He went on: 'They have famished the people and vanquished them.' No reform was possible, unless 'the evil' was 'uprooted'. Finally, he appealed to God: 'I ask him to preserve Lebanon from its enemies, interior and exterior, and protect it from intrigues of evil and corruption. Amen.'[72]

The speech came as a complete surprise to the Chamber. While Sulh was still speaking, all ministers left the government benches and sat down among the rank-and-file deputies to signal their disagreement with his words. Following the speech, Sulh announced that he was about to resign. First, however, he hurried to a meeting with opposition leaders who had apparently known of his intentions.[73] Many Lebanese conjectured that the Syrian leader Shishakli had also been in the picture, citing two meetings he had had with Sulh during August. Rumour had it that after the speech Shishakli phoned Sulh to congratulate him.[74]

Khuri was taken aback. He immediately issued a presidential decree 'accepting' Sulh's resignation and appointing a non-political government of officials.

It included Nizam al-'Akkari, a Sunni who had until then been director-general of the prime minister's office; Basil Trad, a Greek Orthodox official who had held important economic positions; and Musa Mubarak, a Maronite with a similar background in economic and administrative affairs. On 15 September, to preserve the traditional pattern, he made Sunni leader Sa'ib Salam prime minister of the cabinet he had just put together. Next, he asked Salam to form a new cabinet himself. Salam started to negotiate for a new government to be composed of politicians. He wanted a strong cabinet backed by a solid majority in the Chamber. This required hard and prolonged bargaining with prospective ministers. He tried to recruit Sunni notables from Tripoli, from the Karami and Manala families, but they refused to join the cabinet or even promise it their backing. He also turned to ex-president Naqqash and to Charles Malik, Lebanon's ambassador in Washington. Naqqash made his agreement conditional on Malik joining the cabinet; the latter for his part insisted on becoming foreign minister and on being given exclusive control of foreign policy. While these contacts were going on, the opposition gathered strength.[75]

Its leaders, wishing to exploit the momentum created by Sulh's speech, proclaimed a two-day general strike to take place on 15 and 16 September. At first, the public response was no more than partial; in Beirut, about one-third of the city's business premises were closed. But then a group of men (it is not clear whether they were followers of Salim al-Khuri or of Far'un) kidnapped one of the strike leaders, the head of the Beirut greengrocers' union, hoping thereby to end the strike. The Beirut Sunni community reacted furiously. The strike was prolonged and was soon fully observed. It became a lever against Salam, putting him under pressure to abandon his attempts at forming a new cabinet.[76]

The entire attitude of the Sunni community towards Khuri was changing. Sunni notables were no longer content to play the role assigned to them by the president. Sulh's speech in the Chamber had been the starting signal. The next day, Yafi followed suit: he sent Khuri a letter which, in essence, repeated the points Sulh had made in the Chamber. He added that the cabinet and the Chamber no longer ruled Lebanon, as the constitution prescribed. The constitution should either ensure that the president had no executive authority, or else introduce a presidential regime in which the president became the chief executive, but was made accountable to the people and exposed to criticism.[77] A few days later, Rashid Karami and Sa'di al-Manala joined Khuri's critics.

Under pressure from the Sunni community at large as well as from its leaders, Salam decided to return his mandate to the president and not to cooperate with him any longer. He announced his decision at a meeting attended by all the important Sunni leaders. Together they resolved that no Sunni would serve as prime minister under Khuri. This was a heavy blow, worse than any other development during the critical month of September

1952. Without a Sunni to lead the cabinet under him, the president could no longer claim to be the guardian of the National Pact or the guarantor of the country's stability.

On the morning of 18 September, ten opposition leaders submitted a petition to the Chamber demanding the president's resignation. But Khuri was still trying to delay the end. He had his followers prepare a letter of support which was quickly signed by fifty-eight deputies. Yet he was soon forced to acknowledge that not even a majority in the Chamber could save him any longer.[78] In the evening, Salam informed Khuri of his inability to form a new cabinet as well as of his resignation as prime minster of the present cabinet of officials. Khuri then offered the appointment to the commander-in-chief of the army, Fu'ad Shihab. The general consulted with the opposition and then turned the offer down, informing Khuri that the opposition leaders refused to cooperate with him and insisted on his resignation. Next, Khuri turned to an old ally and supporter, Husayn al-'Uwayni, but he, too, refused to accept the premiership. One of the reasons was the hesitant response of Shihab when asked by 'Uwayni whether he could count on the army's loyalty in the event it was required to restore order in the country.

The president was now entirely isolated. At midnight, he signed his letter of resignation in the presence of 'Akkari, informed his associates of his decision, and then handed over power to Shihab. The following morning at 6.30, Khuri's short announcement was read over Radio Beirut. It said: 'I am hopeful that the Chamber of Deputies will succeed in electing in my place a president who will preserve the fatherland's independence and sovereignty and the National Pact which is the main pillar of independence because it guarantees love and peaceful life between all the communities composing our dear fatherland.' Immediately afterwards, the station broadcast an announcement from Shihab, saying: 'While praying to god to grant well-being and happiness to the inhabitants of Lebanon, I appeal to the Lebanese to maintain complete calm, to continue acting in unity and brotherhood and to refrain from demonstrations which might lead to violations of order and might sow discord among the various parts of the fatherland which we hold sacred.' He added that he was determined to keep the army out of politics and that he would not remain acting president longer than necessary. He reminded his listeners that the constitution gave the politicians eight days to elect another president.[79]

Shihab thus played a vital role in ensuring an orderly transfer of power to Khuri's successor, thereby keeping the country from sliding into anarchy. His week-long incumbency in 1952 was to be a prelude to a full term as president from 1958 until 1964. While on good terms with Khuri during the closing years of the latter's presidency, he had kept channels open for a dialogue with opposition figures. During the last days, he had worked for a compromise solution, envisaging a coalition government with a majority of opposition ministers, but with Khuri remaining in office.[80] When the crisis approached its peak, he had refused to promise Khuri the army's backing to keep him in power. When power was temporarily transferred to him he did not exploit his position for political gain and did not aspire to become Khuri's successor. A US diplomatic report commended his honesty and frankness, his resolve to preserve a democratic regime, and the respect he had won from his subordinates.[81] He may have been concerned about the future of the army (to which he had devoted his entire career) if he became a political figure. He may also have convinced himself that he had fewer prospects than the fiercely ambitious and aggressive opposition contestants. Moreover, his descent from so illustrious a family may have made him feel that he was above the fray.

The Chamber convened on 23 September, that is within the prescribed time limit, and the deputies, a great majority of whom had supported Khuri only a week earlier, now elected his bitter rival Camille Chamoun as president. Proposals to exile Khuri or put him on trial were dropped. Both Shihab and Chamoun were against such measures.[82] Those who had hoped Khuri's removal would lead to major reforms in the way the country was being governed were in for a disappointment. Within a few weeks, the opposition front which had brought the president down split up into its original components. Chamoun and Junbalat started quarrelling bitterly about who had done more to remove Khuri and who was, on that account, entitled to greater recompense. Their quarrel made it impossible for Yafi, Chamoun's candidate for the premiership, to form a cabinet. The new president had no choice but to install a temporary government, appointing Khalid Shihab to head it. It governed by decree for the next six months.

At the beginning of this chapter, we referred to the controversy surrounding Khuri's fall and its various possible reasons, domestic or external. This study proposes to account for it by looking at the internal dynamics of Lebanon's elite of notables. The events leading to the president's overthrow took place mostly within this elite and were acted out according to the traditional Lebanese rules of the game among the notables and their representatives in the government and the Chamber. When the growing power of the president and his family threatened to upset the traditional balance and to menace the standing of the notables – and in particular those forming the Maronite and Sunni elite – the 'system' itself, so to speak, found ways and means to restore the equilibrium and restore government to its true form. For just as long as it was necessary to achieve this, the opposition consolidated into a bloc powerful enough to bring Khuri and his relatives down. Once that was done, it fell apart again.

True, Khuri's incumbency was beset by many and varied domestic and external difficulties; we have listed and described them in the preceding chapters. Together, they created the situation that Yafi described as follows in his letter of resignation: 'In these days, Lebanon is suffering a severe psychological crisis which it has never witnessed before. It is dangerous to belittle it, be indifferent about its development or evade it.'[83] But in the final analysis, all these factors were no more than the backdrop to developments occurring within the country's traditional political elite and proceeding according to the traditional rules.

And yet, the end of the Khuri era also signalled a deeper, more fundamental flaw in the Lebanese system. Georges Naqqash (who had remained loyal to Khuri till the end) formulated this clearly when he wrote in his newspaper, *L'Orient*:

> The significance of the 1952 uprising, regardless of how successful or unsuccessful it was, is that it was the first attempt, since independence, to mobilize the country's elites for a single cause. The danger there was that this was done outside Parliament and outside the normal constitutional democratic process. If Lebanese institutions are not reformed to contain future events of that sort they will be done away with at the next occasion. The politics of the area are undergoing structural changes in terms of nationalist and social aspirations, and grievances are leading to extra-parliamentary protest movements. To face this, Lebanon has to adapt itself to modern social and economic trends. The Arab world is ... maintaining a Liberal and stable commercial and monetary policy which would allow Lebanon to fulfill its vocation as an international and touristic center.[84]

As the above passage shows, Naqqash thought that Middle Eastern regional trends, as well as social and economic factors, had greatly influenced events in Lebanon. But the burden of his argument was that the National Pact, and the Lebanese system as a whole, lacked a clear and broadly accepted mechanism for dealing with crisis situations. It was this basic flaw which would trigger the crisis of 1958. And in 1975, the legacy left behind by Khuri over twenty years earlier would still be a contributory factor in the eruption of the civil war.

# Conclusion

Nine years seemed as the day just gone by, they entered between the pages of [the history of] Lebanon and [history] will judge them.

Bishara al-Khuri, *Haqa'iq Lubnaniyya* (Vol. III, p. 483)

Khuri's nine-year incumbency as president of Lebanon lasted longer than that of any other president until Ilyas al-Hirawi (1989–98). Both for Khuri personally and for his country, these nine years were the culmination of a process which had its roots in nineteenth-century Mt Lebanon, passed through the era of the French mandate and encompassed the initial period of independence. During these early years, Lebanon's independence remained threatened and fragile. Khuri's first great task was to continue the struggle of the preceding years, by attempting to safeguard the recently-won independence in the face of threats from within and from without. External threats were the graver of the two, in particular those stemming from overall regional developments. The formative period of modern independent Lebanon co-incided with the formative period of the post-war Middle East as a whole; new ideological fashions and social and economic trends coming to the fore there quickly spilled over into Lebanon. But threatening regional influences continued to make themselves felt for much longer than the 1940s and, in 1952, they contributed to Khuri's downfall. They were to play an equally pivotal role in the commotion of 1958 and the outbreak of civil war in 1975. Alongside international and inter-Arab involvement, the presence of neighbouring Israel and even more so of Syria must be singled out. Both were perceived as a threat by Lebanon for most of the time; some of the time, they actually were. The Khuri era also witnessed the influx of the Palestinian refugees who were later to prove so potently disruptive in the domestic context. Their presence, too, had resulted from regional events outside Lebanon, though on its veritable doorstep.

Khuri himself tended to identify regional and international issues as the main threat to Lebanon and invested his best efforts in dealing with them. Since, by and large, he did so successfully, his efforts brought him handsome political dividends. But the present study of his tenure leads us to recognize the primacy of domestic politics in the history of independent Lebanon.

The initial fundamental problem was whether or not to adopt the format of Greater Lebanon, in the borders drawn by the French in 1920, for the independent state. When it became clear that this would be done, the next question was how it should be achieved.

The solution to this problem was the 1943 National Pact, devised by Khuri and his Sunni partner Riyad al-Sulh. It signalled the acceptance of Greater Lebanon by the various components of the Lebanese population and their readiness to cooperate with each other according to the terms of the pact. But, as with independence, it was up to Khuri to translate the provisions of the pact into actual practice and to adapt the old Ottoman and mandatory rules of the political game to the new realities of the country, the region and the international arena. Moreover, he had to set up a central government and administration of a kind not existent in Lebanon before, make it function, render it durable, and win for it the loyalty of the country's many constituent communities. This transformation was not at all a matter of course. It had to be carried out against a background of vast and rapid changes: modernization, the advent of new ideologies, and the formation of an inter-Arab state system. Khuri did much to make Lebanon find its place in the new circumstances.

Yet it is easy to point to the defects and failures of Khuri as a person and a leader, and to those of the system he devised. He failed to free Lebanon from the fetters of the past, or perhaps did not wish to do so. In perpetuating the ground rules of the old system, he did not act as president of independent Lebanon but rather as the representative of the class of notables, regardless of community. These were men who did not want to see the status quo change to their disadvantage or watch their standing being impaired by a strong central administration. This was one of the reasons why Khuri's government remained comparatively weak. Moreover, officialdom was riddled with corruption and nepotism, to the detriment of administrative skill and efficiency. Since these were the formative years of modern Lebanon, their imprint proved lasting and their flaws were to dominate Lebanese politics for much longer than the duration of Khuri's incumbency; in fact, they became permanent features.

Do we have to conclude, then, that Khuri missed his chance of shaping a thoroughly novel Lebanese polity, one that would have withstood the shocks of 1958 and 1975? Many observers have deduced that he did not even try to grapple with the country's underlying problems. Instead, he sanctified the existing system, rendering it binding on all by making the National Pact the main pillar of the Lebanese state. Inevitably, we must assume that a series of slow, gradual reforms of the administration, of society and of the economy might have created a stronger, more viable state. A cleaner and more efficient administration would have gained greater confidence among the public at large and provided stronger props to buttress the young state.

Even while Khuri was still in office, this gave rise to much criticism by segments of Lebanese public opinion as well as by foreign diplomats. This is the source of Khuri's negative image such as we find it in many historical studies of his period. But there is another side to the coin. It was precisely by clinging to the old system that Khuri succeeded in consolidating newly independent Lebanon. In doing so, he fulfilled his primary, most fundamental mission. His method – regardless of whether he adopted it from lack of choice or of his own free will – was far from perfect, but for all we can see it was the lesser evil. It was best suited to whatever willingness and ability for change the notables possessed. And indeed, the political structure of Lebanon was more solid at the conclusion of Khuri's incumbency than at its outset, even though its administrative performance had not improved. Its political culture was, as it had always been, one of 'live and let live'. But for all the weakness of the central government, Lebanon was a vital and viable state with broadly accepted concepts of legitimacy, discounting the use of force and extolling a broad consensus as the ideal state of affairs.

What, then, were Khuri's failures? Why did he fall? Why did his methods lead to the crisis of 1958 and the civil war of 1975–89? Khuri was a true son of his times. His personality and his ideas reflected the essence of the Lebanese polity, just as his career reflected his country's history during most of the first half of the twentieth century. He was not a man of vision, not a reformer, certainly not a charismatic national leader capable of carrying the masses with him; he did not even possess a strong personal power base in his own community. Rather, he was a faithful representative of his class, gifted with greater manipulative skills than most, but of weak character. During his incumbency, he suffered a physical and mental breakdown. But he turned his weakness into strength and made it the source of his appeal for others, just as the strength and charm of Lebanon as a state resided in its weakness. At least during the early years of his presidency, nobody thought of him as a threat, just as the power of the state, such as it was, did not seem threatening to its citizens, let alone the notables. Therefore, neither the man nor the state aroused real antagonism among the communal elites; both gained a measure of sympathy which they would not have enjoyed had either been stronger.

More than that: during his presidency, Khuri instituted an improved system of checks and balances. At home, this created an equilibrium between the elites of the various communities, sometimes even between several prominent families within the same community. It balanced the authority of the president against that of the prime minister and the Chamber. In foreign affairs, it established an equilibrium between the different Arab blocs as well as between the western powers.

The competition between Sunni notables for pre-eminence in their community – a competition skilfully encouraged by Khuri – ensured their loyalty to the system within which they hoped to rise, and made them dependent on the president in whose gift the highest attainable office, the premiership, was. In turn, the fact that he more than any other Maronite leader had the support of the Sunni camp protected Khuri against challenges from within his own community. The support of Shi'i and Druse notables provided an additional safeguard for his continuing in power.

The system of balances, combined with Khuri's personal weakness, encouraged the perception that his rule was the best possible guarantee for the maintenance of the domestic political, social and economic status quo. It was a perception shared by many Lebanese irrespective of community and it became the real source of Khuri's strength. But gradually Khuri lost control of the scheme of checks and balances he had devised himself. During the late 1940s and, more rapidly, during the early 1950s, the system collapsed layer by layer, until the whole structure came down.

Abroad, Syria, at first a mainstay of independent Lebanon, had turned into an enemy. The fragmentation of the Arab state system, and Egypt's domestic troubles rendered the rest of the Arab world incapable of countering the Syrian threat. The West, now disillusioned with Khuri's regime, could no longer be relied upon. At home, Khuri himself, more than any other figure on the political scene, contributed to his downfall. Largely under the disruptive influence of his brother Salim, he began to aspire to a position of national leadership and to think in terms of a strictly presidential regime. But such a regime conflicted with Khuri's personal qualities, contradicted the task the National Pact had assigned to the president, and went beyond what was feasible in Lebanese politics. The attempt to be the leader he was not capable of being, and to fill a role foreign to the Lebanese system, undermined his legitimacy and cut the ground from under his feet. In the eyes of the notables, he had turned from a political asset into a liability; he had become dangerous.

Paradoxically, his downfall points up the extent of his earlier success. He had laid sound foundations; he fell because he upset the equilibrium he had done so much to consolidate, yet the Lebanese state survived within the bounds of those balances. But the end of his career also underlines the flaw in Lebanese politics we have so often referred to: the absence of an accepted mechanism capable of suiting it to new requirements. This made it impossible for Khuri to realign communal relations (and especially Sunni–Maronite relations) except by a show of force. It was to have still graver consequences on the eve of the civil war.

How, then, shall we assess Khuri's place and that of his regime in the overall course of Lebanon's modern history? We have had occasion before to point to the elements of continuity linking Ottoman, mandatory and independent Lebanon. Khuri's creation of an independent entity was not an artificial act. It was the natural evolution of the stages that had preceded it and was consistent with them. He did not act single-handedly; independence met with broad (though not with total) agreement. But there is no denying that he personally led Lebanon forward from one stage to the next and translated the near-consensus of the public at large into political facts. The course of the country's history was not, after all, governed by an inevitable, predetermined order; at least in part it was the handiwork of Khuri and the men around him. His policy was not devoid of negative aspects, but it led to independence, to the creation of institutions of government (such as they were), and – at least initially – to a more delicately balanced equilibrium of the communities than had existed before. It made it possible for them to co-exist for many years afterwards. Even the civil war of 1975–89 could only modify, not destroy Khuri's system. This, more than anything else, attests to the validity of the ideas underlying his endeavours and those of his political allies. Their enduring effect, for good or for ill, is the measure of his importance for Lebanon.

# Notes

## Abbreviations

| | |
|---|---|
| AD | Les Archives Diplomatiques de Nantes |
| AE (Paris) | Archive du Ministère des Affaires Étrangères |
| AN | Archives Nationales |
| CAB | Cabinet Papers |
| CHEAM | Centre de Hautes Études sur l'Afrique et l'Asie Modernes |
| CLS | Centre for Lebanese Studies |
| CZA | Central Zionist Archive |
| DOS | Department of State |
| FNC | French Committee (1940–43) |
| FO | Foreign Office, London |
| FRUS | Foreign Relations of the United States (documents series) |
| ISA | Israel State Archives |
| MFA | Ministry for Foreign Affairs |
| NA/RG | National Archives/Record Group |
| PREM | Premier's Papers |
| PRO | Public Record Office |
| SAB | Summary of Arab Broadcasting/Library of the Moshe Dayan Center for Middle Eastern and African Studies |
| SHA | Service Historique de l'Armée de Terre |
| SOS | Secretary of State |
| WO | War Office |

## Preface

1. See Ahmad Beydoun, *al-Sira' 'ala Tarikh Lubnan*.

2. Kamal S. Salibi, 'Introduction', in Nadim Shehadi and Danna Haffar Mills (eds), *Lebanon: A History of Conflict and Consensus*; see also Kamal S. Salibi, *A House of Many Mansions: The History of Lebanon Reconsidered*.

3. See Michael C. Hudson, *The Precarious Republic Revisited: Reflections on the Collapse of Pluralist Politics in Lebanon*.

4. See Edmond Rabbath, *La Formation Historique du Liban Politique et Constitutionnel*; Elie Kedourie, 'Lebanon: The Perils of Independence', in his *Islam in the Modern World and Other Studies*, pp. 85–91; Meir Zamir, *The Formation of Modern Lebanon*, pp. 216–23; see also Samir Khalaf, *Lebanon's Predicament*.

5. See Kamal S. Salibi, *The Modern History of Lebanon*; Ghassan Salama, *Al-Mujtama' wal-*

*Dawla fi al-Mashriq al-'Arabi*, pp. 52–9; Nadim Shehadi, *The Idea of Lebanon*; Albert Hourani, *Political Society in Lebanon: A Historical Introduction.* It should be pointed out, however, that in *A House of Many Mansions* Salibi put a series of question marks against conclusions he had himself arrived at in his first book; see Kamal S. Salibi, *A House of Many Mansions*, pp. 151–66, 216–34.

6. See Leonard Binder (ed.), *Politics in Lebanon*; Michael C. Hudson, *The Precarious Republic: Political Modernization in Lebanon*; Elie Adib Salem, *Modernization without Revolution: Lebanon's Experience*; John P. Entelis, *Pluralism and Party Transformation in Lebanon, al-Kata'ib, 1936–1970*; Iliya F. Harik, *Politics and Change in a Traditional Society: Lebanon, 1711–1854*; David R. and Audrey C. Smock, *The Politics of Pluralism: A Comparative Study of Lebanon and Ghana.*

7. Michael W. Suleiman, *Political Parties in Lebanon*; Halim I. Barakat, 'Social and Political Integration in Lebanon: A Case of Social Mosaic'; Leila M. T. Meo, *Lebanon: Improbable Nation: A Study in Political Development.*

8. Meir Zamir, *The Formation of Modern Lebanon*, pp. 216–23; Samir Khalaf, *Lebanon's Predicament*; see also Itamar Rabinovich, *The War for Lebanon, 1970–1985*, pp. 17–33.

9. Emile Khuri, 'Muqaddima', in Bishara al-Khuri, *Haqa'iq Lubnaniyya*, Vol. I, p. 14.

10. For discussion of Khuri's personality and of the years of his incumbency, see e.g. Hudson, *The Precarious Republic*, pp. 105–7, 264–73; Salibi, *The Modern History of Lebanon*, pp. 191–95.

# Introduction

1. See Meir Zamir, *The Formation of Modern Lebanon*, pp. 94–5, 243; Bishara al-Khuri, *Haqa'iq Lubnaniyya*, Vol. I, pp. 310–12.

2. See also Kamal S. Salibi, *A House of Many Mansions: The History of Lebanon Reconsidered*, pp. 72–129; *Maronite Historians of Medieval Lebanon*; and 'The Traditional Historiography of the Maronites' in B. Lewis and P. Holt (eds) *Historians of the Middle East*, pp. 212–25; Zamir, *The Formation of Modern Lebanon*, pp. 1–37; John P. Spagnolo, *France and Ottoman Lebanon, 1861–1914.*

3. See also in Spagnolo, *France and Ottoman Lebanon, 1861–1914.*

4. For more about Fakhr al-Din, see Albert Hourani, *Political Society in Lebanon: A Historical Introduction*, p. 7; 'Aziz al-Ahdab, *Fakhr al-Din – Mu'assis Lubnan al-Hadith.*

5. Kamal S. Salibi, *The Modern History of Lebanon*, pp. 3–17; and 'The Lebanese Emirate, 1667–1841'.

6. Iliya F. Harik, *Politics and Change in a Traditional Society: Lebanon, 1711–1845*; Kamal S. Salibi, 'Mount Lebanon Under the Mamluks', in S. Seiklay, R. Baalbaki and P. Dodd (eds), *Quest for Understanding*, pp. 33–342.

7. See Salibi, 'The Lebanese Emirate'.

8. For the emirate under Shihab II and for the beginnings of modernization, see W. R. Polk, *The Opening of South Lebanon, 1788–1840*; Kamal S. Salibi, *The Modern History of Lebanon*, pp. 18–39.

9. On the civil wars in Mt Lebanon, 1840–60, see, Leila Tarazi Fawaz, *Occasion for War: Civil Conflict in Lebanon and Damascus in 1860*; Salibi, *The Modern History of Lebanon*, pp. 40–105. On the peasant risings, see, Yehoshua Porath, 'The Peasant Revolt of 1858–1861 in Kisrawan'; Edmund Burke III, 'Rural Collective Action and the Emergence of Modern Lebanon: A Comparative Historical Perspective', in Nadim Shehadi and Danna Haffar Mills (eds), *Lebanon: A History of Conflict and Consensus*, pp. 14–30.

10. On the *Mutasarrifiyya*, see Engin Deniz Akarli, *The Long Peace, Ottoman Lebanon, 1861–1920*; Spagnolo, *France and Ottoman Lebanon*; Salibi, *The Modern History of Lebanon*, pp. 106–48.

11. For observations of this kind, see Salibi, *A House of Many Mansions*, pp. 30–3; Zamir, *The Formation of Modern Lebanon*, pp. 216–23.

12. Zamir, *The Formation of Modern Lebanon*, pp. 91–6.

13. The most widely accepted figures put emigration from the Levant between 1880 and 1914 at approximately 350,000; of these more than two-thirds came from Lebanon, and most were Christians; see Charles Issawi, 'The Historical Background of Lebanese Emigration', in his *The Middle East Economy: Decline and Recovery*, pp. 123–40; Albert Hourani and Nadim Shehadi (eds), *The Lebanese in the World: A Century of Emigration*.

14. For further details see C. M. Andrew and A. S. Kanya-Forstner, *France Overseas: The Great War and the Climax of French Imperial Expansion*.

15. On French policy, see Philip S. Khouri, *Syria and the French Mandate: Politics of Arab Nationalism, 1920–1945*, pp. 27–94.

16. Also see Meir Zamir, 'Smaller and Greater Lebanon – The Squaring of a Circle?'.

17. Andrew and Kanya-Forstner, *France Overseas*, pp. 108–64.

18. Zamir, *The Formation of Modern Lebanon*, pp. 38–96.

19. Elie Kedourie, 'Lebanon: The Perils of Independence', in his *Islam in the Modern World*, pp. 85–91; Zamir, *The Formation of Modern Lebanon*, pp. 216–23.

20. See Michael C. Hudson, *The Precarious Republic: Political Modernization in Lebanon*, pp. 17–34.

21. For greater detail, see Albert Hourani, *Arabic Thought in the Liberal Age, 1798–1939*, pp. 95–102, 245–323.

22. Ibid., pp. 237–8; Labib Zuwiyya Yamak, *The Syrian Social Nationalist Party, An Idealogical Analysis*, pp. 18–75.

23. In their testimony before the King-Crane Commission, Greek Orthodox representatives spoke in favour of uniting Lebanon with Syria, but did not altogether reject a western mandate over Lebanon. The Maronite and the Greek Catholic spokesmen, by contrast, supported a French mandate. See Hamdi Badawi al-Tahiri, *Siyasat al-Hukm fi Lubnan*, p. 20; Leila M. T. Meo, *Lebanon: Improbable Nation: A Study in Political Development*, p. 48.

24. Fouad Ajami, *The Vanished Imam, Musa al-Sadr and the Shia of Lebanon*, pp. 52–84.

25. See Shakib Salih, *Toldot Hadruzim*.

26. See Samir Khalaf, *Lebanon's Predicament*, pp. 102–20; Michael Johnson, *Class and Client in Beirut: The Sunni Muslim Community and the Lebanese State, 1840–1985*, pp. 45–81.

27. Marwan Buheiry, *Beirut's Rule in the Political Economy of the French Mandate, 1919–1939*; Leila Tarazi Fawaz, *Merchants and Migrants in Nineteenth-Century Beirut*; Albert Hourani, 'Ideologies of the Mountain and the City', in Roger Owen (ed.), *Essays on the Crisis in Lebanon*, pp. 33–42.

28. See Johnson, *Class and Client in Beirut*, p. 47; Arnold Hottinger, 'Zu'ama in Historical Perspective', in Leonard Binder (ed.), *Politics in Lebanon*, pp. 85–105; Richard Hrair Dekmejian, *Patterns of Political Leadership: Egypt, Israel, Lebanon*.

29. John P. Entelis, *Pluralism and Party Transformation in Lebanon, al-Kata'ib, 1936–1970*; Michael W. Suleiman, *Political Parties in Lebanon*, pp. 227–32.

30. Michael Hudson, *The Precarious Republic Revisited: Reflections on the Collapse of Pluralistic Politics in Lebanon*, p. 4.

31. Hasan al-Hasan, *Al-Qanun al-Dusturi wal-Dustur fi Lubnan*, pp. 128–37; see also Meir Zamir, *The Formation of Modern Lebanon*, pp. 200–15.

32. Farid el-Khazen, *The Communal Pact of National Identities – The Making and Politics of the 1943 National Pact*, pp. 31–3.

33. For biographical details about Riyad al-Sulh see CLS, US Documents, Box 9, RG

84, Box 231, Biographical Sketch of Solh Riad, 22 January 1947; AD (Nantes), 7/1270, Riad Bay Solh; Wade R. Goria, *Sovereignty and Leadership in Lebanon, 1943–1976*, p. 23; el-Khazen, *The Communal Pact*, pp. 22–4; Johnson, *Class and Client in Beirut*, pp. 57–60.

34. For more on the French–Syrian treaty, see Khouri, *Syria and the French Mandate*, pp. 485–93.

35. el-Khazen, *The Communal Pact*, p. 35.

36. Hassan Halaq, *Al-Tiyyarat al-Siyasiyya fi Lubnan, 1943–1952*, pp. 179–81; Raghid Solh, 'The Attitude of the Arab Nationalists towards Greater Lebanon during the 1930s', in Shehadi and Mills (eds), *Lebanon*, pp. 149–65; el-Khazen, *The Communal Pact*, pp. 35–6.

37. Johnson, *Class and Client in Beirut*, p. 58.

38. In 1933, Mubarak had already organized anti-French demonstrations and called for closer cooperation with the leaders of the Syrian National Bloc. 'Arida for his part (his election as Maronite patriarch had been opposed by the French) started receiving Syrian delegations and told them of his support for Lebanese independence and for its close ties with Syria. Khouri, *Syria and the French Mandate*, pp. 485–93; el-Khazen, *The Communal Pact*, p. 8.

39. Meir Zamir, 'Emile Edde and the Territorial Integrity of Lebanon'; and 'Smaller and Greater Lebanon'.

40. CLS, US Documents, Box 8, RG 84, Box 681, al-Khuri Biography, 18 July 1949.

41. For biographical details about Bishara al-Khuri see al-Khuri, *Haqa'iq Lubnaniyya*, Vol. I, pp. 23–4; CLS, US Documents, Box 8, RG 84, Box 681, al-Khuri Biography, 18 July 1949; Goria, *Sovereignty and Leadership*, pp. 20–1, 23–4.

42. al-Khuri, *Haqa'iq Lubnaniyya*, Vol. I, pp. 20–1.

43. W. L. Browne, *The Political History of Lebanon, 1920–1950*, Vol. I, p. 145.

44. al-Khuri, *Haqa'iq Lubnaniyya*, Vol. I, pp. 76, 80–5, 95, 115. See also Salibi, *The Modern History of Lebanon*, pp. 173–4.

45. el-Khazen, *The Communal Pact*, pp. 27–31; see also Carolyn L. Gates, *The Merchant Republic of Lebanon, Rise of an Open Economy*.

46. See Michel Chiha, *Politique Intérieure*; Nadim Shehadi, *The Idea of Lebanon*. See also Albert Hourani, *Arabic Thought in the Liberal Age 1798–1939*, pp. 319–32; see also Gates, *The Merchant Republic*; al-Khazen, *The Communal Pact*.

47. al-Khuri, *Haqa'iq Lubnaniyya*, Vol. I, pp. 175–9.

48. Salibi, *The Modern History of Lebanon*, pp. 176–7; Goria, *Sovereignty and Leadership*, pp. 21–2.

49. al-Khuri, *Haqa'iq Lubnaniyya*, Vol. I, pp. 194–8; Salibi, *The Modern History of Lebanon*, p. 179.

50. Goria, *Sovereignty and Leadership*, pp. 22–3.

## 1. First Steps Along a New Road

1. For French memoirs, see Georges Catroux, *Dans la Bataille de Méditerranée: Egypte – Levant – Afrique du Nord, 1940–1944*; Charles de Gaulle, *Mémoires de Guerre*. British memoirs include: Winston S. Churchill, *The Second World War*; Harold Macmillan, *War Diaries – The Mediterranean 1943–1945*; Edward L. Spears, *Fulfilment of a Mission: The Spears Mission to Syria and Lebanon, 1941–44*. For Lebanese memoirs, see Bishara al-Khuri, *Haqa'iq Lubnaniyya*; Kamil Sham'un (Camille Chamoun), *Marahil al-Istiqlala Lubnan wa-Duwal al-'Arab fi al-Mu'tamarat al-Dawliyya*; Sami al-Sulh, *Ahtakimu 'ila al-Tarikh* and *Mudhakkirat Sami Bak al-Sulh*.

2. A. B. Gaunson, *The Anglo-French Clash in Lebanon and Syria 1940–45*; Yosef Olmert, *British Policy Toward the Levant States, 1940–1945*; Aviel Roshwald, *Estranged Bedfellows: Britain*

*and France in the Middle East During the Second World War*; Asher Susser, *Western Power Rivalry and its Interaction with Local Politics in the Levant, 1941–1946*. Studies by Lebanese researchers include Hassan Halaq, *Al-Tiyyarat al-Siyasiyya fi Lubnan, 1943–1952*; Munir Taqi al-Din, *Wiladat Istiqlal*; Hamdi Badawi al-Tahiri, *Siyasat al-Hukm fi Lubnan*; 'Ali Khalid Fallah, *Mukhadarat fi Tarikh Lubnan*.

3. FO 371/27312-E 6250; FO 371/27369-E 8486, French Texts of the Syrian and the Lebanese Declarations. For the British–French controversy on their publication, see Roshwald, *Estranged Bedfellows*, pp. 92–7.

4. de Gaulle, *Mémoires*, Vol. I, p. 412.

5. SHA, Levant, 4H/299, Nomination du General Catroux comme Délégue Géneral et Plénipotentiare Commandant en Chef des Troupes pour les États du Levant, 24 June 1941.

6. Quoted by Roshwald, *Estranged Bedfellows*, p. 90. See also Spears Papers, Box II/File 4, Record of a Meeting between Churchill and de Gaulle, 12 September 1941.

7. Roshwald, *Estranged Bedfellows*, pp. 81–2.

8. Ibid., pp. 29, 117, 237.

9. Ibid., p. 115.

10. Spears Papers Box III/File 5, 'A Further Note on Peace Terms in the Middle East', Glubb Pasha, 25 May 1943.

11. FO 371/34975-E 3234/2551/65, 'Resolutions on the Political Situation in the Middle East', MEWC (Middle East War Council), May 1943.

12. For the background of Spears's mission in the Levant, see Roshwald, *Estranged Bedfellows*, pp. 85–92.

13. Spears's mission numbered 131 members, 25 of them officers, 37 civilians, the rest other ranks. Its seat was Beirut and it had representatives in Beirut, Tripoli, Zahla and Sidon, as well as in Damascus, Aleppo, Hama, Ladhiqiyya, Suwayda, Dir al-Zur and Hasaka. See FO 921/176-12(4)/44/23

14. FO 371/31468-E 4009/183/89, Minute by Beckett, 8 July 1942.

15. Spears had been a member of parliament for the Conservative Party for many years and kept his seat during his mission to Levant. In 1922 he proposed to Churchill, who had lost his seat in that year's elections, that he, Spears, resign so as to enable Churchill to run in Spears's constituency in a by-election, and thus ensure his return to the House. Churchill declined but was not to forget Spears's generosity. See Roshwald, *Estranged Bedfellows*, p. 86.

16. Macmillan, *War Diaries*, entry for 27 November 1943.

17. SHA, Levant, 4H308/2, 4H311/4, Information, 16 April 1941; see also Roshwald, *Estranged Bedfellows*, p. 50.

18. FO 226/306, Beirut Political Officer, 23 July 1942.

19. FO 371/68495-E 10254, Lebanese Government, 29 July 1948.

20. See FO 226/252-207/94/44, Beirut to FO, 8 June 1944.

21. Ibid.

22. Roshwald, *Estranged Bedfellows*, pp. 103–5.

23. al-Khuri, *Haqa'iq Lubnaniyya*, Vol. I, p. 241.

24. Ibid., pp. 242–3; Tawfiq Wahaba, *Lubnan fi Haba'il al-Siyasa*, Vol. I, p. 98.

25. al-Khuri, *Haqa'iq Lubnaniyya*, Vol. I, pp. 295–6.

26. Ibid., pp. 297–8.

27. CLS, US Documents, Box 8, RG 185, Box 2653, Who's Who in the Lebanon – 1944. Military Attaché, Beirut, 25 February 1944.

28. See also Farid el-Khazen, *The Communal Pact of National Identities: The Making and Politics of the 1943 National Pact*, pp. 8–9.

29. al-Khuri, *Haqa'iq Lubnaniyya*, Vol. I, pp. 295–6.

30. See FO 226/309, Spears to Gen. Wilson, 29 November 1941.

31. al-Khuri, *Haqa'iq Lubnaniyya*, Vol. I, p. 245.

32. Salma Mardam Bey, *Syria's Quest for Independence, 1939–1945*, pp. 56–7.

33. Wahaba, *Lubnan*, p. 109.

34. FO 226/240, British Legation, Beirut, 18 July 1943.

35. Ibid.

36. Ibid.

37. FO 226/235-96/10/42, Beirut to FO, 27 November 1941; Spears Papers, Box IV/ File 4, Spears to Mary Azury, 19 November 1968.

38. Roshwald, *Estranged Bedfellows*, p. 105.

39. al-Khuri, *Haqa'iq Lubnaniyya*, Vol. I, pp. 247–8.

40. See FO 226/233-31/142-42, Note by Furlonge to Spears, 24 July 1942; CLS, US Documents, Box 9-890.0.01/171, Beirut to SD, 21 February 1942; see also al-Sulh, *Mudhakkirat*, p. 52.

41. Roshwald, *Estranged Bedfellows*, p. 125.

42. FO 371/35176-E 1708/27/89, Weekly Political Summary, Syria and the Lebanon, 10 March 1943; FO 371/35175-E 1451, Spears to FO, 9 March 1943.

43. FO 371/35176-E 1774, Weekly Political Summary, Syria and the Lebanon, 24 March 1943.

44. al-Khuri, *Haqa'iq Lubnaniyya*, Vol. I, p. 251.

45. Roshwald, *Estranged Bedfellows*, p. 141.

46. FO 371/35178-E 373, Lascelles to FO, 28 June 1943.

47. FO 371/35179, Weekly Political Summary, Syria and the Lebanon, 14 July 1943; see also Halaq, *Al-Tiyyarat al-Siyasiyya*, pp. 168–71.

48. AD (Nantes), Syrie-Liban, 7/1268, 7/1268, Information, 26 June 1943; see also Halaq, *Al-Tiyyarat al-Siyasiyya*, pp. 170–1.

49. AN, 72 AJ/428, Papiers Catroux, Khouri to Catroux, 30 June 1943.

50. See FO 226/240-9/323/43, Republique Libanaise, les inscriptions de l'année 1932 et celles de 1942.

51. FO 371/35179-E 4142, Weekly Political Summary, Syria and the Lebanon, 14 July 1943.

52. Halaq, *Al-Tiyyarat al-Siyasiyya*, p. 174.

53. FO 371/35179-E 4281, Weekly Political Summary, Syria and the Lebanon, 21 July 1943; see also Halaq, *Al-Tiyyarat al-Siyasiyya*, pp. 174–5.

## 2. The 1943 Elections

1. CLS, US Documents, OOS 226/34139, R. W. McClenahan, Military Intelligence, Cairo, to Washington, 14 April 1943.

2. FO 371/35182-E 6220/27/89, Casey to FO, 16 October 1943.

3. See Mas'ud Dahir, *Lubnan: al-Istiqlal, al-Sigha wal-Mithaq*, p. 148.

4. For the electoral system, see Michael Hudson, *The Precarious Republic: Political Modernization in Lebanon*, pp. 212–19.

5. FO 226/293-31/46/42, Spears to FO, 30 April 1942.

6. See Spears Papers, Box II/File 4, France in the Levant, Memorandum by Spears, 14 May 1954; FO 371/35178-E 3893, Spears to FO, 6 July 1943.

7. FO 226/246-196/16/43, FO to Chargé d'Affaires, Beirut, 8 July 1943.

8. See for example FO 226/241-27/340/43, Spears to FO, 11 November 1943; FO 226/240-9/60/43, Furlonge to Spears, 4 March 1943; FO 226/223 31/141/42, Furlonge to Spears, 24 July 1943; AE (Paris), Guerre 39–45 (Alger), Vol. 1004, pp. 129–35, Vienot to Massigli, 4 November 1943, p. 143, Les Ingérences Britanniques, Cabinet Politique, 20 October 1943.

9. FO 226/252-207/94/44, Beirut to FO, 8 June 1944; see also AE (Paris), Guerre 39–45 (Alger), Vol. 1002, p. 134, Personalities Libanaises; AD (Nantes), Syrie–Liban, 7/1270, 5 August 1943.

10. FO 226/233-31/142/42, Furlonge to Spears, 22 July 1942; FO 371/35183-E 2484, Weekly Political Summary, Syria and the Lebanon, 28 April 1943.

11. FO 226/240-9/60/43, Furlonge to Spears, 4 March 1943.

12. AE (Paris), Guerre 39–45 (Alger), Vol. 1004, p. 138, pp. 143, Les Ingérences Britanniques ou les Élections, Cabinet Politique; FO 226/240-9/621/43, minute by Furlonge, 10 September 1943.

13. Farid el-Khazen, *The Communal Pact of National Identities: The Making and Politics of the 1943 National Pact*, p. 41.

14. *L'Orient*, 28 August 1943; see also FO 226/240-9/610/43, minute by Furlonge, 1 September 1943.

15. FO 226/240-9/621/43, minute by Furlonge, 10 September 1943.

16. *L'Orient*, 28 August 1943; FO 226/240-9/516/43, Lebanese Elections, Furlonge to Spears, 21 August 1943.

17. FO 226/240-9/649/43, Scandals in Beka Elections – Copy of the Petition submitted by the Beka group to the Chamber of Deputies.

18. FO 226/240-9/610/43, Lebanese Elections, Furlonge to Spears, 1 September 1943; AE (Paris), Guerre 39–45 (Alger), Vol. 1004, Les Élections du Liban.

19. FO 226/240-9/502,610/43, Lebanese Élections, Furlonge to Spears, 18 August, 1 September 1943.

20. FO 226/240-9/621/43, minute by Furlonge, 10 September 1943.

21. FO 226/240-9/506/43, minute by Furlonge, 19 August 1943.

22. Spears tried to dismiss the French achievement by attributing it to the low voter participation in Beirut (25 per cent, compared with a country-wide average of 53.6 per cent). Edward L. Spears, *Fulfilment of a Mission: The Spears Mission to Syria and Lebanon, 1941–44*, p. 222.

23. Bishara al-Khuri, *Haqa'iq Lubnaniyya*, Vol. I, p. 193.

24. CLS, US Documents, Box 9, RG84, OOS Special Report No. 1390.

25. FO 371/35210-E3632, Lascelles to FO, 23 June 1943.

26. Spears Papers, Box II/File 4, France in the Levant, Memorandum by Spears, 14 May 1954; see also Aviel Roshwald, *Estranged Bedfellows: Britain and France in the Middle East During the Second World War*, pp. 128–9, 137–8.

27. FO 371/35180-E5230, Spears to FO, 24 August 1943.

28. el-Khazen, *The Communal Pact*, p. 33; see also John Gulick, *Tripoli, a Modern Arab City*.

29. *L'Orient*, 28 August 1943; FO 226/240-9/552/43, minute by Furlonge, 23 August 1943.

30. *L'Orient*, 28 August 1943.

31. See Hassan Halaq, *Al-Tiyyarat al-Siyasiyya fi Lubnan, 1943–1952*, pp. 95–107.

32. AE (Paris), Guerre 39–45 (Alger), Vol. 1004, pp. 201–2.

33. *L'Orient*, 28 August 1943.

34. FO 371/35181-E5421/27/89, Spears to FO, 8 September 1943.

35. FO 226/240-9/621/43, Lebanon Presidency, Furlonge to Spears, 10 September 1943.

36. See FO 226/240-9/502,610/43, Lebanese Presidency, Furlonge to Spears, 10 September 1943.

37. Ibid.

38. FO 226/240-9/641/43, Spears to Casey, 21 September 1943.

39. For Khuri's and Edde's different approaches, see el-Khazen, *The Communal Pact*, p. 25; see also FO 226/252-27/283/44, PIC Paper no. 26, Political Alignments in Lebanon, December 1943.

40. FO 226/240-9/502,610/43, Lebanese Presidency, Furlonge to Spears, 10 September 1943.

41. FO 226/240-9/641/43, Spears to Casey, 21 September 1943.

42. FO 226/240-9/643/43, Spears Diary, 17 September 1943; SHA, Levant, 4H357/1, Le Conseiller Administratif pour le Liban Nord to Helleu, 16 September 1943; AD (Nantes), Syrie–Liban, 7/788, Le Conseilleur Législatif de la Délégation Générale, 5 September 1943; FO 226/240-9/621/43, British Legation, Beirut, 10 September 1943.

43. Spears Papers, Box II/File 4, France in the Levant, Memorandum by Spears, 14 May 1954; Box V/File 4, Spears to Mary Azury, 19 November 1968.

44. FO 226/240-9/643/43, Spears Diary, 17 September 1943.

45. FO 226/240-9/502,610/43, Lebanese Presidency, Furlonge to Spears, 10 September 1943.

46. al-Khuri, *Haqa'iq Lubnaniyya*, Vol. I, p. 261; see also Halaq, *Al-Tiyyarat al-Siyasiyya*, pp. 103–4.

47. FO 226/240-9/643/43, Spears Diary, 17 September 1943.

48. FO 226/240-9/641/43, Spears to Casey, 21 September 1943.

49. FO 226/240-9/643/43, Spears Diary, 16 September 1943.

50. FO 226/240-9/643/43, Spears Diary, 16, 17, 19 September 1943; cf. al-Khuri, *Haqa'iq Lubnaniyya*, Vol. I, p. 261.

51. al-Khuri, *Haqa'iq Lubnaniyya*, Vol. I, pp. 258–9.

52. Ibid.; see also FO 226/240-9/643/43, Spears Diary, 17 September 1943.

53. FO 226/240-9/645/43, Spears to Casey, 21 September 1943.

54. al-Khuri, *Haqa'iq Lubnaniyya*, Vol. I, p. 197.

55. Ibid., p. 231.

56. AD (Nantes), Syrie–Liban, 7/788, Beirut to Algiers, 14 September 1943.

57. AE (Paris), Guerre 39–45 (Alger), Vol. 1004, p. 291, Helleu to de Gaulle, 17 September 1943.

58. FO 226/240-9/645/43, Spears to FO, 20 September 1943.

59. FO 226/240-9/645/43, Spears to Casey, 21 September 1943.

60. al-Khuri, *Haqa'iq Lubnaniyya*, Vol. I, p. 259.

61. FO 226/242-9/645/43, Spears to FO, 20 September 1943; see also AD (Nantes), Syrie–Liban, 7/769, Élection du President de la République Libanaise et de la Formation du Cabinet Riad Solh, 14 October 1943; AE (Paris), Guerre 39–45 (Alger), Vol. 999, p. 18, Helleu to Algier, 22 September.

62. *Al-Anba'*, 30 May 1952.

63. Halaq, *Al-Tiyyarat al-Siyasiyya*, pp. 96–7.

64. Ibid., p. 103.

65. al-Khuri, *Haqa'iq Lubnaniyya*, Vol. II, p. 13.

## 3. The National Pact

1. Bishara al-Khuri, *Haqa'iq Lubnaniyya*, Vol. I, p. 264.

2. *Al-Hayat*, 31 August 1949.

3. Kamal Yusuf al-Hajj, *Al-Ta'ifiyya al-Banna'a aw Falsafat al-Mithaq al-Watani*, p. 140.

4. Itamar Rabinovich, *The War for Lebanon, 1970–1985*, pp. 24–5.

5. Albert Hourani, 'Lebanon: The Development of a Political Society', in Leonard Binder (ed.), *Politics in Lebanon*, p. 28.

6. This last point was not always observed. In 1944, Yusuf Salim, a Greek Catholic, ran for the office of speaker; in October 1944, Habib Abu-Shahla, Greek Orthodox from Beirut, was elected speaker.

7. See al-Khuri, *Haqa'iq Lubnaniyya*, Vol. II, p. 21.

8. For Sulh's speech see Basim al-Jisr, *Mithaq 1943, Limaza Kana waLimaza Saqata*, pp. 485–95.

9. See al-Khuri, *Haqa'iq Lubnaniyya*, Vol. II, p. 21.

10. Hamdi Badawi al-Tahiri, *Siyasat al-Hukm fi Lubnan*, p. 139.

11. See Kamal Salibi, 'The Personality of Lebanon in Relation to the Modern World', in Binder (ed.), *Politics in Lebanon*, pp. 263–70.

12. Farid el-Khazen, *The Communal Pact of the National Identities – The Making and Politics of the 1943 National Pact*, p. 4.

13. Ibid; see also al-Jisr, *Mithaq 1943*; Kamal Yusuf al-Hajj, *Al-Ta'ifiyya al-Banna'a aw Falsafat al-Mithaq al-Watani*; Mas'ud Dhahir, *Lubnan: al-Istiqlal, al-Sigha wal-Mithaq*.

14. Elie Kedourie, 'Lebanon: The Perils of Independence', in his *Islam in the Modern World and Other Studies*, p. 91.

15. Khalid al-'Azm, *Mudhakkirat Khalid al-'Azm*, Vol. II, pp. 11–13.

16. See Michael Hudson, *The Precarious Republic: Political Modernization in Lebanon*, pp. 262–96; Muhammad al-Hassan, *Al-Qanun al-Dusturi wal-Dustur fi Lubnan*, pp. 217–20.

17. FO 226/252-27/283/44, PIC Paper no. 26, Political Alignments in Lebanon, December 1944.

18. FO 226/252-9/315/43, 'Confessionalism and the Lebanese Administration', British Legation, Beirut, 17 June 1944.

19. See Kamal S. Salibi, *The Modern History of Lebanon*, p. 187; Hassan Halaq, *Al-Tiyyarat al-Siyasiyya fi Lubnan, 1943–1952*, p. 180.

20. FO 226/252-9/315/43, 'Confessionalism and the Lebanese Administration', British Legation, Beirut, 17 June 1944.

## 4. The November 1943 Crisis

1. Albert Hourani, 'Lebanon: The Development of a Political Society', in Leonard Binder (ed.), *Politics in Lebanon*, p. 28.

2. FO 371/35182-E6249, Spears to FO, 16 October 1943.

3. SHA, Levant, 4H308/2, Note, Le Directeur du Cabinet Politique, 23 October 1943; see also Aviel Roshwald, *Estranged Bedfellows: Britain and France in the Middle East During the Second World War*, pp. 149–53.

4. Bishara al-Khuri, *Haqa'iq Lubnaniyya*, Vol. II, pp. 21–5; Salma Mardam Bey, *Syria's Quest for Independence, 1939–1945*, pp. 85–93.

5. *Al-Nahar*, 14 November 1943; see also Hassan Halaq, *Al-Tiyyarat al-Siyasiyya fi Lubnan, 1943–1952*, pp. 107–8.

6. Halaq, *Al-Tiyyarat al-Siyasiyya*, p. 109.

7. See al-Khuri, *Haqa'iq Lubnaniyya*, Vol. II, p. 25; FO 226/241-24/297/43, Beirut to FO, 5 November 1943.

8. al-Khuri, *Haqa'iq Lubnaniyya*, Vol. II, p. 24.

9. Ibid., p. 26; FO 226/241-24/297/43, Beirut to FO, 5 November 1943.

10. al-Khuri, *Haqa'iq Lubnaniyya*, Vol. II, p. 26.

11. FO 371/35910-E7207, Spears to FO, 8, 10 November 1943; see also al-Khuri, *Haqa'iq Lubnaniyya*, Vol. II, p. 27.

12. *Al-Nahar*, 9 November 1943; Halaq, *Al-Tiyyarat al-Siyasiyya*, pp. 110–11.

13. FO 226/241-21/214/43, Beirut to FO, 1 October 1943.

14. FO 226/241-27/277/43, Beirut to FO, 30 October 1943.

15. AD (Nantes), Syrie–Liban, 7/771, Information, 14 January 1944.

16. Roshwald, *Estranged Bedfellows*, p. 155.

17. SHA, Levant, 4H308/2, Note, Le Directeur du Cabinet Politique, 23 October 1943.

18. AD (Nantes), Syrie–Liban, 7/788, Note sur le Crise Libanaise, 10–24 November 1943.

19. FO 226/241-27/277/43, Beirut to FO, 30 October 1943.

20. Mardam Bey, *Syria's Quest*, pp. 93–4.

21. A. B. Gaunson, *The Anglo-French Clash in Lebanon and Syria, 1940–45*, p. 122; FO 226/241-27/354/43, Minute by Belgrave, 11 November 1943; Edward L. Spears, *Fulfilment of a Mission: The Spears Mission to Syria and Lebanon, 1941–44*, pp. 224–77.

22. Ibid.

23. Spears Papers, Box III/File 4, Copy of Casey Diary, 11 November 1943.

24. Roshwald, *Estranged Bedfellows*, p. 163.

25. AE (Paris), Guerre 39–45 (Alger), Vol. 1000, pp. 221–33, Chataigneau to Massigli, 9 December 1943.

26. Sami al-Sulh, *Mudhakkirat Sami Bak al-Sulh*, pp. 61, 63.

27. 'Adil Arsalan, *Mudhakkirat al-Amir 'Adil Arsalan*, Vol. I, p. 382.

28. SHA, Levant, 4H308/3, Jean Helleu to Massigli, 20 November 1943.

29. SHA, Levant, 4H308/3, Le Conseilleur Administratif pour Liban-nord to Helleu, 16 November 1943.

30. Roshwald, *Estranged Bedfellows*, pp. 157–8.

31. FO 371/35184-E 6907/27/89, Spears to FO, 12, 13 November 1943.

32. FO 226/241-27/419/43, British Legation Beirut to FO, 13 November 1943.

33. Spears, *Fulfilment of a Mission*, p. 229.

34. Munir Taqi al-Din, *Wiladat Istiqlal*, pp. 88–9.

35. Hamdi Badawi al-Tahiri, *Siyasat al-Hukm fi Lubnan*, pp. 114–5; Halaq, *Al-Tiyyarat al-Siyasiyya*, pp. 114–15.

36. Ibid.

37. al-Tahiri, *Siyasat*, p. 135.

38. Khalid 'Ali Fallah, *Muhadarat fi Tarikh Lubnan*, p. 124.

39. al-Tahiri, *Siyasat*, p. 135.

40. FO 371/35187-E 7052,7096/27/89, Spears to FO, 16, 17 November 1943.

41. Nevertheless, as soon as he was released from detention, Jumayyil met with Edde to

explain to him that despite their conflicting views on Little Lebanon, he had nothing personal against him. He was obviously interested in removing any obstacle likely to prevent Edde's supporters from supporting the Phalanges in the future. SHA (Paris) Levant, 4H320/2, Information, Beirut, 1 December 1943.

42. For further details, see John P. Entelis, *Pluralism and Party Transformation in Lebanon, al-Kata'ib, 1936–1970*, pp. 45–6, 49, 53–5; Michael W. Suleiman, *Political Parties in Lebanon*, pp. 201–12.

43. Roshwald, *Estranged Bedfellows*, p. 275; CZA S25/5577, a letter from Beirut, 25 December 1943.

44. For more information on Arab reactions, see Halaq, *Al-Tiyyarat al-Siyasiyya*, pp. 118–20; cf. AE (Paris), Guerre 39–45 (Alger), Vol. 999, p. 168, 'Abd al-'Aziz to de Gaulle, 13 November 1943; FO 371/35182 E 6219, Spears to FO, 14 October 1943.

45. AE (Paris), Guerre 39–45 (Alger), Vol. 999, p. 179, Helleu to Algier, 15 November 1943.

46. Asher Susser, *Western Power Rivalry and its Interaction with Local Politics in the Levant, 1941–1946*, Part II, pp. 473–4.

47. FO 226/241-27/408/43, British Legation Beirut to FO, 12 November 1943; see also Roshwald, *Estranged Bedfellows*, pp. 156–7.

48. Mardam Bey, *Syria's Quest*, p. 95.

49. Ibid., p. 96.

50. Ibid., p. 97.

51. Susser, *Western Power Rivalry*, Part II, pp. 469–71; Spears Papers, Box II/File 4, Iraq, Syria and Lebanon, 1918–1943, p. 34.

52. Roshwald, *Estranged Bedfellows*, p. 159.

53. FO 226/241-27/340, 583/43, Spears to FO, 11, 15 November 1943; FO 371/35190-E 7203, Spears to FO, 19 November 1943.

54. FO 371/35184-E 6093, C-in-C, Middle East to WO, 12 November 1943.

55. FO 371/35187-E 7102, FO to Minister of State, Cairo, 17 November 1943.

56. Spears, *Fulfilment of a Mission*, p. 243; FO 371/35185-E6964, Spears to FO, 14 November 1943.

57. See Roshwald, *Estranged Bedfellows*, p. 162; Spears Papers Box III/File 4, Casey Diary, 19 and 27 November 1943.

58. Harold Macmillan, *War Diaries – The Mediterranean 1943–1945*, 17 November 1943.

59. FO 226/252, Political Intelligence Summary no. 216, 24 November 1943.

60. Helleu asked correspondents whether, given his age and position, they could really suppose that he had acted on his own. See Spears Papers, Box V/File 4, Spears to Mary Azury, 19 November 1968.

61. Catroux wrote in his memoirs that he first learned of the events in Beirut from a Reuters dispatch at 5 p.m. on 5 November, i.e. twelve hours after they had occurred. His first reaction was to say that this time Reuters had really gone too far. Georges Catroux, *Dans la Bataille de Méditerranée: Egypte–Levant–Afrique du Nord, 1940–1944*, p. 410. See also FO 226/241-27/594/43, Spears to FO, 17 November 1943.

62. Charles de Gaulle, *Mémoires de Guerre*, Vol. II, p. 598.

63. Catroux, *Dans la Bataille*, p. 414.

64. CLS, US Documents, Box 8, RG84, Box 2653, Intelligence Report by Edwin M. Wright, 4 December 1943.

65. Roshwald, *Estranged Bedfellows*, pp. 159–66.

66. AE (Paris), Guerre 39–45 (Alger), Vol. 1005, p. 208, Catroux to de Gaulle, 23 November 1943; Catroux, *Dans la Bataille*, p. 410.

67. *Al-Hayat*, 24 November 1965; see also al-Khuri, *Haqa'iq Lubnaniyya*, Vol. II, pp. 55–58.

68. Being unfamiliar with nineteenth-century regional history, Casey may not have fully grasped Catroux's meaning. FO 371/35188-E 7160, Spears to FO, 19 November 1943; Spears Papers, Box III/File 4, Casey Diary, 19 November 1943.

69. CLS, US Documents, Box 8, RG84, Box 2653, Intelligence Report by Edwin M. Wright, 4 December 1943.

## 5. Between East and West

1. Salma Mardam Bey, *Syria's Quest for Independence, 1939–1945*, pp. 85–8.

2. Aviel Roshwald, *Estranged Bedfellows*, pp. 167–75.

3. FO 371/35196-E 8067, Spears to FO, 23 December 1943; FO 371/40299-E 344, Weekly Political Summary, Syria and the Lebanon, 5 January 1944.

4. FO 371/40301-E 3604/23/89, Weekly Political Summary no. 114, 7 June 1944.

5. Roshwald, *Estranged Bedfellows*, p. 180.

6. FO 371/40313-E 4066/217/89, Eden to Churchill, 29 June 1944.

7. SHA, Levant, 4H308/2, Le Directeur du Cabinet Politique, 23 October 1943; FO 226/245-94/362/43, Spears to FO, 30 November 1943.

8. Bishara al-Khuri, *Haqa'iq Lubnaniyya*, Vol. II, pp. 96–7.

9. FO 371/40347-E 5415/5178/89, Conversation between Eden and Spears, 1 September 1944.

10. Kamil Sham'un (Camille Chamoun), *Marahil al-Istiqlal: Lubnan wa-Duwal al-'Arab fi al-Mu'tamarat al-Dawliyya*, pp. 112–13.

11. FO 371/35194-E 7654/27/89, Spears to FO, 27 November 1943.

12. FO 371/40347-E 5415/5178/89, Conversation between Eden and Spears, 1 September 1944.

13. FO 371/40112-E 5663, 5719, Spears to FO, 13, 18, 21 September 1944.

14. Spears Papers, Box II/File 6, Spears to FO, 8 December 1943.

15. When told of his impending replacement, Spears felt free to follow his own line. He wrote: 'From that time on I considered myself a free man and began to make very open speeches. They were really very good speeches and made a profound impression.' Spears Papers, Box I/File 1, Spears Diary, 1 January 1945.

16. FO 226/254-31/44/44, Record of a conversation between Furlonge and Salim Taqla, 25 September 1944.

17. Mardam Bey, *Syria's Quest*, pp. 85–6.

18. Spears Papers, Box II/File 7, Spears to Churchill, 2 September 1944.

19. Spears Papers, Box II/File 7, Churchill to Spears, 3 September 1944.

20. Spears Papers, Box II/File 7, Spears to Churchill, 24 October 1944; Spears to FO 14 December 1944; Box III/File 6, Record of a meeting between Eden and Spears, 1 January 1945; see also Spears Papers, Box I/File 1, Spears Diary, 1 January 1945.

21. Roshwald, *Estranged Bedfellows*, pp. 188–9; cf. FO 371/45355/88-E 3488, Shone to FO, 28 May 1945.

22. SHA, Levant, 4H375/1, Bulletin d'information, 29 May–1 June 1945; CLS, US Documents, Box 9, RG 84, Box 229/File 851, Wadworth to Secretary of State, 13 August 1945.

23. SHA, Levant, 4H375/1, Bulletin d'information, 29 May–1 June 1945.

24. Sham'un (Chamoun) *Marahil al-Istiqlal*, p. 93.

25. Roshwald, *Estranged Bedfellows*, pp. 154, 156–7, 175–6.

26. FO 226/253-30/28/44, Furlonge to FO, 13 August 1944; FO 371/40112-E 5965, Spears to FO, 28 September 1944.

27. FO 226/273-70/25/45, Shone to FO, 3 March 1945.

28. Hassan Halaq, *al-Tiyyarat al-Siyasiyya fi Lubnan, 1943–1952*, p. 340.

29. FO 371/40112-E 6296, Spears to FO, 14 October 1944.

30. AD (Nantes), 755, Beirut to Paris, 20 October 1944.

31. SHA, Papiers Beynet, 1K230, I, pp. 107–8.

32. For further details, see FO 226/291-249/36/45, Beirut to FO, 4 May 1945; FO 226/287-97/73/45, Beirut to FO, 19 May 1945; FO 226/302 249/90/45, 9th Army to Beirut, 17 May 1945.

33. Mardam Bey, *Syria's Quest*, pp. 197–227; Roshwald, *Estranged Bedfellows*, pp. 197–208.

34. FO 371/45355-E 3571, Beirut to FO, 31 May 1945.

35. FO 226/287-92/253/45, Shone to FO, 30 May 1945.

36. SHA, Levant, 4H303, L'attitude du Liban dans la crise France Syrienne-Libanaise, 2 June 1945; FO 226/291-92/832/45, Shone to FO, 25 August 1945.

37. Ibid.; AE (Paris), Levant, Vol. 35, p. 237, Beirut to Paris, 23 July 1945.

38. FO 226/287-92/117/45, Shone to FO, 22 May 1945.

39. Eden made the note to the House of Commons on the same day. FO 226/287-E 3624/8/94, Extract from House of Commons debates, 31 May 1945.

40. Roshwald, *Estranged Bedfellows*, pp. 206–7.

41. FO 371/45355-E 10276, Copy of a letter from the Lebanese Legation, London, to FO, 28 December 1945.

42. Roshwald, *Estranged Bedfellows*, p. 212.

43. FO 226/302-353/1/45, Record of a conversation between Captain 'Arab and President al-Khouri, 25 July 1945.

44. For more see al-Khuri, *Haqa'iq Lubnaniyya*, Vol. II, p. 218.

45. See protocol of the Security Council debate on the Syrian and Lebanese complaints. Spears Papers, Box IV/File 7.

46. FO 371/52480-E 3771, Beirut to FO, 16 April 1946; Halaq, *Al-Tiyyarat al-Siyasiyya*, p. 155; al-Khuri, *Haqa'iq Lubnaniyya*, Vol. II, p. 218.

47. Spears Papers, Box II/File 4; see also Halaq, *Al-Tiyyarat al-Siyasiyya*, p. 155.

48. See al-Khuri, *Haqa'iq Lubnaniyya*, Vol. II, pp. 216–18.

49. Yehoshua Porath, *In Search of Arab Unity, 1930–1945*, p. 157; Daniel Pipes, *Greater Syria, The History of an Ambition*, pp. 3–100.

50. See Halaq, *Al-Tiyyarat al-Siyasiyya*, pp. 340–1.

51. FO 371/52499/88-E 5046, 7125, Shone to FO, 28 May 1946, Begin to Shone, 31 July 1946.

52. Halaq, *Al-Tiyyarat al-Siyasiyya*, p. 354.

53. Ibid., p. 355.

54. Ibid., p. 361.

55. Ibid.

56. Ibid., pp. 323–4.

57. Porath, *In Search of Arab Unity*, pp. 266–7.

58. Halaq, *Al-Tiyyarat al-Siyasiyya*, p. 325.

59. Porath, *In Search of Arab Unity*, p. 267.

60. Sa'id Murad, *Al-Haraka al-Wahdawiyya fi Lubnan bayna al-Harbayn al-'Alamatayn, 1914–1964*, p. 313.

61. Porath, *In Search of Arab Unity*, p. 283; see also Ahmed Gomaa, *The Foundation of the League of Arab States*, pp. 272–4.

62. Yusuf Salim, *50 Sana ma'a al-Nas*, p. 187.

63. Porath, *In Search of Arab Unity*, p. 285.

64. Ibid., p. 273.

65. FO 226/267-60/402/45, Record of a conversation between Furlonge and President al-Khouri, 8 September 1945; FO 226/276/75/172/45, Beirut to FO, 22 September 1945.

# 6. Domestic Challenges, 1943–47

1. Hassan Halaq, *Al-Tiyyarat al-Siyasiyya fi Lubnan, 1943–1952*, p. 129.

2. AE (Paris), Guerre 39–45 (Alger), pp. 358–9, Beynet to Massigli, 29 March 1944; see also FO 226/252-27/1/44, Furlonge to Spears, 17 January 1944; FO 371/40111-E 2739, Spears to FO, 4 May 1944.

3. FO 371/40111-E 2290/23/89, FO to Spears, 30 April 1944, 1 May 1944.

4. FO 226/252-27/36/44, Furlonge to Spears, 4 March 1944.

5. FO 226/242-27/96/43, Furlonge to Spears, 29 December 1943.

6. Bishara al-Khuri, *Haqa'iq Lubnaniyya*, Vol. II, p. 64.

7. Ibid., p. 82.

8. FO 226/252-20/57/44, Furlonge to Spears, 3 April 1944.

9. For the political come-back of Edde's camp, see FO 226/252-27/183/44, PIC paper, no. 71, Political Alignments in Lebanon, December 1944.

10. FO 226/252-27/71/44, Furlonge to Spears, 15 April 1944; SHA, Levant, 4H303/3, Bulletin d'information politique pour le mois d'Avril 1944.

11. FO 226/252-27/74/44, Beirut to FO, 24 April 1944.

12. FO 226/242-27/96/43, Furlonge to Spears, 29 December 1943.

13. FO 226/252-27/71/44, Furlonge to Spears, 15 April 1944; SHA, Levant, 4H303/3, Bulletin d'information politique pour le mois d'Avril 1944.

14. SHA, Levant, 4H289, Les événements du Liban, Combat, 21 May 1944.

15. FO 226/252-27/84/44, Note on the part of Far'un in the election of Karam, 19 May 1944.

16. FO 226/242-27/96/43, Furlonge to Spears, 29 December 1943.

17. SHA, Levant, 4H289, Les événements du Liban, Combat, 21 May 1944.

18. SHA, Levant, 4H303/3, Bulletin d'information politique pour le mois d'Avril 1944.

19. al-Khuri, *Haqa'iq Lubnaniyya*, Vol. II, p. 86.

20. AE (Paris), Guerre 39–45 (Alger), Vol. 1006, pp. 187–8, 223–7, Beynet to Massigli, Incidents d'Avril, 3, 9 May 1944; al-Khuri, *Haqa'iq Lubnaniyya*, Vol. I, pp. 87–8; cf. FO 371/46301-E 2966, Weekly Political Summary, Syria and the Lebanon, 3 May 1944.

21. al-Khuri, *Haqa'iq Lubnaniyya*, Vol. II, p. 88.

22. FO 371/40301-E 2996, Weekly Political Summary, Syria and the Lebanon, 3 May 1944; AE (Paris), Guerre 39–45 (Alger), Vol. 1006, pp. 129–31, Algiers to Beirut, 28 April 1944.

23. al-Khuri, *Haqa'iq Lubnaniyya*, Vol. II, p. 86.

24. FO 371/40111-E 2733, Beirut to FO, 3 May 1944.

25. Ibid., FO 371/40111-E 2704, Algiers to FO, 1 May 1944, FO to Beirut 3 May 1944.

26. FO 371/40111-E 2704,2771, FO to Beirut, 3 May 1944; Spears to FO, 6 May 1944.

27. AE (Paris), Guerre 39–45 (Alger), Vol. 1006, pp. 206–7, Beirut to Algiers, 5 May 1944.

28. FO 371/40110-E 2655, Spears to FO, 29 April 1944.

29. FO 226/252-27/94/44, Spears Memorandum, 19 June 1944.

30. FO 376/4011-E 2771, Spears to FO, 5 May 1944.

31. Ibid.

32. AE (Paris), Geurre 39–45 (Alger), Vol. 1006, pp. 206–7, Beirut to Algiers, 5 May 1944.

33. FO 371/35182-E 5839/27/88, Beirut to FO, 29 September 1943.

34. FO 371/35182-E 6293, Weekly Political Summary, Syria and the Lebanon, 6 October 1943.

35. *Al-Bayanat al-Wizariyya al-Lubnaniyya waMunaqashatiha fi majlis al-Nuwwab, 1926–1984*, Vol. I, pp. 128–9.

36. FO 226/242-27/996/43, Furlonge to Spears, 29 December 1943.

37. FO 371/35196-E 8104, Weekly Political Summary, Syria and the Lebanon, 15 December 1943.

38. FO 226/252-27/87/44, Furlonge to Spears, 26 May 1944; cf. FO 226/252-27/92/44, Furlonge to Spears, 3 June 1944.

39. FO 224/252-24/102, Furlonge to Spears, 21 June 1944; AD (Nantes), Syrie–Liban, 9/1131/2, Chataigneau to Massigli, 27 March 1944.

40. FO 371/45363-E 3352, Beirut to FO, 24 May 1945.

41. SHA, Levant 4H303/3, Bulletin d'information politique pour le mois de Juin 1944.

42. al-Khuri, *Haqa'iq Lubnaniyya*, Vol. II, p. 111.

43. *Al-Nahar*, 29 July 1944.

44. *Al-Bayanat Al-Wizariyya*, Vol. I, pp. 137–8.

45. FO 371/45354-E 668, Shone to FO, 11 January 1945.

46. AE (Paris), Guerre 39–45, Vol.1031, pp. 283–96, Beynet to Massigli, 22 August 1944.

47. al-Khuri, *Haqa'iq Lubnaniyya*, Vol. II, pp. 111–12.

48. FO 371/45354-E 668, Shone to FO, 11 January 1945.

49. Ibid.

50. CLS, US Documents, Box 9-RG84, Box 229/File 800, James R. Carter to Frank Brown, 4 January 1945; cf. al-Khuri, *Haqa'iq Lubnaniyya*, Vol. II, pp. 112–13.

51. *Al-Bayanat al-Wizariyya*, Vol. I, p. 149.

52. FO 371/45354-E 668, Shone to FO, 11 January 1945.

53. FO 226/252-27/165/44.

54. al-Khuri, *Haqa'iq Lubnaniyya*, Vol. II, p. 124; FO 371/45354-E 247, Shone to FO, 10 January 1945; see also FO 371/45354-E 740, Shone to FO, FO to Shone, 31 January, 5 February 1945.

55. A Jewish agency report attributed Khuri's nervous breakdown to incorrect medical treatment. ISA, MFA 2567/2, Conversation with visitors from Lebanon, 14 February 1945.

56. FO 371/45354-E 740 Shone to FO, FO to Shone, 31 January, 5 February 1945.

57. FO 226/267-60/349/45, Shone to FO, 20 April 1945.

58. al-Khuri, *Haqa'iq Lubnaniyya*, Vol. II, pp. 136–7.

59. Ibid.

60. SHA, Levant, 4H375/2, 9th Army intelligence report no. 3, 13–26 June 1945; see also al-Khuri, *Haqa'iq Lubnaniyya*, Vol. II, p. 145.

61. al-Khuri, *Haqa'iq Lubnaniyya*, Vol. II, p. 146.

62. FO 371/45355-E 5974, Beirut to FO, 15 August 1945.

63. FO 226/267-60/381/45, Shone to FO, 21 August 1945.

64. FO 371/45355-E 6189, Beirut to FO, 23 August 1945.

65. al-Khuri, *Haqa'iq Lubnaniyya*, Vol. II, pp. 238–9.

66. Walter L. Browne, *Lebanon's Struggle for Independence*, Vol. II, pp. 50–2.

67. Sami al-Sulh, *Ahtakim 'Ila al-Tarikh*, p. 57.

68. al-Khuri, *Haqa'iq Lubnaniyya*, Vol. II, p. 237.

69. *L'Orient*, 5 May 1945; Michael Hudson, *The Precarious Republic: Political Modernization in Lebanon*, pp. 266–8.

70. SHA, Levant, 4H375/1, Information, 17 March 1945.

71. Hudson, *The Precarious Republic*, pp. 266–8; see also al-Khuri, *Haqa'iq Lubnaniyya*, Vol. II, p. 238.

72. Hudson, *The Precarious Republic*, pp. 268–9; Halaq, *Al-Tiyyarat al-Siyasiyya*, p. 158.

73. al-Khuri, *Haqa'iq Lubnaniyya*, Vol. II, p. 234.

74. For more details, see Hudson, *The Precarious Republic*, pp. 266–9.

75. CLS, US Documents, Box 8, RG 319, 'P' file, Box 2180, Lebanon: Cabinet Crisis, 13 December 1946; Browne, *Lebanon's Struggle*, pp. 86–93, Monthly Political Review, Lebanon, June 1946.

76. FO 371/52480-E 4046, Beirut to FO, 3, 22 May 1946; FO 226/252-60/392/45, Shone to FO, 23 August 1946.

77. CLS, US Documents, Box 8, RG 319, 'P' file, Box 2180, Lebanon: Cabinet Crisis, 13 December 1946.

78. Browne, *Lebanon's Struggle*, pp. 86–93, Monthly Political Review, Lebanon, June 1946; also FO 371/61723-E 2346/2346/88, Annual Report of the Lebanon for 1946, Houstoun Boswall to Bevin, 18 March 1947.

79. Browne, *Lebanon's Struggle*, p. 121, Monthly Political Review, Lebanon, October 1946; cf. al-Khuri, *Haqa'iq Lubnaniyya*, Vol. II, p. 271.

80. FO 371/61723-E 2346/2346/88, Annual Report of the Lebanon for 1946, Houstoun Boswall to Bevin, 18 March 1947.

81. al-Khuri, *Haqa'iq Lubnaniyya*, Vol. II, p. 238.

82. *Al-Hayat*, 25 March 1946.


# 7. At the Peak of Power

1. The due date was August 1947, precisely four years after the preceding elections, but it was decided to set an earlier date because of the death on 16 February of Ayub Thabit whose seat had thus fallen vacant. The electoral law laid down that a vacant seat must be filled within three months. Bishara al-Khuri, *Haqa'iq Lubnaniyya*, Vol. III, p. 13.

2. FO 371/61710-E 5207/9909/88, Lebanon: Summary for the Month of May 1947.

3. CLS, US Documents, Box 8, RG84, Box 229/File 800, Pinkerton to Department of State, 3 April 1947.

4. al-Khuri, *Haqa'iq Lubnaniyya*, Vol. III, p. 36.

5. See CLS, US Documents, Box 8, 890E.00/4-3047, The general elections, 25 May 1947, Pinkerton to Secretary of State, 28 April 1947; al-Khuri, *Haqa'iq Lubnaniyya*, Vol. III, pp. 34–5.

6. Ibid.; Yusuf Salim, *50 Sana ma'a al-Nas*, pp. 270–94.

7. See CLS, US Documents, Box 8, 890E.00/4-3047, The general elections, 25 May 1947, Pinkerton to Secretary of State, 28 April 1947; al-Khuri, *Haqa'iq Lubnaniyya*, Vol. III, pp. 31–2.

8. FO 1018/26-139/32/47, List of candidates in the elections; *Al-Hayat*, 24 May 1947.

9. al-Khuri, *Haqa'iq Lubnaniyya*, Vol. III, p. 41.

10. CLS, US Documents, Box 8, 890E.00/4-3047, The general elections, 25 May 1947, Pinkerton to Secretary of State, 28 April 1947; 0097.3/0092-54439/47, Beirut to Department of State, 30 June 1947; FO 1018/26-139/25/47, The electionary situation in the North Lebanon district, 29 April 1947.

11. FO 371/61710-E 3364, 4304, Lebanon: Summaries no. 8, 9–23 April, 21 May 1947.

12. FO 1018/26-139/25/47; 139/47/47, The electionary situation in the North Lebanon district, 29 April 1947; Conditions in Tripoli, 2 June 1947.

13. Ibid.

14. Ibid.; also al-Khuri, *Haqa'iq Lubnaniyya*, Vol. III, pp. 23–5.

15. FO 1018/21-80/9/47, Beirut to FO, 28 April 1947.

16. FO 1018/26-139/25/47; 139/47/47, The electionary situation in the North Lebanon district, 29 April 1947; Conditions in Tripoli, 2 June 1947.

17. FO 1018/26-139/33/47, T. E. Evans to Bevin, 24 May 1947; al-Khuri, *Haqa'iq Lubnaniyya*, Vol. III, pp. 32–4.

18. al-Khuri, *Haqa'iq Lubnaniyya*, Vol. III, p. 37; cf. CLS, US Documents, Box 8, 890E.00/4-3047, The general elections, 25 May 1947, Pinkerton to Secretary of State, 28 April 1947.

19. See FO 1018/21-80/1/47, Beirut to FO, 6 January 1947; 80/5/47, Beirut to FO, 24 March 1947; 80/6/47, Beirut to FO, 2 April 1947.

20. FO 1018/26-139/19/47, British Legation, Beirut, 10 May 1947.

21. CLS, US Documents, Box 9, 890E.00/4-3047, Pinkerton to Secretary of State, 28 April 1947.

22. CLS, US Documents, Box V, Box 4076, 783A.00/4-451, Pinkerton to Secretary of State, 4 April 1951; FO 1018/21-80/37/47, Lebanon: Summary for the Month of November 1947.

23. CLS, US Documents, Box V, Box 4076, 890E.00/4-3047, Pinkerton to Secretary of State, 28 April 1947.

24. FO 371/61710-E 4307/909/88, Lebanon: Summary no. 9, 21 May 1947.

25. FO 371/61710/88-E 4307, Beirut to FO, 30 April 1947.

26. Hassan Halaq, *Al-Tiyyarat al-Siyasiyya fi Lubnan*, p. 555.

27. al-Khuri, *Haqa'iq Lubnaniyya*, Vol. III, pp. 37–40.

28. Ibid.; FO 371/61710/88-E 4307, Beirut to FO, 30 April 1947.

29. See CLS, US Documents, Box V, Box 4076, 783A.00/2-1352, Minor to State Department, 13 February 1952.

30. al-Khuri, *Haqa'iq Lubnaniyya*, Vol. III, pp. 40–2; CLS, US Documents, Box 8, RG84, Box 231, Pinkerton to Secretary of State, 28 May 1947.

31. Halaq, *Al-Tiyyarat al-Siyasiyya*, p. 242; Walter L. Browne, *Lebanon's Struggle for Independence*, pp. 204–7; CLS, US Documents, Box 890E.00/5-1347, Pinkerton to Secretary of State, 13 May 1947; FO 371/61710-E 5207/9909/88, Lebanon: Summary for the Month of May 1947.

32. Members of the National Bloc published a severe indictment against the regime, entitled *The Black Book*. It came out in an Arabic as well as in an English edition, the latter for the benefit of Lebanese émigrés abroad. See George Akl (ed.), *The Black Book of the Lebanese Elections of May 25, 1947*, p. 14.

33. Ibid.

34. Ibid., pp. 23, 36–7.

35. al-Khuri, *Haqa'iq Lubnaniyya*, Vol. III, pp. 41, 49; FO 371/61710-E 5207/9909/88, Lebanon: Summary for the Month of May 1947.

36. AE (Paris), Guerre 39–45 (Alger), Vol. 1001, Chataigneau to Massigli, 1 January 1944.

37. FO 1018/26, copy of letter from Mubarak to Khuri.

38. CLS, US Documents, Box 8, RG84, Box 231, Pinkerton to Secretary of State, 28 May 1947; cf. FO 371/61710-E 5207/909/88, Lebanon: Summary for the Month of May 1947, 18 June 1947.

39. al-Khuri, *Haqa'iq Lubnaniyya*, Vol. III, pp. 30–1.

40. FO 371/68455-E 2922, Summary of events in the Lebanon during the year 1947, 25 February 1948.

41. FO 371/61710-E 6621, 8742/909/88, Lebanon: Summary for the Month of June 1947, August 1947.

42. CLS, US Documents, Box 8, RG84, Box 232, File 800, Beirut to Department of State, 5 February 1948; *Al-Nahar*, 5 February 1948.

43. FO 371/68485-E 3952, Beirut Summary for the Month of February 1948, E 10947, Beirut Monthly Summary for the Month of July 1948.

44. Sami al-Sulh, *Mudhakkirat Sami Bak al-Sulh*, p. 68.

45. al-Khuri, *Haqa'iq Lubnaniyya*, Vol. III, pp. 121–2.

46. Ibid., p. 122.

47. CLS, US Documents, Box 8, RG84, Box 220, Pinkerton to SD, 26 May 1948.

48. FO 371/6849-E 10301, Beirut Monthly Summary for the Month of June 1948.

49. *Al-Hayat*, 28 May 1948.

50. CLS, US Documents, Box V, RG84, Box 232, 801.1/800.1-5-2648, Pinkerton to Secretary of State, 26 May 1948.

51. FO 371/68485-E 7508, Houstoun Boswall to Bevin, 30 May 1948.

52. al-Khuri, *Haqa'iq Lubnaniyya*, Vol. III, p. 123; FO 1018/80, Beirut Monthly Summary for the Month of May 1948.

53. FO 371/68489-E 12619, Beirut Monthly Summary for the Month of August 1948.

54. al-Khuri, *Haqa'iq Lubnaniyya*, Vol. III, p. 153.

55. FO 371/68495-E 16175, British Legation, Beirut, 15 December 1948.

56. CLS, US Documents, Box V, RG84, Box 232, 801.1/800.1-5-2648, Pinkerton to Secretary of State, 26 May 1948.

57. FO 1018/80, Beirut Monthly Summary for the Month of May 1948.

58. al-Khuri, *Haqa'iq Lubnaniyya*, Vol. III, p. 131.

59. Ibid., pp. 261–2.

60. FO 371/75318-E 13102, Beirut Monthly Summary for the Month of September 1948.

61. FO 1030/91-E 12447, Houstoun Boswall to Attlee, 5 October 1949.

62. CLS, US Documents, Box 8, 890E.00/8-1748, American Legation, Beirut, to Department of State, 17 August 1948; FO 371/68489-E 7086, Beirut Monthly Summary for the Month of June 1948.

63. CLS, US Documents, Box 8, 890E.00/8-1748, American Legation, Beirut, to Department of State, 17 August 1948; FO 371/68489-E 7086, Beirut Monthly Summary for the Month of April 1948; also al-Khuri, *Haqa'iq Lubnaniyya*, Vol. III, pp. 114–16.

## 8. The 1948 War in Palestine

1. Hassan Halaq, *Al-Tiyyarat al-Siyasiyya fi Lubnan, 1943–1952*, p. 14; FO 226/277-76/69/45, Beirut to FO, 4 September 1945.

2. David Ben-Gurion, *Yoman Hamilhama*, Vol. I, p. 339; Halaq, *Al-Tiyyarat al-Siyasiyya*, p. 14; ISA, MFA, 2565/12-159/403/G, The last elections campaign in Lebanon. A. Ilani to Moshe Sharett, 2 May 1951; SHA, Levant, 4H/375, Délégation Générale, bulletin d'information no. 45, 5–12 November 1945; 4H/298-9, Cabinet Politique, 4 June 1944.

3. For more details on Druze and Shi'i attitudes on Palestine see Halaq, *Al-Tiyyarat al-Siyasiyya*, pp. 444–90.

4. Laura Zittrain Eisenberg, *My Enemy's Enemy. Lebanon in the Early Zionist Imagination 1900–1948*, pp. 64–6.

5. For more details, see Ian Black, *Zionism and the Arabs, 1936–1939*; Eisenberg, *My Enemy's Enemy*, pp. 63–4, 76–94; Hassan Halaq, *Mawqif Lubnan min al-Qadiyya al-Falastiniyya, 1918–1952*.

6. ISA, MFA, 2567/2-32/1/71, 92, Letters from Beirut, 1 July 1945; Spears, 1 March 1944.

7. More details in Laura Zittrain Eisenberg, 'Desperate Diplomacy: The Zionist–Maronite Treaty of 1946'.

8. Eyal Zisser, 'The Maronites, Lebanon and the State of Israel: Early Contacts'.

9. Eisenberg, 'Desperate Diplomacy: The Zionist–Maronite Treaty of 1946', pp. 141–2; 75. Ya'akov Shim'oni, 'Jordanian, Egyptian and Palestinian "Orientations" in the Policies of the Jews in Palestine, the Zionist Movement and the Nascent Israel', p. 54.

10. Eisenberg, 'Desperate Diplomacy', pp. 155–8.

11. ISA, MFA, 2567/12 , copy of Mubarak's memorandum to UNSCOP, 13 October 1947.

12. Halaq, *Al-Tiyyarat al-Siyasiyya*, pp. 461–2, 465.

13. See ISA, MFA, 2567/12-11/1/32, the Mubarak affair, 7 October 1947; FO 371/61710-E 11425, Beirut Monthly Summary for the Month of September 1947.

14. Bishara al-Khuri, *Haqa'iq Lubnaniyya*, Vol. III, p. 518.

15. CLS, US Documents, RG84, Box 232/File 800, Pinkerton to Secretary of State, 26 November 1948.

16. FO 371/91437-E 1052/3, Chapman Andrews to FO, 25 July 1951.

17. FO 371/82250-E 1053/10, British Legation, Beirut, to FO, 6 November 1951.

18. CLS Documents, Box V, Box 4076, 783A.00/5-1451, Bruins to Department of State, 14 May 1951.

19. See more, William Haddad, 'The Christian Arab Press and the Palestine Question: A Case Study of Michel Chiha of Beirut's Le Jour'.

20. ISA, MFA, 1454/12, T. Arazi (Paris) to MFA, 19 February 1949.

21. Ibid.

22. See FO 371/68487-E 12169, Beirut Monthly Summary for the Month of August 1948.

23. Halaq, *Mawqif Lubnan*, p. 81.

24. Ibid., pp. 81–2; *Al-Nahar*, 7 August 1946.

25. ISA, MFA, 2565/12-159/403/G, The last elections campaign in Lebanon. A. Ilani to Moshe Sharett, 2 May 1951; FO 371/61741/88-E 11816, Houstoun Boswall to FO, 9 December 1947; Halaq, *Al-Tiyyarat al-Siyasiyya*, p. 14.

26. FO 371/61710-E 11425, Beirut Monthly Summary for the Month of October 1947.

27. FO 371/68489-E 1744, 2855, Beirut Monthly Summary for the Month of December 1947.

28. Bruce Maddy-Weitzman, *The Crystallization of the Arab State System, 1945–1954*, pp. 48–70.

29. al-Khuri, *Haqa'iq Lubnaniyya*, Vol. III, p. 105.

30. Ibid., p. 109.

31. CLS, US Documents, Box 8, RG84, Box 232, Pinkerton to Secretary of State, 16 February 1948.

32. al-Khuri, *Haqa'iq Lubnaniyya*, Vol. III, p. 102.

33. Jon and David Kimchie, *Both Sides of the Hill*, pp. 145–78.

34. See Guy Ma'ayan, *Lebanon, the Arab World and the Zionist Yishuv/The State of Israel: 1945–1949*; IDF, Historical Branch, *Toldot Milhemet Hakomemiyut*, pp. 175–6; see also al-Khuri, *Haqa'iq Lubnaniyya*, Vol. III, p. 159; FO 371/68493-E 13713, British Legation, Beirut to FO, 22 October 1948.

35. IDF, Historical Branch, *Toldot Milhemet Hakomemiyut*, pp. 322–60.

36. ISA, MFA, 186/17, Shim'oni to Eytan, 18 November 1948, Shim'oni to Elyas, 2 November 1948.

37. CLS, US Documents, Box 8, RG84, Box 232, Pinkerton to Secretary of State, 26 November 1948; al-Khuri, *Haqa'iq Lubnaniyya*, Vol. III, p. 159.

38. CLS, US Documents, Box 8, RG84, Box 232, Pinkerton to Secretary of State, 26 November 1948.

39. FO 371/75310/31, Beirut to FO, 14 January 1948; Halaq, *Al-Tiyyarat al-Siyasiyya*, pp. 484–5.

40. FO 371/68489-E 16176, Beirut Monthly Summary for the Month of November 1948.

41. Ben-Gurion, *Yoman Hamilhama*, Vol. III, p. 870.

42. ISA, MFA, 2454/12, Tuvia Arazi to Elyas Sasson, 14 December 1948.

43. Ben-Gurion, *Yoman Hamilhama*, Vol. III, p. 870.

44. CLS, US Documents, Box 8, RG84, Box 232, Pinkerton to Secretary of State, 26 November 1948.

45. ISA, MFA, 2454/12, Sasson to Sharett, 31 May 1949.

46. See Halaq, *Mawqif Lubnan*, p. 285; *Al-Tiyyarat al-Siyasiyya*, pp. 493–6.

47. al-Khuri, *Haqa'iq Lubnaniyya*, Vol. III, p. 197; FO 371/75318-E 2636, Beirut Summary for the Month of January 1949.

48. al-Khuri, *Haqa'iq Lubnaniyya*, Vol. III, p. 148.

49. IDF, Historical Branch, *Toldot Milhemet Hakomemiyut*, p. 368.

50. A US diplomatic report of the meeting attributes it to Lebanon's desire for border tensions to abate. The Lebanese side stated that if the present meeting was kept secret, further useful contacts might follow. ISA, MFA, 2454/12, 27 February 1950; CLS, US Documents, Box VI, Box 4077, 783.00(W)/3-752, Beirut, Military Attaché, 7 March 1952.

51. CLS, US Documents, Box V, Box 2984, 683A.54/7-2750, American Legation, Beirut, to SD, 27 July, 3 August 1950; see also Kirsten E. Schulze, 'Coercive Diplomacy: The 1950 Israeli Attack on a Lebanese Airliner'.

52. Hassan Halaq, *Al-Tiyyarat al-Siyasiyya*, p. 488.

53. See Benny Morris, 'Israel and the Lebanese Phalanges: The Birth of a Relationship, 1948–1951'.

54. ISA, MFA, 2565/12, Y. Zeligson to Y. Shim'oni, a conversation with Emile Edde on 3 July 1948, 13 July 1948.

55. ISA, MFA, 2565/12, T. Arazi to E. Sasson, a conversation with Emile Edde in Paris, 22 May 1948.

56. Itamar Rabinovich, *The Road Not Taken*, pp. 209–10. Cf. his description of a friendly meeting between Sasson and Shukri al-Quwatli. Quwatli was then a political exile and the meeting took place in Geneva. The atmosphere was similar.

57. FO 371/68489, E 1744, Beirut Monthly Summary for the Month of December 1947.

58. FO 1018/21-08/38/47, Amman to FO, 29 December 1947.

59. ISA, MFA, 2403/5, a meeting with an envoy of Archbishop Mubarak, S. Ya'ari, 30 March 1949.

60. Ibid.

61. Morris, 'Israel and the Lebanese Phalanges', pp. 125–6.

62. ISA, MFA, 2408/16 Ben Hurin (New York) to M. Shertok (Tel Aviv), 18 December 1948.

63. ISA, MFA, 2565/12 E. Sasson (Ankara) to M. Sasson (MFA), 18 December 1950.

64. Gideon Rafael met with Rababi in December 1950 and recommended making him a grant of 5,000–10,000 Lebanese lira. In March 1951, Yehoshua Palmon gave Rababi $2,000 at a meeting in Paris. ISA, MFA, 2565/12, E. Sasson, 28 December 1950, Y. Palmon to MFA, 26 March 1951, Gideon Rafael to the director-general of the MFA, 23 December 1950.

65. ISA, MFA, Gideon Tadmor, the MFA, the research branch to the minister, assistance to the Lebanese Phalanges, 2 January 1951.

66. ISA, MFA, 2565/12, S. Divon (Paris) to A. Najar (MFA), 6 June 1951; see also ISA, MFA, 2565/12, Gideon Rafael to the director-general of the MFA, a conversation with Elyas Rababi, 28 December 1950.

67. *Talaghraf*, 26 June 1949.

68. ISA, MFA, E. Sasson (Rome) to R. Shiloah (MFA), 29 March 1959.

69. ISA, MFA, 2565/12, Sharett to the director-general of the MFA, 12 November 1950.

70. ISA, MFA, 2565/12, Assistance to the Lebanese Phalanges, Gideon Tadmor, MFA, the research branch, 21 January 1951.

71. ISA, MFA, 2565/12, S. Sasson, 18 December 1950, Y. Palmon to Sharett, 26 March 1952; Gideon Rafael to the director-general of MFA, 28 December 1950.

72. Moshe Sharett, *Yoman Ishi*, Vol. VIII, pp. 2397–400.

73. Y. Shim'oni, 'Jordanian, Egyptian and Palestinian "Orientations"', p. 54.

# 9. The Syrian–Lebanese Crisis

1. The Lebanese Finance Minister, Muhammad al-'Abud to American diplomats. See CLS, US Documents, Box 8, RG84, Box 232, Pinkerton to Secretary of State, 16 February 1948.

2. FO 371/75318-E 6549, Beirut Political Summary for the Month of April 1949.

3. al-Khuri, *Haqa'iq Lubnaniyya*, Vol. III, p. 206.

4. Ibid., p. 526.

5. FO 371/75322-E 5199, Houstoun Boswall to FO, 19 April 1949.

6. Ibid; cf. FO 371/75318-E 6549, Beirut Political Summary for the Month of April 1949; al-Khuri, *Haqa'iq Lubnaniyya*, Vol. III, p. 211.

7. Itamar Rabinovich, *The Road Not Taken*, pp. 65–110.

8. FO 1018/48-2/554/49, 2/559/59, Beirut to FO, 14 April 1948.

9. al-Khuri, *Haqa'iq Lubnaniyya*, Vol. III, p. 206.

10. FO 371/75322-E 5199, Houstoun Boswall to FO, 19 April 1949.

11. al-Khuri, *Haqa'iq Lubnaniyya*, Vol. III, pp. 212–13.

12. Ibid., p. 207.

13. ISA, MFA, 2454/12, a conversation with Charles Malik, T. Arazi, 30 April 1949.

14. al-Khuri, *Haqa'iq Lubnaniyya*, Vol. III, pp. 207–8.

15. Ibid., p. 221; FO 371/75318-E 6549, Beirut Political Summary for the Month of April 1949.

16. al-Khuri, *Haqa'iq Lubnaniyya*, Vol. III, pp. 207–8.

17. FO 371/75318-E 7778, Beirut Political Summary for the Month of May 1949; *Al-'Alaqat al-Lubnaniyya al-Suriyya, 1943–1958*, Vol. I, pp. 46–7; see also Andrew Rathmell, *Secret War in the Middle East: The Covert Struggle for Syria, 1949–1961*, p. 46.

18. Radio Damascus, 25 May 1949, SAB.

19. al-Khuri, *Haqa'iq Lubnaniyya*, Vol. III, p. 225; FO 371/75318-E 7778, Beirut Political Summary for the Month of May 1949.

20. al-Khuri, *Haqa'iq Lubnaniyya*, Vol. III, p. 225.

21. Ibid., p. 227; FO 371/75318-E 9483, Beirut Political Summary for the Month of June 1949.

22. al-Khuri, *Haqa'iq Lubnaniyya*, Vol. III, p. 230.

23. See Radio Near East, 15 August 1948, SAB; FO 371/75318-E 12196, Beirut Political Summary for the Month of August 1949.

24. See Nadim Shehadi, *The Idea of Lebanon*, pp. 9–10; Carolyn L. Gates, *The Merchant Republic of Lebanon, Rise of an Open Economy*; *The Historical Role of Political Economy in the Development of Modern Lebanon*; 'Laissez-faire, Outward Orientation, and Regional Economic Disintegration: A Case Study of the Dissolution of the Syrio-Lebanese Customs Union', in Youssef M. Choueiri (ed.), *State and Society in Syria and Lebanon*, pp. 75–7.

25. Gates, 'Laissez-Faire', pp. 75–9.

26. FO 371/61726-E 7989, Beirut to FO, 25 August, 30 September 1947.

27. al-Khuri, *Haqa'iq Lubnaniyya*, Vol. III, pp. 87–93; FO 371/68489-E 3952, Beirut Monthly Summary for the Month of February 1948.

28. Rathmell, *Secret War in the Middle East*, pp. 46–7; al-Khuri, *Haqa'iq Lubnaniyya*, Vol. III, pp. 237–8.

29. Gates, 'Laissez-Faire', pp. 79–80; al-Khuri, *Haqa'iq Lubnaniyya*, Vol. III, pp. 286–7; Khalid al-'Azm, *Mudhakkirat Khalid al-'Azm*, Vol. II, p. 47.

30. See *Al-Hayat*, 18 March 1950; Kamal Junbalat, *I Speak for Lebanon*, p. 85.

31. al-'Azm, *Mudhakkirat*, Vol. II, p. 11–14.

32. Gates, 'Laissez-Faire', p. 52.

33. FO 371/98543-E 10389/2, Beirut to FO, 10 October 1950.

34. Gates, 'Laissez-Faire', p. 80.

35. *Al-Hayat*, 10 February 1950.

## 10. The Confrontation with the PPS

1. See Andrew Rathmell, *Secret War in the Middle East: The Covert Struggle for Syria, 1949–61*, pp. 44–50; Jubran Jurayj, *Ma'a Antun Sa'ada*, pp. 87–8.

2. Labib Zuwiyya Yamak, *The Syrian Social Nationalist Party, An Ideological Analysis*, pp. 51–5.

3. For more details on the SSNP see Yamak, *The Syrian Social Nationalist Party*; Michael W. Suleiman, *Political Parties in Lebanon*, pp. 91–119; Daniel Pipes, *Greater Syria, The History of an Ambition*, pp. 100–11.

4. Suleiman, *Political Parties in Lebanon*, pp. 94, 111–12; Yamak, *The Syrian Social Nationalist Party*, p. 60.

5. Antun Sa'ada, *The Principles of the Syrian Social Nationalist Party*, p. 8.

6. Antun Sa'ada, *Nushu' al-'Umam*, p. 178.

7. Sa'ada, *Principles of the Syrian Social Nationalist Party*, p. 15; Yamak, *The Syrian Social Nationalist Party*, pp. 84–5.

8. Yamak, *The Syrian Social Nationalist Party*, pp. 84–5.

9. Suleiman, *Political Parties in Lebanon*, pp. 117; Patrick Seale, *The Struggle for Syria: A Study of Post-War Arab Politics, 1945–1958*, p. 68; see also, Antun Sa'ada, 'Al-'Uruba Aflasat'; 'Harabna al-'Uruba al-Wahmiyya Linuqima al-'Uruba al-Waqi'iyya', *Kull Shay'*, 21 January, 11 February 1949.

10. Yamak, *The Syrian Social Nationalist Party*, p. 107.

11. Ibid., p. 106.

12. Suleiman, *Political Parties in Lebanon*, p. 107.

13. Ibid., pp. 111–12; Yamak, *The Syrian Social Nationalist Party*, p. 56.

14. Yamak, *The Syrian Social Nationalist Party*, p. 58.

15. AD (Nantes), 1930–1940, Syrie–Liban, pp. 503–4, De Martel, 25 May 1937.

16. Yamak, *The Syrian Social Nationalist Party*, p. 60.

17. Ibid., p. 61.

18. FO 226/252-27/45/44, British Legation Beirut, 15 March 1944; Yamak, *The Syrian Social Nationalist Party*, p. 62.

19. SHA, Levant, 4H314/3, Le Parti Populaire Syrie, P.P.S., Note d'information, April 1942.

20. CLS, US Documents, Box 8, RG84, Box 231, American Military Attaché, Beirut, 5 March 1947.

21. FO 226/252-27/45/44, British Legation, Beirut, 15 March 1944.

22. Suleiman, *Political Parties in Lebanon*, p. 94.

23. Walter L. Browne, *Lebanon's Struggle for Independence*, Vol. II, pp. 166–7; CLS, US Documents, 890.00/3-1847, Pinkerton to Secretary of State, 18 March 1947; cf. Suleiman, *Political Parties in Lebanon*, p. 96.

24. *Al-Hayat*, 4, 7 March 1947.

25. FO 371/61710-E 3360, Lebanon: Summary no. 8.

26. Antun Sa'ada, *Al-Athar al-Kamila*, Vol. XIV, 1947, pp. 57–60, 74–8.

27. Ibid., pp. 74–8, 93–7.

28. Yamak, *The Syrian Social Nationalist Party*, p. 63; FO 371/75318-E 9986, Beirut Monthly Summary for the Month of September 1947.

29. Yamak, *The Syrian Social Nationalist Party*, p. 64.

30. Suleiman, *Political Parties in Lebanon*, p. 95.

31. FO 371/75318-E 3717, 371/68489-E 12619, Beirut Summaries for the Months of August 1948, February 1949.

32. See Sa'ada, 'Al-'Uruba Aflasat', and 'Harabna al-'Uruba al-Wahmiyya'; Yamak, *The Syrian Social Nationalist Party*, p. 65.

33. Ibid.

34. Bishara al-Khuri, *Haqa'iq Lubnaniyya*, Vol. III, pp. 228–9.

35. *Al-Nahar*, 11 June 1949; FO 371/75318-E 9483, Beirut Political Summary for the Month of June 1949.

36. Yamak, *The Syrian Social Nationalist Party*, p. 67.

37. Suleiman, *Political Parties in Lebanon*, p. 96.

38. FO 371/75320-E 7211, British Legation, Beirut, to FO, 11 June 1949; See also, Rathmell, *Secret War in the Middle East*, pp. 46–7.

39. FO 371/75320-E 7211, British Legation, Beirut, to FO, 11 June 1949.

40. FO 371/75328-E 10339, Political Summary for the Month of July 1949.

41. *Al-Bayraq*, 20 July 1949; *Talaghraf*, 20 August 1949.

42. FO 371/75318-E 9483, Beirut Political Summary for the Month of June 1949; cf. Rathmell, *Secret War in the Middle East*, pp. 46–7.

43. Ibid.

44. al-Khuri, *Haqa'iq Lubnaniyya*, Vol. III, p. 238.

45. Ibid.; see also Radio Beirut, 5 July 1949; FO 371/75318-E 9483, Beirut Political Summary for the Month of May 1949; al-Khuri, *Haqa'iq Lubnaniyya*, Vol. III, pp. 238–9.

46. This point was made by Sulh in a conversation with the British minister. FO 371/75318-E 10399, Political Summary for the Month of July 1949; see also FO 371/75320-E 8852/1017/88, Beirut to FO, 20 July, Annual Review for 1949, Houstoun Boswall, 7 February 1950.

47. al-Khuri, *Haqa'iq Lubnaniyya*, Vol. III, pp. 236–7.

48. FO 371/75320-E 7211, British Legation, Beirut, to FO, 11 June 1949.

49. Radio Near East, 3 July 1949, SAB.

50. Rathmell, *Secret War in the Middle East*, p. 46.

51. Seale, *The Struggle for Syria*, p. 70.

52. al-Khuri, *Haqa'iq Lubnaniyya*, Vol. III, p. 237.

53. Ibid., pp. 231–3.

54. Rathmell, *Secret War in the Middle East*, p. 49.

55. See Seale, *The Struggle for Syria*, p. 89; Jurayj, *Ma'a Antun Sa'ada*, pp. 188–9; Nadhir Fansa, *Ayam Husni al-Za'im; 137 Yawm Hazzat Suriya*, pp. 86–9.

56. Rathmell, *Secret War in the Middle East*, pp. 49–50, 185.

57. Fansa, *Ayyam Husni al-Za'im*, pp. 77–82.

58. Rathmell, *Secret War in the Middle East*, p. 46; Seale, *The Struggle for Syria*, p. 87.

59. Jurayj, *Ma'a Antun Sa'ada*, pp. 181–2; al-Khuri, *Haqa'iq Lubnaniyya*, Vol. III, p. 241.

60. FO 371/75318-E 10339, Beirut Political Summary for the Month of July 1949.

61. al-Khuri, *Haqa'iq Lubnaniyya*, Vol. III, pp. 238–43; Hassan Halaq, *Mawqif Lubnan min al-Qadiyya al-Falastiniyya, 1918–1952*, p. 285.

62. FO 371/75321-E 8359, Beirut to FO, 8 July 1949.

63. Ibid.

64. *Al-Hayat*, 9 July 1949.

65. al-Khuri, *Haqa'iq Lubnaniyya*, Vol. III, p. 243.

66. Ibid., pp. 240–1.

67. Hassan Halaq, *Al-Tiyyarat al-Siyasiyya fi Lubnan, 1943–1952*, pp. 272–3.

68. Khalid al-'Azm, *Mudhakkirat Khalid al-'Azm*, Vol. II, p. 43.

69. al-Khuri, *Haqa'iq Lubnaniyya*, Vol. III, pp. 285–6.

70. See Rathmell, *Secret War in the Middle East*, p. 183.

71. Pipes, *Greater Syria*, pp. 175–88.

## 11. Khuri and Sulh

1. FO 371/82268-E 1016/6, Houstoun Boswall to Younger, 12 July 1950.

2. Bishara al-Khuri, *Haqa'iq Lubnaniyya*, Vol. III, pp. 339–40.

3. Ibid., p. 340.

4. For the full text of the song see Nadim Abu-Isma'il, *Bishara al-Khuri, Taghiya Akhar Yazulu*, pp. 53–7.

5. al-Khuri, *Haqa'iq Lubnaniyya*, Vol. III, pp. 311.

6. Ibid., pp. 311–12; FO 371/82266-E 1013/8, Beirut Political Summary for the Month of July 1950.

7. FO 371/82266-E 1013/7, 10, Beirut Political Summaries for the Months of June and September 1950; see also al-Khuri, *Haqa'iq Lubnaniyya*, Vol. III, pp. 313; *Al-Hayat*, 21 June 1950.

8. FO 371/82266-E 1013/8, Beirut Political Summary for the Month of July 1950; FO 371/91433-E 1011/1, Lebanon: Annual Review for 1950, Houstoun Boswall to Bevin.

9. FO 371/91434-E 1016/1, Beirut to FO, 15 February 1951; al-Khuri, *Haqa'iq Lubnaniyya*, Vol. III, p. 300.

10. FO 371/82266-E 1013/7, 8, Beirut Political Summaries for the Months of June and July 1950; al-Khuri, *Haqa'iq Lubnaniyya*, Vol. III, p. 320.

11. FO 82266-E 1013/9, Beirut Political Summary for the Month of August 1950.

12. FO 371/91433-E 1011/1, Lebanon: Annual Review for 1950, Houstoun Boswall to Bevin.

13. CLS, US Documents, Box 13, 883A/12-2750, Beirut to Department of State, 27 December 1950.

14. CLS, US Documents, Box VI, Box 4076, 783A.00/2-2851, Pinkerton to Department of State, 28 February 1951.

15. CLS, US Documents, Box VI, Box 4074, 783A.00/3-2151, Pinkerton to Department of State, 21 March 1951; *Al-Hayat*, 14 March 1951.

16. *Al-Hayat*, 19 March 1951; FO 371/91434, Memorandum by Kamal Junbalat.

17. Radio Beirut, 19 March 1951, SAB.

18. FO 371/91434-E 1016/4,5, Beirut to FO, 18, 20 March 1951; Radio Beirut, 20 March 1951.

19. *Al-Hayat*, 23 March, 17 April 1951.

20. Radio Beirut, 14 April 1951, SAB.

21. CLS, US Documents, Box V, Box 4076, 783A.00/4-1251, Pinkerton to Department of State, 12 April 1951.

22. FO 371/98523-E 1011/1, Lebanon: Annual Review for 1951, Chapman Andrews to Eden, 22 February 1952.

23. *The Economist*, 28 April 1951.

24. FO 371/91434-E 1016/6, Beirut to FO, 29 May 1951.

25. CLS, US Documents, Box XIX, 611.883A.64/6-551, Beirut to Department of State, 6 May 1951.

26. al-Khuri, *Haqa'iq Lubnaniyya*, Vol. III, pp. 324; *L'Orient*, 17 April 1951.

27. Ibid.

28. Ibid.; al-Khuri, *Haqa'iq Lubnaniyya*, Vol. III, pp. 326–30; see also FO 371/91434, Houstoun Boswall to Morrison, 4 April 1951.

29. *L'Orient*, 17 May 1951.

30. FO 371/82266-E 1013/3, Beirut Political Summary for the Month of February 1950.

31. FO 371/82266-E 1013/9, Beirut Political Summary for the Month of August 1950. CLS, US Documents, Box V, Box 4076, 783A.00/9-2250, Pinkerton to Department of State, 22 September 1950.

32. FO 371/91434, Houstoun Boswall to FO, 24 April 1951; see also John P. Entelis, *Pluralism and Party Transformation in Lebanon, al-Kata'ib, 1936–1970*, p. 134.

33. al-Khuri, *Haqa'iq Lubnaniyya*, Vol. III, p. 326; CLS, US Documents, Box V, Box 4076, 783A.00/4-2551, Bruins to Department of State, 25 April 1951.

34. Ibid.; Entelis, *Pluralism and Party Transformation in Lebanon*, p. 135.

35. CLS, US Documents, Box V, Box 4076, 783A.00/11-2350, Pinkerton to Department of State, 28 November 1950; *L'Orient*, 17 May 1951.

36. *L'Orient*, 17 May 1951; CLS, US Documents, Box V, Box 4076, 783A.00/4-2551, Bruins to Department of State, 25 April 1951, Box XIX, Box 6111, 983A.64/6-551, 5 June 1951.

37. See al-Khuri, *Haqa'iq Lubnaniyya*, Vol. III, p. 326.

38. Hassan Halaq, *Al-Tiyyarat al-Siyasiyya fi Lubnan*, p. 577.

39. Radio Beirut, 16 July 1951, SAB.

40. FO 371/91434-E 1016/26,33, Beirut to FO, 17, 19 July 1951; Halaq, *Al-Tiyyarat al-Siyasiyya*, pp. 577–83.

41. Sami al-Sulh, *Ahtakimu 'ila al-Tarikh*, p. 96.

42. See Halaq, *Al-Tiyyarat al-Siyasiyya*, pp. 577–83; Andrew Rathmell, *Secret War in the Middle East: The Covert Struggle for Syria, 1949–1961*, p. 596.

43. CLS, US Documents, Box V, Box 4076, 783A.00/7-1951, Bruins to Department of State, 19 July 1951.

44. *Al-Hayat*, 1 August 1951.

45. al-Khuri, *Haqa'iq Lubnaniyya*, Vol. III, pp. 395–7.

46. Ibid., p. 391.

47. Ibid., pp. 409–10.

48. FO 1018/80, Political Summary for the Month of September 1951; CLS, US Documents, Box V, Box 4076, 783A.00/7-1951, Bruins to Department of State, 19 July 1951; *Al-Hayat*, 19 July 1951.

49. CLS, US Documents, Box V, Box 4076, 783A.00/919-522, Beirut to Department of State, 19 September 1952.

50. FO 371/91434-E 1052/1, 3, Chapman Andrews to FO, 23, 25 July 1951; E 1052/4 Furlonge to Chapman Andrews, 25 July 1951.

51. al-Khuri, *Haqa'iq Lubnaniyya*, Vol. III, pp. 399–400.

52. *Al-Hayat*, 15 July 1952.

53. al-Khuri, *Haqa'iq Lubnaniyya*, Vol. III, p. 388, Khalid al-'Azm, *Mudhakkirat Khalid al-'Azm*, Vol. II, p. 76.

## 12. Rift with the West

1. Bishara al-Khuri, *Haqa'iq Lubnaniyya*, Vol. III, pp. 420, 426, 471.

2. See Douglas Little, 'Cold War and Covert Action: The US and Syria, 1945–1958'; Shimon Shamir, 'The Collapse of Project Alpha', in W. Roger Louis and Roger Owen (eds), *Suez 1956*, pp. 73–100; Itamar Rabinovich, *The Road Not Taken*, pp. 65–110; see also Andrew Rathmell, *Secret War in the Middle East: The Covert Struggle for Syria*; Irene L. Gendzier, *Notes from the Minefield: United States Intervention in Lebanon and the Middle East*.

3. FO 371/61726-E 7953/2686/93, Anglo-United States Relations in the Lebanon, Houstoun Boswall to Ernest Bevin, 29 August 1947.

4. Elie Kedourie, 'The Transition from a British to an American Era in the Middle East', in Itamar Rabinovich and Haim Shaked (eds), *The Middle East and the United States: Perceptions and Policies*, pp. 5–6.

5. CLS, US Documents, Box 8, RG84, Box 232/File 800, George Wadsworth to Loy Henderson, 11 July 1945.

6. CLS, US Documents, Box 8, RG84, Box 229/File 863.3, John H. Leavell, Petroleum Attaché, Cairo, 25 January 1945.

7. CLS, US Documents, Box IX, 890E.00/6-848, SWNCC (State, War, Navy Coordination Committee), Country Study on Long-Range Assistance to Lebanon, 8 June 1948.

8. CLS, US Documents, Box X, 883A.00TA/11-350, Pinkerton to Department of State, 3 November 1950.

9. FO 371/52500-E 8455, Young to FO, 22 August 1946; E 9912, Washington to FO, 27 September 1946; FO 371/61703 E 230, Beirut to FO, 2 January 1947; E 286, FO to Beirut, 22 January 1947.

10. CLS, US Documents, Box XXII, Box 2850, 611-831A/10-1150, Pinkerton to Secretary of State, 11 October 1950.

11. CLS, US Documents, Box VIII, Box 4079, 783A/1-1851, Pinkerton to Secretary of State, 18 January 1951.

12. FO 371/98523-E 1011/1, Lebanon Annual Review for 1951, Chapman Andrews to Eden, 22 February 1952; FO 371/91442-E 1201/1, Beirut to FO, 9 February 1951.

13. *Al-Bayraq*, 2 June 1950; al-Khuri, *Haqa'iq Lubnaniyya*, Vol. III, pp. 310–11.

14. FO 371/61742-E 11391, Beirut to FO, 2, 17 December 1947.

15. FO 371/68499-E 14505, Beirut to FO, 9 November 1948.

16. ISA, MFA, K/29, a conversation with Alfons Ayub, First Secretary in the Lebanese Legation in Paris, E. Sasson, 14 October 1948.

17. FO 371/82280-E 1053/9, Record of a conversation between Wright and Takla, 6 November 1950.

18. CLS, US Documents, Box XXII, Box 2850, 611.83A/8-3051, Department of State to Beirut, 30 August 1951.

19. FO 371/82269-E 1022/1, Beirut to FO, 2 January 1950.

20. FO 1018/80, Political Summary for the Month of October 1951; CLS, US Documents, Box V, Box 4076, 783A.00/11-1351, Minor to Secretary of State, 14 November 1951.

21. FO 1018/80, Political summary for the Month of November 1951.

22. al-Khuri, *Haqa'iq Lubnaniyya*, Vol. III, pp. 427–8; *Al-Hayat*, 25 November 1951.

23. CLS, US Documents, Box XXII, Box 2850, 611.83A/10-451, Bruins to Department of State, 4 October 1951.

24. CLS, US Documents, Box V, Box 4076, 783A.00/11-1351, Minor to Secretary of State, 14 November 1951.

25. AD (Nantes), Vol. 1003, pp. 19–20, Bulletin de Renseignements, 20 July 1944.

26. For more on the Communist Party in Lebanon, see Tareq Y. and Jacqueline S. Ismael, *The Communist Movement in Syria and Lebanon*; Michael W. Suleiman, *Political Parties in Lebanon*, pp. 57–91; Walter Z. Laqueur, *Communism and Nationalism in the Middle East*, pp. 276–7; see also Mustafa al-'Aris, *Mustafa al-'Aris Yatadhakkaru*.

27. See ISA, MFA, 2569/19, 32/36, the Communist Party, October 1947; CLS, US Documents, Box IX, 890E.00/6-848, SWNCC, Country Study on Long-Range Assistance to Lebanon, 8 June 1948; FO 371/68496-E 2092, Houstoun Boswall to FO, 21 January 1948.

28. CLS, US Documents, Box VII, Box 4078, 783A.001/2-1951, John B. Bruins to Department of State, 19 February 1951.

29. CLS, US Documents, Box IX, 890E.00/6-848, SWNCC, Country Study on Long-Range Assistance to Lebanon, 8 June 1948.

30. See CLS, US Documents, Box VII, Box 4078, 783A.001/3-653, Minor to Department of State, 6 March 1952.

31. See a conversation between Bruins and the Lebanese prime minister 'Abdallah al-Yafi concerning communism in Lebanon, CLS, US Documents, Box XVII, Box 4078, 783A.001/8-751, Bruins to Department of State, 7 August 1951; see also al-Khuri, *Haqa'iq Lubnaniyya*, Vol. III, pp. 22, 25–6, 418.

32. See FO 371/684961-E 2097, 13803, 14571, Houstoun Boswall to FO, 21 January 1948, Beirut to FO, 21 October, 29 November 1948.

33. Radio Near East, 5 September 1950, SAB; CLS, US Documents, Box V, Box 4076, 783A.001/8-3050, Pinkerton to Secretary of State, 30 August 1950; Box VI, Box 4078, 783A.001/10-2450, Pinkerton to Department of State, 24 October 1950.

34. CLS, US Documents, Box VII, Box 4078, 783A.001/3-2752, Minor to Secretary of State, 27 March 1952.

35. CLS, US Documents, Box XXII, Box 2850, 611.83A/10-1150, Pinkerton to Department of State, 11 October 1950.

36. CLS, US Documents, Box XII, Box 2850, 611.83A/1-2951, Department of State, 29 January 1951.

37. CLS, US Documents, Box VIII, RG319, 'P' File, Box 2180, File 850, Economic and Financial Annual Review – Syria and Lebanon, 1946, Lane Clayton, American Legation, Beirut.

38. FO 371/98437, Furlonge to Chapman Andrews, 24 July 1951.

39. CLS, US Documents, Box XII, Box 2850, 611.83A/9-1151, Department of State, 11 September 1951.

40. CLS, US Documents, Box V, Box 4076, 783A.00/10-1452, Minor to Department of State, 14 October 1952.

# 13. The Overthrow

1. Michael C. Hudson, *The Precarious Republic: Political Modernization in Lebanon*, p. 264.

2. Bishara al-Khuri, *Haqa'iq Lubnaniyya*, Vol. III, p. 483.

3. See for example, 'Abd al-Rahman Mahmud al-Huss, *Lubnan fi 'Ahd al-Ra'is Sham'un*; *Ma'asat al-Qati'a bayna Suriyya waLubnan*; Nadim Abu-Isma'il, *Bishara al-Khuri, Taghiya Akhar Yazulu*.

4. Kamal Junbalat, *Rub' Qarn min al-Nidal*, p. 187; see also Labib Zuwiyya Yamak, *The Syrian Social Nationalist Party: An Ideological Analysis*, p. 69.

5. Fahim I. Qubain, *Crisis in Lebanon*, pp. 24–5.

6. Philip K. Hitti, *Lebanon in History: From the Earliest Times to the Present*, p. 506.

7. CLS, US Documents, Box V, Box 4078, 783A.11/10-1452, Minor to Secretary of State, 14 October 1952.

8. Hudson, *The Precarious Republic*, p. 273.

9. Kamal S. Salibi, *The Modern History of Lebanon*, pp. 195–6.

10. al-Khuri, *Haqa'iq Lubnaniyya*, Vol. II, p. 289, Vol. III, pp. 64–6, 254.

11. CLS, US Documents, Box V, Box 4076, 783A.00/2-1352, Minor to Department of State, 13 February 1952.

12. See CLS, US Documents, Box VI, Box 4077, 783A.00(W)/7-1351, 6-2951, Military Attaché, 29 June, 13 July 1951; Abu-Isma'il, *Bishara al-Khuri*, pp. 20, 23.

13. *Al-Hayat*, 27 June 1950.

14. The point was made in a US legation report from before the time US–Lebanese relations deteriorated. See CLS, US Documents, Box 8, RG84, Box 681, 59A543/7-1849, Beirut to Department of State, 18 July 1949.

15. 'Adil Arsalan, *Mudhakkirat al-Amir 'Adil Arsalan*, Vol. II, p. 761.

16. Junbalat, *Rub' Qarn al-Nidal*, p. 121; for more on the party see Michael W. Suleiman, *Political Parties in Lebanon*, pp. 213–27.

17. See CLS, US Documents, Box V, Box 4076, 783A.00/4-451, Pinkerton to Secretary of State, 4 April 1951.

18. FO 371/98524, Monthly Review of the Lebanese Press, May 1952.

19. FO 371/98524, Beirut Political Summary for the Month of May 1952.

20. FO 1018/80, Political Summary for the Month of June 1951.

21. CLS, US Documents, Box V, Box 4076, 783A.00/1-1552, Minor to Department of State, 15 January 1952.

22. FO 1018/80, Political Summary for the Month of July 1951.

23. *Al-Bayanat al-Wizariyya al-Lubnaniyya wa Munaqashatiha fi Majlis al-Nuwwab, 1926–1984*, Vol. I, p. 230.

24. FO 371/91937-E 1052/3, Furlonge to Chapman Andrews, 27 July 1951.

25. FO 371/91937-E 1016/5, Chapman Andrews to Morrison, 13 June 1951; al-Khuri, *Haqa'iq Lubnaniyya*, Vol. III, p. 387.

26. CLS, US Documents, Box V, Box 4076, 783A.00/8-2951, Bruins to Department of State, 29 August 1951; FO 1018/80, Political Summary for the Month of August 1951; see also al-Khuri, *Haqa'iq Lubnaniyya*, Vol. III, p. 411.

27. FO 371/88525-E 1015/1, Beirut to FO, 28 October 1951.

28. FO 371/98523-E 1011/1, Lebanon Annual Review for 1951, Chapman Andrews to Eden.

29. CLS, US Documents, Box VI, Box 4077, 783A.00(W)/7-1351, 6-2951, Military Attaché, Beirut, 29 June, 13 July 1952; FO 1018/80, Political Summary for the Month of August 1951.

30. CLS, US Documents, Box VII, Box 4078, 783A.21/12-2051, Beirut to Department of State, 20 December 1951.

31. Radio Beirut, 9 February 1952, SAB; FO 371/98524, Political Summary for the Month of February 1952.

32. al-Khuri, *Haqa'iq Lubnaniyya*, Vol. III, p. 449.

33. CLS, US Documents, Box V, Box 4076, 783A.00/5-1252, Beirut to Department of State, 12 May 1952.

34. CLS, US Documents, Box V, Box 4076, 783A.00/2-1352, Minor to Department of State, 13 February 1952.

35. CLS, US Documents, Box VII, Box 4078, 783A.12/3-2552, Minor to Secretary of State, 25 March 1952; *Al-Hayat*, 19 December 1951.

36. See Carolyn L. Gates, *The Merchant Republic of Lebanon, Rise of an Open Economy*; see also CLS, US Documents, Box XIII, 883.A80/7-2254, Consumption Patterns in Lebanon, 22 July 1954; for more, see CLS, US Documents, Box 8, 883A.06/3-3050, Annual Economic Review for the Year 1949; Box 9, Box 5439, 883A.00/3-850, 1-3151, 2-652, Annual Economic Reviews for the Years 1950, 1951, 1952.

37. FO 371/93524, Political Summary for the Month of April 1952.

38. CLS, US Documents, Box V, 783A.00(W)/7-1152, Military Attaché, Beirut, 11 July 1952.

39. For more, see FO 1018/52-17/110, 148/49, Beirut to FO, 9 May, 3 July 1949; FO 1018/50-14/185/49, Beirut to FO, 20 July 1949; FO 1018/85-10/323/2152, Beirut to FO 2 April 1952.

40. CLS, US Documents, Box VI, Box 4077, 783A.61/5-952, Minor to Department of State, 9 May 1952; *Al-Hayat*, 9 May 1952.

41. al-Khuri, *Haqa'iq Lubnaniyya*, Vol. III, p. 284.

42. *Al-Anba'*, 30 May 1952.

43. al-Khuri, *Haqa'iq Lubnaniyya*, Vol. III, pp. 449–51.

44. FO 371/98524, Monthly Review of the Lebanese Press, June 1952.

45. *Al-Hayat*, 24 May 1952; CLS, US Documents, Box V, Box 4076, 783A.00/5-3152, Minor to Secretary of State, 31 May 1952.

46. *L'Orient*, 27 May; *Le Jour*, 28 May 1952; CLS, US Documents, Box VII, Box 4077, 963A.61/6-452, Weekly News Summary, 25 May–1 June, Beirut to Department of State, 4 June 1952.

47. CLS, US Documents, Box V, Box 4076, 783A.00/2-2052, Minor to Secretary of State, 20 February 1952.

48. CLS, US Documents, Box V, Box 4076, 783A.00/1-3152, Beirut to Department of State, 31 January 1952; see also al-Khuri, *Haqa'iq Lubnaniyya*, Vol. III, p. 451.

49. FO 371/98526-E 1015/26, Chapman Andrews to Eden, 13 June 1952; CLS, US Documents, Box VII, Box 4078, 783A.1/6-2052, Beirut to Department of State, 20 June 1952.

50. FO 1018/80, Political Summary for the Month of June 1952; *Al-'Amal*, 17, 28 June 1952.

51. CLS, US Documents, Box V, Box 4076, 783A.00/6-752, Minor to Secretary of State, 7 June 1952.

52. CLS, US Documents, Box V, Box 4076, 783A.00/7-852, Minor to Department of State, 8 July 1952.

53. CLS, US Documents, Box V, Box 4076, 783A.00/6-752, Minor to Department of State, 7 June 1952.

54. CLS, US Documents, Box V, Box 4076, 783A.00/6-1752, Department of State to Minor, 17 June 1952.

55. FO 371/98525-E 1015/22, Chapman Andrews to FO, 28 May 1952.

56. FO 371/98525-E 1015/24, Chapman Andrews to Eden, 10 June 1952.

57. FO 371/98526-E 1015/24, Chapman Andrews to Churchill, 20 August 1952.

58. Ibid.

59. al-Khuri, *Haqa'iq Lubnaniyya*, Vol. III, p. 457.

60. Ibid., p. 455.

61. *Al-Hayat*, 26, 31 July, 20 August 1952.

62. CLS, US Documents, Box VII, Box 4078, 783A.13/8-1952, Minor to Department of State, 19 August 1952.

63. FO 371/98524-E 1015/32, Chapman Andrews to Ross, 8 August 1952.

64. FO 371/98526-E 1015/31, Beirut to FO, 18 August 1952.

65. al-Khuri, *Haqa'iq Lubnaniyya*, Vol. III, p. 459.

66. CLS, US Documents, Box V, Box 4076, 783A.00/8-1852, Minor to Department of State, 18 August 1952.

67. CLS, US Documents, Box V, Box 4076, 783A.00/8-1452, Minor to Department of State, 14 August 1952; *Al-Bayraq*, 17 April 1952.

68.  al-Khuri, *Haqa'iq Lubnaniyya*, Vol. III, p. 459.

69.  CLS, US Documents, Box VII, Box 4078, 783A.21/8-2352, Minor to Department of State, 23 August 1952; FO 371/98526-E 1015/37, Chapman Andrews to Eden, 28 August 1952.

70.  *Al-Hayat*, 24 August 1952.

71.  See al-Khuri, *Haqa'iq Lubnaniyya*, Vol. III, p. 464; Sami al-Sulh, *Mudhakkirat Sami Bak al-Sulh*, p. 71.

72.  al-Huss, *Lubnan fi 'Ahd al-Ra'is Sham'un*, pp. 29–39.

73.  al-Khuri, *Haqa'iq Lubnaniyya*, Vol. III, pp. 464–5.

74.  See CLS, US Documents, Box V, Box 4076, 783A.00/9-1252, Minor to Secretary of State, 12 September 1952; ISA, MFA, 2408/12, S. Divon to R. Shiloah, 29 October 1951; al-Khuri, *Haqa'iq Lubnaniyya*, Vol. III, p. 471.

75.  CLS, US Documents, Box VII, Box 4078, 783A.13/9-952, Minor to Department of State, 9 September 1952.

76.  CLS, US Documents, Box V, Box 4076, 783A.00/9-1752, Minor to Secretary of State, 17 September 1952; FO 371/98527-E 1015/60, Chapman Andrews to Eden, 19 September 1952.

77.  For Yafi's letter see CLS, US Documents, Box VII, Box 4078, 783A.00/9-1152, Minor to Secretary of State, 11 September 1952.

78.  Khuri gives a detailed description of the day's events in his memoirs, *Haqa'iq Lubnaniyya*, Vol. III, pp. 476–7.

79.  Radio Beirut, 18 September 1952, SAB.

80.  CLS, US Documents, Box VII, Box 4078, 783A.13/9-952, Minor to Department of State, 9 September 1952.

81.  CLS, US Documents, Box VII, Box 4076, 783A.00/5-2150, Beirut to Department of State, 29 May 1950.

82.  CLS, US Documents, Box VII, Box 4078, 783A.11/10-1452, Minor to Secretary of State, 14 October 1952; FO 371/98526-E 1015/57, Chapman Andrews to Eden, 20 September 1952.

83.  For Yafi's letter see CLS, US Documents, Box VII, Box 4078, 783A.00/9-1152, Minor to Secretary of State, 11 September 1952.

84.  Naqqashe's article is quoted in Nadim Shehadi, *The Idea of Lebanon*, pp. 27–8.

# Bibliography

## Archival Sources

BRITISH SOURCES

Public Record Office

Foreign Office Papers
FO 226 (Foreign Office Papers – Beirut Legation and Spears Mission 1942–45)
FO 371 (general correspondence)
FO 684 (Damascus consulate)
FO 921 (Minister of State Cairo's office)
FO 1018 (Embassy and consular archives – Lebanon)

War Cabinet
CAB 65 War Cabinet meetings
CAB 66 War Cabinet print [memoranda]

Prime Minister
PREM3 Prime Minister's Office Operational Papers

Middle East Centre, St Antony's College, Oxford
Private Papers Collection: Spears Papers

Centre for Lebanese Studies, Oxford
Collections of American Archives Documents
890.D and 890.E Political Correspondence – Department of State – Syria and Lebanon


FRENCH SOURCES

Archive du Ministère des Affaires Étrangères, Paris

Archives Nationale, Papiers Catroux (72 AJ 428)

Levant 1918–1929, Syrie–Liban: 2ème partie, 1922–1929, Syrie–Liban, 1930–1940; Guerre 1939–1945, Alger CFLN–GPRF, Londres CNF, Vichy–Levant

Les Archives Diplomatiques de Nantes, Ministère des Affaires Étrangères: Mandat Syrie-Liban, 1918–1948.

Centre de Hautes Études sur l'Afrique et l'Asie Modernes, Paris

Ministère de la Guerre, Service Historique de l'Armée de Terre, Vincennes: Papiers Beynet (1K 230)

Cabinet militaire à Beirut 1941–1946
2ème Bureau 1940–1941, 1941–1946


ISRAELI ARCHIVES

Central Zionist Archives, Jerusalem
S25 Papers (Jewish Agency – Political Department)
Israel State Archives, Jerusalem
Ministry for Foreign Affairs
The Moshe Dayan Center for Middle Eastern and African Studies, the Library – Summaries
of Arab Broadcasting

## Newspapers and Periodicals Cited

*Al-Ahram*, Cairo

*Al-Anba'*, Beirut

*Al-Bayraq*, Beirut

*Bayrut*, Beirut

*The Economist*, London

*Al-Hayat*, Beirut

*Jerusalem Post*

*Le Jour*, Beirut

*Kull Shay'*, Beirut

*Al-Nahar*, Beirut

*New York Times*

*L'Orient*, Beirut

*Talaghraf*, Beirut

## Published Documents

*Al-'Alaqat al-Lubnaniyya al-Suriyya, 1943–1958, Waqa'i' Bibliyughrafiyya* (Syrian–Lebanese Relations, 1943–1958). Vols I, II. Beirut: Markaz al-Tawthiq wal-Buhuth al-Lubnani.

*Al-Bayanat al-Wizariyya al-Lubnaniyya waMunaqashatiha fi Majlis al-Nuwwab, 1926–1984* (The Governments' Addresses to the Chamber of Deputies, 1926–1984). Vol. 1. Beirut: Dar al-Matbu'at al-Sharqiyya.

Browne, Walter L. *The Political History of Lebanon, 1920–1950; Lebanon's Struggle for Independence*, Vols I, II. (Collections of Documents relating to Lebanon in the State Department, including dispatches from the American consul-general in Beirut.) Salisbury, NC, 1976.

Great Britain, Parliamentary Debates, House of Commons. Various volumes from the Years 1941–52.

Al-Hizb al-Suri al-Qawmi al-Ijtima'i. *Antun Sa'ada, Al-'Athar al-Kamila* (Collection of Antun Sa'ada's articles). Beirut, 1975.

*Lubnan wa Faransa* (Lebanon and France). (Collection of Documents relating to the Maronite Church's role in Lebanese–French Relations.) Beirut: Dar al-Farabi, 1987.

Muruwwa, Kamil. *Qul Kalimatak walmshi* (Say Your Words and Go Away). Vol. I. (Collection of editorials by Kamil Muruwa published in *Al-Hayat*.) Beirut: Dar al-Hayat lil-Tiba'a wal-Nashr, 1986.

*Nidal al-Hizb al-Shuyu'i al-Lubnani min Hilal Wathai'iqihi* (The Struggle of the Lebanese Communist Party Through Its Documents). Vol. I. Beirut: Manshurat al-Hizb al-Shuyu'i al-Lubnani, 1971.

Nuwar, 'Abd al-'Aziz Sulayman. *Watha'iq al-Siyasa min Tarikh Lubnan al-Hadith, 1517–1920* (Political Documents on Lebanon's Modern History, 1517–1920). Beirut: Dar al-Buhayri, 1974.

US, Department of State. *Foreign Relations of the United States* (*FRUS*). Various volumes from the years 1942–52.

# Memoirs

al-'Aris, Mustafa. *Mustafa al-'Aris Yatadhakkaru* (Memoirs of Mustafa al-'Aris). Beirut: Dar al-Farabi, 1982.

Arsalan, 'Adil. *Mudhakkirat al-Amir 'Adil Arsalan* (Memoirs of Amir 'Adil Arsalan).Vols I, II. Beirut: Al-Dar al-Taqaddumiyya lil-Nashr, 1983.

al-'Azm, Khalid. *Mudhakkirat Khalid al-'Azm* (Memoirs of Khalid al-'Azm). Vols I–III. Beirut: Al-Dar al-Muttahida lil-Nashr, 1973.

Ben-Gurion, David. *Yoman Hamilhama* (The War of Independence, Ben Gurion's Diary). Tel Aviv: Defense Ministry Publishing House, 1982.

Casey, R. *Personal Experience, 1940–1946.* New York: D. McKay, 1962.

Catroux, Georges. *Dans la Bataille de Méditerranée: Egypte–Levant–Afrique du Nord, 1940–1944.* Paris: René Julliard, 1949.

Churchill, Winston S. *The Second World War*, Vols IV, V, VI, VIII, XI. London: Cassel, 1964.

de Gaulle, Charles. *Mémoires de Guerre*, Vols I–III. Paris: Plon, 1959.

Dov, Yosef. *Qirya Neemana* (Faithful City). Jerusalem: Schocken Publishing House, 1960.

Fansa, Nadhir. *Ayyam Husni al-Za'im: 137 Yawm Hazzat Suriya* (The Days of Husni al-Za'im, 137 Days that Shook Syria). Beirut: Manshurat Dar al-'Afaq al-Jadida, 1982.

Farajallah, Hilu. *Kitabat Mukhtara* (Selected Articles). Beirut: Dar al-Farabi, 1974.

Glubb, John B. *The Story of the Arab Legion.* London: Hodder and Stoughton, 1948.

Junbalat, Kamal. *Haqiqat al-Thawra al-Lubnaniyya* (The Reality behind the Lebanese Revolution). Beirut: Manshurat al-Hizb al-Taqaddumi al-Ishtiraqi, 1959.

— *I Speak for Lebanon.* London: Zed Books, 1982.

— *Rub' Qarn min al-Nidal* (Twenty-five Years of Struggle). Al-Mukhtara: Al-Dar al-Taqaddumiyya, 1987.

Jurayj, Jubran. *Ma'a Antun Sa'ada* (With Antun Sa'ada). n. p.: n. d.

al-Khuri, Bishara. *Haqa'iq Lubnaniyya* (Lebanese Realities). Vols I–III. Beirut: Manshurat Awraq Lubnaniyya.

Macmillan, Harold. *War Diaries – The Mediterranean 1943–1945.* London: Macmillan, 1984.

Salim, Yusuf. *50 Sana ma'a al-Nas* (Fifty Years with the People). Beirut, 1975.

Sham'un, Kamil (Chamoun, Camille). *Marahil al-Istiqlal; Lubnan wa-Duwal al-'Arab fi al-Mu'tamarat al-Dawliyya* (On the Road to Independence, Lebanon and the Arab States in the International Conferences). Beirut: Maktabat Sadir, 1949.

— *Mudhakkarati* (My Memoirs). Beirut, 1969.

Sharett, Moshe. *Yoman Ishi* (Personal Diary). Tel Aviv: Ma'ariv, 1978.

Spears, Edward L. *Fulfilment of a Mission; The Spears Mission to Syria and Lebanon, 1941–44.* London: Leo Cooper, 1977.

al-Sulh, Sami. *Mudhakkirat Sami Bak al-Sulh* (Memoirs of Sami al-Sulh). Beirut: Maktabat al-Fikr al-'Arabi, 1960.

— *Ahtakimu 'ila al-Tarikh* (I Ask History to Judge Me). Beirut: Dar al-Nahar lil-Nashr, 1970.

## Secondary Sources

Abu-Isma'il, Nadim. *Bishara al-Khuri, Taghiya Akhar Yazulu* (Bishara al-Khuri, Another Dictator Disappears). Beirut, n.d.

'Abud, Marun. *Al-Shaykh Bishara al-Khuri.* Beirut: Manshurat Dar al-Makshuf, 1950.

al-Ahdab, 'Aziz. *Fahr al-Din – Mu'assis Lubnan al-Hadith* (The Founder of Modern Lebanon). Beirut, 1973.

Ajami, Fouad. *The Vanished Imam, Musa al-Sadr and the Shia of Lebanon.* Ithaca, NY: Cornell University Press, 1986.

Akadimiyat al-'Ulum fi al-Ittihad al-Sufyati, Ma'had al-Istishraq. *Tarikh al-Aqtar al-'Arabiyya al-Mu'asir, 1918–1975.* (The Modern History of the Arab States, 1918–1975). Vol. I. Moscow: Dar al-Taqaddum, 1975.

Akarli, Engin Deniz. *The Long Peace, Ottoman Lebanon, 1861–1920.* London: Centre for Lebanese Studies and I.B. Tauris, 1993.

Akl, George (ed.) *The Black Book of the Lebanese Elections of May 25, 1947.* New York: Phoenicia Press, 1947.

— *The Black Book of the Lebanese Elections.* New York: Phoenicia Press, 1947.

Alin, Erika G. *The United States and the 1958 Lebanon Crisis.* Lanham, MD: University Press of America, 1993.

Andrew, Christopher M. and A. S. Kanya-Forstner. *France Overseas: The Great War and the Climax of French Imperial Expansion.* London: Thames and Hudson, 1981.

'Awd, Walid. *Ashab al-Fahama Ru'asa Lubnan* (The Presidents of Lebanon). Beirut: Al-Ahliyya lil-Nashr wal-Tawzi', 1980.

Azar, Edward E. (ed.) *The Emergence of a New Lebanon – Fantasy or Reality?* New York: Praeger Publishers, 1984.

Barakat, Halim (ed.) *Toward a Viable Lebanon.* London: Croom Helm, 1988.

— 'Social and Political Integration in Lebanon: A Case of Social Mosaic', *Middle East Journal*, Vol. 27, no. 3 (Summer 1973), pp. 301–18.

Binder, Leonard (ed.) *Politics in Lebanon.* New York: John Wiley, 1966.

Beydoun, Ahmad. *Al-Sira' 'ala Tarikh Lubnan.* (The Struggle over the History of Lebanon). Beirut: Manshurat al-Jami'a al-Lubnaniyya, 1989.

Black, Ian. *Zionism and the Arabs, 1936–1939.* PhD Dissertation, University of London, 1978.

Buheiry, Marwan. *Beirut's Role in the Political Economy of French Mandate, 1919–1939.* Oxford: Centre for Lebanese Studies, n.d.

Bulus, Jawad. *Tarikh Lubnan* (The History of Lebanon). Beirut: Dar al-Nahar lil-Nashr, 1972.

Burke, Edmund III, 'Rural Collective Action and the Emergence of Modern Lebanon: A Comparative Historical Perspective', in Nadim Shehadi and Dana Haffar Mills (eds) *Lebanon – A History of Conflict and Consensus*. London: I.B.Tauris, 1988.

Chiha, Michel. *Le Liban d'Aujourd'hui*. Beirut: Editions du Trident, 1942.

— *Politique Intérieure*. Beirut: Éditions du Trident, 1964.

Choueiri, Youssef M. (ed.) *State and Society in Syria and Lebanon*. Exeter: University of Exeter Press, 1993.

Cobban, Helena. *The Making of Modern Lebanon*. London: Hutchinson, 1985.

Dahir, Mas'ud. *Lubnan: al-Istiqlal, al-Sigha wal-Mithaq* (Lebanon: The Independence and the Pact). Beirut: Ma'had al-Inma' al-'Arabi, 1977.

Davis, Helen Miller. *Constitution, Electoral Laws, Treaties of States in the Near and Middle East*. Durham, NC: Duke University Press, 1953.

Daw, Butrus. *Tarikh al-Mawarna al-Dini wal-Siyasi wal-Khadari*. (The Political and Cultural History of the Maronites) Vols I–V, 1977. Beirut: Dar al-Nahar lil-Nashr.

Dekmejian, R. Hrair. *Patterns of Political Leadership: Egypt, Israel, Lebanon*. Albany, NY: State University of New York Press, 1975.

Eisenberg, Laura Zittrain. *My Enemy's Enemy. Lebanon in the Early Zionist Imagination, 1900–1948*. Detroit: Wane State University Press, 1994.

— 'Desperate Diplomacy: The Zionist–Maronite Treaty of 1946', *Studies in Zionism*, Vol. 13, no. 2 (1992), pp. 147–63.

Entelis, John P. *Pluralism and Party Transformation in Lebanon, al-Katai'b, 1936–1970*. Leiden: E. J. Brill, 1974.

Fallah, 'Ali Khalid. *Mukhdarat fi Tarikh Lubnan* (Lectures on Lebanese History). Beirut, 1979.

Faris, Hani. *Al-Niza'at al-Ta'ifiyya fi Tarih Lubnan al-Hadith* (The Communal Conflicts in Lebanon's History). Beirut: Al-Ahliyya lil-Nashr wal-Tawzi', 1980.

Fawaz, Leila Tarazi. *Merchants and Migrants in Nineteenth-Century Beirut*. Cambridge, MA: Harvard University Press, 1983.

— *Occasion for War, Civil Conflict in Lebanon and Damascus in 1860*. London: I.B.Tauris, 1994.

Gates, Carolyn L. *The Historical Role of Political Economy in the Development of Modern Lebanon*. Oxford: Centre for Lebanese Studies, 1989.

— 'Laissez-Faire, Outward-Orientation, and Regional Economic Disintegration: A Case Study of the Dissolution of the Syro-Lebanese Customs Uunion', in Youssef M. Choueiri (ed.) *State and Society in Syria and Lebanon*. Exeter: University of Exeter Press, 1993, pp. 74–83.

— *The Merchant Republic of Lebanon: Rise of an Open Economy*. London: I.B.Tauris, 1998.

Gaunson A. B. *The Anglo-French Clash in Lebanon and Syria 1940–45*. New York: St Martin's Press, 1987.

Gendzier, Irene L. *Notes from the Minefield: United States Intervention in Lebanon and the Middle East, 1945–1958*. New York: Columbia University Press, 1997.

Gilsenman, Michael, *Lords of the Lebanese Marches: Violence and Narrative in an Arab Society*. Berkeley and Los Angeles: University of California Press, 1996.

Gomaa, Ahmed. *The Foundation of the League of Arab States*. London: Longman, 1977.

Gordon, David C. *The Republic of Lebanon – Nation in Jeopardy*. London: Croom Helm, 1983.

Goria, Wade R. *Sovereignty and Leadership in Lebanon, 1943–1976*. London: Ithaca Press, 1985.

Grassmuck, George and Kamal Salibi. *A Manual of Lebanese Administration*. Beirut: Catholic Press, 1955.

Gulick, John. *Tripoli, A Modern Arab City.* Cambridge, MA: Harvard University Press, 1967.

Haddad, Wadi D. *Lebanon – The Politics of Revolving Doors.* Washington Papers no. 14. New York: Praeger Publishers, 1985.

Haddad, William. 'The Christian Arab Press and the Palestine Question: A Case Study of Michel Chiha of Beirut's *Le Jour*', *Muslim World*, Vol. 65, no. 2 (April 1975), pp. 119–31.

Haffar, Ahmed Rafiq. *France in the Establishment of Greater Lebanon – A Study of French Expansionism on the Eve of the First World War.* Ann Arbor, MI: University Microfilms, 1980.

al-Hajj, Kamal Yusuf. *Falsafat al-Mithaq al-Watani* (The Philosophy of the National Pact). Beirut, 1961.

Halaq, Hassan. *Mawqif Lubnan min al-Qadiyya al-Falastiniyya, 1918–1952* (Lebanon's Attitude Towards the Palestinian Question). Beirut: Markaz al-Abhath, Munazzamat al-Tahrir al-Falastiniyya, 1982.

—— *Al-Tiyyarat al-Siyasiyya fi Lubnan, 1943–1952* (Political Trends in Lebanon, 1943–1952). Beirut: Ma'had al-Inma al-'Arabi, 1988.

Haley, P. Edward and Lewis W. Snider (eds). *Lebanon in Crisis.* Syracuse, NY: Syracuse University Press, 1979.

Hanna, Zakhem Samir. *Lebanon between East and West: Big Power Policies in the Middle East.* Ann Arbor, MI: University Microfilms, 1979.

Harik, Iliya F. *Politics and Change in a Traditional Society: Lebanon, 1711–1845.* Princeton, NJ: Princeton University Press, 1968.

—— 'Voting Participation and Political Integration in Lebanon, 1943–1974', *Middle Eastern Studies*, Vol. 16 (January 1980).

—— *Al-Tahawul al-Siyasi fi Tarikh Lubnan al-Hadith* (Political Change in the Modern History of Lebanon). Beirut: Al-Ahliyya lil-Nashr wal-Tawzi', 1982.

Harris, William. *Faces of Lebanon.* Princeton, NJ: Marcus Weiner Publishers, 1997.

al-Hasan, Hasan. *Al-Qanun al-Dusturi wal-Dustur fi Lubnan* (Law and Constitution in Lebanon). Beirut: Manshurat Dar Maktabat al-Hayat, 1959.

Haydar, Ahmad Mustafa. *Al-Dawla al-Lubnaniyya, 1920–1953* (The Lebanese State, 1920–1953). Beirut: Matba'at al-Najma, 1954.

Hitti, Nasif. *The Foreign Policy of Lebanon.* Oxford: Centre for Lebanese Studies, 1989.

Hitti, Philip K. *Lebanon in History: From the Earliest Times to the Present.* London: Macmillan, 1957.

Hottinger, Arnold. 'Zu'ama in Historical Perspective', in Leonard Binder (ed.) *Politics in Lebanon.* New York: John Wiley, 1966, pp. 85–105.

Hourani, Albert. *Syria and Lebanon, A Political Essay.* Oxford: Oxford University Press, 1946.

—— *Minorities in the Arab World.* London: Oxford University Press, 1947.

—— 'Lebanon from Feudalism to State', *Middle Eastern Studies*, Vol. 2 (1960), pp. 256–63.

—— 'Lebanon: The Development of a Political Society', in Leonard Binder (ed.) *Politics in Lebanon.* New York: John Wiley, 1966, pp. 13–29.

—— 'Ottoman Reform and the Politics of the Notables', in William R. Polk and Richard L. Chambers (eds) *The Beginnings of Modernization in the Middle East.* Chicago: University of Chicago Press, 1968, pp. 41–68.

—— 'Ideologies of the Mountain and the City', in Roger Owen (ed.) *Essays on the Crisis in Lebanon.* London: Ithaca Press, 1976, pp. 33–42.

—— *Arabic Thought in the Liberal Age, 1798–1939.* Cambridge: Cambridge University Press, 1983.

— *Political Society in Lebanon: A Historical Introduction*. Oxford: Centre for Lebanese Studies, 1985.

Hourani, Albert and Nadim Shehadi (eds) *The Lebanese in the World: A Century of Emigration*. London: Centre for Lebanese Studies and I.B.Tauris, 1992.

Hudson, Michael C. *The Precarious Republic Revisited: Reflections on the Collapse of Pluralist Politics in Lebanon*. Seminar Paper no. 2. Washington, DC: Institute of Arab Development, Center for Contemporary Arab Studies, 1977.

— *The Precarious Republic: Political Modernization in Lebanon*. Boulder, CO: Westview Press, 1985.

al-Huss, 'Abd al-Rahman Mahmud. *Lubnan fi 'Ahd al-Ra'is Sham'un* (Lebanon Under President Chamoun). Beirut, 1953.

— *Ma'sat al-Qati'a bayna Suriyya waLubnan* (The Tragedy of the Dissolution of the Syro-Lebanese Customs Union). Beirut: Maktabat al-Ma'arif, 1953.

IDF (Israel Defense Forces), Historical Branch. *Toldot Milhemet Hakomemiyut* (The History of the War of Independence). Tel Aviv: Ma'arachot, 1975.

Ismael, Tareq Y. and Jacqueline S. Ismael. *The Communist Movement in Syria and Lebanon*. Gainesville, FL: University Press of Florida, 1998.

Issawi, Charles. *The Middle East Economy: Decline and Recovery*. Princeton, NJ: Marcus Weiner Publishers, 1995.

al-Jisr, Basim. *Ri'asa waSiyasa waLubnan al-Jadid* (Presidency and Politics in New Lebanon). Beirut: Manshurat Dar Maktabat al-Hayat, 1964.

— *Mithaq 1943, Limaza Kana waLimaza Saqata* (The National Pact of 1943). Beirut: Dar al-Nahar lil-Nashr, 1978.

Johnson, Michael. *Class and Client in Beirut: The Sunni Muslim Community and the Lebanese State, 1840–1985*. London: Ithaca Press, 1986.

Karami, Nadya and Nawaf Karami. *Waqi' al-Thawra al-Lubnaniyya* (The Lebanese Revolution). Beirut: 1959.

Kedourie, Elie. *Arabic Political Memoirs and Other Studies*. London: Frank Cass, 1974.

— 'The Transition from a British to an American Era in the Middle East', in Itamar Rabinovich and Haim Shaked (eds) *The Middle East and the United States: Perceptions and Policies*. Boulder, CO Westview Press, 1978.

— *Islam and the West and Other Studies*. New York: Holt, Rinehart and Winston, 1980.

— 'Lebanon: The Perils of Independence', in his *Islam in the Modern World and Other Studies*. London: Mansell, 1980.

— *The Chatham House Version and Other Middle Eastern Studies*. University Press of New England, 1984.

al-Khajj, Kamal Yusuf. *Al-Ta'ifiyya al-Banna'a aw Falsafat al-Mithaq al-Watani* (The Constructive Confessionalism or The Philosophy of the National Pact). Beirut: Matb'at al-Rahbaniyya al-Lubnaniyya, 1961.

Khalaf, Samir, *Persistence and Change in 19th Century Lebanon*. Beirut: American University of Beirut, 1979.

— *Lebanon's Predicament*. New York: Columbia University Press, 1987.

Khalidi, Walid. *Conflict and Violence in Lebanon: Confrontation in the Middle East*. Cambridge, MA: Center for International Affairs, Harvard University, 1983.

Khalil, Ahmad Khalil. *Kamal Junbalat – Thawrat al-Amir al-Hadith* (Kamal Junbalat – The Revolution of the Modern Emir). Beirut: Dar al-Matbu'at al-Sharqiyya, n.d.

Khashan, Hilal. *Inside the Lebanese Confessional Mind*. Lanham, NY: University Press of America, 1992.

el-Khazen Farid, *The Communal Pact of National Identities – The Making and Politics of the 1943 National Pact*. Papers on Lebanon no. 12. Oxford: Centre for Lebanese Studies, 1991.

Khouri, Philip S. *Syria and the French Mandate: the Politics of Arab Nationalism, 1920–1945*. Princeton, NJ: Princeton University Press, 1987.

Khoury, A. *The Foreign Policy of Lebanon*. Ann Arbor, MI: University Microfilms, 1968.

Khoury, Enver M. *The Crisis in the Lebanese System, Confessionalism and Chaos*. Foreign Affairs Study no. 38. Washington DC: American Enterprise Institute for Public Policy Research, 1976.

Khoury, Gérard D. *La France et L'Orient Arabe, Naissance du Liban Moderne 1914–1920*. Paris: Armand Colin Éditeur, 1993.

al-Khusus, Badr al-Din 'Abbas. *Al-Qadiyya al-Lubnaniyya fi Tarikhiha al-Hadith wal-Mu'asir* (The Lebanese Question in its Modern History). Cairo: Matba'at Sijil al-'Arab, 1978.

Khuwayri, Antun. *The Operational Capability of the Lebanese Political System*. Beirut: Catholic Press, 1972.

— *Kamil Sham'un fi Tarikh Lubnan* (Camille Chamoun in Lebanon's History). Beirut: Dar al-Abjadiyya, 1987.

Kimche, David and Jon. *Both Sides of the Hill* (2nd edn, in Hebrew). Tel Aviv: Ma'arachot, 1979.

Kuthrani, Wajih. *Al-Ittijahat al-Ijtima'iyya wal-Siyasiyya fi Jabal Lubnan wal-Mashriq al-'Aarabi, 1860–1920* (Social and Political Trends in Mt Lebanon and the Arab East, 1860–1920). Beirut: Ma'had al-Inma' al-'Arabi, 1978.

Laqueur, W. Z. *Communism and Nationalism in the Middle East*. London: Routledge and Kegan Paul, 1956.

Lesch, David W. *The Middle East and the United States*. Boulder, CO: Westview Press, 1996.

Little, Douglas. 'Cold War and Covert Action: The US and Syria, 1945–1958', *Middle East Journal*, Vol. 44, no. 1 (Winter 1990), pp. 51–75.

Longrigg, Stephen Hemsley. *Syria and Lebanon under French Mandate*. London: Oxford University Press, 1958.

Louis, W. Roger. *The British Empire in the Middle East, 1945–1951*. Oxford: Clarendon Press, 1984.

Louis, W. Roger and Roger Owen (eds). *Suez 1956*. Oxford: Clarendon Press, 1991.

Ma'ayan, Guy, *Levanon, haYishuv haZiyuni/Medinat Yisrael veHa'Ulam ha'Aravi, 1945–1949* (Lebanon, the Arab World and the Zionist Yishuv/The State of Israel, 1945–1949). M.A. thesis submitted to the Hebrew University, Jerusalem, 1997.

Maddy-Wietzman, Bruce. *The Crystallization of the Arab State System, 1945–1954*. Syracuse, NY: Syracuse University Press, 1993.

Maghayzal, Josef. *Lubnan wal-Qadiyya al-'Arabiyya* (Lebanon and the Arab Question). Beirut: Manshurat 'Uwaydat, 1959.

al-Marayati, Abid A. *Middle Eastern Constitution and Electoral Laws*. New York: Praeger Publishers, 1968.

Mardam Bey, Salma. *Syria's Quest for Independence, 1939–1945*. London: Ithaca Press, 1994.

Meo, Leila M. T. *Lebanon: Improbable Nation: A Study in Political Development*. Bloomington: Indiana University Press, 1968.

Moosa, Matti. *The Maronites in History*. Syracuse, NY: Syracuse University Press, 1986.

Morris, Benny. 'Israel and the Lebanese Phalanges: The Birth of a Relationship, 1948–1951', *Studies in Zionism*, Vol. 5, no. 2 (1984), pp. 125–44.

Murad, Sa'id. *Al-Haraka al-Wahdawiyya fi Lubnan bayna al-Harbayn al-'Alamtayn, 1914–1964* (The Unionist Movement in Lebanon, 1914–1964). Beirut: Ma'had al-Inma' al-'Arabi, 1986.

al-Naqqash, Zay. *Lubnan bayna al-Haqiqa wal-Dallal, Dirasa Thliliyya waNaqd Mawdu'i lil-Kitab Haqa'iq Lubnaniyya* (Lebanon between Light and Darkness, Analysis of the Book Haqa'iq Lubnaniyya). Beirut: Manshurat al-Maktab al-Tijari lil-Tiba'a wal-Tawzi' wal-Nashr, 1965.

Oden, B. J. *Lebanon: Dynamic of Conflict*. London: Zed Books, 1985.

Olmert, Yosef. 'British Policy Toward the Levant States, 1940–1945', PhD dissertation, Department of Government, London School of Economics, 1983.

Owen, Roger (ed.) *Essays on the Crisis in Lebanon*. London: Ithaca Press, 1976.

Petran, Tabitha. *The Struggle Over Lebanon*. New York: Monthly Review Press, 1987.

Phares, Walid. *Lebanese Christian Nationalism: The Rise and Fall of an Ethnic Resistance*. London: Lynne Rienner Publishers, 1995.

Picard, Elizabeth. *Lebanon, a Shattered Country*. New York: Holmes and Meier, 1996.

Pipes, Daniel. *Greater Syria: The History of an Ambition*. Oxford: Oxford University Press, 1990.

Polk, W. R. *The Opening of South Lebanon, 1788–1840*. Cambridge, MA: Harvard University Press, 1963.

Porath, Yehoshua. 'The Peasant Revolt of 1858–1861 in Kisrawan' (in Hebrew), *Hamizrah Hahdash*, Vol. XV, no. 4 (1965), pp. 379–400; Vol. XVI, no. 1 (1966), pp. 31–57.

— *In Search of Arab Unity, 1930–1945*. London: Frank Cass, 1986.

Qubain, Fahim I. *Crisis in Lebanon*. Washington DC: Middle East Institute, 1961.

Rabbath, Edmond. *La Formation Historique du Liban Politique et Constitutionnel*. Beirut: Publications de l'Université Libanaise, 1973.

Rabinovich Itamar, *The War for Lebanon, 1970–1985*. Ithaca, NY: Cornell University Press, 1985.

— *The Road Not Taken*. Oxford: Oxford University Press, 1991.

Rathmell, Andrew. *Secret War in the Middle East: The Covert Struggle for Syria, 1949–1961*. London: I.B.Tauris, 1995.

al-Riyashi, Iskandar. *al-Ayyam al-Lubnaniyya* (Lebanese Days). Beirut, 1957.

— *Ru'asa Lubnan Kama 'Araftuhum* (The Presidents of Lebanon Whom I Knew). Beirut: Manshurat al-Maktab al-Tijari lil-Tiba'a wal-Tawzi' wal-Nashr, 1961.

Rizq, Charles. *Le Régime Politique Libanais*. Paris: Libraire Générale de Droit et de Jurisprudence, 1966.

Rizq, Rizq. *Rashid Karami*. Beirut: Mukhtarat, n.d.

Rondot, Piere. *Les Institution Politiques du Liban*. Liban: Institut d'Études de L'Orient Contemporain, 1947.

— 'Lebanese Institutions and Arab Nationalism', *Journal of Contemporary History*, Vol. III, no. 3 (July 1968).

Roshwald, Aviel. *Estranged Bedfellows: Britain and France in the Middle East During the Second World War*. Oxford: Oxford University Press, 1990.

Rubin, Barry. *The Arab States and the Palestine Conflict*. Syracuse, NY: Syracuse University Press, 1981.

Sa'ada, Antun, *Nushu' al-Umam* (The Genesis of Nations). Beirut, 1938.

— 'Al-'Uruba Aflasat' (The Failure of Arabism), *Kull Shay'*, 21 January 1949.

— *The Principles of the Syrian Social Nationalist Party* (in English). Beirut: al-Hizb al-Suri al-Qawmi al-Ijtima'i, 1949.

— 'Harabna al-'Uruba al-Wahmiyya Linuqima al-'Uruba al-Waqi'iyya' (We Fought the Unrealistic Arabism in Order to Establish Real Arabism), *Kull Shay'*, 11 February 1949.

Sachar, Harward M. *Europe Leaves the Middle East, 1936–1954.* New York: Alfred A. Knopf, 1972.

Salama, Ghassan. *Al-Mujtama' wal-Dawla fi al-Mashriq al-'Arabi* (Society and State in the Arab East). Beirut: Markaz Dirasat al-Wahda al-'Arabiyya, 1987.

Salama, Ghassan (ed.) *The Foundations of the Arab State.* London: Croom Helm, 1987.

Salem, Elie Adib. *Modernization without Revolution: Lebanon's Experience.* Bloomington: Indiana University Press, 1973.

Salibi, Kamal S. *Maronite Historians of Medieval Lebanon.* Beirut: American University of Beirut Press, 1959.

— 'The Traditional Historiography of the Maronites', in B. Lewis and P. Holt, *Historians of the Middle East.* London: Oxford University Press, 1962, pp. 212–25.

— 'The Personality of Lebanon in Relations to the Modern World', in Leonard Binder (ed.) *Politics in Lebanon.* New York: John Wiley, 1966, pp. 263–70.

— 'The Lebanese Emirate, 1667–1841', *Al-Abhath*, Vol. XX, no. 3 (September 1967), pp. 1–16.

— 'The Lebanese Identity', *Journal of Contemporary History*, Vol. 6, no. 1 (1971), pp. 76–88.

— *The Modern History of Lebanon.* Delmar, NY: Caravan Books, 1977.

— *Cross Roads to Civil War, Lebanon 1958–1976.* Delmar, NY: Caravan Books, 1976.

— *A House of Many Mansions: The History of Lebanon Reconsidered.* London: I.B.Tauris, 1988.

— *Lebanon and the Middle East Question.* Oxford: Centre for Lebanese Studies, 1988.

— 'Mount Lebanon under the Mamluks', in S. Seikaly, R. Baalbaki and P. Dodd (eds) *Quest for Understanding.* Beirut: American University of Beirut Press, 1991.

Salih, Shakib. *Tuldot Hadruzim* (The History of the Druze). Jerusalem: Bar Ilan University Press, 1989.

Schulze, Kirsten E. *Israel's Covert Diplomacy in Lebanon.* London: Macmillan, 1998.

— 'Coercive Diplomacy: The 1950 Israeli Attack on a Lebanese Airliner', *Middle Eastern Studies*, Vol. 31, no. 4 (October 1995), pp. 919–31.

Seale, Patrick. *The Struggle for Syria: A Study of Post-War Arab Politics, 1945–1958.* New Haven: Yale University Press, 1987.

Shamir, Shimon. 'The Collapse of Project Alpha', in W. M. Roger, V. Louis and Roger Owen (eds) *Suez 1956.* London: Clarendon Press, 1989, pp. 73–100.

Shehadi, Nadim. *The Idea of Lebanon.* Oxford: Centre for Lebanese Studies, 1987.

Shehadi, Nadim and Danna Haffar Mills (eds). *Lebanon: A History of Conflict and Consensus.* London: Centre for Lebanese Studies and I.B.Tauris, 1988.

Shehadi, Nadim and Bridget Harney (eds). *Politics and the Economy in Lebanon.* Oxford: Centre for Lebanese studies and Centre of Near and Middle Eastern Studies, SOAS, University of London, 1989.

Shim'oni, Ya'akov. 'Jordanian, Egyptian and Palestinian "Orientations" in the Policies of the Jews of Palestine, the Zionist Movement and Nascent Israel' (in Hebrew), *Iyunim Bitkumat Israel*, Vol. 4 (1994), pp. 54–65.

Smock, David R. and Audrey C. Smock. *The Politics of Pluralism: A Comparative Study of Lebanon and Ghana.* New York: Elsevier, 1975.

Solh, Raghid. 'The Attitude of the Arab Nationalists towards Greater Lebanon during the 1930s', in Nadim Shehadi and Dana Haffar Mills (eds) *Lebanon: A History of Conflict and Consensus.* London: I.B.Tauris, 1988, pp. 149–65.

Spagnolo, John P. 'Constitutional Change in Mt. Lebanon, 1861–1914', *Middle Eastern Studies* (January 1971), pp. 25–48.

— *France and Ottoman Lebanon, 1861–1941.* Oxford: St Antony's College, 1977.

Stoten, D. (ed.) *A State without a Nation.* Occasional Paper Series no. 41. University of Durham, Centre for Middle East and Islamic Studies, 1992.

Suleiman, Michael W. *Political Parties in Lebanon.* Ithaca, NY: Cornell University Press, 1967.

Susser, Asher. *Western Power Rivalry and Its Interaction with Local Politics in the Levant 1941–1946.* PhD Dissertation, Tel Aviv University, June 1986.

Swanson, John Robert. *Soviet and Local Communist Perceptions of Syrian and Lebanese Politics 1944–1964.* Ann Arbor, MI: University Microfilms, n.d.

al-Tahiri, Hamdi Badawi. *Siyasat al-Hukm fi Lubnan* (The Policy of Governing in Lebanon). Cairo: al-Dar al-Qawmiyya lil-Tiba'a wal-Nashr, 1966.

al-Tamawi, Sulayman Muhammad. *Al-Sulutat al-Thalath fi al-Dasatir al-'Arabiyya wafi al-Fikr al-'Arabi al-Islami, Dirasa Muqarina* (The Executive, Legislature and Judiciary in the Arab Constitutions and in Arabic and Islamic Thinking). Cairo: Al-Fikr al-'Arabi, 1973.

Taqi al-Din, Munir. *Wiladat Istiqlal* (The Birth of Independence). Beirut: Dar al-'Ilm lil-Malayin, 1953.

— *Lubnan … Madha Dahak* (What Happened to Lebanon?) Beirut: Manshurat Dar Maktabat al-Hayat, 1979.

Torrey, G. H. *Syrian Politics and the Military, 1945–1958.* Ohio: Ohio State University Press, 1964.

Van Leeuw, Michel. 'Analyse de la Politique Française au Liban en 1943, au Travers des Archives Diplomatiques Belges', *Brismes* (1989).

Wahaba, Tawfiq. *Lubnan fi Haba'il al-Siyasa* (Lebanon in World Politics). Beirut, n.d.

Weinberger, Naomi Joy. *Syria's Intervention in Lebanon.* Oxford: Oxford University Press, 1986.

Winslow, Charles. *Lebanon, War and Politics in a Fragmented Society.* London: Routledge, 1996.

Yamak, Labib Zuwiyya. *The Syrian Social Nationalist Party, An Ideological Analysis.* Cambridge, MA: Harvard University Press, 1966.

Zamir Meir. 'Emile Eddé and the Territorial Integrity of Lebanon', *Middle Eastern Studies,* Vol. 14, no. 2 (May 1978), pp. 232–35.

— 'Smaller and Greater Lebanon – The Squaring of a Circle?' *Jerusalem Quarterly,* no. 23 (Spring 1982), pp. 34–53.

— *The Formation of Modern Lebanon.* Ithaca, NY: Cornell University Press, 1988.

— *Lebanon's Quest. The Road to Statehood. 1926–1939.* London: I.B.Tauris, 1997.

— 'Faisal and the Lebanese Question, 1918–1920', *Middle Eastern Studies,* Vol. 27, no. 3 (July 1991), pp. 402–26.

Zeine, N. *The Emergence of Arab Nationalism.* New York: Caravan Books, 1973.

Ziadeh, Nicola A. *Syria and Lebanon.* New York: Praeger Publishers, 1956.

— *Ab'ad al-Tarikh al-Lubnani al-Hadith* (The Modern History of Lebanon). Beirut: Ma'had al-Buhuth wal-Dirasat al-'Arabiyya, 1972.

Zisser, Eyal. 'The Downfall of the Khuri Administration: A Dubious Revolution', *Middle Eastern Studies*, Vol. 30, no. 3 (July 1994), pp. 486–511.

— 'The Maronites, Lebanon and the State of Israel: Early Contacts', *Middle Eastern Studies*, Vol. 31, no. 5 (October 1995), pp. 889–918.

# Index

## DATE DUE

| | | |
|---|---|---|
| MAY 1 4 2003 | | |
| APR 3 0 2003 | | NOV 1 6 2003 |
| APR 0 7 2004 | | |
| | JAN 0 6 2004 | |
| | APR 1 9 2005 | |
| JAN 0 2 2007 | | |
| | | APR 2 3 2006 |
| | | |
| | | |
| | | |
| | | |
| | | |
| | | |
| | | |
| | | |
| | | |

Printed
in USA

HIGHSMITH #45230